Paleoindian Geoarchaeology
of the Southern High Plains

TEXAS ARCHAEOLOGY AND ETHNOHISTORY SERIES

Thomas R. Hester, Editor

PALEOINDIAN

Geoarchaeology of the
Southern High Plains

VANCE T. HOLLIDAY

UNIVERSITY OF TEXAS PRESS
Austin

First edition, 1997

Requests for permission to reproduce material from this work should be sent to
Permissions, University of Texas Press, Box 7819, Austin, TX 78713-7819.

⊗ The paper used in this publication meets the minimum requirements
of American National Standard for Information Sciences—Permanence
of Paper for Printed Library Materials, ANSI Z39.48-1984.

LIBRARY OF CONGRESS CATALOGING-IN-PUBLICATION DATA
Holliday, Vance T.
    Paleoindian geoarchaeology of the southern High Plains / Vance T. Holliday. —
1st ed.
        p.   cm. — (Texas archaeology and ethnohistory series)
    Includes bibliographical references (p.   ) and index.
    ISBN 0-292-73109-4 (alk. paper). — ISBN 0-292-73114-0 (pbk. : alk. paper)
    1. Paleo-Indians—High Plains (U.S.)   2. Excavations (Archaeology)—High
Plains (U.S.)   3. Archaeological geology—High Plains (U.S.)   4. High Plains
(U.S.)—Antiquities.   I. Title.   II. Series.
E78.G73H63   1997
978—dc20   96-25213

I dedicate this volume to Vance Haynes with respect and admiration. His work in geoarchaeology and Paleoindian archaeology first inspired me as an undergraduate, and I was fortunate to have the opportunity to follow in his footsteps when I began working on the High Plains. During my graduate and subsequent professional career he became a source of ideas and inspiration, a great colleague, and, above all, a friend.

Contents

Illustrations

Figures

Tables

Foreword

In 1952, the University of Texas Press published one of the classic volumes in New World archaeology, *Early Man in America*, authored by E. H. Sellards. Sellards was the director of the Texas Memorial Museum and had been involved for decades in the study of early human prehistory, especially in Texas and the Southwest. He and his field teams excavated many significant sites of this early era, known as Paleoindian, and laid the groundwork for future research. Indeed, a number of the sites described in this present book by Holliday were first published by Sellards and his associates. Holliday's book is a fitting sequel to *Early Man in America*. While not as broad in scope, it emphasizes the interpretation of the archaeological remains in their geologic context. Holliday's research in this area is much more sophisticated given some of the approaches that he has used and that were not available in Sellards' time. But Sellards was a geologist, and most of his field team were similarly trained, especially Glen Evans, Grayson Meade, and Gene Mear. Geology was critical in determining how the site was formed, and in the years predating radiocarbon analysis (which was still in its early stages at the time Sellards' book appeared), knowledge of local geological formations was essential in assigning an age to the archaeological remains.

Vance Holliday has taken on a major task in putting together this volume. It focuses on the Southern Plains of the United States, where many Paleoindian sites have been dug, published, dug again, reanalyzed, and otherwise scrutinized within the past twenty to thirty years. Holliday brings his extensive training in geoarchaeology to the discussion of these sites. While we have better chronometric or numerical dating techniques these days, it is still essential to work out the stratigraphy and the geomorphology of archaeological sites. This is especially true with Paleoindian sites, since their great antiquity—some of them going back 11,200 years—means that they have sometimes been greatly modified by later geological processes.

Holliday's work puts the faunal remains and associated artifacts in context by examining the processes that led to the formation or burial of the site and those that caused subsequent erosion or other geological modification.

Holliday's review of the history of Paleoindian research on the Southern Plains is a great resource for archaeologists and students of the history of archaeology; it also reflects the prominent role played by Sellards. The current terminology, dating, and cultural aspects related to Southern Plains Paleoindian cultures are usefully reviewed. But many archaeologists and certainly students of archaeology, both avocational and professionals-in-training, will seek out the summaries of the major Paleoindian sites, several of them among the best known in the Western Hemisphere. Holliday has sorted the sites according to their topographic occurrence, in draws, playas, or dunes. These summaries are accompanied by illustrations of the sites and their cultural remains; the reader will note that some of the original illustrations are those that appeared in Sellards' book, deftly and accurately drawn by the late Hal Story. Overall, Holliday's focus on site stratigraphy helps provide a clearer picture of the ancient environments of the Southern Plains and a refined view of classic Plains Paleoindian cultural chronology. Those archaeologists and geologists seeking detailed stratigraphic information will find such data in Appendix 1. In Appendix 2, there is a very useful survey of the raw material resources used for making stone tools in the Southern Plains, adding to Holliday's earlier studies and a monograph published several years ago by Larry Banks.

The archaeology of Paleoindians is cloaked in a type of mystique—the sites are old, reaching back into the Pleistocene in many cases; the artifacts are skillfully made; the animals are of species long extinct. Such sites, with their mammoth or large bison remains, grab public attention (witness the development of the Lubbock Lake Landmark Historical Site). Yet what Holliday has done here is to demonstrate that these sites are understood only through tenacity, hard work, long-term research efforts, and interdisciplinary teamwork. New Paleoindian sites continue to be found in the Southern Plains; some, like Wilson-Leonard and Gault, in central Texas (on the southern edge of the Southern Plains), have been excavated fairly recently and have not yet been fully published. Others are threatened by urban expansion and by relic-collectors. If we are to continue to unravel the story of this early phase of the human occupation of the New World, it is critical that these sites be documented thoroughly and interpreted in the fashion exemplified by this book.

THOMAS R. HESTER

Preface and Acknowledgments

This volume represents almost two decades of thinking about and working on Paleoindian research and geoarchaeology on the Southern High Plains. My interests in both subjects began when I was an undergraduate in Anthropology at the University of Texas at Austin, inspired by the late Dave Dibble and Elton Prewitt at the Texas Archeological Salvage Project (now part of the Texas Archeological Research Laboratory). In 1973 I took the opportunity to work as a volunteer in the first season of the Lubbock Lake Project, run under the auspices of the Museum of Texas Tech University. That field season resulted in a permanent relationship when I entered graduate school in Museum Science at Texas Tech (1974). As I began my graduate training and became more involved at Lubbock Lake I was encouraged to explore both geoscience and Paleoindian interests by Chuck Johnson and especially by Eileen Johnson, who were co-directing the project. With training in soils from B. L. Allen and in geomorphology from C. C. "Tex" Reeves, both at Texas Tech, I then fully immersed myself in geosciences as a PhD student in Geology at the University of Colorado (1978–1982). Once I graduated, my training in soil–geomorphology and Quaternary studies from Pete Birkeland served me well in active pursuit of the geoarchaeological aspects of Paleoindian occupations on the Southern High Plains. This work began as an informal part of other geoscientific research I started in the 1980s. In the course of investigating the late Quaternary stratigraphic record of the Southern High Plains, I took advantage of occasional opportunities to study some of the many reported Paleoindian sites in the region. By the late 1980s I was attempting to systematically investigate as many Paleoindian localities on the Southern High Plains as I could gain access to, incorporating the work into broader questions of regional stratigraphy and paleoenvironments. Beginning with my graduate work at Colorado, I also took the opportunity to visit (and ideally work on) as many Paleoindian sites as I could in neighboring regions such as the Rolling Plains, Edwards Plateau, and northern Plains.

This journey has been fascinating and about as much fun as I can stand, in large measure because of the colleagues and friends I've made along the way, and especially because of the archaeologists and geoscientists who have struggled to keep me honest. I am pleased to have this opportunity to identify and thank the individuals and agencies that have been of such help.

Support for the 1988–1995 research was provided largely by the National Science Foundation (grants EAR-8803761 and EAR-9218593). Additional funding was provided by the University of Wisconsin Graduate School in 1991 and 1992. Prior to 1988, most of my work was under the auspices of the Lubbock Lake Project, Eileen Johnson (Museum of Texas Tech University), Director, funded by the National Science Foundation, Moody Foundation, West Texas Museum Association, and the Institute of Museum Research and the Museum, Texas Tech University. The writing phase of this research got off to an excellent start thanks to a sabbatical leave granted by the College of Letters and Sciences of the University of Wisconsin–Madison (Fall 1993) and as the result of a Visiting Professorship I was offered by the Alaska Quaternary Center at the University of Alaska–Fairbanks (Spring 1994). My thanks to E. James Dixon (Denver Museum of Natural History, formerly with the AQC) and to Mary Edwards (AQC Director) for arranging my stay in Fairbanks.

The 1988–1995 field work was successfully completed thanks to the field and lab assistance of my graduate students Peter Jacobs, Ty Sabin, Garry Running, and James Jordan. Their efforts, insights, and good cheer added immensely to the enjoyment of the work. Others who helped prior to 1988 include Dan McGrath, Dave Swanson, and Curt Welty.

Eileen Johnson is due special thanks for the 20-plus years (!) as a research partner, for much of the intellectual stimulation that led to this volume, and for unending encouragement and support. Dave Meltzer (Southern Methodist University) and Jack Hofman (University of Kansas) became valued research partners and great pals during the course of my geoarchaeological efforts. In particular, Dave involved me in his work at Mustang Springs and got us into the Midland site, and Jack invited me to join in on his work at the Lipscomb site. Their archaeological wisdom has been invaluable, their friendship incomparable (and such fun). Dave also planted an idea that led to the writing of this volume, and both Dave and Jack reviewed the manuscript and urged me to attempt a broader approach. Others who provided valued commentary on parts of the manuscript include Reid Ferring, Vance Haynes, Diane Holliday, Eileen Johnson, and Fred Wendorf. Thomas R. Hester (Texas Archeological Research Laboratory) provided valuable advice from the early stages of writing to final publication.

Many other colleagues, friends, and landowners provided critical assistance in the field. Vance Haynes (the University of Arizona) shared considerable insight on the Clovis site and other sites in the area. John Montgomery and Joanne Dickenson (both of Eastern New Mexico University, Portales) always provided a cheerful welcome at the Clovis site as well as considerable logistical assistance. Jim Warnica (Portales, New Mexico) freely shared his exceptional knowledge of the Clovis site and many other localities in the region. Richard Rose (Midland, Texas) and Jay Blaine (Dallas, Texas) likewise provided considerable insights into the archaeology of the Andrews/Monahans Dunes. Eddie Guffee (Wayland Baptist University, Plainview) first showed me the Plainview site area and arranged for access. Dave Brown (Hicks & Co., Austin) shared the data we collected at the Lubbock Landfill, under contract with the City of Lubbock, and Eric Schroeder helped with the radiocarbon sampling at the Landfill.

Access to archaeological sites often is a problem, but I was fortunate in getting to most thanks to a number of individuals: George Arrington, Don Jenkins, and Effie Jenkins (Miami); the William Barnett family (Car Body); Jay Blaine (Winkler-1); Mike Burns (Burns Ranch); Richard and Lorene Callison (San Jon); Denny Carley (Carley-Archer); J. T. Gibson, Hollis Cain, and Charlotte Gibson Cain (Marks Beach/Gibson Ranch); Sonny Lupton (Ryan's site); Shane McCormick (Bedford Ranch); Jerry and Hollene Perry (Lipscomb); Richard Rose (Bedford Ranch, Shifting Sands, Seminole-Rose, and Wyche Ranch); Clarence Scharbauer III (Midland); Rick Walter (Poverty Hill); Rick Walter and the late Wayne Parker (Robertson); Jim Warnica (Elida, Ro-16, and Tatum); and Ted Williamson (Milnesand and Ted Williamson).

I also thank those who helped with archival and historical information and other valuable data: Carolyn Spock, Darrell Creel, and Lynn Denton (the University of Texas at Austin) provided information on the work of E. H. Sellards; Glen Evans (Austin) shared observations and insights based on his long association with Sellards and on his own field work on the High Plains; Fred Wendorf (Southern Methodist University) and Vance Haynes helped put together the history of the High Plains Paleoecology Project; Salvatore Valastro (the University of Texas Radiocarbon Laboratory) provided information on the dating of bone from Lake Theo; the late Dorothy Meade (Agate Springs Ranch, Nebraska) kindly shared memories of her late husband Grayson Meade, and provided insights on other members of her fascinating family; Matthew G. Hill (University of Wisconsin) and Dennis Stanford (Smithsonian Institution) supplied information on Frank H. H. Roberts' work at San Jon, and Stanford provided access to the San Jon collections; Sheldon Judson (Princeton) also shared some memories of work at San Jon with Frank Roberts and Kirk Bryan; Douglas Drake (the University of Texas at Austin) provided samples from plaster jackets of the Milnesand bone bed collected by Sellards; Roberta Speer (West Texas A&M University) provided insights on Sellards' work at Plainview and also supplied samples of the Plainview bone bed taken from plaster jackets collected by Sellards.

I appreciate the help of many individuals who supplied photographs that appear in this book and who allowed photographs and artifact drawings to be reproduced: Thomas R. Hester and Carolyn Spock (Texas Archeological Research Laboratory, Austin) for the Miami photo; Joanne Dickenson for the Clovis photos from the early 1960s; Fred Wendorf for the Midland artifact drawings; LeRoy Johnson, Jr. (Texas Historical Commission) for the Texas Golondrina drawings; Ellen Sue Turner (San Antonio) for the Angostura drawings; Dee Ann Story (the University of Texas at Austin) for all of Hal Story's drawings of Sellards' collections. Rebecca Hinrichs (Texas Tech Museum) photographed the Plainview and Clovis bone blocks and printed all Lubbock Lake photos supplied by the Museum.

The line drawings were prepared with support from the Cartography Laboratory of the Department of Geography at UW-Madison. This chore was patiently and expertly carried out by Joshua Hane and Scott Wiand. Onno Brouwer, Director of the Cartography Lab, put in many hours scanning and manipulating the old artifact drawings so they could be reproduced.

Finally, my gratitude and love to my wife Diane, who shares my interest in Paleoindian archaeology and supported the work I report.

Paleoindian Geoarchaeology
of the Southern High Plains

CHAPTER ONE

Paleoindian Studies, Geoarchaeology, and the Southern High Plains

Introduction

The discoveries at the Folsom site in New Mexico from 1926–1928 clearly established human antiquity in the New World to late Pleistocene times (Wormington 1957; Meltzer 1983). The discoveries also ushered in a new era in North American archaeology: Paleoindian studies on the Great Plains. Some of the best-known and most intensively studied early sites in the Western Hemisphere are on the open grasslands of the midcontinent, and they have provided archaeologists with many presently held concepts— and biases—regarding Paleoindian typologies, chronologies, and subsistence (Wormington 1957; Wilmsen 1965; Meltzer and Smith 1986; Meltzer 1993).

Within the Great Plains, one of the highest concentrations of Paleoindian sites and research is on the Southern High Plains of northwestern Texas and eastern New Mexico (FIGS. 1.1, 1.2). The first excavations at the Clovis site, New Mexico, just a few years after the Folsom finds, began one of the longest traditions of Paleoindian archaeological studies in any region in North America. Moreover, the work at Clovis established a tradition of integrating geoscientific studies with Paleoindian research that still thrives on the Southern High Plains over 60 years later. Interdisciplinary Paleoindian research has been almost continuous in the region since 1933 and has included work at several type localities (Clovis, Plainview, San Jon, Midland, Milnesand), other well-known, key sites (Lubbock Lake, Miami), and a number of lesser-known but nevertheless significant sites (FIG. 1.3).

This volume is a synthesis of the available data on the stratigraphic, geomorphic, chronologic, and paleoenvironmental contexts of Paleoindian occupations on the Southern High Plains. The data base includes information from many previous studies as well as new data that I gathered from most of the reported, stratified Paleoindian sites. The results of this study are intended to provide a physical and temporal basis for more expressly archaeological investigations of Paleoindian occupation. Some archaeological interpretations dealing with issues of artifact chronologies, site settings, and environmental changes are offered, but this study is not an exhaustive treatment of Paleoindian archaeology. Such a task is left to archaeologists.

A synthetic treatment of Paleoindian studies on the Southern High Plains is warranted because of the long and varied history of Paleoindian research in the region and because of the importance of this research in North American archaeology. The archaeological and geoscientific investigations of Paleoindian sites on the Southern High Plains are significant for several reasons. These studies were the first to: establish the stratigraphic

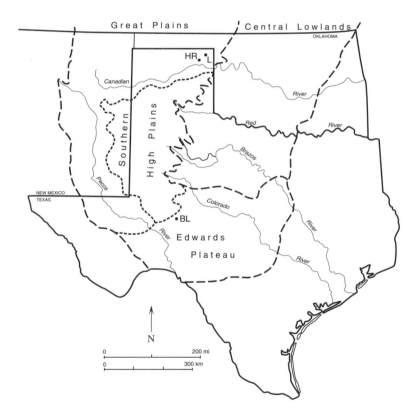

FIGURE 1.1. Map showing the location of the Southern High Plains relative to Texas, New Mexico, and Oklahoma, and relative to neighboring physiographic provinces and sections (based on Fenneman 1931 and Hunt 1974; modified from Holliday 1995b:fig. 1). Paleoindian sites bordering Southern High Plains include Lipscomb (L), Horace Rivers (HR), and Big Lake (BL).

FIGURE 1.2. Physiographic map of the Southern High Plains with the principal draws, dune fields, rivers, and salinas (unlabeled), and selected cities (modified from Holliday 1995b:fig. 3).

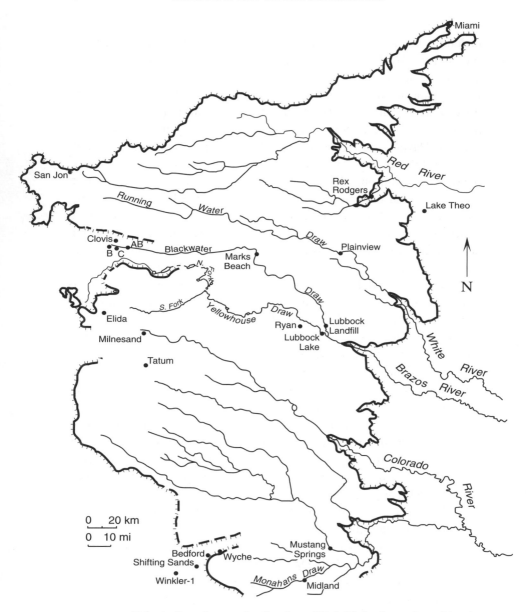

FIGURE 1.3. Paleoindian sites on the Southern High Plains investigated by the author (1980–1995). In the Clovis area are the Burns site (B), the Car Body site (C), and Anderson Basin #1 and #2 (AB). The Ted Williamson site is immediately adjacent to the Milnesand site. See FIG. 3.61 (p.144) for RO-16, Robertson, and Poverty Hill sites; FIG. 3.42 (p.111) for Carley-Archer and Seminole Rose.

relationships among some of the various Plains Paleoindian occupations, including the now-classic sequence of Clovis-Folsom-Lanceolate projectile points; provide radiocarbon age control for Paleoindian occupations; and yield clues to the very different and changing environments in which Paleoindians lived. Paleoindian discoveries at several sites also led to broader investigations of late Quaternary geohistory and paleoenvironments, such as the decades of geoarchaeological work at Clovis by C. V. Haynes (Haynes and Agogino 1966; Haynes 1975, 1995; Stanford et al. 1990), and the first systematic treatment of playa basin origins and development by S. Judson, which began with his research at San Jon (Judson 1950, 1953). Paleoindian finds also led to two of the few systematic, regional studies of Paleoindian archaeology and paleoenvironments in North America by E. H. Sellards and colleagues (late 1930s through 1950s) (Sellards 1952; Sellards and Evans 1960), and by F. Wendorf and his associates (late 1950s and 1960s) (Wendorf 1961a; Wendorf and Hester 1975).

Since 1933 there have been scores of investigators working on dozens of Paleoindian sites on the Southern High Plains under a variety of conditions with varying aims. As a result, there are more data on Paleoindian archaeology, geology, and paleoenvironments than for most other regions of comparable size in the Americas. However, there have been few attempts to synthesize the results. The first summaries of the cultural sequence and integration of the geologic framework were by Sellards (1952) in his well-known volume *Early Man in America* and by Sellards and Evans (1960), who proposed the classic Paleoindian cultural and environmental succession for the region. Subsequent investigators (Wendorf 1961b; Kelley 1964; Collins 1971; Hester 1975a; Wendorf and Hester 1975; Hester and Grady 1977) discuss and synthesize aspects of the Paleoindian cultural succession, geoarchaeology, social patterns, and environments on the Llano Estacado, but these studies now are dated, summarizing work completed before or in the 1960s. Haynes (1968a, 1975) and Stafford (1981) deal with the geologic environments of Paleoindians, but in geographically limited areas of the Southern High Plains. Hofman (1989a) presents the most comprehensive chronology of Paleoindian occupations, based on the considerable research by many investigators in the 1970s and 1980s, but this study is not within a geologic framework and the paleoenvironmental context is limited.

Another goal of this volume is to synthesize the paleoenvironmental data for reconstruction of regional environments during the Paleoindian occupation. Most of the data on Paleoindian environments of the Southern High Plains are site-specific, and regional paleoenvironmental reconstructions are relatively rare and based on comparatively sparse data. This point is well illustrated by the results of COHMAP (1988; Wright et al. 1993). As part of the COHMAP research, the vegetation reconstructions based on proxy data for western and eastern North America (Thompson et al. 1993; Webb et al. 1993) display very little information for the Great Plains and essentially none for the southern Plains.

Regionally, a synthesis of the data for the Southern High Plains is timely, given the record of Paleoindian occupations emerging from the northern Plains (Frison 1991a, 1993). Moreover, many of the "well-known" sites and "classic" studies on the Southern High Plains are not all that well known or well reported (similar to the situation on the northern Plains; Tiffany 1993:2–3). The stratigraphic and geochronologic data from many of these sites are decades old, and much of the data received only cursory discussion or none at all. A reexamination of the geologic record of each site for its implications regarding paleoenvironments and cultural chronology is warranted in view of the considerable interdisciplinary research in the area since the early 1970s.

The long record of interdisciplinary Paleoindian research on the Southern High Plains is unique in North America and is due to several circumstances. Following the discoveries at the Folsom site, the impetus for Paleoindian studies on the Great Plains resulted from repeated finds of Folsom or Folsom-like artifacts or additional discoveries of human artifacts associated with Pleistocene fauna. On the Southern High Plains these finds included the Clovis site (Howard 1935a,b), the Lipscomb site (Barbour and Schultz 1941), and the Miami site (Sellards 1938).

Perhaps more important to the development of interdisciplinary studies on the Southern High Plains, many of the archaeological sites investigated have thick, well-stratified deposits that provide evidence of markedly different depositional environments in the past (e.g., meandering streams where arroyos now prevail or perennial, freshwater lakes in presently dry basins) owing to the dramatically different environmental conditions at the end of the Pleistocene (Haynes 1990; Ferring 1994). These striking contrasts between past and present depositional environments drew the attention of archaeologists and earth scientists alike who recognized the paleoenvironmental implications. Indeed, during the first excavations at Clovis, E. B. Howard (1935a:62) was explicit in his belief that interdisciplinary research was a prerequisite to understanding Paleoindian archaeology, and especially focused on geology:

> Geology, particularly its allied branches of palaeontology, physiography, and glacial geology, must be called upon to explain many phases of the

subject [of the peopling of the New World] that involve a wide variety of converging lines of research, presenting many peculiar difficulties. The archaeologist, starting from the point where the historian usually leaves off, soon finds it necessary to lengthen his perspective, and eventually he is faced, so far as America is concerned, with a geological problem. The recognition on his part of the importance of special studies relating to such factors as climatic changes, studies of invertebrates, analysis of diatoms, or pollen that may be found in a given deposit marks a step in the right direction. Therefore the archaeologist must familiarize himself with these and other phases of geology which bear upon the problem, such as the study of terraces, buried soil levels, loess deposits, varved clays, ancient lakes and shore lines, and any other factors which may give a clue to the environment in which early man lived in America . . . [T]he importance of a field of investigation which lies somewhere between geology and archaeology . . . is becoming increasingly apparent as a number of scientists recognize.

Rephrased in a more contemporary context, "the prominent role of geology in Paleoindian archaeology . . . is explained [in part] by . . . the distinctive archaeological, paleoenvironmental, and evolutionary problems that are addressed by students of the Paleoindian period" (Ferring 1994:57).

The geologic records at the Paleoindian sites stimulated interdisciplinary geoarchaeological research for several other reasons. One of the most direct applications of earth science in the early decades of Paleoindian studies was for dating. Geologists and paleontologists were called upon to provide age estimates of sites in the absence of other forms of numerical age control such as radiocarbon dating (Hofman 1989a:44; Ferring 1990a; Haynes 1990). More significantly, however, the Paleoindian sites were inviting because many investigators had interests in Pleistocene stratigraphy and paleontology (e.g., Haynes 1990). The presence of a Pleistocene archaeological record in North America was "an enormous stimulus to research" (Bryan 1941a:508) by geologists on Paleoindian sites (Wilmsen 1965). Many of the Paleoindian investigators on the Southern High Plains had academic backgrounds in geology in addition to an abiding interest in human prehistory, especially the issue of "Early Man" (Claude C. Albritton, Glen L. Evans, F. Earl Green, C. Vance Haynes, Jr., E. B. Howard, Grayson E. Meade, and E. H. Sellards). Geologic research was inseparable from their approach to archaeology. Such backgrounds also added immeasurably to their interpretations of paleoenvironments and geochronology. The Paleoindian archaeology of the Southern High Plains also happened to attract the attention of archaeologists trained in an interdisciplinary approach (E. B. Howard, Eileen Johnson, and Fred Wendorf). Geoarchaeology was an integral part of their research programs.

Interdisciplinary Paleoindian investigations on and near the Southern High Plains in recent decades provide considerable new data on archaeology, chronology, and paleoenvironments, and this volume is a summary of much of this work along with the older data in light of the new information. The emphasis is on summarizing and comparing the geoarchaeology of Paleoindian occupations. From 1980 to 1995 I investigated most Paleoindian sites in the region for which data are published, focusing on the relationships of the archaeology to the soils, stratigraphy, and geochronology. These and previously published data are used for stratigraphic correlation, for paleoenvironmental summaries, and for refining or redefining the cultural chronology.

There are four main components to this study. Following introductory material on the physiography of the Southern High Plains, Chapter 2 provides a history of Paleoindian research in the region. Many Paleoindian researchers worked in the area between 1933 and 1995, usually independent of one another, resulting in a vast and often confusing array of data and ideas. The chapter, focusing on geoarchaeological and geochronological aspects of Paleoindian studies, provides an historical perspective on the individuals and institutions involved, on the discoveries, and on the evolving interpretations. Chapter 3 is a discussion of the geoarchaeology of the individual Paleoindian sites that integrates the new and old data on site geomorphology, stratigraphy, geochronology, and paleoenvironments. Chapter 4 is a survey of Paleoindian geoarchaeology and cultural chronology in neighboring areas of the Great Plains. The discussion is intended to place the Paleoindian record of the Southern High Plains into a broader chronological and paleoenvironmental perspective, in light of long-term and well-known Paleoindian studies from the continental interior of North America. Chapter 5 then presents my views on Paleoindian cultural chronology and paleoenvironments on the Southern High Plains based on the stratigraphic and geochronologic data along with other archaeological and paleoenvironmental data. Two appendixes also are included, presenting descriptions of site settings and stratigraphy (Appendix 1) and a discussion of stone-tool resources (Appendix 2).

Environmental Setting

The Southern High Plains or Llano Estacado probably is the most environmentally homogeneous region of its size in North America, with flat topography, relatively stable, uniform regional geology, and low, smooth environmental gradients. The Llano Estacado is a vast, level plateau covering approximately 130,000 km^2 and comprising the southernmost portion of the High Plains physiographic section (Fenneman 1931; Hunt 1974) (FIGS. 1.1, 1.2). The plateau is defined by escarpments 50 to 200 m high on three sides. The western escarpment separates the plateau from the Pecos River valley, and the northern escarpment separates the plateau from the Canadian River valley. The eastern escarpment, formed by headward erosion of tributaries of the Red, Brazos, and Colorado rivers, separates the Southern High Plains from the Rolling (or Osage) Plains. The eastern escarpment provided the name Llano Estacado or "stockaded plains"—the prominent topographic break took on the appearance of an immense stockade to Spanish explorers traveling west across the Rolling Plains (Bolton 1990:243). To the south, the surface of the Southern High Plains merges with the surface of the Edwards Plateau province of Central Texas with no topographic demarcation. The southern boundary is defined by the northernmost outcrops of Edwards Limestone (Fenneman 1931; Hunt 1974).

The climate of the Southern High Plains is continental and semiarid, classified as BScDw: steppe with dry winters, mainly mesothermal years (mean temperature of the coldest month is 32–64° F) with occasional microthermal years (mean temperature of the coldest month is below 32° F) (Russell 1945). There are relatively uniform gradients in precipitation and temperature across the region: precipitation generally increases from west to east and temperature usually increases from northwest to southeast (Lotspeich and Everhart 1962; Carr 1967).

The natural vegetation of the Llano Estacado is a mixed-prairie grassland (Blair 1950; Lotspeich and Everhart 1962). The dominant native plant community is short-grass, which includes types of grama (*Bouteloua* sp.) and buffalo grass (*Buchloe dactyloides*). Trees are absent except along the escarpments and reentrant canyons. The floristic composition varies somewhat from north to south due to changes in climate and soil texture. Native plant communities of the region occur in very few areas today, however, because most of the Southern High Plains is under cultivation. On a geologic time scale, the Llano Estacado probably was a grassland throughout the Holocene and probably varied from a subhumid to semiarid savanna to semiarid grassland in the Pleistocene as effective precipitation varied (Johnson 1986, 1987a; Holliday 1987a, 1989a).

The Southern High Plains is an almost featureless plain, ". . . the largest level plain of its kind in the United States" (NOAA 1982:3). There is a regional slope to the southeast with altitudes ranging from 1700 m in

are considered members of the Tahoka Formation, but other late Pleistocene fills are not Tahoka and all of the Holocene sediment is considered
post-Tahoka (Reeves 1991), further illustrating the difficulties in using
formal lithostratigraphic terminology for lake sediments of the region.

Dunes on the Southern High Plains occur as sand dune fields or as
lunettes in or adjacent to some playa basins and most salina basins (Holliday 1995a). These two types of dunes have different origins and different
stratigraphic records. The lunettes are localized accumulations of eolian
sediment deflated from playas in the late Pleistocene and Holocene. They
are on the northeast, east, or southeast sides of the lake basins. The dune
fields primarily consist of Holocene sands that probably originated in the
Pecos Valley, immediately west of the Llano Estacado (FIGS. 1.1, 1.2). There
are three sets of extensive dunes on the western side of the Southern High
Plains (Hawley et al. 1976; Holliday 1985a, 1995a) (FIG. 1.2).

Stone-Tool Resources

Geoarchaeologists, especially in Paleoindian studies, traditionally have not
dealt with issues of lithic resources in a systematic, regional manner (e.g.,
Waters 1992:xix–xx). Although geoscientists have been involved in studies of stone-tool resources, this work usually either is locality-specific (focused on a single resource or type of resource or a particular type of
method) (e.g., Bryan 1950; Godfrey-Smith et al. 1993) or is done by archaeologists (e.g., Luedtke 1992; Church 1994). Indeed, the focus of this
monograph is on aspects of geoarchaeology and Paleoindian studies far
removed from the study of stone-tool resources. Nevertheless, the source
areas and types of rocks used to fashion artifacts clearly are geoarchaeological issues, and with regard to the Southern High Plains, matters of resource availability frequently are raised in studies of artifact manufacture,
reuse, and typology (Hofman 1992; Johnson and Holliday 1980, 1981; see
Chapter 5), as well as matters of settlement, mobility, and adaptations
(Meltzer 1986; Hofman 1992). To provide some background and perspective on the location and types of knappable stone resources available
to prehistoric inhabitants of the Southern High Plains, Appendix 2 was
prepared.

Field work aimed at gathering new data on lithic resources was not a
part of the research that led to this monograph, and little new data are presented in Appendix 2. Rather, this discussion is a summary of the literature published on stone-tool resources on, near, or otherwise available to
Paleoindians on the Llano Estacado. There have been no systematic stud-

ies specifically focusing on this topic, but there are several regional over-
views (Holliday and Welty 1981; Banks 1990) and numerous site-specific
or lithology-specific studies that form the basis for the presentation.

A variety of materials suitable for manufacturing lithic artifacts are
available along or beyond the margins of the Southern High Plains. The
material includes flint, chert, agate, jasper, various quartzites, and some
opal (Appendix 2). Paleoindians in particular favored the high-quality
Alibates agate, Tecovas jasper, and so-called Edwards chert (Hester 1975a;
Hofman 1989b, 1991, 1992). The Ogallala Formation has the greatest variety and abundance of material in the area, however. The availability of
such a variety of material places some limitations on the use of rock types
found in archaeological sites for estimating possible interregional contact.
A notable example is the gravel of high-quality chert and flint in the
Ogallala and in the gravel derived from the Ogallala and redeposited in terraces on the Rolling Plains. The material is macroscopically identical to
chert found on the Edwards Plateau in Central Texas and probably was derived from outcrops of Cretaceous limestone in the area during deposition
of the Ogallala. Hofman (1989b:7) suggests that the Ogallala and younger
gravels were not exposed until post-Paleoindian times by drying conditions and erosion. No stratigraphic or geomorphic evidence is available to
support this hypothesis, however. Such a cover over Ogallala outcrops
along the High Plains escarpment should be preserved locally, but is not,
and massive stripping of a conjectured cover along the escarpments seems
unlikely. Moreover, the extensive gravel deposits on the Rolling Plains almost certainly have been exposed since deposition.

The importance of raw material availability and types has long been
recognized as a factor in determining the quality and quantity of tools and
debitage in archaeological sites on the Southern High Plains (e.g., Green
and Kelley 1960). Of particular significance is the paucity of suitable material for stone-tool manufacture except along or beyond the margins of the
region (Collins 1971; Hester 1975a; Holliday and Welty 1981; Johnson and
Holliday 1987b). This geological characteristic of the region is a direct result of the late Cenozoic landscape evolution. The region was blanketed by
relatively young eolian sediments (the Blackwater Draw Formation) and
has undergone very limited erosion except along the margins in the past
few million years (Holliday 1989a, 1990b; Holliday and Gustavson 1991).
Rock outcrops, therefore, are common only along the escarpments that
form the west, north, and east boundaries of the Llano Estacado. Other
rock outcrops that were sources or potential sources are found on the Rolling Plains and possibly in the mountains of western Oklahoma to the east,

the Edwards Plateau to the southeast and south, the mountains of far western Texas and central New Mexico to the southwest and west, and the Pecos River valley, immediately west (Appendix 2). Besides raw material available as *in situ* outcrops, gravel derived from suitable stone-tool materials also is gaining recognition as an important source (e.g., Holliday and Welty 1981; Wyckoff 1993). But the gravel sources also are available only at or beyond the boundaries of the region. In any event, to procure material, inhabitants of the interior of the Southern High Plains had to travel some distance to the outcrops or engage in trade for the resources.

Terminology

Paleoindian studies, like other areas of archaeology and most other disciplines, have a confusing array of terms and jargon. This monograph focuses on Paleoindian archaeology, but is not intended to resolve definitional matters. These issues must be dealt with by archaeologists who focus on artifact technology and subsistence (e.g., Hofman 1989a). However, by focusing on the cultural stratigraphy and chronology in a geographically restricted area containing key Paleoindian sites, some order may appear that will help resolve some issues of typology and dating. In order to proceed with the discussion some terminological matters are addressed. Additional typological discussion is presented in Chapter 5.

Roberts (1940) was the first to use the term "Paleo-Indian." It was introduced in the title of his paper ("Development on the Problem of the North American Paleo-Indian") and used a few times in the lengthy article (65 pages), but nowhere was it explicitly defined. The paper reviews all sites in North America of "some antiquity" (Roberts 1940:54), however, summarized as consisting

> of artifacts and skeletal materials in deposits dateable by geologic means, in association with bones of extinct species of animals and invertebrates . . . and also of indications of cultures that were adapted to conditions totally unlike those prevailing in modern times. (Roberts 1940:54)

In later usage he provided a more explicit though broader definition, using "Paleo-Indian" simply to refer to "older" or "early" Indians (Roberts 1953:256).

The term "Paleoindian" did not come into wide use for over a decade after its introduction. Indeed, Roberts (1951) did not use the term in his review of "Early Man" radiocarbon ages. In the 1950s several definitions appeared, as did alternate terms (Krieger 1964:51–52). For example,

Sellards (1952) continued to use the term "Early Man," though considering it the equivalent of Paleoindian (Sellards 1952:10). Sellards, like Roberts (1940), considered Early Man sites to be "of some appreciable antiquity in a geologic sense" (Sellards 1952:5). "Paleoindian" probably gained its biggest foothold in archaeological terminology when used by H. M. Wormington in the fourth edition of her influential book *Ancient Man in North America* (Wormington 1957), although she did not use the term in her third edition (1949). By 1965 the term was "firmly entrenched" (Wilmsen 1965:182).

Though well established as a term, the concept of "Paleoindian" still is poorly defined, probably because Paleoindian archaeology is so poorly known relative to later occupations. For the purposes of this study the Paleoindian stage, occurring in the very late Pleistocene and very early Holocene, is a time of ameliorated climate when humans coexisted with now-extinct large mammals and prepared a variety of distinctive, lanceolate, unnotched projectile points (modified from Hofman 1989a:25). "Big-game hunting" often is cited as a characteristic of the Paleoindian stage (e.g., Stephenson 1965; Willey 1966; Wedel 1983), but the native inhabitants of the Great Plains hunted "big game" until the nineteenth century, and there is ample evidence of a more diverse Paleoindian subsistence (Johnson 1986a, 1991; Meltzer 1993; Meltzer and Smith 1986).

The Paleoindian stage is subdivided on the basis of projectile point styles (e.g., Wormington 1957; Hofman 1989a), due to the lack of other obvious archaeological traits. The principal subdivisions used in this monograph are Clovis, Folsom, and Late Paleoindian. The Clovis and Folsom periods are defined by the presence of distinctive fluted point styles that occupy relatively discrete time intervals. Archaeological sites or features that date to one of these two discrete time intervals but lack diagnostic artifacts are referred to as "Clovis age" or "Folsom age." The Late Paleoindian period is defined by the occurrence of a variety of generally lanceolate, unfluted, well-made projectile points. "Late Paleoindian" is equivalent to the "Plano Complex" of Jennings (1955, cited in Krieger 1964). There seems to be considerable temporal overlap among some of the unfluted, lanceolate styles and some temporal overlap with fluted styles (Chapter 5). Moreover, Late Paleoindian projectile point types, typology, and nomenclature present some vexing problems in dealing with this period (Chapter 5). In the absence of more or other kinds of data, however, these gross subdivisions based on artifact styles provide the best first approximation of Paleoindian culture history on the Llano Estacado.

The Paleoindian period was one of dramatic environmental change.

These changes were of such magnitude that they are the basis for some definitions of major chronostratigraphic units used in the earth sciences and in archaeology. In general, the Paleoindian period includes the last millennia of the Pleistocene and first few thousand years of the Holocene, although the age of the Pleistocene-Holocene boundary is the subject of some debate (Fairbridge 1983; Farrand 1990). Chronostratigraphic conventions in this monograph are: the Pleistocene-Holocene boundary is 10,000 yrs BP (after Hageman 1972); early Holocene is 10,000÷7500 yrs BP.

Methods

Some of the data synthesized in this monograph are from the work of other investigators, but the rest is the result of my field research. Most of the archaeological research and some of the geoscientific information are from others, but no other individual investigator studied all of these sites or integrated the archaeological data base with interpretations from stratigraphy, sedimentology, pedology, geomorphology, and geochronology. Geoarchaeological investigations were conducted at all sites on the Llano Estacado discussed in Chapter 3. At Clovis, however, most field work focused on strata older than the Clovis occupation. Geoarchaeological research at the site has been in the hands of C. V. Haynes for the past 30 years. Off the Llano Estacado, I conducted no work at Rex Rodgers or Horace Rivers (Chapter 3), but did investigate the Lake Theo and Lipscomb sites (Chapter 4).

Most of the field work focused on the three principal sites of late Quaternary deposition: draws, playas, and dunes. Paleoindian sites are found elsewhere on the Llano Estacado (e.g., Hester 1975a; Hester and Grady 1977; Meltzer 1986; Polyak and Williams 1986; Largent et al. 1991), but not in settings that allow stratigraphic or chronometric evaluation. These settings are on uplands, resting on or mixed (via bioturbation) into older Pleistocene deposits such as the Blackwater Draw Formation, or buried by thin layers of sediment lacking stratigraphic distinctiveness. Archaeologists have long recognized the problem of interpreting sites found on the vast, long-stable upland surface of the Llano Estacado (Kelley 1964; Collins 1971; Kibler 1991, 1992). Given the focus of the present study on dating and environmental reconstruction, therefore, most work reported in this monograph emphasizes settings which yielded *in situ* Paleoindian sites. The sand dunes of the region present special problems of interpretation because they have the potential of yielding archaeology in place, but more often produce early sites in deflated and disturbed contexts (e.g.,

Pearce 1936; Fritz and Fritz 1940; Polyak and Williams 1986). As a result, the only dune sites discussed are those where Paleoindian materials were found in place or where reasonable stratigraphic inferences could be made.

A variety of field and laboratory techniques were used in this study. The primary stratigraphic correlations and environmental interpretations are based on lithologic and pedologic characteristics of the sediment preserved at each site. The lithologies allow a first approximation of both stratigraphic relationships and depositional environments. The degree and nature of soil development also are useful indicators for dating and correlating some strata, for reconstructing landscape evolution, and for making some paleoenvironmental reconstructions (Holliday 1985b,c,d,e, 1995a,b).

The field data that I gathered came from investigation of natural and artificial exposures, from cores, and from hand-auger samples. All cores and sections were measured and minimum basic descriptive data (i.e., pedologic horizonation and structure, boundary, bedding, and color characteristics) were recorded in the field. Samples from most sections and cores also were brought back to the laboratory for further description and characterization using standard pedologic and geologic nomenclature (Soil Survey Division Staff 1993; AGI 1982; Birkeland 1984; Birkeland et al. 1991) with several modifications noted in Holliday (1995b).

Most of the samples were subjected to a variety of analyses for further assessment of sedimentologic and pedologic characteristics, although the field characteristics and descriptions were the most informative kinds of data (e.g., Holliday 1985b,c,d,e). Laboratory analyses included particle-size distribution (sand–silt–clay content), carbonate content, organic-carbon content, bulk density, and clay mineralogy, following methods described in Singer and Janitzky (1986) and Jacobs (1995). Thin–sections were prepared for some samples and were analyzed under a petrographic microscope. The results of the laboratory analyses are available on request from the author.

Significant clues to the Paleoindian paleoenvironment of the Llano Estacado also come from paleontological and paleobotanical studies, which were an important component of many Paleoindian research programs in the region (e.g., Stock and Bode 1936; Patrick 1938; Wendorf and Hester 1975). The study of large vertebrates has been an especially important component of Paleoindian studies owing to the recovery of such remains in most of the Paleoindian sites in the region (e.g., Stock and Bode 1936; Lundelius 1972; Slaughter 1975; Johnson 1986a, 1987c, 1991). Microvertebrate studies are a relatively recent phenomenon in the region, however, pioneered largely by Johnson (1986a, 1987c) at Lubbock Lake. Beetle studies in the region also were pioneered at Lubbock Lake by Elias and Johnson (1988) and attempted at other sites (Elias 1995a), but the recovery was very low. Recovery and analysis of gastropod, bivalve, and diatom remains have been a part of some research programs on the Llano Estacado, including the early work at Clovis (e.g., Patrick 1938), the High Plains Paleoecology Project (Hohn and Hellerman 1961; Wendorf 1961c; Drake 1975; Hohn 1975), the more recent research at Lubbock Lake (Pierce 1987), and the recent regional study of the draws (Neck 1995; Winsborough 1995).

Paleobotanical research also has been an important component of Quaternary research on the Southern High Plains, focusing on pollen. Most of the palynological research was conducted during the High Plains Paleoecology Project (e.g., Hafsten 1961; Oldfield and Schoenwetter 1975), with subsequent work at Lubbock Lake (Stafford 1981; Bryant and Schoenwetter 1987). The results varied significantly and were largely unreproducible (Bryant and Schoenwetter 1987). Additional attempts at pollen recovery from draw samples were made by Hall (1995), and the results largely were negative. The problems with pollen recovery appear to be related to differential pollen production, differential pollen preservation, and extraction techniques (Hall in Holliday, Johnson, Hall, and Bryant 1985; Bryant and Schoenwetter 1987; Holliday 1987a; Hall 1995). In particular, the late Quaternary deposits on the Southern High Plains are conducive to pollen degradation because they are typically alkaline and well drained (and oxidized), but occasionally saturated. These characteristics are among the worst for pollen preservation (Hall 1981; Bryant and Holloway 1983; Bryant and Schoenwetter 1987; Bryant and Hall 1993; Bryant et al. 1994).

In light of the problems associated with pollen preservation and recovery, other approaches to paleobotany were attempted, including examination of seeds from Lubbock Lake (Thompson 1987) and recovery of phytoliths from several other draw localities (Bozarth 1995). The results of these attempts at non-pollen-based paleofloral recovery are encouraging.

An especially promising approach to paleovegetation and paleoenvironmental reconstructions is the analysis of stable-carbon isotopes from soil organic matter. There is a strong and positive correlation between $\delta^{13}C$ in soils and the proportions of C_3 and C_4 biomass (Kelly et al. 1993; Nordt et al. 1994). The two groups of plant species are broadly indicative of two distinct environments and therefore can provide clues to past environments. The C_4 plants are mainly warm-season grasses and indicative of warm, semiarid environments, whereas the C_3 plants include cool-season grasses, most aquatic plants, and all trees, and are linked to cooler, more temperate settings (Kelly et al. 1993; Nordt et al. 1994). Isotopic data are available from paludal and lacustrine mud in a few draw localities (Holliday 1995b), from buried A-horizons in some lunettes, and from lacustrine mud in several playas (Chapter 5). These settings vary in their drainage characteristics and lithologies, so direct comparisons of specific isotopic values from them cannot be made, because each could have inherently different vegetation assemblages. Comparison of isotopic trends, however, should reveal evidence of significant vegetation changes.

An important component of this study is better documentation of the geochronology and especially the cultural chronology of Paleoindian occupations. To achieve these goals, and in addition to previously reported ages, a number of new radiocarbon ages were determined for many of the sites discussed in Chapter 3. Most of the ages were determined by the Southern Methodist University (SMU) radiocarbon laboratory. Others were determined by the University of Arizona radiocarbon laboratories (A, the conventional lab, and AA, the AMS lab). A few ages were determined by the Smithsonian Institution (SI) and by Beta Analytic, Inc. (Beta), the latter for Brown (1993).

All of the recently determined or earlier unpublished ages are from samples of organic-rich sediments and soil horizons. Both humate (NaOH-soluble) and residue (NaOH-insoluble) fractions were extracted and dated. Preferred materials for radiocarbon dating such as charcoal or wood are very rare on the Llano Estacado. Shell and bone are locally more abundant but were avoided due to the uncertainties in interpreting ages from these materials (Taylor 1987). There are problems in dating organic-rich sediments and soil horizons (e.g., Campbell et al. 1967; Scharpenseel 1971, 1979; Matthews 1985), but with proper care in sampling, laboratory processing, and interpretation they can provide reliable age control, particularly in nonleaching environments. Organic-rich sediment occurs as silty and clayey, homogeneous deposits that accumulated in slowly aggrading, probably marshy settings and as clayey lenses interbedded with sand or diatomite. Dating these types of samples at Lubbock Lake, where archaeological data and ages on wood and charcoal are also available, shows that they usually yield reasonable, approximate ages of deposition, but sometimes provide only minimum ages (Holliday, Johnson, Haas, and Stuckenrath 1983, 1985; Haas et al. 1986; see also Holliday et al. 1994). In situations where ages appear reversed or where two ages are available from a single sample (e.g., for residue and humate fractions), the older age is assumed to be a better indication of the age of the sediment (Matthews 1980; Hammond et al. 1991; Martin and Johnson 1995). Contamination with dead carbon from groundwater, precipitated in calcium carbonate, is the only known, common means of yielding falsely old ages in the region. Calcium carbonate is removed during processing of samples, however.

Organic matter in the A-horizons of buried soils was incorporated into the surface of the soil parent material during a period of landscape stability and pedogenesis. A radiocarbon age from such "homogenized" horizons is the "mean residence time" of organic material from this zone, plus the time since burial by overlying sediments (Scharpenseel 1971). Data from Lubbock Lake show that the maximum age of burial (and therefore the approximate age of the overlying sediments) can be reasonably estimated by collecting samples from the top of these zones (Haas et al. 1986). More younger carbon appears to be preserved at the top of the buried A-horizons. Older carbon probably was oxidized or mixed via bioturbation deeper in the profile. Radiocarbon ages from the lower portions of a buried A-horizon provide an intermediate age between the beginning and end of pedogenesis (Haas et al. 1986), indicating that some of the older carbon (and probably most of the oldest) were oxidized.

All of the ages determined on samples that I collected are based on a radiocarbon half-life of 5568 years and are corrected for $\delta^{13}C$ fractionation. Tree-ring calibration of radiocarbon ages can have a significant effect on the dating of Paleoindian occupations on the Great Plains (Eighmy and LaBelle 1996), but the radiocarbon ages presented in this volume are not calibrated for several reasons. (1) Calibrations would confuse comparisons with other dated sequences from the region and surrounding areas, none of which is calibrated. (2) Calibrations often require correction (especially the more recently published calibrations), rendering published calibrated ages inaccurate (e.g., Stuiver and Pearson 1992; Stuiver 1993). (3) Many of the radiocarbon ages from Paleoindian sites are in the range of only tentative calibrations (>10,000 yrs BP) (Becker 1993; Stuiver 1993). Calibration of only part of the sequence is not a useful exercise. Eighmy and LaBelle (1996) show that calibrated ages for Plains Paleoindian complexes are ca. 2000 years older than uncalibrated ages, but that the chronological sequence and duration of individual artifact styles are not significantly changed.

CHAPTER TWO

History of Paleoindian Research on the Southern High Plains

Introduction

For over 60 years archaeologists, geologists, pedologists, paleontologists, and paleobotanists have investigated the rich Paleoindian record of the Southern High Plains. As in Paleoindian research elsewhere and in most scientific endeavors, there were relatively few individuals involved at first. But as the disciplines matured and expanded, and the data base grew, the Llano Estacado became nationally known for its Paleoindian archaeology and more investigators were drawn to the region and to the research questions emerging there. The growth and evolutionary pathways of scientific research are by their nature unplanned, but in retrospect key events, key players, and the influence of each can be identified. This is certainly the case with Paleoindian studies on the Llano Estacado.

This chapter presents a brief outline of Paleoindian research on the Llano Estacado. The emphasis is on (1) highlighting the long and important role of geoscience in this research, in particular regarding stratigraphic, paleoenvironmental, and geochronological applications, and (2) examining the evolution of various Paleoindian artifact chronologies offered for the region, because of the impact they had on Paleoindian studies throughout North America. The first 30 years of research can be divided fairly evenly into decadal phases, with a key figure emerging from each decade. After about 1963, however, the historical record becomes more difficult to manage, as first there is a relative lull in research, lasting about a decade, and then a boom that continued into 1995.

The First Decade

The results of the Folsom excavations (1926–1928) prompted widespread research on Paleoindians in the New World. This work focused on further documentation of extinct fauna associated with human activity and on the artifact typology and chronology of those early occupations (Wormington 1957; Wilmsen 1965). There are several significant aspects of these research orientations beyond the immediate results of site excavations. Published papers and monographs suggest that little of this work was systematic; as sites were reported they were tested, particularly if they offered the prospect of yielding both artifacts and extinct fauna. Few regional surveys were conducted to locate sites. Surface finds or buried sites with low visibility, due to lack of megafauna remains, often were overlooked. The excavations at Lindenmeier (Wilmsen and Roberts 1978) and the long-term collection and typological study of Paleoindian points by E. B. Renaud (1931, 1932) are exceptions. Moreover, the relatively high visibility of sites with megafauna remains and the emphasis on recovery of megafauna with artifacts resulted in long-held but probably skewed ideas about Paleoindian subsistence (Meltzer 1993).

The first Paleoindian research on the Llano Estacado is an example of the serendipitous nature of the work. Edgar B. Howard of the University of Pennsylvania Museum, one of the pioneering Paleoindian researchers, was pursuing "the problem of early man" (Howard 1935a:61) at Burnet Cave in southern New Mexico (1930–1932). The work at the cave apparently was the result of a systematic survey of caves in the region. Howard instituted the survey, probably the first and one of the few aimed specifically at finding Paleoindian sites, because he believed the dry caves offered the best opportunity of finding evidence of early human occupation, based on discoveries of Paleolithic sites in caves in Europe and on the well-preserved finds of later occupations in caves throughout the Southwest (Howard 1935a:62). At the close of the 1932 season at the cave, Howard learned of fluted points found with extinct fauna near Clovis, New Mexico, in and near upper Blackwater Draw (FIG. 1.3). He decided to investigate the area further because of the extensive local collections of fluted points, additional finds of Pleistocene fauna, and excavation of a gravel pit at one of the find spots. In 1933 Howard began field work in the Clovis area (FIG. 2.1), and the results were such that he continued the field program until 1937 (Howard 1935a,b; Hester 1972).

The work in the Clovis area was directly supervised by Howard in 1933 and 1934 and by John L. Cotter, a graduate student at the University of Pennsylvania (FIG. 2.2), in 1936 and 1937 (no field work was conducted in 1935) (Hester 1972; Boldurian 1990). All of the research was co-sponsored by the Academy of Natural Sciences of Philadelphia (Howard 1935a; Cotter 1937, 1938; Hester 1972). The field work focused on a gravel pit opened in

FIGURE 2.1. Visitors to the Clovis gravel pit in the summer of 1933. The view is to the southeast, and the party is inspecting an excavation area on the southeast side of the south pit (FIG. 3.7). At center right are concrete posts constructed for the mining of gravel in 1932. Reproduced with the permission of the University of Pennsylvania Museum, Philadephia (Neg. #54-141406).

FIGURE 2.2. E. B. Howard (left) and John Cotter (right) examine artifacts from the Clovis site at the Philadelphia Academy of Natural Sciences. Courtesy Library, The Academy of Natural Sciences of Philadelphia.

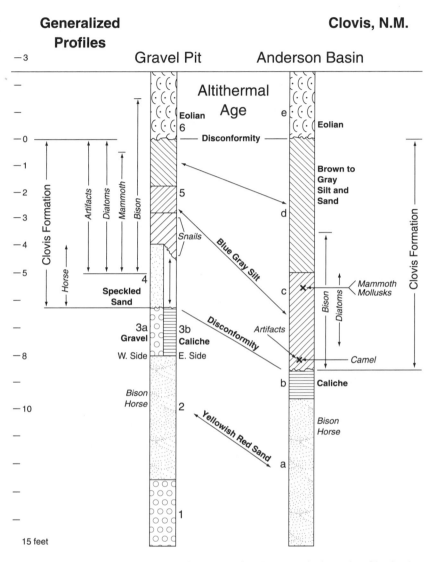

FIGURE 2.3. Stratigraphic correlation chart for the gravel pit at the Clovis site and the Anderson Basin area prepared by Ernst Antevs (from Antevs 1949: 186; with slight modification). His "Blue Gray Silt" is the "Blue Sand" of Howard (1935a) and Stock and Bode (1936), which contained most of the Paleoindian archaeology and much of the extinct fauna.

1932 between the towns of Clovis and Portales. The investigations also included nearby deflation basins ("blowouts"), most notably two basins referred to as the Anderson Lakes (now known as the Anderson Basin localities) (FIG. 1.3), which yielded a stratigraphic sequence, artifact styles, and extinct fauna similar to those found in the gravel pit (FIG. 2.3).

From the outset in 1933 the field work at Clovis went beyond archaeology. Other investigators were incorporated into the research, including geologists (Antevs 1935, 1949; Stock and Bode 1936), vertebrate and invertebrate paleontologists (Lohman 1935; Stock and Bode 1936; Clarke 1938; Patrick 1938), and paleobotanists (Howard 1935b). Howard's interdisciplinary approach reflected his broad interests in geology, paleontology, and archaeology, and an academic background that included advanced degrees in both anthropology and geology (Roberts 1943). Howard's unusually comprehensive disciplinary breadth is best reflected in the papers of an international symposium on "Early Man" (MacCurdy 1937), which he organized while the work at Clovis was still under way (Roberts 1943).

Thus began the long history of Paleoindian studies on the Llano Estacado. Moreover, this work at Clovis and neighboring localities was the first interdisciplinary archaeological project in the region (perhaps the first in North America) and established an interdisciplinary tradition on the Llano Estacado that continues today.

The finds at Clovis and surrounding sites came from sediments that filled Blackwater Draw and, at the gravel pit, deposits filling a basin that drained into the draw. The research produced some spectacular finds and provided some early clues to Paleoindian chronology, typology, and environments. Of primary importance to Howard was further documentation of the association of artifacts with extinct vertebrates. This goal was amply met. The remains of two mammoths and five extinct bison were found in several strata along with a variety of artifacts that included fluted points and bone foreshafts and points, providing clear evidence of butchering and probably killing (FIG. 2.4). The research also demonstrated that during the fluted-point occupations the environment was wetter, with flowing or standing fresh water, although a drying trend was in evidence.

The fluted points found during Howard's research now are classified as Clovis and Folsom types, but were not so differentiated at the time. Beginning with the Folsom discovery and through the 1930s, most fluted points were referred to as "Folsom," "Folsom-like," "Folsomoid," or "Generalized Folsom" (Wormington 1957: 30). By the late 1930s the typological and chronological distinctions between Clovis and Folsom were all but formalized. Cotter (1938:117), in summarizing the 1936 and 1937 excavations at the Clovis site, observed:

> it is evident that the . . . points associated . . . with mammoth bones were typically long and heavy for the Folsom pattern, with very slight channeling at the base. . . . finds made in the [overlying] . . . clay associated with bison bones were typically of a slighter design, with and without channeling.

In 1937, about one month after the close of Howard's excavations at Clovis, another field project was under way that also would have profound impact on Paleoindian studies on the Southern High Plains. In 1933 large bone fragments were found exposed in a field on the C. R. Cowan Ranch, near Miami, Texas, on the northeastern Llano Estacado (Sellards 1938) (FIG. 1.3). J. A. Mead of Miami, an amateur archaeologist and fossil collector, tested the site in 1934 and then arranged for full-scale excavations under the auspices of E. H. Sellards, geologist and paleontologist at the

FIGURE 2.4. Mammoth vertebra and Clovis point (base is visible protruding from the sand to the lower left of the vertebra) found during Cotter's excavations in 1936. Note the sandy matrix. This is a small part of an extensive mammoth bone bed (the "mammoth pit") at the far southwestern corner of the south pit, immediately north of and adjacent to the area now called the South Bank (FIG. 3.7). Reproduced from Cotter (1937:plate 6.3) with the permission of the University of Pennsylvania Museum, Philadephia (Neg. #54-141403).

FIGURE 2.5. The Miami site at the end of Sellards' excavations in 1937. Most of the bone, in plaster jackets, has been removed, but the position of the jackets and bones is apparent from the debris left behind (see Holliday et al. 1994: fig. 2A). Below the bone bed are deep test pits that yielded poorly preserved, unidentifiable bone fragments, some from a large animal (G. L. Evans, pers. comm. 1992). The light zone on the far side of the nearest pit (arrow) is probably the loess. Courtesy of the Texas Archeological Research Laboratory, the University of Texas at Austin.

University of Texas at Austin. The work at Miami, in 1937, was directed by Sellards' chief assistant Glen L. Evans. Parts of five mammoths were recovered from a small playa (FIG. 2.5). Three fluted points, identified as "Folsom or Folsom-like" but now known to be Clovis, were found among the bones along with a scraper (Sellards 1938). The site is the third documented co-occurrence of Clovis points and mammoths on the Great Plains after the finds near Dent, Colorado (Wormington 1957), and Clovis. In addition to Clovis, the study also was one of few Paleoindian investigations of the decade to deal with site stratigraphy.

Perhaps more importantly, the work at Miami marked the beginning of almost a quarter century of research by Sellards into the Quaternary geology and paleontology and Paleoindian archaeology of the Southern High Plains. Miami was important to Sellards for the additional proof it furnished of Pleistocene humans in the New World. Twenty years earlier Sellards became involved in that debate when he thought he found human skeletal remains directly associated with Pleistocene megafauna near Vero, Florida (Sellards 1916, 1917). Sellards probably was wrong and was harshly criticized (Hrdlicka 1918; Meltzer 1983). He became embarrassed and embittered by the affair, and upon moving to Texas he continued to seek evidence of human association with extinct Pleistocene species (Ferguson 1981:88; Evans 1986). Miami was his first opportunity, and he was able to take advantage of it in his capacity as Director of the Bureau of Economic Geology.

The first excavations of a Folsom site in Texas came shortly after the Miami work, north of the Llano Estacado, but not far from Miami. In 1939 C. Bertrand Schultz of the University of Nebraska Museum investigated the Lipscomb Bison Quarry (now simply the Lipscomb site) on the Central High Plains in the extreme northeast corner of the Texas Panhandle, north of the northeast corner of the Llano Estacado (Barbour and Schultz 1941; Schultz 1943) (FIG. 1.1). Schultz, a vertebrate paleontologist, was attracted to the site because it contained a bed of extinct bison remains exposed in a gully along a small creek. Upon investigation, however, Folsom artifacts were found in association with the bone; Lipscomb became the fourth Folsom bison kill found in North America, after Folsom, Lindenmeier, and Clovis. Additional field work was carried out at Lipscomb in 1946. The Lipscomb research primarily was paleontological, however, and little stratigraphic or paleoenvironmental data were published, although such data apparently exist (Hofman et al. 1989).

Another important Paleoindian site in a playa came to light a few years after the Miami excavations. Near San Jon, New Mexico, on the northwestern edge of the Llano Estacado (FIG. 1.3), a local rancher found some bone and stone artifacts eroding out of deep ravines cut into playa sediments along the Caprock Escarpment. He showed the specimens to individuals at the Laboratory of Anthropology in Santa Fe and the University of New Mexico in Albuquerque. In the spring of 1940, Frank Hibben of the University tested the locality (Roberts 1942; Judson 1953). Hibben's crew recovered additional archaeological materials but was unable to take on full-scale excavations. The work was turned over to Frank H. H. Roberts of the Smithsonian Institution, who conducted field work at San Jon from June to September 1941 (FIG. 2.6). Roberts was a veteran field archaeologist for the Smithsonian Institution, fresh from his work at the Lindenmeier site, Colorado. Stratigraphic studies at and in the vicinity of the San Jon site were conducted by Sheldon Judson, a graduate student in geology at Harvard University (Judson 1953:3). Judson's involvement in the project resulted from his study with Kirk Bryan, a pioneer in geoarchaeology, as well as geomorphology and Quaternary stratigraphy (Haynes 1990). Archaeological research at San Jon was cut short by the

FIGURE 2.6. Frank H. H. Roberts' excavations at the San Jon site early in the 1941 season, sponsored by the Smithsonian Institution. The crew is beginning to dig in Area II. The view is to the north, probably taken from near Area I (see FIG. 3.49). The deep arroyo between Area II and Area I is apparent in the middleground, and the breach in the High Plains escarpment is obvious at the upper right (the Canadian River valley is visible in the distance). Reproduced with permission of the National Anthropological Archives, Smithsonian Institution.

Second World War, but Judson conducted additional geologic work in 1943 and 1947.

Roberts was interested in the San Jon site because the surface collection and testing yielded "fossil bone" associated with artifacts and because the artifact collection included the lanceolate "so-called Yuma type, a form purported to be of some antiquity but about which further data are needed to determine its true status" (Roberts 1942:2). Geologic investigations by Judson were a significant component of the work at San Jon, due to the spectacular stratigraphic exposures at the site. In particular, geologic investigations were intended to answer questions about the antiquity of the "Yuma type" points and to address questions concerning stratigraphic and climatic correlations with other regions (Judson 1953:2).

Two bone beds with Paleoindian artifacts were found at San Jon. The lower bed contained remains of extinct bison in lacustrine clay associated with a lanceolate point named San Jon by Roberts (1942:8). A Folsom point recovered from another part of the site was correlated with this horizon. The upper bed contained bones of modern bison in slopewash associated with the then newly named lanceolate "Eden Valley Yuma" (later termed the Eden style) (see below). The results were important for documenting the association of a lanceolate style with extinct fauna, the first of such finds on the Llano Estacado, but raised questions concerning the relationship of lanceolate styles with modern bison, and did not clarify the stratigraphic relationship between Folsom and lanceolate styles (Wormington 1957: 113, 122–123; Wheat 1972: 143).

At the close of the San Jon field season Roberts attended a symposium on Paleoindian terminology held in Santa Fe and sponsored by the University of Pennsylvania Museum and the Laboratory of Anthropology (Ray 1942; Howard 1943; Wormington 1948). The group decided to differentiate the various fluted types, thus defining the Folsom and Clovis types so familiar today (Howard 1943; Wormington 1948). The Santa Fe conference also resulted in one of the earliest and one of the few systematic attempts to differentiate the many lanceolate styles. The catchall "Yuma" category was discarded and new classificatory names, such as "Eden Valley Yuma," were designated on the basis of type collections.

The Sellards Years

After completion of the work at Miami, E. H. Sellards, as Director of the Bureau of Economic Geology and the Texas Memorial Museum (each part of the University of Texas at Austin), instituted several statewide paleontological and strategic mineral surveys (funded by the Depression-era Works Progress Administration, or WPA) (Ferguson 1981: 105) that had a significant impact on postwar Paleoindian research (Evans 1986). Sellards and his associates did not conduct archaeological surveys in the modern sense (they were geologists and paleontologists carrying out geological surveys), but these surveys, particularly the paleontological ones, provided ample opportunities to search for and find Paleoindian sites, especially high-visibility ones with megafauna remains. As Evans (1986: 10) emphasizes, "Sellards was not an archaeologist . . . , but a geologist and paleontologist—a fact worth keeping in mind when reading his papers on early man, which often reveal a geologist's preoccupation with man's *antiquity*, rather than with his cultural traits" (emphasis in original).

Much of the field work instituted by Sellards was under the direction of Glen Evans, who sometimes worked in association with Grayson Meade of Texas Technological College (now Texas Tech University). Evans was a geologist who began working for Sellards in the 1930s (Evans 1986). Under Sellards' influence, Evans' initial archaeological interests were allowed to grow and to merge with his geological duties until he became intimately involved in Sellards' quest (and enthusiasm) for Paleoindian sites. Evans worked with Sellards until 1953 and continued informal collaborations afterward. Meade was a vertebrate paleontologist who studied with Erwin H. Barbour, a prominent paleontologist in Nebraska who also had interests in the issue of "Early Man" and human associations with extinct fauna (Schultz 1948; Evans 1995; D. Meade, pers. comm. 1995). Meade was not only influenced by Barbour (who was also Meade's grandfather-in-law), but, perhaps more significantly, Meade's father-in-law was Harold Cook, excavator of the Folsom site. Prior to Meade's association with Sellards and Evans, therefore, his appreciation of issues regarding "Early Man" was already fully established (D. Meade, pers. comm. 1995). Sellards hired Grayson Meade onto the paleontological surveys in 1939. Meade joined the faculty at Texas Tech in 1941, but continued his summer field work for the Texas Memorial Museum until 1952.

Evans and Meade were close collaborators throughout the period 1939–1952, and gathered considerable stratigraphic and paleontological data. They presented the results of much of their research in the first comprehensive summary of the Quaternary history of the Llano Estacado (Evans and Meade 1945). During the surveys they investigated several archaeological sites. In 1942 they visited a reservoir excavated in Lubbock, Texas, where Paleoindian artifacts were reported. The site, in a meander of Yellowhouse Draw (FIG. 2.7), was their "Locality 12," but later became known as the Lubbock Lake site (FIG. 1.3). The reservoir was constructed in 1936, and the dredging unearthed Folsom artifacts and bones of extinct animals (Johnson and Holliday 1987a). These finds resulted in WPA-sponsored excavations in 1939 and 1941, but a high water table (FIG. 2.7) prevented investigation of the Paleoindian levels (Wheat 1974; Johnson and Holliday 1987a). Sellards first learned of the site in 1938 from Adolfe Witte (one of several local informants cultivated by Sellards), who found a Folsom point there (Sellards 1940; letter on file, Museum of Texas Tech University). As a result, Evans visited the site in 1939 and found a "Yuma" point (accession records on file, Texas Archeological Research Laboratory, Austin). The water table was declining due to mining of the Ogallala Aquifer, however, and by the time Evans and Meade visited the reservoir in 1942, it was drying. In 1944 Evans and Meade discovered fossil bone at their "Locality 8," a quarry along Running Water Draw in Plainview, Texas (later known as the Plainview site) (FIG. 1.3). The site apparently was known to a few local inhabitants who collected artifacts there for some years prior to 1944 (Speer 1990). Both Lubbock Lake and Plainview were excavated during the most intense phase of Paleoindian studies in Sellards' career, even though he was 70 by the summer of 1945.

Paleoindian research on the Southern High Plains was dominated by Sellards and his associates in the decade following World War II, and resulted in some of the best-known and most influential Paleoindian discoveries in North America. Their first efforts were directed at the Plainview bone bed. The bed was associated with alluvium near the base of a sedimentary sequence filling Running Water Draw (FIG. 1.3). From June to October 1945, much of the bone bed was removed (Sellards et al. 1947). More of the bed was taken out on a return trip in November 1949 (Sellards 1952:61–62; Speer 1990). The bed consisted of bone from extinct bison in association with stone artifacts, including a number of lanceolate projectile points. These points became the type specimens for the Plainview projectile point style (Krieger 1947). At the time it was the largest collection of lanceolate points in the region found in place. The matrix containing the bone provided evidence of a competent perennial stream in the now-dry valley, an indication of a substantial environmental change. The excavations, however, did not shed light on the relationship of the lanceolate style to fluted points. This vexing problem was soon to be solved by Sellards and Evans.

In the late 1940s and early 1950s, Sellards, Evans, and Meade directed their attention to Lubbock Lake and to the Clovis gravel pit. Both sites had similar stratigraphy and held the promise of multiple Paleoindian occupations. By the late 1940s the reservoir at Lubbock Lake was completely dry. The crews directed by Sellards and Evans were the first to explore the Paleoindian features (Kelley 1974; Johnson and Holliday 1987a). Excavations at Lubbock were in June to October 1948, August 1950, and May to August 1951 (TARL files). The work at Clovis was in July, August, November, and December 1949, and May to July 1950 (Hester 1972).

The results of the work at Clovis and Lubbock Lake were profound. At Clovis a stratified succession of stone tools with bones of extinct fauna finally confirmed the superposition of Folsom over Clovis. Moreover, bone beds with lanceolate points were recovered stratigraphically above Folsom features, first establishing unfluted Paleoindian styles as later than the fluted points. The lanceolate styles were grouped together as the "Portales Complex" (Sellards 1952:72–74). Sellards' (1952) data, combined with that of Howard and Cotter, resulted in the most definitive descriptions of the Paleoindian assemblages from the site as of 1952 (Hester 1972:39).

FIGURE 2.7. The Lubbock Lake site in Yellowhouse Draw (looking north). The photo was taken by J. B. Wheat in August 1939, during WPA excavations that he directed (Wheat 1974). Visible are the reservoir (filled with water), the dike created from dredge spoil, the valley walls, and the limit of late Quaternary valley fill (denoted by the darker vegetation in the valley). Courtesy of the Lubbock Lake Landmark, Museum of Texas Tech University.

Geologically, Glen Evans' stratigraphic work in the gravel pit was the first to provide an indication of the extent and history of ancient, spring-fed streams, ponds, and marshes that once existed in the basin.

Lubbock Lake also yielded stone artifacts associated with extinct fauna within deposits from ancient streams, ponds, and marshes (Sellards 1952; Johnson 1987a). These deposits, generally similar to those at Clovis, provided additional evidence of Paleoindian environments significantly different from that of the present dry valley. Of particular interest was the discovery of two bison bone beds with Folsom points in place. In 1950 burned bone was collected from another bone bed and submitted to Willard Libby for radiocarbon analysis (FIG. 2.8), one of the first applications of the new dating method to Paleoindian archaeology (Roberts 1951). The resulting

FIGURE 2.8. View along the west side of the reservoir cut at Lubbock Lake (looking north) (see FIG. 3.20), probably in the summer of 1950. Figure in the middle of the photo is standing on the west side of the "island" left by the dredging and above "Station M" (see FIG. 3.29), where burned bone was secured from stratum 2 to yield radiocarbon sample C-558 from Willard Libby's laboratory. The sample was long believed to be from a Folsom occupation (and to be the first radiocarbon age for Folsom), but subsequent work showed that the level was Late Paleoindian. Courtesy of the Texas Memorial Museum, the University of Texas at Austin.

age of 9883 ± 350 yrs BP (C-558) later was correlated with the Folsom bone beds (discovered in the 1951 season) and was believed to be the first radiocarbon determination for the Folsom tradition (Holliday and Johnson 1986). Later research determined that the age and the correlation were in error (Holliday and Johnson 1986), but the work nevertheless helped bring Lubbock Lake into archaeological prominence.

Several events in 1952 and 1953 had a significant impact on Paleoindian studies in North American and also changed the direction of Paleoindian research on the Southern High Plains. In 1952 Sellards published *Early Man in America*, for its time the most comprehensive statement on the topic. The volume was the first to document the classic typological sequence of Clovis–Folsom–unfluted lanceolate. The book also contained Sellards' only published account of his Paleoindian work at Clovis and Lubbock Lake and the return trip to Plainview. Also in 1952, the ownership of the Clovis site changed and gravel mining resumed (Hester 1972). In 1953 human remains were found in proximity to some apparent Paleoindian projectile points near Midland, Texas (FIG. 1.3), an unusually rare and potentially important discovery discussed below.

Also in 1953 Glen Evans left the Texas Memorial Museum (TMM) to work in the oil industry, and Sellards lost his principal collaborator. Evans was Sellards' primary field director for Quaternary studies, including the Paleoindian research, and, in particular, was responsible for most of the geoarchaeological field work (e.g., Hester 1972:6). Evans produced stratigraphic sections and maps for all of the TMM Paleoindian projects, data notably absent from Sellards' subsequent field work. Evans' field notes (unpublished) also contain the most detailed documentation of the TMM Paleoindian research beyond field maps and the artifact accession records. For example, the meticulous description and documentation by Evans (1951) of Archaic wells at Clovis stand in marked contrast to the much more general and cursory discussion of Paleoindian features at Clovis and Lubbock Lake by Sellards (1952). Evans also prepared detailed maps of bone beds (albeit incomplete), beginning with work at Miami, which was an unusual field procedure for its time (Holliday and Johnson 1996). The maps included placement of the artifacts in relation to the bones, and the assigning of individual numbers to the objects correlated with the mapped material. This procedure allowed the collection to be useful to other researchers interested in different questions raised by subsequent theoretical perspectives.

From 1953 to 1957 Sellards continued his Paleoindian field work and Evans occasionally joined him. Sellards directed sporadic excavations at the Clovis gravel pit during this period, and in 1954 he participated in work at the Midland site, discussed below. The work at Clovis primarily emphasized the salvage of archaeological materials as they were exposed by gravel mining (Hester 1972:7). This phase of Sellards' work at Clovis suffered from the absence of Evans' "precise knowledge of the stratigraphy of the site" (Hester 1972:6). Fortunately, most of the 1953–1957 field work at Clovis was conducted by two talented amateur archaeologists from the local area: Oscar Shay and James M. Warnica (Hester 1972:6). Warnica's interest in Paleoindian archaeology and the high standards of his field work played an important role in subsequent research at the gravel pit and in work throughout the Clovis-Portales area and other areas of eastern New Mexico, as indicated below and in Chapter 3.

Sellards excavated at two other sites in eastern New Mexico: Milnesand and Ted Williamson (FIGS. 1.3, 2.9). Both of these sites were beds of

FIGURE 2.9. Excavations at the Milnesand site in 1953. Exposed bone is visible in the left middleground and foreground (see also FIG. 3.59). The photo also illustrates the open, low-relief character of the Lea-Yoakum dune field. Courtesy of the Texas Memorial Museum, the University of Texas at Austin.

extinct bison in sand dune fields and were exposed by wind erosion during severe drought in the early 1950s. They are significant because they produced a new artifact type and because they yielded two of the most extensive Paleoindian bone beds and the two largest collections of individual Paleoindian projectile point styles on the Southern High Plains. These sites also are two of the few formally reported from the extensive dune fields of the region, although many Paleoindian sites are known to exist in these areas. For example, deflation exposed the Tatum and Barber sites (FIG. 1.3), which were visited by Sellards and noted by Sellards and Evans (1960), but never formally investigated (J. Warnica, pers. comm. 1995).

Sellards excavated Milnesand in 1953 (Sellards 1955a, n.d.a) and tested Ted Williamson at about the same time (Sellards, n.d.b; J. Warnica, pers. comm. 1994). The field work at Milnesand yielded 23 lanceolate projectile points among an unknown number of extinct-bison remains. The artifact collection became the type specimens for the Milnesand projectile point style, and it was believed related to the post-Folsom assemblage found at Clovis (Sellards 1955a, n.d.a). Before and after excavations the landowner collected over 100 additional points (Warnica and Williamson 1968). Little is known about the Ted Williamson site except for a brief discussion by Sellards (n.d.b), and that the landowner collected about 130 projectile points (Johnson et al. 1986; Buchanan et al. 1995). Sellards found little during his testing and devoted most of his attention to Milnesand (J. Warnica, pers. comm. 1994). The Ted Williamson site apparently was very similar to Milnesand, with the stone artifacts scattered among an extensive *Bison antiquus* bone bed. Most of the points are of the Plainview style, but a few are Milnesand (Johnson et al. 1986). Milnesand and Ted Williamson are spectacular for the large artifact collections they produced, but essentially nothing is known about the bone beds themselves. Blocks of bone were recovered from Milnesand but not Ted Williamson, and there are no maps of either bone bed and no provenience data on the artifacts other than a sketch and a general comment by Sellards (1955a:337, fig. 97).

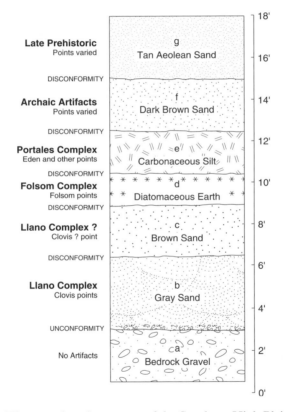

Late Prehistoric Points varied	g Tan Aeolean Sand	18' 16'
DISCONFORMITY		
Archaic Artifacts Points varied	f Dark Brown Sand	14'
DISCONFORMITY		
Portales Complex Eden and other points	e Carbonaceous Silt	12'
DISCONFORMITY		
Folsom Complex Folsom points	d Diatomaceous Earth	10'
DISCONFORMITY		
Llano Complex ? Clovis ? point	c Brown Sand	8'
DISCONFORMITY		6'
Llano Complex Clovis points	b Gray Sand	4'
UNCONFORMITY		
No Artifacts	ca Bedrock Gravel	2' 0'

FIGURE 2.10. The geocultural sequence of the Southern High Plains proposed by E. H. Sellards and Glen Evans (Sellards and Evans 1960: fig. 2; with very slight modification), based on geoarchaeological research at the Clovis and Lubbock Lake sites. This is the first geologically oriented cultural chronology for the region.

Sellards' Paleoindian field studies largely ended by 1957. He spent most of his remaining years analyzing his data, focusing especially on the large collections from Clovis (Hester 1972:7), and also preparing a second edition of his book. Sellards and Evans (1960) produced the first comprehensive summary of the Paleoindian archaeology of the Llano Estacado. The stratigraphy at Clovis and Lubbock Lake was an important component of the discussion, and the strata were identified on the basis of associated artifact styles, as in the "Folsom stratum" or the "Portales unit" (Sellards and Evans 1960:643, 645) (FIG. 2.10). The similarities in the stratigraphic sequences at these two sites also were noted and used to support interpretations of regional environmental changes. The revision of *Early Man in America* was not completed at the time of Sellards' death in 1961, however, and it was never published.

Sellards' passing marked the end of the first major phase of Paleoindian research on the Southern High Plains. This work, beginning at Clovis in 1933, was not systematic and tended to be driven by chance discoveries. The research also tended to emphasize individual sites, recovery of megafauna associated with stone tools, and artifact chronologies and typologies. There were few attempts to recover animal remains except those of the extinct megafauna, and only a few paleoenvironmental reconstructions were attempted, most notably at Clovis by Howard, Cotter, and associates, and based on a variety of data. The trends in environmental change proposed by Sellards and Evans (1960) were based largely on stratigraphic information. The field studies started by others at the Midland site began a new phase in more broadly based (geographically and methodologically), interdisciplinary approaches to the study of Paleoindians on the Llano Estacado, reflecting national and international trends in archaeological method and theory.

Midland, Wendorf, and the High Plains Paleoecology Project

The Midland discovery in 1953, fully discussed by Wendorf and others (1955), was made by Keith Glasscock, an artifact collector. The human remains were found in a blowout in sand dunes on the floor of Monahans Draw (FIGS. 1.3, 2.11A). Near the skeleton were several projectile points with attributes similar to Paleoindian styles. Glasscock contacted Fred Wendorf, then at the Laboratory of Anthropology, Santa Fe, and in October 1953 Glasscock, Wendorf, and others tested the Midland site (also known as the Scharbauer Ranch site). All evidence suggested that the human remains were Paleoindian. Given the rarity of such finds Wendorf

FIGURE 2.11A. Locality 1 at the Midland site during the initial visit by Fred Wendorf and colleagues on October 29, 1953, looking north across the north end of the blowout and toward the main belt of dunes. Figures in the center-ground are near the find spot of the human remains. Courtesy of the Texas Memorial Museum, the University of Texas at Austin.

FIGURE 2.11B. Coring in Locality 1 at the Midland site on July 4, 1990. The view is northwest across the north end of the blowout. The Giddings rig is near the area where the human bone was recovered. The margins of the blow-out moved to the northwest and north since 1953. Note the heavy brush (largely salt cedar) around the margins of the basin. The vegetation and muddy floor are the result of dumping of tertiary sewage effluent into Monahans Draw by the City of Odessa, which results in a high water table in the draw and regular flooding of the valley floor.

conducted full-scale excavations in 1953–1954 and in 1955 (Wendorf et al. 1955; Wendorf and Krieger 1959). Sellards also conducted excavations at Midland in 1954, and Evans assisted with the stratigraphic interpretations (Sellards 1955b; G. L. Evans, pers. comm. 1990).

Wendorf's work at Midland represented only the second truly interdisciplinary Paleoindian study on the Southern High Plains (after Howard's work at Clovis). Wendorf's inspiration for this approach was one of his advisors at Harvard University, Hallam Movius, who was impressed by interdisciplinary archaeology under way in Britain and had himself experienced it in Ireland (F. Wendorf, pers. comm. 1995). Movius' approach and experience reflected broader trends in archaeological research, in particular the emerging field of interdisciplinary "environmental archaeology" (Butzer 1971:6–11). With respect to the Midland site specifically, the stratigraphic complexity and the importance of stratigraphy in dating the human remains convinced Wendorf that a geoscientific approach was required in his research at the site (F. Wendorf, pers. comm. 1995). The geology of the site was investigated by Claude C. Albritton, Jr., on the faculty of Southern Methodist University. Albritton was another student of Kirk Bryan and had previously worked on problems of Quaternary stratigraphy and archaeological geology in western Texas (Albritton and Bryan 1939; Kelley et al. 1940; Huffington and Albritton 1941; Ferring 1989). Albritton's work with R. M. Huffington on dune stratigraphy west of Midland was especially germane to the stratigraphic problems that confronted Wendorf's team at the Midland site.

The contrast between Wendorf's field methods and those of Sellards epitomizes the broader contrast between the first several decades of Paleoindian research in the region and those that were to follow. Wendorf's excavations were based on careful recording of all archaeological and geological associations and on observations made in hand-excavated trenches and pits. Sellards' approach was to mechanically trench the greater part of the area producing the human bone (FIG. 2.12). His interest focused on further documentation of human artifacts in association with extinct fauna. There was almost no recording of this work. The only surviving field documentation was provided by Evans, as in their earlier collaboration, who produced a stratigraphic drawing of one of the trenches. This section ultimately proved important in subsequent research at the site (discussed in Chapter 3).

The geological investigations by Albritton provided initial age estimates of the human remains. Near the human remains were small projectile points (later termed Midland) similar to unfluted Folsom points. The

FIGURE 2.12. Trenching at the Midland site (Locality 1) by E. H. Sellards, in late 1954 (see Sellards 1955b:fig. 35). View is north across the north end of the site, probably taken from just east of the excavations around the original site of the human bone (compare with FIG. 2.11A). Courtesy of the Texas Memorial Museum, the University of Texas at Austin.

unfluted types as well as Folsom points were recovered in adjacent dunes and blowouts. Dating of the human remains, therefore, relied largely on correlating the strata and the archaeology among blowouts. Radiocarbon dating and the newly devised uranium-series method also were applied to the problem (Rosholt 1958; Wendorf and Krieger 1959). The initial interpretations of the Midland finds were that the skeletal material pre-dated the Folsom occupation and was perhaps as old as 20,000 yrs BP.

The discovery of possible Paleoindian human remains was a significant development in Paleoindian studies, but the research at Midland had a more far-reaching impact. The work at Midland produced "several intriguing clues about the past climate" of the Southern High Plains (Wendorf 1961a:9). Wendorf's subsequent work at the Clovis site (Hester 1972:7) and his exposure to the record at Lubbock Lake while he was at Texas Tech convinced him that the stratigraphic complexities of the region and questions of late Quaternary environments could only be resolved using an interdisciplinary natural sciences approach (F. Wendorf, pers. comm. 1995). In particular, Wendorf came into contact with Kathryn Clisby (Oberlin College) and Paul Sears (Yale University), who encouraged

Wendorf to pursue the paleoenvironmental questions raised by his work and that of others on the Southern High Plains (Wendorf 1961a:9; pers. comm. 1995). Clisby and Sears were especially enthusiastic about palynology based on their research in New Mexico (Clisby and Sears 1956).

As a result of this series of events and encounters, Wendorf launched the High Plains Paleoecology Project (HPPP). The primary goal of the project was "to bring the data and methodology from a variety of disciplines to bear on the study of the sequence of environmental changes on the Llano Estacado during the Late Pleistocene" (Wendorf and Hester 1975:vii). Another important goal of the project "was to delimit precisely the environment of this region during the period when the first known human occupation occurred and during the several thousand year interval immediately following" (Wendorf and Hester 1975:viii). The research involved archaeology, vertebrate and invertebrate paleontology, geology, and paleobotany, with particular emphasis on palynology, and was conducted in two phases: 1957–1959, reported in Wendorf (1961a), and 1961–1962, discussed by Wendorf and Hester (1975). The project ended in 1962 when Wendorf began research in Egypt and the Sudan (F. Wendorf, pers. comm. 1995).

There were several significant aspects of the High Plains Paleoecology Project and its results. This interdisciplinary venture was and remains one of the few regional studies of late Quaternary history in North America that incorporated archaeology, stratigraphy, geochronology, paleobotany, and paleontology. The paleoecological studies included investigation of most of the well-known Paleoindian sites of the area. Pollen samples were collected from Clovis, Lubbock Lake, San Jon, the Anderson Basin sites, and Plainview (Hafsten 1961, 1964; Green 1961a; Hester 1975b; Wendorf and Hester 1962; Oldfield 1975; Schoenwetter 1975; Oldfield and Schoenwetter 1975) (FIG. 1.3).

The principal outcomes of this research included the definition of a sequence of late Quaternary "climatic intervals" (Wendorf 1961b) and "pollen-analytical episodes" (Oldfield 1975; Schoenwetter 1975), along with environmental reconstructions for the various "intervals" and "episodes" (Oldfield and Schoenwetter 1975; Wendorf 1970, 1975b). An especially important outcome of the paleoecological research was evidence for coniferous forest on the Southern High Plains at the close of the Pleistocene, coeval with some of the Paleoindian occupations (Wendorf 1961b, 1970; Wendorf and Hester 1975). Indeed, clarification of this issue based on the results of the first phase of the study was one of the driving forces behind the second phase (Wendorf and Hester 1975:viii). "The suggestion that a boreal forest had once covered the southernmost section of the High Plains was highly controversial" (Wendorf and Hester 1975:viii). The prevailing view at the time was that the High Plains always was a grassland, even during so-called "pluvial maxima" (Antevs 1954). If the Southern High Plains was a boreal forest at times in the past, then more northerly regions probably were as well, requiring a "climatic change of much greater magnitude than previously estimated" (Wendorf and Hester 1975:viii).

Considerable geological and archaeological research focused on the Paleoindian sites of the region as both direct and indirect results of the project. There is no more intense period of such research in the 60-plus years of Paleoindian studies on the Southern High Plains. F. Earl Green, who had training in geology and paleontology, considerable experience on the Southern High Plains, and a long interest in archaeology, was brought into the HPPP at its beginning in 1957. Green was responsible for geologic research in the early stages of the project, resulting in his archaeological and geological work at Lubbock Lake (Green 1962b) and at Clovis (Green 1962a, 1963, 1992), perhaps best known for the discovery of Clovis blades (Green 1963).

C. Vance Haynes, Jr., also became involved in geoarchaeological work at the Clovis site and surrounding localities during the later stages of the HPPP. Like many others who worked on the Southern High Plains, Haynes was trained in geology (particularly mining geology and geochemistry) but had a long-standing interest in archaeology (Albritton 1985). By the late 1950s he was devoting increasing amounts of time to geoarchaeology and less and less to mining geology (C. V. Haynes, pers. comm. 1995). Haynes' training in geochemistry led him to begin a systematic attempt to date Paleoindian sites with radiocarbon, a method just barely a decade old. A significant outcome of the dating project was publication of a report on the geochronology of the Lindenmeier site (Haynes and Agogino 1960). Haynes' background, interests, and abilities were known to Wendorf, so he was invited to join the second phase of the HPPP (C. V. Haynes, F. Wendorf, pers. comm. 1995). Haynes' work at Clovis led to the most comprehensive statements on the geoarchaeology of the area to date (Haynes and Agogino 1966; Haynes 1975) and a continuing research program at the gravel pit (e.g., Stanford et al. 1990; Haynes 1995). In particular, Haynes' work resulted in documentation of the very important role of spring discharge in the site formation processes at Clovis (Haynes and Agogino 1966). Haynes also was the first to synthesize all of the geologic observations made at the gravel pit and neighboring sites (such as Anderson Basin) between 1933 and 1963, and to fit the local paleoenvironmental interpretations into regional paleoclimatic reconstructions.

Other work of the HPPP focused on Paleoindian sites in eastern New Mexico. Jerry Harbour (1975) conducted stratigraphic research at the San Jon site as part of a larger study of Pleistocene stratigraphy, updating the work of Judson (1953) and providing additional insights into the processes of playa-basin formation in general and formation of the San Jon site in particular. A Folsom site near Elida, New Mexico, also was first reported at this time (Warnica 1961; Hester 1962) (FIG. 1.3). The site, one of the few Folsom campsites reported in the region, was exposed in a deflating dune field and yielded an extensive Folsom lithic assemblage.

Wendorf also was involved with attempts to protect several Paleoindian sites from destruction. In 1956 he was among a group of scientists that tried to set aside part of the Clovis site, rapidly undergoing destruction by quarrying, as a scientific preserve. These efforts were unfortunately unsuccessful (Hester 1972:14–15). Wendorf also was concerned about the future of Lubbock Lake, where an increase in quarrying for caliche near the old reservoir raised the specter of wholesale destruction such as that continuing at Clovis (Museum of Texas Tech University records). In 1958 Wendorf assisted in convincing the City of Lubbock, which owned the site, to protect and preserve the locality. The city arranged a long-term lease with Texas Tech for the area surrounding the reservoir (Museum of Texas Tech University records). Over 35 years later the site still remains protected, and in 1990 became part of the state park system of Texas.

The protection of Lubbock Lake and loss of Clovis are reflected in the data for each site surviving from that time. Excavations by Green and Jane Holden (an archaeologist and daughter of W. C. Holden, the discoverer of the site) in 1959 and 1960, unhurried by impending destruction, included careful observation and documentation of geologic stratigraphy, archaeological features, and artifact associations (F. E. Green, ms. on file, Museum of Texas Tech University; Kaczor 1978). Years later, these field methods allowed analysis and reconstruction of individual features and relatively precise correlations with subsequently excavated features (Kaczor 1978).

The resumption of gravel mining at Clovis resulted in considerable field work between 1957 and 1963 (Dittert 1957; Green 1962a, 1963, 1992; Haynes and Agogino 1966; Warnica 1966; Agogino 1968; Hester 1972: 7–10), beyond that generated directly by the HPPP, and aimed at salvaging archaeological materials (mostly Paleoindian) (FIGS. 2.13A,B). The work included groups from the Museum of New Mexico (the HPPP),

Eastern New Mexico University, Texas Tech, and the El Llano Archaeological Society (Hester 1972:7–10; Stevens 1973:6–8). There were some spectacular finds, the best known being bone beds from Clovis mammoth kills (Warnica 1966) (FIG. 2.13A) and the Clovis blades (Green 1963), but these were made amid confusion, personal rancor, and wholesale site destruction (Hester 1972:8–10, 85–86). The data recovered and preserved were meager compared to what was lost. One result of these difficulties was that Eastern New Mexico University was given responsibility for coordinating the work at the site and in 1963 hired George A. Agogino, a Paleoindian archaeologist then at the University of Wyoming, to direct the work (Stevens 1973:7–8). In late 1963 the owner of the gravel pit (Sam Sanders) decided that only Eastern New Mexico University would work at the site, and beginning in early 1964 Agogino became the principal investigator (Agogino 1968; Stevens 1973:8).

1964–1994

From 1964 to 1972, Paleoindian research on the Southern High Plains was relatively limited and involved little geological or other paleoenvironmental studies. Most of the work in this period was at the Clovis site. Gravel mining ended in the late 1960s (J. Warnica, pers. comm., March 1994), and a long-term field school directed by George Agogino operated in most summers from 1964 to 1974, largely focused on the South Bank (Agogino and Rovner 1969; Stevens 1973; Agogino et al. 1976) (FIG. 2.13B). Below the Clovis site, well down Blackwater Draw, Kenneth Honea, an archaeologist then at Texas Tech University, directed field schools at the Marks Beach site (FIG. 1.3) from 1968 to 1970 (Honea 1980). A stratigraphic sequence somewhat similar to that known from Clovis and Lubbock Lake was discovered, including the remains of extinct bison, possibly butchered, in ancient lake beds. The stratigraphic similarities among Marks Beach, Clovis, and Lubbock Lake strengthened the arguments for regional similarities in late Quaternary depositional environments, if not regional paleoclimates. Jay Blaine (1968) also reported on his careful, systematic, long-term collecting of Midland points from deflating sand dunes at the Winkler-1 site in extreme southeastern New Mexico (FIG. 1.3). This site was the only other one besides Midland to produce an apparently "pure" Midland lithic assemblage, and it produced a much larger collection than Midland. James Warnica (pers. comm. 1994) also conducted additional testing at the Ted Williamson Plainview site in 1965.

Archaeological activity throughout North America experienced rapid

FIGURE 2.13A. Aerial view of the mammoth excavations on the North Bank by the El Llano Archaeological Society in 1963. A total of four mammoths were recovered. One of them was jacketed by F. E. Green and taken to Texas Technological College (now Texas Tech University) and prepared for display (FIG. 3.14). Reproduced with permission of the Blackwater Draw Site Photo Archives, Gordon Greaves, Photographer (BWD 2107).

growth beginning in the 1970s as a result of legislation for the protection or mitigation of endangered archaeological resources. But on the Llano Estacado most of the Paleoindian studies continued to be systematic, problem-oriented investigations. Beginning in 1972 the tempo of such research increased in the region. The principal development was establishment of the Lubbock Lake Project. The project began in 1972 when Craig Black, a vertebrate paleontologist at the University of Kansas, became director of the Museum of Texas Tech University, bringing with him Eileen Johnson, a zooarchaeologist, and Charles A. Johnson II, a geoarchaeologist. All three brought an interdisciplinary approach to Lubbock Lake. Eileen Johnson remained at Texas Tech to direct the project. Thomas W. Stafford, Jr., a geologist, became the site geoarchaeologist in 1976 and continued in this role through 1978. I became project geoarchaeologist in 1979 after joining the excavations as an archaeologist in 1973. The continuing, interdisciplinary research program at Lubbock Lake initially focused on the record of human adaptation to late Quaternary environmental change, especially during the Paleoindian occupation, as preserved at the Lubbock Lake site. The research program included archaeology, stratigraphy, pedology, paleontology, and paleobotany (e.g., Black 1974; Johnson and Holliday 1980, 1981, 1986, 1989; Stafford 1981; Holliday 1985b,c,d, 1988b; Holliday and Allen 1987; Johnson 1986a, 1987a) and yielded the most complete record of late Quaternary human occupation and paleoenvironments in the south-central United States. In particular, the site has an unusually rich record of sequential Paleoindian occupations, similar to Clovis, and research focused on the cultural chronology, subsistence, and bone technology of the Paleoindians and the changing environments of their times. Several symposia dealing with Paleoindian themes also were sponsored under the auspices of the Lubbock Lake Project (Black 1974; Johnson 1977, 1995a).

In the past two decades there have been a number of other archaeological and geological investigations of Paleoindian occupations in the region. Research continued at the Clovis gravel pit in 1974 (Agogino et al. 1976), in 1983 and 1984 (Stanford et al. 1990; Haynes 1995), and in 1985 and

FIGURE 2.13B. Early stages of excavation on the South Bank of the Clovis site in October 1964. View is northeast across the south end of the south pit (see FIG. 3.7) toward the gravel sorting operation above the east wall of the south pit (note standing water on the floor of the quarry). The archaeologists are at most 3 m above the Paleoindian levels, providing an indication of how much deeper the commercial sand and gravel lay. Reproduced with permission of the Blackwater Draw Site Photo Archives, Vance Haynes, Photographer (BWD 2196).

1986 (Boldurian 1990). The research in the 1980s proved especially significant. Stanford et al. (1990) and Haynes (1995) demonstrated that substantial Paleoindian deposits are preserved in the channel that connects the
now-destroyed paleobasin with Blackwater Draw proper. Boldurian (1990)
explored an extensive Folsom campsite on the uplands adjacent to the paleobasin. Few such campsites are known, and this particular feature is the
only such setting investigated at the Clovis site.

In research elsewhere, testing at the Plainview site revealed that some
remnants of the Paleoindian bone bed are still preserved (Guffee 1979),
and a cache of Plainview points, along with a large collection of other tools,
was recovered from the Ryan site in a small playa near Lubbock (Johnson
et al. 1987; Hartwell 1995) (FIG. 1.3). Testing at the Milnesand and Williamson sites documented the presence of some remaining occupation debris
surrounding the long since destroyed bone beds (Buchanan et al. 1995).
Amick and Rose (1990) and Hofman and others (1990) documented
Shifting Sands, a significant Folsom-Midland site in stratified lake and
dune sediments on the southwestern Llano Estacado (FIG. 1.3), based on
surface collections and preliminary field studies. Paleoindian artifacts
commonly are found in these dunes (e.g., Fritz and Fritz 1940; Polyak and
Williams 1986), but Shifting Sands and Winkler-1 are the only documented and well-recorded sites. In addition to field work there also were
several studies of projectile point technology, variability, and distribution
(e.g., Wheat 1972; Knudson 1983; Meltzer 1986; Hofman 1992).

Several other Paleoindian sites immediately adjacent to the Southern
High Plains were investigated during the period 1963–1994 and are important to understanding the archaeology of the region. The Lake Theo
site, on the Rolling Plains immediately east of the High Plains escarpment
(FIG. 1.3), was tested in 1974 and 1977 (Harrison and Smith 1975; Harrison and Killen 1978). The site contains two beds of bone from extinct bison associated with Folsom artifacts (lower bed) and Plainview artifacts
(upper bed) (Harrison and Killen 1978). The site is one of the few Plainview sites with a stratified archaeological record. Subsequent studies at
Lake Theo yielded significant paleoenvironmental data (Johnson et al.
1982; Neck 1987). Near Lake Theo, in Tule Creek where it flows out onto
the Rolling Plains, another Paleoindian bone bed was excavated in 1973
and 1974 as a result of reservoir mitigation. The Rex Rodgers site (FIG. 1.3)
contained a bed of extinct bison bone and an unusual combination of
projectile point styles: side-notched points similar to southeastern styles
along with several more "Plains-like" lanceolate points (Willey et al. 1978;
Speer 1978). In the Canadian River valley just north of the Llano Esta-

cado, testing of the Horace Rivers Plainview site was conducted in 1992 (Mallouf 1994; Mandel 1994a) (FIG. 1.1).

In 1988, Jack Hofman, archaeologist with the Oklahoma Archeological Survey and subsequently on the faculty of the University of Kansas, began a reinvestigation of the Lipscomb site (Hofman et al. 1989) (FIG. 1.1). This work entailed study of the bone and stone recovered in the 1939 and 1946 research and also included additional excavation at the site. The project was an interdisciplinary one aimed at reconstructing the site setting, paleoenvironment, and site formation processes.

As a part of the resurgence of interest in Paleoindian archaeology on the Southern High Plains, I began geoarchaeological investigation of many of the sites in the late 1970s, and the work is continuing. Initially the field studies focused on Lubbock Lake (Holliday 1985b,c,d, 1988b), but expanded to the other draw localities at Plainview and Clovis (Holliday 1985e), the dunes at Milnesand and Williamson (Johnson et al. 1986), and also Lake Theo, just east of the High Plains (Johnson et al. 1982) (FIG. 1.3). Beginning in 1988, as part of systematic studies of the paleoenvironmental significance of draw, dune, and playa stratigraphy, additional work was conducted at Plainview, Clovis, Anderson Basin, Marks Beach, Milnesand and Williamson, Elida, Tatum, Midland, Winkler-1, Shifting Sands, Miami, and San Jon (FIG. 1.3), along with several hitherto unreported localities (Holliday 1995b), and, off the Llano Estacado, at the Lipscomb site (FIG. 1.1). The data derived from these studies, combined with the information available from all previous investigations of Paleoindian sites on the Llano Estacado, form the basis for this monograph.

CHAPTER THREE

Stratigraphy, Soils, and Geochronology of Paleoindian Sites

Introduction

The best-documented *in situ* Paleoindian sites of the Southern High Plains are found in the three loci of late Quaternary deposition: draws, playas, and dunes (Chapter 1). This chapter presents a discussion of the geology of individual Paleoindian sites grouped by these three settings (listed alphabetically within each setting). At the end of the chapter is a brief discussion of two Paleoindian sites (Rex Rodgers and Horace Rivers) found off but near the Llano Estacado that provide significant information on Paleoindian chronologies and geoarchaeology.

For each site there is a presentation of the geologic background, a summary of previous findings and interpretations, and a presentation of data gathered by the writer. Information for most sites that I investigated includes field descriptions and stratigraphic measurements (Appendix 1), laboratory data (available on request), and radiocarbon ages. Correlations of previous stratigraphic schemes with mine also are presented.

Draws

The draws are the most intensively studied and best known of late Quaternary stratigraphic localities on the Southern High Plains. This close scrutiny historically is linked to archaeological research. The most widely known and most carefully studied sites in the region, Clovis and Lubbock Lake, are in draws, as are the well-known sites at Plainview and Midland. A regional, systematic investigation of 10 draws by the writer (Holliday 1995b) was a direct result of these geoarchaeological studies. All of the Paleoindian sites in draws are in the Brazos River and Colorado River systems (FIGS. 1.1, 1.3). There are 15 named draws that feed into these systems, but stratified Paleoindian sites are known only from four draws:

Running Water (with the Plainview site), Blackwater (with the Clovis, Anderson Basin #1 and #2, Marks Beach, and Lubbock Landfill sites), Yellowhouse (with Lubbock Lake), and Monahans (with the Midland site) (FIG. 1.3). Paleoindian artifacts commonly are found on uplands adjacent to many of the draws, however (Hester and Grady 1977; Hester 1975a; Wendorf and Hester 1962; Johnson and Stafford 1976; Kibler 1991, 1992).

The draws filled with a variety of sediments following their final phase of incision, which occurred between 20,000 and 12,000 yrs BP (Holliday 1995b). All of the 10 draws that I investigated (Holliday 1995b) have a similar stratigraphic sequence that permitted identification of 5 principal lithostratigraphic units: strata 1–5, oldest to youngest, all of which are asynchronous (FIGS. 3.1, 3.2). Of these 5, strata 1, 2, and 3 are pertinent to the Paleoindian geoarchaeology. Stratum 1 is sandy and gravelly alluvium. The beginning of alluviation is undated, but the end varied from ca. 11,000 yrs BP to ca. 9500 yrs BP. Stratum 2, resting conformably on stratum 1, contains beds of lacustrine diatomaceous earth (2d) and paludal mud (2m) along valley axes with sandy, valley-margin eolian and slopewash facies (2s). Stratum 2 is famous for containing abundant Paleoindian archaeological material (e.g., Howard 1935a; Sellards 1952; Haynes and Agogino 1966; Johnson 1987d), but is discontinuous and quite rare regionally. Of over 100 study localities in 10 draws, only 12 contain stratum 2 (Holliday 1995b). The beginning of stratum 2 sedimentation varied from ca. 11,000 to ca. 10,000 yrs BP and the end of deposition varied from ca. 10,000 to ca. 8500 yrs BP (FIG. 3.2). Stratum 3 most commonly has a lacustrine carbonate (marl) facies (3c) along the valley axes and a sandy, relatively low-carbonate, eolian facies (3s) along valley margins. Stratum 3 is conformable with stratum 1 (where stratum 2 is absent), and therefore the beginning of stratum 3 deposition varies from ca. 11,000 to ca. 9500 yrs BP, but both the beginning and end of deposition are time-transgressive. Where stratum 2 occurs, stratum 3 sometimes is separated from it by an unconformity indicated by a soil in upper stratum 2. The beginning of stratum 3 deposition on top of stratum 2 varied from 8500 to 6500 yrs BP. The end of stratum 3 deposition varied from ca. 9500 to ca. 7500 yrs BP (FIG. 3.2). Stratum 4, largely a sand to sandy loam deposited by wind, locally is old enough to contain Paleoindian archaeology, but none is reported.

The late Quaternary fill in the draws, along with other proxy data, provides evidence of significant environmental change (Holliday 1995b). From the latest Pleistocene to the early Holocene there was a hydrologic shift from flowing water (deposition of stratum 1) to standing water (deposition of stratum 2 and/or 3c) and then almost complete disappearance

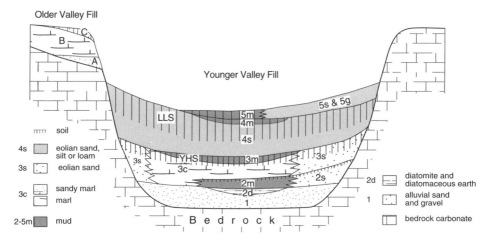

FIGURE 3.1. Schematic illustration of stratigraphic relationships in the valley fill on the Southern High Plains (LLS Lubbock Lake soil; YHS Yellowhouse Soil) (from Holliday 1995b: fig. 6). No vertical or horizontal scale is implied.

of surface water and the accumulation of eolian sediment (stratum 3s and/or 4). Very broadly, the shifts in depositional environment were time-transgressive (younger down draw). These environmental changes resulted from a decrease in effective regional precipitation from the late Pleistocene to the middle Holocene. In the late Pleistocene and early Holocene, local variability in the types and ages of the deposits was controlled by the presence or absence of springs and by time-transgressive decline in spring discharge. The early-to-middle Holocene eolian fill resulted from desiccation and wind deflation of the High Plains surface.

In the following discussion of draw localities, the above-outlined stratigraphic nomenclature established for the valley fill will be followed except for the Clovis site, where most of the geologic research was by C. V. Haynes. Correlations of the regional stratigraphic scheme with Haynes' nomenclature for Clovis and with stratigraphic schemes erected for other sites are provided.

ANDERSON BASIN

Anderson Basin refers to a reach of Blackwater Draw 12 to 16 km below the Clovis site (FIGS. 1.3, 3.3). The archaeological sites in Anderson Basin are exposed in a series of blowouts among dunes on the floor of the draw. The valley fill is sufficiently coarse and unconsolidated to allow wind to scour the sediment down to the local bedrock (Holliday 1995b). The area

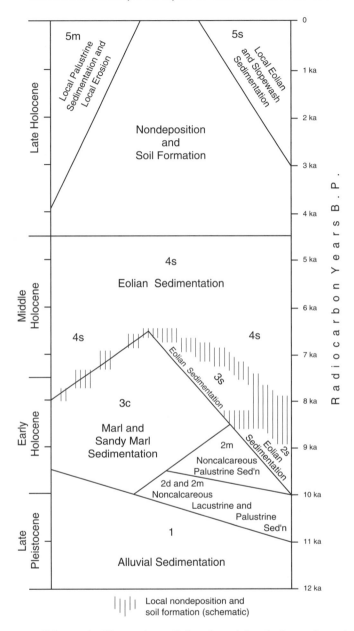

FIGURE 3.2. Schematic illustration of the depositional chronology (vertical axis) and relative dominance of depositional environments (horizontal axis; not to scale) in draws on the Southern High Plains (from Holliday 1995b: fig. 19).

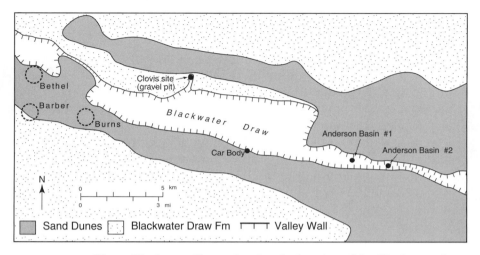

FIGURE 3.3. Upper Blackwater Draw, showing the location of the Clovis gravel pit, Anderson Basin #1 and #2, and the Car Body, Burns, Bethel, and Barber sites in or near the western Muleshoe Dunes.

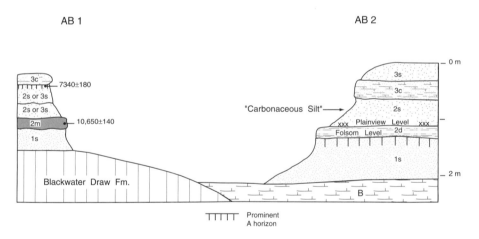

FIGURE 3.4. Stratigraphic sections at Anderson Basin with locations of radiocarbon samples. Anderson Basin #1 (AB1) is to the left and Anderson Basin #2 (AB2) is to the right. The horizontal relationship is schematic and not to scale; the sections are ca. 2.5 km apart (modified from Holliday 1995b: fig. 23).

was referred to as "Anderson Lakes" by Howard (1935a:95). His efforts were concentrated in a series of blowouts that he and subsequent workers called Anderson Basin #2 (AB2) (Howard 1935a:95–97; Hester 1975b:20, 28–31; Haynes 1975:70–71), which is the eastern of two sites investigated during the High Plains Paleoecology Project (FIGS. 3.3, 3.4, 3.5). Howard (1935a:95–97) is unclear whether he investigated the blowouts farther west, termed Anderson Basin #1 (Hester 1975b:27–28; Haynes 1975:70–71) (FIG. 3.3). Anderson Basin #1 (AB1) did not yield archaeological materials, but does expose a dated stratigraphic sequence similar to AB2 and Clovis (Hester 1975b; Holliday 1995b) (FIG. 3.4). The following geo-archaeological discussion is based on the work of Howard (1935a), Stock and Bode (1936), Hester (1975b), Haynes (1975), and field work by the author (Holliday 1995b) (Table 3.1).

The valley fill at Anderson Basin apparently was originally continuous throughout the area of the site, disappearing only at the valley margins as the sediments thinned. Much of the valley fill was removed by wind erosion, leaving exposures around the margins of the blowouts (FIG. 3.5). The oldest valley fill in Anderson Basin is late Pleistocene indurated lake-carbonate (stratum B). These deposits are exposed across the floor of AB2. Fossils of late Pleistocene megafauna are abundant in these carbonates, but there are no indications that the bone is associated with human activity. The carbonates are more localized in AB1, where they are inset against the local bedrock, which is the Blackwater Draw Formation (FIG. 3.4).

TABLE 3.1. Correlation of stratigraphic terminology for the area of Anderson Basin[1]

Anderson Basin #1		Anderson Basin #2		
Haynes 1975	Holliday this volume	Stock & Bode 1936	Haynes 1975	Holliday this volume
Unit G2				
Unit G1	[nr]	Eolian Sand	Unit G	Stratum 5s
Unit F			Unit F	Stratum 4s
Unit E	Stratum 2s	Brown Sand	Unit E	Stratum 2s
Unit D	Strata 2s & 2d	Blue Sand	Unit D	Strata 2d & 2s
Unit C	Stratum 1	Caliche	Unit B1	Stratum 1
Units B1 & B2	[nr]	Yellow Sand	Units A6–A13	[nr]

[1] From Holliday (1995b:table 6B). nr = Strata not recognized.

FIGURE 3.5. Anderson Basin #2, probably in 1933, showing one of several mammoth tusks weathering out of upper stratum 1 in a blowout on the floor of the draw. This particular blowout exposed so many tusks that Howard (1935a:91) referred to it as "Elephant Tusk Lake." The ledge just above the bone and in the right middleground probably is the base of the more resistant stratum 2 mud. Reproduced from Howard (1935a:plate xxviii) with the permission of the University of Pennsylvania Museum, Philadephia (Neg. #54-141370).

TABLE 3.2. Recently determined radiocarbon ages for sites in upper Blackwater Draw

Site	^{14}C Age Years BP	Lab. No.	Material Dated & Remarks
Anderson Basin #1[1]			
	7340±180	SMU-2691	Humates; buried A-horizon in stratum 3s
	10,650±140	SMU-2703	Humates; muddy marsh facies (2m) of diatomite
Clovis			
	8690±70	SMU-1671	Humates; Unit E, sampled from block removed during Sellards' 1949 excavations
	8970±60	SMU-1672	Humates; Unit E, sampled from block removed during Sellards' 1949 excavations
	10,780±110	SMU-1880	Humates; Unit C, sampled from block removed during Jelinek's 1956 excavations

[1] Holliday (1995b).

The oldest archaeologically significant valley fill throughout Anderson Basin is fine alluvial sand with localized concentrations of gravel (stratum 1). The sands yielded no diagnostic artifacts, but Howard (1935a:97) indicates that both mammoth and some stone tools or debitage were found in this zone at AB2 (FIG. 3.5). Also at AB2, the sands in the upper 20–30 cm of stratum 1 are heavily stained by organic matter (the "dark gray sand" of Hester 1975b:fig. 2-25) (FIG. 3.4). This zone is an A-horizon developed in stratum 1 and represents the establishment of a stable (i.e., nonaggrading) and perhaps marshy landscape denoting the onset of conditions that resulted in deposition of stratum 2.

Stratum 1 is overlain conformably by lacustrine diatomaceous earth and paludal mud at both sites. At AB1, stratum 2 is pure diatomite (2d) along the valley axis and paludal mud (2m) along the valley margin. A sandy eolian facies of stratum 2 (2s) rests on the mud in AB1. The mud facies is dated to ca. 10,600 yrs BP and the sand dated to ca. 7300 yrs BP (Table 3.2; FIG. 3.4). At AB2 only the valley-axis facies is exposed. It consists of 2d (resting on the stratum 1 A-horizon) overlain by "carbonaceous silt" (Hester 1975b:28), an A-horizon cumulized by eolian sedimentation similar to Unit E at Clovis (discussed below). Folsom artifacts and fragments of bison bone were found in 2d, and a Plainview point associated with a *Bison antiquus* bone bed was found at the top of 2d (Howard 1935a: 95, 97; Hester 1975b:28, 31; Haynes 1975:71).

CLOVIS

The Clovis site is in an ancient basin 2 km north of and draining into upper Blackwater Draw, connected to it by a small channel (the "shallow ravine" of Haynes 1975:66; the "outlet channel" of Stanford et al. 1990; "Spring Draw" of Haynes 1995:318) (FIGS. 3.3, 3.6). Late Quaternary fill in the upper reaches of the draw proper largely was removed by wind deflation, well illustrated by the blowouts at Anderson Basin (discussed above). The archaeologically significant sediments buried in the tributary basin and in the outlet channel were protected by their unique topographic setting.

The site was an active gravel pit in 1932 and from 1952 to the late 1960s, and sometimes is referred to as "the Clovis gravel pit." The site also is known as the Blackwater Draw site, Blackwater Locality No. 1, Blackwater No. 1, or Blackwater Draw Locality 1, derived from Sellards (1952: 29). During the first phase of research in the 1930s, however, the site was referred to by its proximity to Clovis, New Mexico, and known as the Clovis site both before and after Sellards proposed his designation (e.g.,

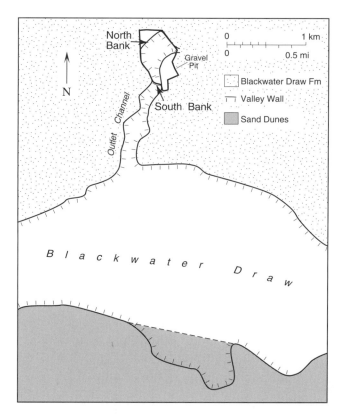

FIGURE 3.6. Map of upper Blackwater Draw in the area of the Clovis site, showing the location of the gravel pit at the site (including the North Bank area and
the South Bank section at the north end of the "Outlet Channel") and the
relationship of the paleobasin to Blackwater Draw (modified from Holliday
1995b:fig. 12A).

Krieger 1950:182; Green 1962a). The name "Clovis site" is used here to
refer to the gravel pit and outlet channel, as proposed by Green (1963).

   The Clovis site witnessed the largest number of extensive excavations
of Paleoindian features on the Llano Estacado and probably in all of North
America. These numerous and extensive excavations largely were the result of salvage ahead of and in some cases during mining, however, and the
resulting data bases often leave much to be desired (Hester 1972). The
mining also provided many stratigraphic exposures in the basin, but because this activity proceeded more or less continuously beginning in 1952,
while archaeological field work was intermittent, many investigators saw
stratigraphic and archaeologic relationships not observed by earlier or later

investigators. The research directed by Howard and Sellards through 1952 was on the floor of the paleobasin in quarry pits that did not change size or shape significantly (FIG. 3.7). Subsequent work followed the expanding gravel pit until the walls were at the edge of the paleobasin by the early 1960s (FIGS. 3.7, 3.8). The mining, the chaos during much of the archaeological work (well described by Hester 1972 and Stevens 1973), and the variability in field documentation methods (if used at all) hamper in-depth discussion of the geological relationships of the archaeology, in particular the depositional environments or the immediate landscape setting of individual features.

In spite of the many problems that plagued research at the Clovis site, considerable data are available. The site has proven to be one of the most significant localities in Plains Paleoindian research. The long-term research at the site yielded the most complete well-dated Paleoindian projectile point chronology of any site in the region, among other achievements. This summary discussion of the geoarchaeology of the site is based on the site synthesis prepared by Hester (1972), on the additional historical data from Stevens (1973), on the considerable and long-term research of C. V. Haynes (Haynes and Agogino 1966; Haynes 1975, 1995; Stanford et al. 1990), and on the precultural stratigraphic research (Holliday 1995b) (Table 3.3).

The present configuration of Blackwater Draw in the area of the gravel pit is at least several tens of thousands of years old (Holliday 1995b), but the ancient basin of the Clovis site is considerably younger. The basin is inset into the Blackwater Draw Formation and underlying gravels, probably of the Ogallala Formation (FIGS. 3.9, 3.10). These gravels were the object of the mining operations that led to the discovery and destruction of the site. Resting on top of the Blackwater Draw Formation is a lacustrine carbonate (stratum B of Holliday 1995b; Unit A9 of Haynes 1995; stratum I of Boldurian 1990) (Table 3.3). Between stratum B and the underlying Blackwater Draw Formation is a buried A-horizon that yielded radiocarbon ages between 23,000 and 17,000 yrs BP. The basin containing the archaeological materials therefore is quite young, post-dating stratum B but older than 13,000 yrs BP, the age of the oldest basin fill (Haynes 1995).

The paleobasin of the Clovis site contains a stratified sequence of late Quaternary deposits (FIGS. 3.10, 3.11). These layers essentially were continuous throughout the basin, but there was considerable facies variation, especially at the microstratigraphic (i.e., archaeological) scale. The oldest fill is spring-laid sand divided into Unit B (13,000–11,500 yrs BP) and Unit C (11,500–11,000 yrs BP) and separated by an erosional unconformity. Near the basin margins these sands have complex facies relationships

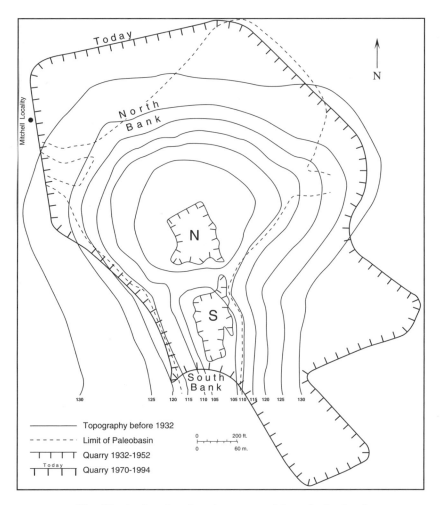

FIGURE 3.7. The Clovis site, showing the extent of the paleobasin, the topography before mining (contour interval is 5 feet), the quarry limits as they existed from 1933 to 1952 (consisting of a north pit "N" and a south pit "S"), the quarry limits once mining ceased around 1970, and the Mitchell Locality (modified from Hester 1972:fig. 15). The locations of the South Bank and North Bank sections are also indicated. The North Bank area marks the location of the north limit of the quarry as of the early 1960s.

FIGURE 3.8. Aerial photo of the Clovis site in 1991. View is south down the outlet channel (OC), toward Blackwater Draw. The South Bank area (SB) and Mitchell Locality (M) are indicated (see FIG. 3.7). Courtesy of the Lubbock Lake Landmark, Museum of Texas Tech University.

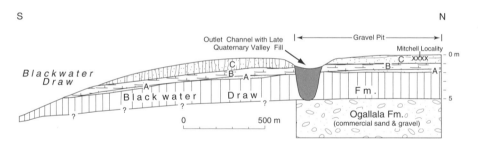

FIGURE 3.9. Geologic cross section through the west side of the Clovis site and south into Blackwater Draw, illustrating the stratigraphic relationships of the late Quaternary basin fill (here shown as fill in the outlet channel), the older valley fill (strata A, B, and C of Holliday 1995b), the Mitchell Locality in stratum C, and the older upper Cenozoic units (Ogallala and Blackwater Draw formations) (modified from Holliday 1995b:fig. 12B).

TABLE 3.3. Correlation of selected stratigraphic terminology for the Clovis site[1]

Stock & Bode 1936	Sellards & Evans 1960	Haynes 1975[2]	Haynes 1995[2]	Holliday this volume
Eolian Sand	Tan Eolian Sand	Units G1,G2	Units G2, G3	Stratum 5s
	Jointed Sand	Unit F	Unit G1	Stratum 4s
			Unit F	Stratum 3s
Blue Sand	Carbonaceous Silt	Unit E	Unit E	Stratum 2s
	[nr]	Unit D	Units Do, D2z	Stratum 2s
	Diatomaceous Earth	Unit D	Units D1, D2	Stratum 2d
Caliche?	Brown Sand Wedge	Unit C	Units D2x, D2y	Strata 1–2
Speckled Sand?	Gray Sand	Unit B1	Unit C	Stratum 1s2
Speckled Sand	Gray Sand?	Unit B1	Units B1–B3	Stratum 1s1
				Stratum C[3]
[nr]	[nr]	[nr]	Unit A9	Stratum B[4]
[nr]	[nr]	[nr]	[nr]	Stratum A
[nr]	[nr]	Units A5–A13, B2	Units A3–A8	Blackwater Draw Fm
Yellow Sand	Bedrock Gravel	Units A1–A4	Units A1, A2	Ogallala Fm (commercial sand & gravel)

[1] From Holliday (1995b: table 6A).
[2] Stratigraphic nomenclature primarily applies to "South Bank" and "West Bank."
[3] Stratum II of Boldurian (1990).
[4] Stratum I of Boldurian (1990).
nr = Strata not recognized.

with sand and rubble derived from the valley walls and with sand discharged directly from spring throats (FIG. 3.11). The stratigraphic relationships of these sands along the basin margins, particularly the "Brown Sand Wedge" of Sellards (1952) (Unit C), are problematic, however, owing to destruction of sections by gravel mining. The sand beds also are highly convoluted at the basin margins due to soft-sediment deformation from fluctuating spring discharge and the deposition of slopewash. Toward the center of the basin the sands are bedded and have stratigraphic relationships more typical of stream deposits. The erosional unconformity between B and C and another at the top of C are believed the result of wind deflation (Haynes 1995).

The Unit B and C sands are significant archaeologically because they

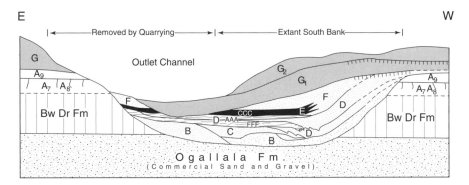

FIGURE 3.10. Generalized east-west geologic cross section (looking south) of the south end of the Clovis site paleobasin (FIG. 3.7), illustrating the stratigraphic relationships of the Paleoindian levels (FFF Folsom; AAA Agate Basin, exact provenience uncertain; CCC Cody/Firstview) to the basin fill preserved in the South Bank area (see FIG. 3.7). Note the complex relationship of the sandy basin-margin facies of Units D and F (stipple pattern) to Units C, D, and E on the basin floor. Not to scale. Modified from Haynes (1995:fig. 7).

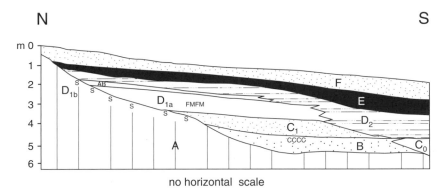

no horizontal scale

FIGURE 3.11. Generalized cross section of the North Bank area of the Clovis site in the early 1960s (FIG. 3.7), illustrating the stratigraphic relationships of the Paleoindian levels (CCCC Clovis with mammoths; FMFM Folsom and Midland; AB Agate Basin), and their relationship to spring-laid strata (Units C_1, D_{1a}, D_{1b}) (S spring conduits). Based on Haynes and Agogino (1966:fig. 5), Haynes, Saunders, Stanford, and Agogino (1992:fig. 2), and C. V. Haynes, Jr. (pers. comm. 1995).

yielded the type Clovis artifacts (FIG. 3.12) and associated bone assemblages. Most of the Clovis features are from Unit C, but some Clovis materials are found on top of and in upper B. Whether the materials in upper B are *in situ* or intrusive still is debated (e.g., Green 1992; Haynes, Saunders, Stanford, and Agogino 1992), exemplifying the confusion imposed by the quarrying and by the destruction of stratigraphic sections.

Clovis features recovered from the sands include the remains of at least eight mammoths, two *Bison antiquus* bone beds, and two camp areas (Table 3.4; FIG. 3.13). The mammoth features, each consisting of one individual, all were near the margins of the paleodepression (Hester 1972) (FIG. 3.13). The spectacular series of mammoth kills reported by Warnica (1966) were associated with spring conduits (Haynes and Agogino 1966) on the "North Bank" (FIGS. 2.13A, 3.11, 3.13, 3.14). Near the south side of the paleobasin margin two mammoths were recovered at the head of the outlet channel (FIG. 3.13). The mammoths excavated in 1936 and 1937 (Cotter 1937, 1938), which yielded most of the Clovis type collection (FIG. 3.12), were in the outlet channel, just south of the paleobasin and in proximity to the channel margins (FIG. 3.13).

The mammoths found at Clovis in 1936 (Cotter 1937) are the "fossils

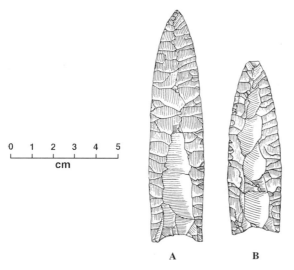

FIGURE 3.12. The type specimens for the Clovis point, recovered during excavations of the Philadelphia Academy of Natural Sciences. Modified from Sellards (1952:figs. 17a,b). Drawn by Hal Story and reproduced courtesy of the Texas Memorial Museum, the University of Texas at Austin.

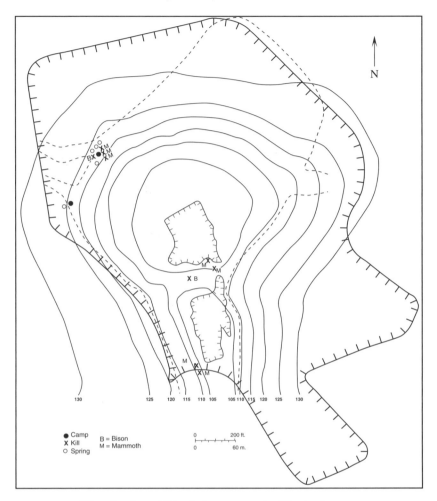

FIGURE 3.13. Distribution of Clovis features at the Clovis site.

upon which the concept of mammoth hunting in North America was established" (Saunders and Daeschler 1994:1). But as Saunders and Daeschler (1994) show, the mammoths from this famous feature probably were
scavenged rather than hunted by Clovis people.

Two Clovis-age bison bone beds were recovered at the Clovis site, both
at the south margin of the paleobasin, near the head of the outlet channel
(Hester 1972) (FIG. 3.13). The bison bone bed excavated by Sellards in 1955
(Hester 1972:46–47) included the remains of seven individuals with an
associated Clovis point. The Jelinek excavations of 1956–1957 focused
on a bison bone bed (Johnson and Holliday 1996), initially reported as a

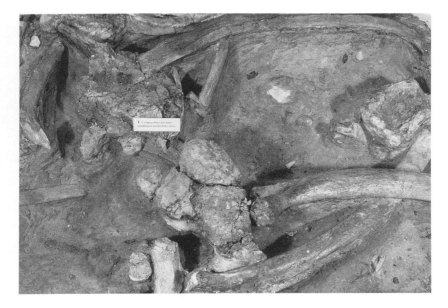

FIGURE 3.14. A Clovis point (center left, just below the card) among mammoth bone in a block removed during the 1962–1963 "El Llano excavations" at the Clovis site (Warnica 1966). This block is part of "Mammoth No. 2," which was found by F. E. Green late in 1962 and led to the discovery of the other mammoth kills on the North Bank (see FIG. 2.13A). The point is a cast of "EL-10" in Hester (1972:figs. 89a, 90a). The swirled, convoluted, and pebbly nature of the "Gray Sand" can be seen below the bone; probably the "contorted sand" in Hester (1972:fig. 77) and Fryxell (in Hester 1972:81), and Unit C_0 in Haynes and Agogino (1966:813) and Haynes, Saunders, Stanford, and Agogino (1992:340–341, fig. 3). Courtesy of the Lubbock Lake Landmark, Museum of Texas Tech University.

mammoth feature (Hester 1972:51–53). The remains of four butchered, extinct bison were found in the Brown Sand Wedge, along with a few scattered mammoth bones with no obvious evidence of human modification (Johnson and Holliday 1996). A sediment sample for radiocarbon dating, taken from near the top of a plaster-jacketed block, provides a minimum age of ca. 10,800 yrs BP for the Jelinek bone bed (Table 3.2) (Johnson and Holliday 1996).

Hester (1972:170) suggests that the basin-margin settings were attractive to Clovis hunters because they afforded access to the paleobasin (either through arroyos known to have existed in Clovis time or via the south outlet channel). Another possibility is that all of the kills were near springs, but the geologic evidence for most of them was not observed or recorded. The outlet channel also was a site where all water, either spring-derived or from runoff, converged and was discharged from the basin.

Two Clovis campsites are reported from the basin margin (Hester 1972: 167). The localities were at or near the uplands of the paleobasin, and both areas were near spring conduits (FIG. 3.13). The largest collection of Clovis camping debris was found near the North Bank conduits. The North Bank materials were redeposited, however, probably derived from the northwest edge of the paleobasin (FIG. 3.13). The camping material on the west side was near a conduit and also near paleoarroyos that drained into the ancient basin (FIG. 3.13).

Most of the Paleoindian features at Clovis were found in the pond and marsh deposits of Units D and E. Unit D is diatomaceous earth, which includes beds of pure diatomite, lenses of diatomite interbedded with mud or sand, and diatomaceous mud. The mud and diatomite were best expressed in the center of the basin, where additions of coarse clastics were minimal and where water was deepest or marshes the wettest, supporting luxuriant plant growth. Unit D becomes sandy toward the basin margin. On the "South Bank," where a cross section of the outlet channel is preserved (FIG. 3.10), Haynes (1995:372) identifies "20 subunits [of D] ranging from nearly pure lacustrine diatomite to bank facies of fine to medium sand." The interbedding resulted from fluctuating pond levels, expansion and contraction of marshes, and periodic addition of sand from spring discharge, eolian deposition, and slopewash. Some of the spring-laid sands are a component of the problematic "Brown Sand Wedge" of Sellards (1952), i.e., the Brown Sand Wedge, Unit C, underlies Unit D and also is, in part, a facies of D (FIG. 3.10).

An upland eolian deposit on the northwest side of the paleobasin and containing a Folsom feature (the Mitchell Locality, FIG. 3.7, discussed below) is reported by Boldurian (1990). Haynes (1995) suspects that the layer is an upland facies of Unit D. This deposit (Stratum II of Boldurian 1990, and Stratum C of Holliday 1995b) is a sheet-like eolian layer of loamy to sandy sediment up to 130 cm thick containing a well-expressed soil (A–Bt–Btk horizonation) that is the modern surface soil of the uplands surrounding the gravel pit (FIG. 3.9).

Unit E is the "carbonaceous silt," which is an organic-rich sandy mud, representing the accumulation of both silt and sand in an aggrading, marshy environment. Locally, Unit E is a cumulic A-horizon, overthickened due to slow eolian additions during pedogenesis. Along the basin margins Unit E, like D, includes organic-rich silt and sand interbedded with eolian sand

TABLE 3.4. Paleoindian features at the Clovis site[1]

Artifact Chronology	Feature Type	Feature Identification[2]
Late Paleoindian	Bison bone bed	TMM Station A
("Portales")	Bison bone bed multiple kills	TMM Station E[3]
	Bison bone bed	HPPP Locality 2[4]
("Cody")	Bison bone bed processing station	ENMU South Bank[5]
("Cody")	Bison bone bed	ENMU South Bank[6]
Agate Basin	Bison bone bed	ENMU South Bank[7]
Folsom	Bison bone bed	ANSP/ENMU South Bank[8]
	Bison bone bed	TMM Station E[9]
	Bison bone bed	HPPP North Bank[10]
	Bison bone bed	HPPP Locality 3[11]
	Bison bone bed	HPPP Locality 5[12]
	Bison bone bed	El Llano[13]
	Camp	HPPP Locality 4[14]
	Camp	El Llano[15]
	Camp	Mitchell Locality[16]
Clovis	Mammoth bone bed	Cotter, Mammoth 1[17]
	Mammoth bone bed	Cotter, Mammoth 2[17]
	Mammoth bone bed	TMM Station A[18]
	Mammoth bone bed	Shay, North Pit[19]
	Mammoth bone bed	El Llano, Mammoth 1[20]
	Mammoth bone bed	El Llano, Mammoth 2[20]
	Mammoth bone bed	El Llano, Mammoth 3[20]
	Mammoth bone bed	El Llano, Mammoth 4[20]
	Bison bone bed	TMM North Pit[21]
	Bison bone bed	Jelinek[3,22]
	Camp	HPPP Locality 4[14]
	Camp	El Llano[15]

[1] Green (1963), Haynes and Agogino (1966), and Hester (1972) indicate the presence of features besides those in the table, but so little documentation is available on age and artifact associations that they are not listed.

[2] ANSP = Academy of Natural Sciences of Philadelphia; TMM = Texas Memorial Museum (University of Texas at Austin); HPPP = High Plains Paleoecology Project; ENMU = Eastern New Mexico University.

[3] Johnson and Holliday (1996).

[4] Hester (1972:54–55).

[5] This feature, in the upper Carbonaceous Silt, appears to be the zone identified as possibly "Frederick" by Agogino and Rovner (1969), but later considered "Firstview" (but part of the Cody Complex) by Agogino et al. (1976), although the correlation between the two publications is unclear.

[6] The "Eden-Scottsbluff" level of Agogino and Rovner (1969) at the base of the Carbonaceous Silt.

[7] Agogino and Rovner (1969).

[8] Found in lower diatomite by Cotter (1937), but no diagnostic artifacts were recovered; assumed to be Folsom by Hester (1972:167–172); equivalent to Folsom bone bed reported from South Bank by Agogino and Rovner (1969) and Stanford et al. (1990)?

[9] Hester (1972:36–41).

[10] "Green and Wendorf salvage," Hester (1972:53, 167–172).

[11] Hester (1972:54–57, 167–172).

[12] Hester (1972:59–64, 167–172).

[13] Hester (1972:167–170).

[14] Folsom and Clovis camping debris mixed together, Hester (1972:65–66, 167).

[15] Folsom and Clovis camping debris mixed together, Hester (1972:86, 167).

[16] Stanford and Broilo (1981); Boldurian (1990).

[17] Cotter (1937, 1938); Hester (1972:18–29); Saunders and Daeschler (1994).

[18] Hester (1972:33–36).

[19] Hester (1972:49).

[20] Warnica (1966); Hester (1972:71–86).

[21] Hester (1972:46–47).

[22] Hester (1972:51–53).

(FIG. 3.10). Some of the sand interbeds are traceable directly into dune sands on the uplands of the basin margin. Unit D dates from 10,800 to 10,000 yrs BP. Unit E is not well dated but at most spans the period 10,500 to 8500 yrs BP.

Most of the Folsom features in the gravel pit were associated with Unit D, and most were *Bison antiquus* bone beds (Table 3.4). Hester (1972: 170) records six such features (FIG. 3.15), including those excavated by Sellards' TMM crew, which demonstrated the stratigraphic superposition of Folsom above Clovis (Chapter 2). The excavations by TMM yielded some unfluted points that could be considered Midland artifacts (FIG. 3.16). Stanford et al. (1990) and Haynes (1995) report a Folsom bone bed in Unit D along the South Bank area of the outlet channel, but this feature may be the same one mentioned by Agogino and Rovner (1969) and investigated by Cotter (1937). For those features where data are available, the number of bison involved varies from one to five. The bone beds were found in muddy interbeds of the diatomite, denoting times of low or subsurface water, or found in basin margin settings away from deep water or mud. The diatomite ponds undoubtedly were fed by some of the spring conduits on

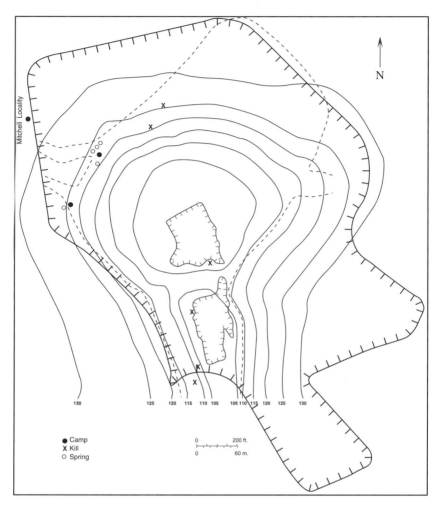

FIGURE 3.15. Distribution of Folsom features at the Clovis site.

the northwest side of the basin, which were active during Folsom time (Haynes and Agogino 1966).

Three Folsom camping areas are known. Two of the sites are in the same area as the Clovis camps, near spring conduits and paleoarroyos along the northwest and west sides of the paleobasin (FIG. 3.15). An extensive Folsom campsite is in the sheet-like eolian layer on the uplands on the northwest side of the ancient basin (referred to as "Frank's Folsom site" by Stanford and Broilo 1981, and as the "Mitchell Locality" by Boldurian 1990) (FIGS. 3.7, 3.8, 3.9). The site yielded thousands of stone artifacts and

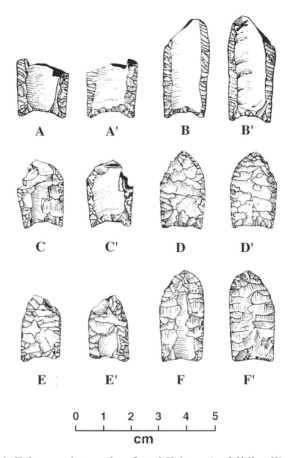

FIGURE 3.16. Folsom points and unfluted Folsom (or Midland?) points found by Sellards' crew at the Clovis site. Modified from Sellards (1952:fig. 25). Drawn by Hal Story and reproduced courtesy of the Texas Memorial Museum, the University of Texas at Austin.

is interpreted as a base camp used by Folsom hunters (Boldurian 1990). Boldurian (1990:44, 47) proposes that the sediment and soil containing the Folsom occupation (his Stratum II) represent "part of a soil that was slowly aggrading during Folsom time" and that the "Folsom occupation zone was probably buried at a relatively slow, but continuous rate, and in certain areas, with little disturbance through time." The soil is typical of Bt-horizons in sandy parent material in both upland and lowland settings on the Llano Estacado (Holliday 1985a,c,e, 1995b). Pedogenic features indicative of slowly aggrading profiles such as a thick zone of dark gray

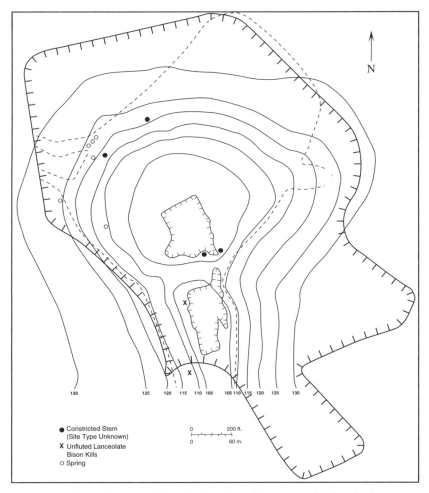

FIGURE 3.17. Distribution of Late Paleoindian features at the Clovis site.

(A-horizon) coloration overprinted by B-horizon characteristics (Holliday 1985a, 1988b, 1995b) are not apparent. More likely, and as suggested by Haynes (1995), the Folsom people lived on a sand sheet (an upland facies of Unit D) deposited just before or during occupation, and their artifacts were mixed into the sediment by bioturbation. Most of the illuvial clay of the Bt-horizon probably post-dates the Folsom occupation; a considerable amount of clay could move through the sandy parent material in 10,000 years (Holliday 1985a, 1988b, 1995b).

Late Paleoindian occupations generally are associated with Unit E. The Late Paleoindian features (Table 3.4) are characterized by a variety of unfluted, lanceolate projectile point styles. The oldest of these artifact styles are identified as Agate Basin, but they have poor association with activity areas. Some Agate Basin material was recovered from spring conduits on the North Bank (FIGS. 3.11, 3.17) in association with Folsom material, suggesting a temporal overlap of the two styles and likely occurrence of Agate Basin material in Unit D (Haynes and Agogino 1966). Additional Agate Basin material was found directly above Folsom occupations on the North Bank (FIGS. 3.11, 3.17) in Unit D and in spring-laid sands, but no associated features are reported (Green 1963:160; Hester 1972:59; J. Warnica, pers. comm. 1994). Agate Basin artifacts also were recovered from Unit E in a bison bone bed along the South Bank area of the outlet channel (Agogino and Rovner 1969; Stanford et al. 1990) (FIG. 3.17).

Five Late Paleoindian bone beds of *Bison antiquus* are reported or at least noted in Unit E (Table 3.4). The best-known and best-documented are features excavated by Sellards (1952:72–74; Hester 1972:36–39) and Agogino et al. (1976). The bone uncovered by Sellards' team was near the head of the outlet channel (FIG. 3.17) and covered over 100 m^2 (Hester 1972:37), leading to the conclusion that "this particular bison kill was one of the largest ever found at the site . . . [though] the number of bison that were killed is not known" (Hester 1972:37). Some bones and blocks of bones were removed from the bone bed. Johnson (1986b; Johnson and Holliday 1996) examined these materials and, based on weathering and other taphonomic characteristics, radiocarbon ages, the thickness of the bed, and discussions with Glen Evans, concluded that the feature represents a jumble of at least two and perhaps three bone beds, possibly churned by trampling. Photographs of the bone bed (FIG. 3.18) also suggest vertical mixing. The feature probably is a mixture of several kills and perhaps natural deaths.

The artifact assemblage from Sellards' Unit E bone bed formed the basis for defining the "Portales Complex" (Sellards 1952:72–74) (FIG. 3.19), which includes types similar to Eden, Scottsbluff, Plainview, and San Jon, according to Sellards, but more like Angostura, Eden, Scottsbluff, Milnesand, and "parallel flaked points" according to Hester (1972:37). The mixing of bone beds likely resulted in mixing of artifact styles (Johnson 1986b; Johnson and Holliday 1996), supporting a conclusion also reached by Agogino and Rovner (1969). Heavy reworking of many points also probably contributed to the identification of many point "types" (Johnson and Holliday 1996). Two radiocarbon ages were secured on sediment excavated from near the tops of the preserved blocks (Table 3.2), dating the upper portion of the bone bed to ca. 8700 yrs BP (Johnson and Holliday 1996).

FIGURE 3.18. A section of the jumbled and mixed bone bed in the "Carbonaceous Silt" (Unit E of Haynes 1975, 1995) at the Clovis site found during the 1949–1950 excavations on the south wall of the north pit (FIG. 3.7). Courtesy of the Texas Memorial Museum, the University of Texas at Austin.

Several Late Paleoindian features are reported from the outlet channel, ca. 100 m south of Sellards' bone bed (FIG. 3.17). Agogino and Rovner (1969) note a bone bed with unfluted lanceolate points at the base of Unit E, but provide no details. Stevens (1973) and Haynes (1995) refer to excavations of Cody Complex features in lower Unit E in the same area, but again no details are forthcoming. Upper Unit E yielded another Late Paleoindian bison bone bed, described by Agogino et al. (1976). The fully disarticulated nature of the bone and degree of bone breakage suggest that the zone probably was a bone processing station. The surface on which the event occurred probably was very firm, though damp, because there is no evidence for vertical displacement.

The youngest Paleoindian features at Clovis may be from Unit F, which buries Unit E (Haynes 1995). The features are in the South Bank, along the outlet channel, and associated with weakly developed buried soils formed in eolian sediments. The stratigraphy is indicative of increased eolian sedimentation on the surrounding uplands, but also of vegetated and perhaps damp lowlands. The latest Paleoindian features are not well-dated but are in the range of 8500 to 8000 yrs BP (Haynes 1995).

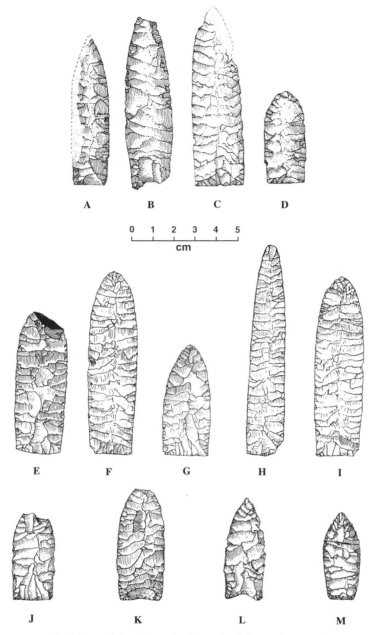

FIGURE 3.19. Artifacts of the "Portales Complex" found in the "Carbonaceous Silt" by Sellards' crew at the Clovis site. Modified from Sellards (1952:figs. 35, 36, 37). Drawn by Hal Story and reproduced courtesy of the Texas Memorial Museum, the University of Texas at Austin.

LUBBOCK LAKE

Lubbock Lake is in and above an entrenched meander of lower Yellow-house Draw (FIGS. 1.3, 3.20). The "lake" refers to the U-shaped reservoir excavated in the draw in 1936 (FIG. 2.7), also giving rise to the name Lubbock Reservoir site (Green 1962b; Johnson and Holliday 1987a). The reservoir dredging cut through the valley fill along the inside of the meander (FIGS. 2.7, 3.20, 3.21) and yielded evidence for Paleoindian occupations. Most of the Paleoindian archaeological research at the site focused on the walls of the reservoir cut (FIG. 2.8). As a result, all known Paleo-indian features are near or on the inside of the meander. Geological studies since 1973, however, included trenching and coring of the valley fill across the draw above, at, and below the old reservoir. The following geoarchaeo-logical discussion is summarized from Stafford (1981), Holliday (1985b,d), and Holliday and Allen (1987) (Table 3.5). The archaeological summaries are based on Sellards (1952), unpublished data from F. E. Green (discussed by Kaczor 1978), Johnson (1987a), and Johnson and Holliday (1989). The geochronology is provided by Holliday and others (1983, 1985), and Haas and others (1986).

Lubbock Lake, like Clovis, yielded evidence for dozens of archaeological features spanning the Paleoindian period. Although relatively few diagnostic artifacts have been recovered from the features, the closely spaced archaeological record has the potential for refining the regional cultural chronology and in particular for addressing transitional periods such as Folsom-to-post-Folsom time and the Late-Paleoindian-to-Archaic periods. Moreover, the geocultural microstratigraphy provides many clues to discrete behavioral changes over short periods of time for the entire Paleo-indian period. Research at the site also yielded the most detailed microenvironmental record for Paleoindian times of any locality on the southern Great Plains, based on vertebrate and invertebrate paleontology, geology, and paleobotany.

In the Lubbock Lake area Yellowhouse Draw cut through the Blackwater Draw Formation and into the Blanco Formation, the latter forming the local bedrock of the site. Incision occurred in at least three phases, based on occurrence of three terraces. All terraces are cut on the Blanco Formation, and the two highest terraces are exposed at the surface (FIGS. 3.20, 3.21). The lowest terrace is underlain by up to 1 m of sand and gravel (stratum 1; stratum 03 of Stafford 1981) and buried by valley fill (Holliday 1985b) (FIG. 3.21). Johnson and Stafford (1976) also report a buried terrace down draw from Lubbock Lake. The archaeological record at Lubbock

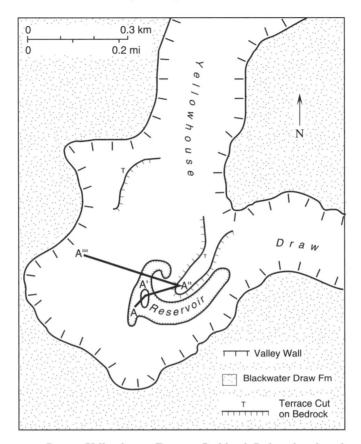

FIGURE 3.20. Lower Yellowhouse Draw at Lubbock Lake, showing the reservoir excavated in 1936 along the entrenched meander, terraces cut on bedrock, and line of sections A'''–A'' (FIG. 3.21) and A–A'–A'' (FIG. 3.23) (modified from Holliday 1995b:fig. 28A).

Lake is found in sediment that fills Yellowhouse Draw and post-dates the two highest terraces. The stratigraphic units described below are continuous along the draw at and below the site, although facies variations, especially at the microstratigraphic scale, are common.

Alexander (1978:21) suggests that pre-Clovis material was found at Lubbock Lake in "middle or early Pleistocene . . . clays" based on statements by Kelley (1974:68), who discusses finds from excavations in 1939 and 1941. The clays referred to are lacustrine sediments of the Blanco Formation (Pliocene). In the first excavations at the site (1939, 1941), before the bedrock stratigraphy was understood, artifacts were found just

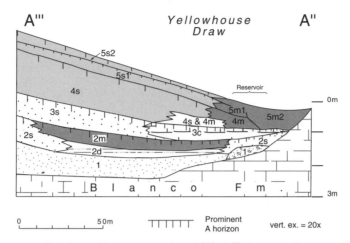

FIGURE 3.21. Stratigraphic cross section A‴–A″ (FIG. 3.20) across Yellowhouse Draw at the Lubbock Lake site (modified from Holliday 1995b: fig. 28B).

below the weathered surface of the clays along the sloping valley margin (Wheat 1974). The Pliocene clays were exposed at the surface for at least 6000 years prior to burial by middle-Holocene sediments, however. Upon subaerial exposure these clays typically become blocky and highly friable. Undoubtedly the combined effects of surface weathering and bioturbation resulted in mixing of late Quaternary occupation debris into the Pliocene bedrock.

Filling of Yellowhouse Draw began with deposition of alluvial sand and gravel (stratum 1) inset against the buried terrace. Discharge of stratum 1 probably was maintained both by runoff and spring flow along the draw. The time of initial deposition of stratum 1 is unknown, but the end of deposition was ca. 11,100 yrs BP.

Stratum 1 contains the oldest well-documented archaeological feature at Lubbock Lake (Table 3.6). The final phase of stratum 1 deposition coincided with the occupation of a gravelly point bar (FIG. 3.22). Distributed across the bar are bones of late Pleistocene megafauna, a feature (identified as FA2-1) resulting from the human activity. The bar and bones were buried by fining-upward sands. Additional bone (FA2-4) was recovered from this overlying sand. The animal remains from FA2-1, some of which exhibit evidence of butchering, include mammoth (*Mammuthus columbi*), extinct bison (*Bison antiquus*), extinct horse (*Equus mexicanus* and *Equus francisci*), extinct camel (*Camelops hesternus*), extinct giant armadillo

TABLE 3.5. Correlation of selected stratigraphic terminology for the Lubbock Lake site[1]

Stafford 1981	Holliday 1985b	Holliday this volume
Stratum 5C	Strata 4B1, 5A1, and 5B1	Strata 4m and 5m
Stratum 5B	Stratum 5B	Strata 5s2 and 5g2
Stratum 5A	Stratum 5A	Strata 5s1 and 5g1
Stratum 4C	A-horizon	Stratum 4s
Stratum 4B	Stratum 4B	
Stratum 4A	Stratum 4A	Stratum 4s
Stratum 3C clay		Stratum 4m
Stratum 3C A-horizon	A-horizon	
Stratum 3B	Stratum 3l	Stratum 3m
Stratum 3A	Stratum 3e	Stratum 3s
Stratum 2C	A-horizon	Stratum 2s or 2m
Stratum 2E	Stratum 2s	Stratum 2s
Stratum 2F	Strata 2e and 2F	
Stratum 2B	Stratum 2B	Stratum 2m
Stratum 2A	Stratum 2A	Stratum 2d
Stratum 1C		
Stratum 1B	Stratum 1	Stratum 1
Stratum 1A		

[1] From Holliday (1995b : table 9A).

(*Holmesina septentrionale*), and extinct short-faced bear (*Arctodus simus*). Among the bones were several large (from 30 to 70 cm, maximum width) calcrete boulders, which are sedimentologically anomalous among fine sands and likely represent anvils for bone breakage. A few stone tools and butchered bone were found in stratum 1 in other localities, providing scattered evidence for Clovis-age occupation of the active stream bed elsewhere in the site.

Stafford (1981) suggested that FA2-1 consisted entirely of bone redeposited across the gravel bar by fluvial activity, indistinguishable from FA2-4, but subsequent research shows that the feature essentially is intact. The particle-size of the sediment that buries the feature indicates that the water that flowed over the bone was not competent enough to move most

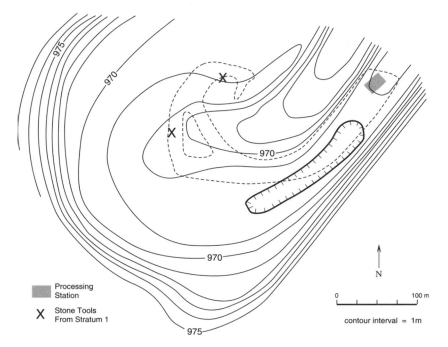

FIGURE 3.22. Distribution of Clovis features at Lubbock Lake on a paleotopographic base map of the entrenched meander (contour interval 1 m). The position of the reservoir is shown with a dashed line.

of the remains, and that easily transported fragments of mammoth skull remained in anatomical position during burial (Holliday 1985b; Kreutzer 1988). Kreutzer (1988), in a taphonomic analysis, could not demonstrate that the bone was in a secondary context but suggested orientation of some of the bone by fluvial action. In a more complete analysis of the bone on and above the gravel bar (i.e., a study of FA2-1 and FA2-4), Johnson (1995b) shows that: (1) the two groups of bones represent two discrete events; (2) FA2-1 was in primary context (although some realignment of bone did occur, but not transport); (3) FA2-4 bone was in secondary context; and (4) discrete cultural activity areas are discernable in FA2-1.

Remains of *Bison antiquus*, some with cut marks, were found at the top of the stratum 1 buried terrace (Holliday and Johnson 1984; Johnson and Holliday 1985; Johnson and Shipman 1986; Johnson 1991) (FIG. 3.23). This terrace must be older than the inset deposits of stratum 1, i.e., >11,100 yrs BP. Data are not available, however, to determine whether the terrace and bone bed are earlier Clovis-age features or of pre-Clovis age.

TABLE 3.6. Paleoindian features at the Lubbock Lake site[1]

Artifact Chronology	Feature Type	Feature Identification[2]
Late Paleoindian	Bison bone bed	GA12-4
	Bison bone bed	GA12-3
	Bison bone bed	GA12-12
	Bison bone bed	FA5-12
	Bison bone bed	FA5-8/GA5-1
	Bison bone bed	FA5-7/GA5-3
	Bison bone bed	FA5-5/TMM Station M
	Bison bone bed	FA4-1
(Firstview)	Camp and bone bed	FA6-3[3]
(Plainview age)	Bison bone bed	FA5-13
	Bison bone bed	FA9-1
	Bison bone bed	FA5-17 ("constricted stem")
	Bison bone bed	GA12-5
(Plainview)	Bison bone bed	FA6-11[4]
Folsom Age	Bison bone bed	FA6-8
	Bison bone bed	FA6-15
	Bison bone bed	FA2-2
Folsom	Bison bone bed	TMM, near Station I[5]
	Bison bone bed	TMM, near Station D[5]
Clovis Age	Pleistocene megafauna bone bed	FA2-1[6]
	Pleistocene megafauna bone bed	FA6-9

[1] Notes on file at the Texas Memorial Museum and Vertebrate Paleontology Laboratory (both at the University of Texas at Austin) suggest that TMM investigators (1948–1951) encountered other features besides those in the table, but so little documentation is available on age and artifact associations that they are not listed.

[2] Features identified as "FA" are from the Lubbock Lake Project (1973–1994) (Johnson 1987; unpub. data); features identified as "GA" are from West Texas Museum (now Museum of Texas Tech University) excavations of F. E. Green (Green, manuscript on file at MTTU; Kaczor 1978).

[3] Johnson and Holliday (1981); Bamforth (1985).

[4] Johnson and Holliday (1980).

[5] Sellards (1952); Holliday and Johnson (1996).

[6] Johnson (1987d, 1989, 1991); Kreutzer (1988).

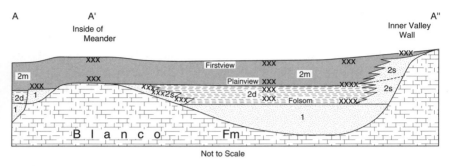

FIGURE 3.23. Schematic geologic cross section at Lubbock Lake along line A–A′–A″ (FIG. 3.20), showing the relationship of Paleoindian features (xxx with typological association indicated where known) within stratum 2 along the inside of the entrenched meander.

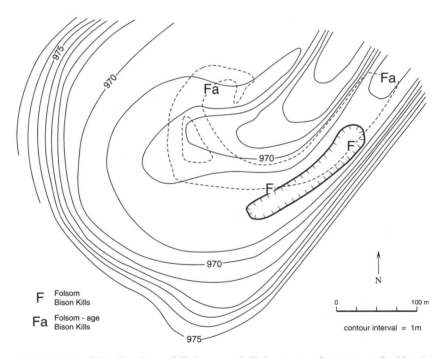

FIGURE 3.24. Distribution of Folsom and Folsom-age features at Lubbock Lake on a paleotopographic base map of the entrenched meander (contour interval 1 m). The position of the reservoir is shown with a dashed line.

Conformably above stratum 1 are various deposits comprising stratum 2, which is up to 2 m thick. Like Clovis, Lubbock Lake is perhaps best known geoarchaeologically for the diatomaceous earth of stratum 2, which includes beds of pure diatomite, lenses of diatomite interbedded with mud or sand, and diatomaceous mud. These deposits (2d) are on the valley floor. The diatomite beds were deposited under standing lake waters (decimeters to meters deep), and the muddy interbeds reflect marshy conditions when water was at or below the surface, based on sedimentology and invertebrate paleontology (Holliday 1985b, 1995b; Winsborough 1995; R. Forrester, pers. comm. 1994). The sand lenses were derived from slopewash off the bedrock valley walls. Tufas and heavily contorted and convoluted lenses of sand and mud interfacing with 2d along the valley margins are indicative of soft sediment deformation induced by spring discharge during 2d accumulation (Stafford 1981; C. V. Haynes, pers. comm. 1983). Sandy slopewash and sandy eolian facies (2s) also are located along the valley margin (FIGS. 3.21, 3.23). Stratum 2d and its facies date from 11,000 to 10,000 yrs BP.

The physical mechanism for impounding the stratum 2 waters is unknown. No evidence is available to suggest that beavers constructed dams in the draw (Johnson 1987c). Some indirect evidence indicates that at the end of stratum 1 deposition, alluvial sand from the top of the unit was reworked by wind, producing dunes that constricted drainage along narrow reaches of Yellowhouse Draw (Holliday 1985b).

Most of the Paleoindian archaeology at Lubbock Lake is in stratum 2. The various facies of the deposit, particularly strata 2d and 2m along the inside of the entrenched meander, contain a geocultural sequence dating to all post–Clovis Paleoindian stages. Not all of these features contain stylistically diagnostic artifacts, however, and typological affiliations of some features are unknown. Five Folsom or Folsom-age bone beds of butchered *Bison antiquus* are known from strata 2d and 2s (Table 3.6; FIGS. 3.23, 3.24, 3.25A,B). These features include two bone beds excavated by Evans and Meade (Sellards 1952) that yielded several Folsom points (FIGS. 3.25A, 3.26). The Folsom features date between 10,800 and 10,200 yrs BP. Five Plainview or Plainview-age bison bone beds are known from the top of 2d or its valley margin facies (Johnson and Holliday 1980; Holliday and Johnson 1981; Johnson 1987d) (Table 3.6; FIGS. 3.23, 3.27, 3.28). The Plainview feature dates to ca. 10,000 yrs BP. One of the Plainview-age features included a group of untyped constricted-stem projectile points (Holliday and Johnson 1984).

FIGURE 3.25A. Bison bone and a Folsom point exposed in the diatomite (stratum 2d) at Lubbock Lake during excavations by Sellards' crew in 1951 along the southeast side of the reservoir (FIG. 3.24). Note the lack of deformation, indicating that the lake beds provided a firm surface for killing and butchering bison. Courtesy of the Texas Memorial Museum, the University of Texas at Austin.

FIGURE 3.25B. A portion of a Folsom-age bone bed (FA6-8 in Johnson 1987d) exposed on the inside of the northwest end of the reservoir cut (FIG. 3.24), the area also shown in FIG. 3.28. The bone is in a mud interbed of stratum 2d and crushed to a few centimeters thick, probably during dewatering of the sediment. Courtesy of the Lubbock Lake Landmark, Museum of Texas Tech University.

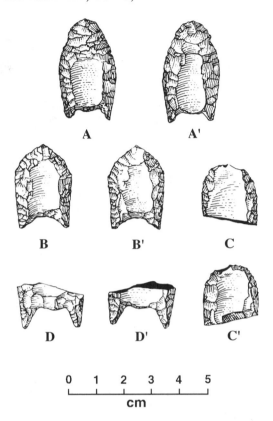

FIGURE 3.26. Artifacts from the "Folsom horizon" in the "Diatomaceous Earth" (stratum 2d) found by Sellards' crew at Lubbock Lake (modified from Sellards 1952:fig. 24). Drawn by Hal Story and reproduced courtesy of the Texas Memorial Museum, the University of Texas at Austin.

The Folsom, Folsom-age, Plainview, and Plainview-age features are in the muddy layers interbedded between deposits of pure diatomite (FIGS. 3.25A,B, 3.28) or in muddy to sandy valley-margin facies, and all represent localities where bison were killed and butchered when water was at or below the surface. Each bone bed represents at least two and as many as six individuals (with more bone yet to be excavated in all of these features), killed and butchered adjacent to marshes extant in the deepest part of the draw during low water phases of the diatomite ponds. Very little mixing of the diatomite layers and mud lenses is apparent below these features (FIGS. 3.25A,B, 3.28), indicating that the surfaces must have been very firm to support the weight of a bison and the hunters. One Folsom-age bone

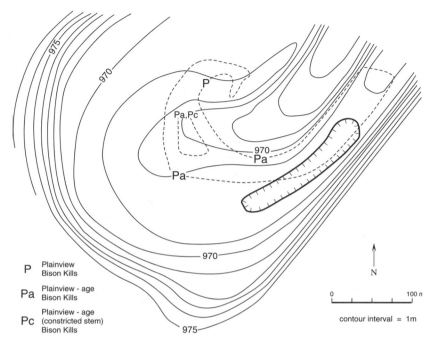

FIGURE 3.27. Distribution of Plainview and Plainview-age features at Lubbock Lake on a paleotopographic base map of the entrenched meander (contour interval 1 m). The position of the reservoir is shown with a dashed line.

bed was found choking a small channel (100 cm wide) at the base of 2d, directly above FA2-1, the Clovis-age bone scatter (FIGS. 3.22, 3.24). The channel is related to the final stages of stratum 1 alluviation in this reach of the draw.

Conformably above stratum 2d along the valley axis is a more homogeneous paludal mud (2m). Sandy eolian and slopewash facies of 2m (2s) are in valley-margin positions (FIGS. 3.21, 3.23). A weakly developed soil formed in the top of stratum 2 (A–C and A–Cg profiles in the valley-axis facies; A–C and A–Bw profiles in the better-drained valley-margin facies). Deposition of 2m and its sandy facies largely was from 10,000 to 8500 yrs BP, followed by soil formation from 8500 to 6300 yrs BP (i.e., continuing into the Early Archaic). The pedogenesis in upper 2m is indicative of general landscape stability within the draw, although localized eolian deposition occurred intermittently during soil formation.

Nine Late Paleoindian archaeological features are known from stratum 2m and its facies (Table 3.6). Most are bone beds of extinct bison in topographic settings similar to the Folsom- and Plainview-age features, found on both the valley floor and the valley margin along the inside of the meander (Johnson and Holliday 1981; Johnson 1987d) (FIGS. 3.23, 3.29). One feature is a camp or possibly a plant-harvesting and processing area (Johnson and Holliday 1981; Bamforth 1985) in stratum 2m and dating to ca. 8600 yrs BP. The feature is located on the gently sloping wall of the inner valley margin, immediately adjacent to a kill site on the flat valley floor (Johnson and Holliday 1981) (FIG. 3.29). Diagnostic artifacts are rare in these features, but when found typically are Late Paleoindian lanceolate projectile points, usually reworked, including Firstview points from the

FIGURE 3.28. Excavations at Lubbock Lake in the summer of 1974 on the inside of the northwestern end of the reservoir (FIG. 3.27). The crew is working at several levels in the bedded diatomite (stratum 2d), which shows up as the distinct, horizontal, lighter (diatomite) and darker (mud) beds. The top of the diatomite (on which most of the crew stands) in this area contains the Plainview bone bed reported by Johnson and Holliday (1980). The top of stratum 1 sand is exposed throughout the area in the lower right. The smaller excavated area low in the diatomite contains the Folsom-age bone bed shown in FIG. 3.25B. The homogeneous mud of stratum 2m is about 50 cm thick on top of 2d, exposed low along the back wall of the excavations. The light gray marl of stratum 3c rests on 2m. Note the lack of deformation of the beds in 2d despite the multiple bison butchering activities.

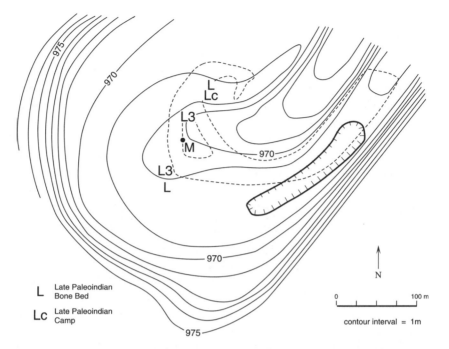

FIGURE 3.29. Distribution of Late Paleoindian features at Lubbock Lake on a paleotopographic base map of the entrenched meander (contour interval 1 m). The position of the reservoir is shown with a dashed line. Three Late Paleoindian bone beds are known from each of the two areas with "L3." The area marked "M" is "Station M" of Sellards (see FIG. 2.8).

camp/kill feature (Johnson and Holliday 1981). As with the Folsom and Plainview features, the latest Paleoindian bone beds represent localities where small groups of *Bison antiquus* (two to seven individuals) were killed and butchered in or near the margins of a marsh.

All of the features in stratum 2 (Folsom, Plainview, and latest Paleoindian) are on or near the gently sloping valley walls on the inside of the entrenched meander of the draw, where both animals and hunters had easy access to the ponds and marshes on the flat valley floor (FIGS. 3.23, 3.24, 3.27, 3.29). There is no evidence for a natural means of trapping the animals, such as in an arroyo, or of stampeding them off a cliff into the draw. As noted, however, all of the excavated Paleoindian features at Lubbock Lake were along the walls of the old reservoir cut, providing a very restricted view of the activities and landscape settings of the Paleoindian occupation of the site. Little is known of Paleoindian activity along the outside of the meander, where the valley wall is steeper, but stratum 2 is thicker and better drained, or along the more narrow, steep-walled, downstream end of the meander.

Burned bison bone found in 1950 by G. Evans and G. Meade and submitted for radiocarbon dating was believed to be from a Folsom occupation, based on stratigraphic correlation (Roberts 1951; Sellards 1952) (FIG. 2.8). The resulting age (9883±350 yrs BP, C-558) was considered to be the first date for the Folsom occupation of North America and one of the first applications of radiocarbon dating to Paleoindian archaeology (Roberts 1951; Taylor 1987). Diagnostic artifacts were not recovered from the feature, however, and subsequent geoarchaeological investigations showed that the feature was a Late Paleoindian bison kill/processing station near the base of stratum 2m, where the diatomaceous sediments are missing and the younger muds rest directly on stratum 1 (Holliday and Johnson 1986).

The geocultural stratigraphy at Lubbock Lake is very similar to that reported from Clovis. The principal differences between the two sites are (1) Clovis is in a tributary paleobasin and Lubbock Lake is directly in a draw, and (2) the Clovis record largely was destroyed, but the Lubbock Lake record largely is intact. The relatively large number of Paleoindian features reported from the relatively small area of the old reservoir cut at Lubbock Lake suggests that the Paleoindian record preserved at the site is as rich as the record lost at Clovis.

LUBBOCK LANDFILL

Geologic investigations at the Lubbock Landfill in lower Blackwater Draw (FIG. 1.3) revealed a stratigraphic sequence similar to that reported from Clovis and Lubbock Lake (Holliday 1995b). Very limited archaeological testing yielded evidence for a Paleoindian occupation (Brown 1993). The site is exposed in a large pit excavated for the landfill (the "Wind Pit," FIG. 3.30), which is 10 km above the confluence with Yellowhouse Draw and 8 km northeast of Lubbock Lake (FIG. 1.3).

The Landfill is in an entrenched meander of Blackwater Draw (FIG. 3.30), which cut through the Blackwater Draw Formation and into lacustrine carbonate. The Wind Pit exposed these older bedrock units and the inset late Quaternary valley fill (FIG. 3.31A). The oldest valley fill is alluvial sand and gravel of stratum 1, which is up to 1.6 m thick. Above stratum 1 is stratum 2, also up to 1.6 m thick and composed of three facies: diatomite and diatomaceous earth (2d), organic-rich mud (2m), and sand (2s) (FIGS. 3.31A,B).

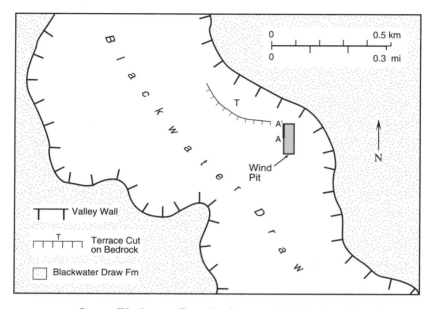

FIGURE 3.30. Lower Blackwater Draw in the area of the Lubbock Landfill with the location of the Wind Pit and section A–A' (FIG. 3.31) along the valley margin and the locations of terraces cut on bedrock (modified from Holliday 1995b: fig. 27A).

Stratum 2 is very limited in areal extent and is exposed only in the Wind Pit (FIG. 3.31A). Extensive trenching and coring above the Wind Pit, beginning 100 m up draw and continuing up draw for about 1 km, located no other deposits of stratum 2 (Brown 1993; Holliday 1995b). Down draw 2 km, stratum 2 was not exposed in any of the large pits excavated at the BFI Landfill (Holliday 1985a, 1995b). Stratum 2 is confined to a relatively short and narrow reach along the outside of an entrenched meander of the draw.

The most prominent stratigraphic feature exposed in the Wind Pit is a channel in the top of stratum 1 that is filled with stratum 2 (FIG. 3.31B). The channel probably represents a cutoff meander from the final stages of stratum 1 alluviation. Relatively minor alluvial activity, including both cutting and filling, alternated with sedimentation under ponds and marshes (probably spring-fed) in the early stages of stratum 2 accumulation. The oldest layer of stratum 2 is organic-rich mud (2m1) exposed north of the channel. The top of the mud includes a thin but prominent A-horizon traceable to the channel margin (FIG. 3.31B). A layer of pure diatomite (2d) caps stratum 1 and forms the base of stratum 2 south of the channel. Stratum

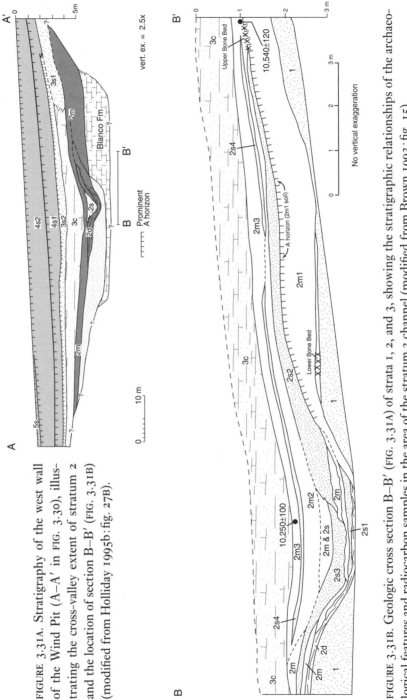

FIGURE 3.31A. Stratigraphy of the west wall of the Wind Pit (A–A' in FIG. 3.30), illustrating the cross-valley extent of stratum 2 and the location of section B–B' (FIG. 3.31B) (modified from Holliday 1995b: fig. 27B).

FIGURE 3.31B. Geologic cross section B–B' (FIG. 3.31A) of strata 1, 2, and 3, showing the stratigraphic relationships of the archaeological features and radiocarbon samples in the area of the stratum 2 channel (modified from Brown 1993: fig. 15).

2d interfingers with thin lenses of alluvial sand (2s1) in the channel and suggests intermittent alluviation (or perhaps localized spring discharge) during ponding. The diatomite and associated sand lenses are buried by interbedded layers of massive sand (2s2, 2s3, 2s4) and mud (2m2, 2m3) that also fill the channel. These deposits denote intermittent and waning alluviation as marsh muds accumulated in the draw. The oldest of the sand layers (2s2) covers some of the buried soil and 2m1 to the south of the channel, and the overlying mud (2m2) covers the rest of the soil and 2m1. The youngest layer of mud (2m3) is buried by marl (stratum 3c) with a thick, cumulic A-horizon lithologically similar to Unit E ("carbonaceous silt") at the Clovis and Anderson Basin sites.

Two bone beds were found in stratum 2 (FIG. 3.31B). The lower bone bed, consisting of several disarticulated bones of *Bison antiquus*, is at the base of the oldest mud (2m1), resting on a bench (small terrace?) of stratum 1 gravel. The bone is intimately mixed with the gravel and, therefore, probably is not in primary context. No stone artifacts were recovered from this feature. The upper bone bed rests on the A-horizon of 2m1 and yielded a few disarticulated elements of *Bison antiquus*. Stratum 2s2 is roughly contemporaneous with the bone bed. The muds of 2m2 bury the feature. The stable, low-energy setting indicates that the upper bone bed is *in situ*. Lithic debitage was scattered among the bone. Bone and stone artifacts recovered by water-screening stratum 2 hint at the presence of camping or food processing features, but no evidence was noted in the field (Johnson 1993, 1994).

The stratum 2m2 muds that bury the upper bone bed date to ca. 10,500 yrs BP (FIG. 3.31B; Table 3.7). The top of stratum 2m dates to ca. 10,250

TABLE 3.7. Radiocarbon ages from Paleoindian levels and bracketing levels on lower and middle Blackwater Draw

Site	^{14}C Age Years BP	Lab. No.	Material Dated & Remarks
Lubbock Landfill[1]			
	8840±120	Beta-43009	Humates; buried A-horizon at top of 3c
	10,250±100	Beta-57226	Humates; top of stratum 2 (2m3)
	10,540±120	Beta-61962	Humates; stratum 2m2 (burying bone bed)
Marks Beach (Gibson Ranch)			
	9710±80	SMU-2247	Humates; OM-rich mud within 2d[1]
	9920±380	GX-1458	Bone in 2d[2]

[1] Holliday (1995b).   [2] Honea (1980).

yrs BP (FIG. 3.31B; Table 3.7), and the top of stratum 3c, sampled elsewhere in the site, dates to ca. 8800 yrs BP (Table 3.7) (Brown 1993). The upper bone bed, therefore, is of Folsom age.

The Paleoindians that produced the upper bone bed occupied a relatively stable landscape (denoted by the A-horizon) near the paleochannel (FIG. 3.31B). The disarticulated nature of the remains suggests that the feature was a butchering station rather than a primary kill (Johnson 1993, 1994), although very little of it was exposed. The floor of the draw to the south of the bone bed (toward the center of the draw) probably was marshy during occupation. The channel itself probably held a marsh (wetter, perhaps, than the surrounding marsh) at this time, but it also could have held a small flowing stream. Vertebrate microfauna indicate that stratum 2 accumulated as a boggy marsh with sedgebeds along its margins, surrounded by a riparian wet-meadow grading into an open prairie along the draw margins (Johnson 1993, 1994). The microstratigraphic data available at this time do not allow a more precise reconstruction of the bone bed environment.

MARKS BEACH (GIBSON RANCH)

Marks Beach is in a short, straight reach of Blackwater Draw between two broad entrenched meanders, and in the only east-to-west-flowing reach of any draw on the Southern High Plains (Holliday 1995b) (FIGS. 1.3, 3.32). The site is a blowout along the north margin of the draw, a small part of a larger study locality referred to as Gibson Ranch. The blowout is a basin deflated into valley-margin facies of the valley fill. The geoarchaeological discussion is summarized from Honea (1980) and based on field research by the writer and D. J. Meltzer (Table 3.8).

Blackwater Draw in the Gibson Ranch area incised through Pleistocene lake carbonate (stratum B of Holliday 1995b) and into the Blackwater Draw Formation. The strata comprising the valley fill are continuous through the Marks Beach area and are more or less continuous through the Gibson Ranch area. The oldest valley fill at Marks Beach and throughout this reach of the draw is sand and gravel alluvium of stratum 1 (FIG. 3.33). No bones or stone artifacts were found in stratum 1 at Marks Beach, but some mammoth remains in possibly archaeological contexts were recovered during test excavations 4 km up draw (Honea 1980, addendum: 329).

Cultural remains and possible archaeological features were found in stratum 2 at Marks Beach. The 1968–1970 excavations at the site penetrated a sandy, valley-margin facies (2s) of diatomaceous earth (2d), which is common along the axis of the draw south of the site (FIG. 3.33). Stratum 2

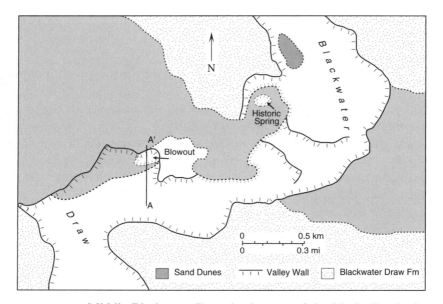

FIGURE 3.32. Middle Blackwater Draw in the area of the Marks Beach site ("Blowout") on Gibson Ranch, with the location of section A–A' (FIG. 3.33) across the valley (modified from Holliday 1995b: fig. 29A). The location of a spring which fed historic ponds in the draw (and prehistoric diatomite ponds?) is also indicated.

TABLE 3.8. Correlation of stratigraphic terminology for the Marks Beach site[1]

Honea 1980	Holliday this volume
Zone V	Stratum 5s
Zone IV	
Zone IIIB	Stratum 3s
Zone IIIA	
	Stratum 2s
Zone II	
	Stratum 2d
Zone I	Stratum 1

[1] From Holliday (1995b: table 8A).

is continuous for at least 1.5 km below Marks Beach, but does not extend along the draw above the site. Stratum 2s in the site consists of interbedded laminae of sandy diatomite, organic-rich sand, and clean sand. Honea encountered a bone bed of a single disarticulated and possibly butchered *Bison antiquus* in upper 2s, 30 m from the north valley wall. Honea proposed that the kill was near a spring outlet, similar to settings described at the Clovis site (e.g., Haynes and Agogino 1966). Examination of published profiles and coring through the area do not support this interpretation, however. The microstratigraphy reported in and near the bone bed consists of finely bedded, horizontal layers of sand, mud, and diatomite, in strong contrast to the heavily convoluted and largely sandy bedding associated with spring discharge (e.g., Haynes and Agogino 1966). A historic spring is known from about 2 km up draw (Holliday 1995b), and it likely fed the diatomite ponds as well. The bone bed probably was located where it is because of proximity to the pond, and the area is accessible and well drained.

No stone artifacts were found in the bone bed, but test excavations by D. J. Meltzer in 1991 100 m southwest of the test pits with the bone bed yielded about 80 small chert flakes, some with evidence of retouch, and some charcoal flecks at the same level as the bone bed. Burned bone from the feature was dated to ca. 9900 yrs BP (Honea 1980) (Table 3.7). Sediment from lower 2d along the valley axis, stratigraphically below the bone bed,

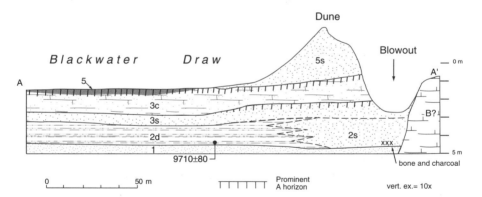

FIGURE 3.33. Stratigraphic cross section A–A′ (FIG. 3.32) through the Marks Beach site and across middle Blackwater Draw, showing the stratigraphic position of the Paleoindian bone bed (xxx) and the radiocarbon sample (modified from Holliday 1995b: fig. 29B).

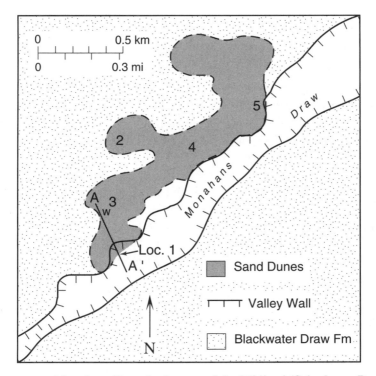

FIGURE 3.34. Monahans Draw in the area of the Midland (Scharbauer Ranch) site, showing Locality 1 in the draw and Locality 3 in the dunes, the distribution of the dunes fringing the draw, and the location of section A–A′ (FIG. 3.35) (modified from Holliday 1995b: fig. 24A).

was dated to ca. 9700 yrs BP (Table 3.7). The bone bed, therefore, is a Late Paleoindian, Plainview-age feature.

MIDLAND

The Midland site is along Monahans Draw, a tributary of the Colorado River system, at the south end of the Llano Estacado (FIG. 1.3). The site is renowned in archaeology because it yielded some of the best-documented human remains of possible Paleoindian age and because it is the type site for the Midland point. The age of the human remains is not agreed upon, however, owing to difficulties in dating the bone or associated deposits and artifacts. The initial arguments in support of its age relied largely on geo-archaeological data. Renewed investigations by the author and D. J. Meltzer also focused on stratigraphic relationships (Holliday and Meltzer 1996).

Midland (also known as the Scharbauer Ranch site) is in a small

($<$5 km^2) dune field that rests on the Blackwater Draw Formation and, significantly, overlaps Monahans Draw (FIGS. 2.11A, 3.34). Midland often is referred to as a dune locality (e.g., Wormington 1957:242; Smith 1976:125; Jennings 1983:40, 1989:65; Haynes 1993:230), and the major geologic emphasis of Wendorf and others (1955) is dune stratigraphy and history, but important areas of the site are in valley fill (Holliday 1995b) (FIGS. 3.34, 3.35). The following geoarchaeological summary is based on the work of Wendorf and others (1955), Wendorf and Krieger (1959), Wendorf (1975b), and the work of the author and D. J. Meltzer (Holliday and Meltzer 1996; Holliday 1995b, unpub. data) (Table 3.9).

The site includes five blowouts (Localities 1–5 of Wendorf et al. 1955) in the active portion of the dunes. Locality 1, which yielded the human remains, is where the dunes overlap Monahans Draw (FIGS. 2.11A,B, 3.34). There, wind eroded through the dunes and into the valley-margin facies of the draw fill (FIG. 3.35). Much of the recent geoarchaeological work concentrated in Locality 1. The other four localities are entirely within the dunes north of the draw (FIG. 3.34). Most of the recent work outside of Locality 1 focused on the west end of Locality 3 (3w) (FIGS. 3.34, 3.35). In both the original site studies and the recent reinvestigations, this was a key

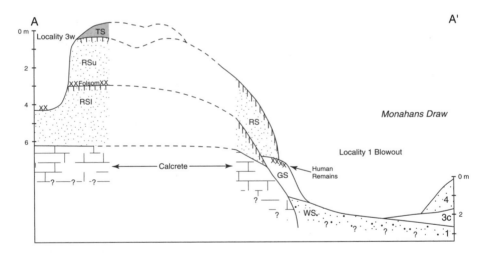

FIGURE 3.35. Geologic cross section A–A′ (FIG. 3.34) at the Midland site, showing the stratigraphic relationships of deposits and archaeology (xxx) in Localities 1 and 3w (WS = White Sand, GS = Gray Sand, RS = Red Sand; RSl = lower Red Sand, RSu = upper Red Sand, TS = Tan Sand). Note the wedge of sand (probably the lower Red Sand) between the Red Sand (as originally identified by Wendorf et al. 1955) and the calcrete.

TABLE 3.9. Correlation of stratigraphic terminology for the Midland site[1]

Wendorf et al. 1955			Holliday this volume
		Unit 5	
Monahans Fm			Stratum 5s
		Unit 4	
Judkins Fm	Red Sand	Unit 3	Stratum 4s
	Gray Calcareous Sand	Unit 2b	Stratum 3s2
		Unit 2a	Stratum 3s1
	White Calcareous Sand	Unit 1	Stratum 1

[1] From Holliday (1995b: table 13A).

area for correlating the Paleoindian archaeology and dune stratigraphy with the human remains and draw stratigraphy.

Monahans Draw is cut into a massive calcrete in the area of the Midland site. The small dune field at the site buries the calcrete and the valley fill (FIG. 3.35). There are three valley-fill strata (1, 3, 4) pertinent to the interpretations of the Paleoindian archaeology. The oldest valley fill (stratum 1), the "White Sand" of Wendorf and others (1955), is calcareous silty and clayey loam, interbedded with thin lenses of low-carbonate sands and gravels. The sand and gravel is alluvial, but some of the more calcareous zones are nodules and fragments of carbonate rock, probably derived from the bedrock calcrete. Stratum 1 contains the remains of late Pleistocene megafauna (*Mammuthus columbi, Camelops* sp., *Equus* sp., *Canis dirus, Capromeryx, Bison antiquus*).

Above stratum 1 in Locality 1 is a calcareous sand (stratum 3s), the "Gray Sand" of Wendorf and others (1955), which is an eolian, valley-margin facies of lacustrine carbonate (marl; stratum 3c) found along the valley axis. Fossils in stratum 3 include *Equus* sp., *Capromeryx*, and *Bison antiquus*, along with the famous *Homo sapiens* remains. Some lithic artifacts, including the type Midland points (FIG. 3.36), also were found in stratum 3s in Locality 1. The points initially were identified as "unfluted Folsom" (Wendorf et al. 1955:49). The term "Midland point" was proposed following subsequent excavations at the Midland site (Wendorf and Krieger 1959), but only as a typological category. The relationship of Folsom to Midland was unknown (Wendorf and Krieger 1959:67).

Burying stratum 3s in Locality 1 is a massive eolian sand (stratum 4s), the "Red Sand" of Wendorf and others (1955). *Equus* sp., *Capromeryx*, and *Bison antiquus* also are reported from stratum 4s. In the valley-margin set-

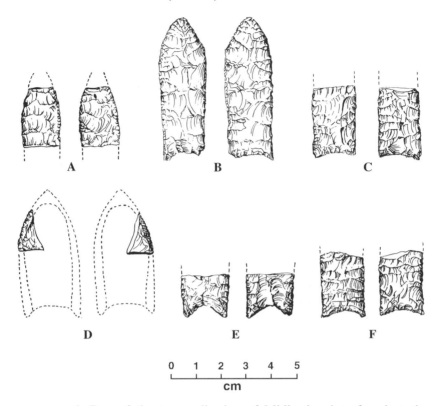

FIGURE 3.36. Part of the type collection of Midland points found at the Midland site (A–C from Locality 1, D–F from Locality 2) in 1953 and 1954 (from Wendorf et al. 1955:figs. 12, 17). Reproduced with the permission of Fred Wendorf.

ting of Locality 1 a weakly developed soil (A–Bw profile) formed in stratum 4. Along the valley axis soil development is stronger (A–Bt profile), which is typical of soil variability between valley-axis and valley-margin facies in the draws (Holliday 1985a,c, 1995b). Above stratum 4 are historic or modern sands, which constitute the prominent, active dunes of the area.

The Red Sand was recognized in the other localities, where it was capped by a buried soil (Wendorf et al. 1955:32; Wendorf and Krieger 1959:66). No artifacts were recovered from within the lower portion of the Red Sand, but it appeared that Folsom and Midland points, along with other evidence for human occupation, were associated with the buried soil at the top of the Red Sand (Wendorf et al. 1955:43–48; Wendorf and Krieger 1959:67). Because of the apparent association of Midland points with the upper portion of the Red Sand in the dune localities, Wendorf et al. (1955:45) concluded that the Midland point associated with the skeletal remains in the draw was intrusive, the result of deflation of overlying Red Sand (Wendorf and Krieger 1959:67).

Wendorf and Krieger (1959) discuss attempts to date the site using radiocarbon and the then-new "uranium daughter-product" method (Rosholt 1958) (now known as uranium-thorium or U-series disequilibrium) (Table 3.10). The results were ambiguous, and in the end three scenarios were offered for the age of the human remains: (1) ca. 13,400–10,000 yrs BP, considered "most plausible," (2) ca. 7000 yrs BP, considered "least plausible," and (3) ca. 20,000 yrs BP, which "should not be entirely discounted" (Wendorf and Krieger 1959:78). As of 1959, therefore, the Midland skull was believed to pre-date Folsom occupations and possibly be 20,000 years old. As a result, the site generally was accorded an age "substantially pre-Folsom" (Willey 1966:44) or "more than 10,000, and possibly as much as 20,000 years old" (Jennings 1989:66).

The stratigraphic work at Midland by Holliday and Meltzer (1996) resulted in several significant conclusions. There are two Red Sands in Area 3, a lower Red Sand and an upper Red Sand. The lower Red Sand is redder, more compact, has stronger structural development, and is higher in clay content than the upper Red Sand. These characteristics are the result of pedogenic processes and formation of a moderately to strongly developed soil (A–Bt profile). The buried humic zone noted by Wendorf and others (1955:33) is at the top of this soil. The upper Red Sand is similar in color to the lower Red Sand, but exhibits substantially less pedogenic alteration with only a weak A–Bt profile. The secondary clay in this soil is in the form of four to six 1–3 mm thick, illuvial "clay bands" (cf. Gile 1979). The lower Red Sand is stratigraphically below the White Sand (FIG. 3.35) (as suggested by Glen Evans, pers. comm. 1991, and drawing on file, Texas Memorial Museum, Austin). The Folsom material in Locality 3 is from the buried surface at the top of the lower Red Sand. The upper Red Sand in Locality 3 is the same layer as stratum 4s (the Red Sand) in Locality 1. The human remains, therefore, are younger than the lower Red Sand, but their relationship to the Folsom artifacts cannot be determined. Wendorf (1975b) also suggested this possibility.

The stratigraphic sequence exposed in Locality 1 now is recognized as the valley-margin facies of the fill in Monahans Draw. The valley-axis stratigraphy is essentially identical to that observed in other reaches of the draw and in other draws (Holliday 1995b). Stratum 3c is not dated in Monahans Draw, but over 25 radiocarbon assays bearing on the age of 3c are available from other localities throughout the Southern High Plains

TABLE 3.10. Radiocarbon and U-series ages from the Midland site

Age Years BP	Lab No.	Material Dated & Remarks
[14]C		
8,670±600	M-388	"Turtle bones and other bones from white sand"[1]; also reported as M-389, M-390 & M-391, "mammoth tusk and two others of fossil bone" from the top of the White Sand[2]
7,100±1000	M-411	"Concentrated carbon . . . from animal bone from the grey sand"[1]; "fossil bone fragments" from the Gray Sand[2]
20,400±900	L-347	"Carbon extracted from [burned] caliche . . . found in Gray Sand"[3]; "Several pounds of . . . burned caliche . . . processed"[4]
23,500	L-347?	Apparent age determined on "calcium carbonate from the caliche itself [L-347]"[3]; also reported as 23,800 on "caliche residue"[4]
13,400±1200	L-304C	"Pond snail shells from the white sand"[5]
U-Series		
17,000	249088	"fragmentary bone" from the Gray Sand[6]
18,000	229122	"fossil bone"[6]; "rib"[7]
20,000	253502	"small section from the human skull"[6]
10,600±1000		recalculation of 253502[7]
12,030±1000		recalculation of 229122[7]
12,300±500	SMU-133B1	"cranial bone"[7]

[1] Crane (1956:670).
[2] Wendorf et al. (1955:9, 99–100).
[3] Olson and Broecker (1959:22).
[4] Wendorf and Krieger (1959:71).
[5] Broecker and Kulp (1957:1329); Wendorf and Krieger (1959:71).
[6] Wendorf and Krieger (1959:72); see also Rosholt (1958).
[7] McKinney (1992).

(Holliday 1995b), in addition to dozens of ages available from the Lubbock Lake site and Mustang Springs site (Holliday, Johnson, Haas, and Stuckenrath 1983, 1985; Meltzer 1991) (FIG. 1.3). The deposit is time-transgressive, but rarely dates to >10,000 yrs BP and is <10,000 yrs BP at all dated localities in the draws of the Colorado system.

One of the goals of the work at Midland by D. J. Meltzer and the author was recovery of material suitable for dating. We were unable to obtain

charcoal or bone that might permit radiocarbon dating. Moreover, this ef-
fort was severely hampered by a high water table in the draw, resulting
from seasonal groundwater fluctuations, and the pumping of sewage effluent
into Monahans Draw by the city of Odessa (FIG. 2.11B), some 20 miles
"upstream" of the site. Had samples of charcoal or bone been recovered,
the potential for effluent contamination would have rendered the resulting
dates suspect.

Several other lines of evidence were offered that the Gray Sand and the
human remains are of Folsom age (>10,000 yrs BP) or older, but the data
are ambiguous. Similarities in fluorine content and degree of fossilization
among the bone from the White and Gray sands, including the human remains, were used to argue in support of the contemporaneity of the human
bone and the Pleistocene fauna (Wendorf et al. 1955:91–95). Similarities
in such postdepositional characteristics do not necessarily indicate contemporaneity and can result in erroneous conclusions (e.g., Cotter 1991).
Fragments of teeth and bone from extinct horse and extinct antelope found
in the Gray Sand and Red Sand may be deflated from stratum 1 (as suggested by Wendorf et al. 1955; Wendorf and Krieger 1959) or eroded off
the nearby valley walls. A fragment of extinct antelope (*Capromeryx*) may
have been in place within the Gray Sand, but provides only a general clue
to the minimum age of the Gray Sand. Extinct antelope was found at
Lubbock Lake in deposits of Folsom age (>10,000 yrs BP) or possibly
younger (<10,000 yrs BP) (Johnson 1987c). Some new U-series ages from
the site, based on recalculations of the original ages, suggested that the
bone from stratum 3 was late Pleistocene (McKinney 1992). This approach to U-series dates has not been shown to provide reliable, repro-
ducible results, however.

In summary, the available stratigraphic data suggest that the Midland
skeletal material and Midland points are Folsom age or younger (probably
<10,000 yrs BP). Stratum 3 at most other localities on the Southern High
Plains is of early Holocene age, and the human remains may be Late Paleoindian or possibly Early Archaic, still the oldest human remains known in
the region.

Regardless of the age of the human remains, however, the Midland site
clearly was the locus of relatively intense Paleoindian occupation. Folsom,
Midland, and other unfluted lanceolate artifacts were found on deflated
surfaces in most localities, and hearths of possible Midland age were excavated in Locality 1 (Wendorf and others 1955; Wendorf and Krieger 1959).
Local artifact collectors report numerous additional surface finds of Paleoindian artifacts, including Folsom, Midland, and unfluted lanceolate

points. The reason for this relatively high concentration of Paleoindian materials is not clear. Stratigraphic studies in the draw provide no indication of any particular attractions such as springs or ponds. Artifacts simply may be more visible here because of the dune field, which is devoid of ground cover and easily eroded, conditions that do not obtain in other areas along Monahans Draw.

PLAINVIEW

The Plainview site is in a broad, gently meandering reach of Running Water Draw, now within the city limits of Plainview, Texas (FIGS. 1.3, 3.37). The site was discovered after a quarry was opened along the south side of the draw (Pit 1, FIGS. 3.37, 3.38) for mining of the Ogallala Caprock (Sellards et al. 1947; Speer 1990). Some years after the archaeological excavations ended two more pits were opened, providing excellent, long stratigraphic exposures of the valley fill (Pits 2,3, FIG. 3.37). Air photos and topographic maps show that Pit 1 was enlarged after 1945, destroying evidence of the precise stratigraphic relationship between the bone bed and the valley fill, which is important for dating the Plainview occupation. In the 1970s Pit 1 was filled with garbage, and the original excavation area and related exposures were buried. Guffee (1979), however, determined that some of the bone bed still is preserved east of Pit 1 (FIG. 3.37). In the west wall of Pit 3 (FIG. 3.37) is a cross section of valley fill closest to the original archaeological excavations, and it provided much of the data for the observations and interpretations presented below (Table 3.11). The southwest wall of Pit 2 (FIG. 3.37) provided a lateral section of valley fill close to the archaeological site, and some data were gathered along it, too, before burial under garbage (Holliday 1985e, 1990a).

In the Plainview area, Running Water Draw cut through the Blackwater Draw Formation and into the Ogallala Caprock (FIGS. 3.38, 3.39). At the site the caprock is a massive, brecciated, pisolitic, locally highly silicified, pedogenic calcrete up to 3 m thick. The exposures in Pit 3 (FIGS. 3.37, 3.39) demonstrate that incision occurred in at least two stages. Along the south side of the valley is a bench (terrace?) cut on the calcrete. The surface of the bench is about 1 m above the deepest point of valley incision, which produced a broad, flat floor cut into the calcrete. A channel 1 m deep was cut into the bench and then filled with stratum 1m, an organic-rich, loamy mud facies of stratum 1 alluvium and dated from ca. 12,000 to 11,000 yrs BP (Table 3.12; FIG. 3.39). The fine-grained and organic-rich nature of the sediments and their paleotopographic position suggest that they formed in a marsh that occupied a channel of Running Water Draw,

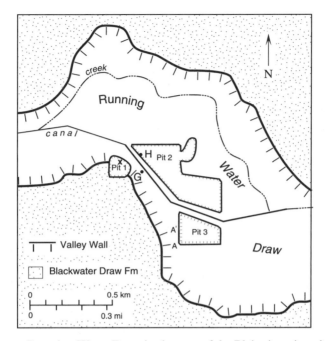

FIGURE 3.37. Running Water Draw in the area of the Plainview site with the locations of the three caliche quarries (Pits 1–3), location of the Plainview bone bed in Pit 1 (x), location of test by Guffee (1979) (G) and section described by Holliday (1985e) (H), and section A–A′ in Pit 3 (FIG. 3.39) (modified from Holliday 1995b: fig. 26A).

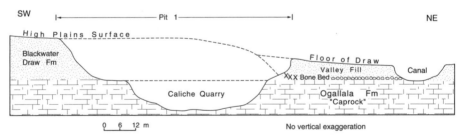

FIGURE 3.38. Generalized geologic cross section of Running Water Draw through Pit 1 and the Plainview bone bed (xxx) (FIG. 3.37) (modified from Evans 1949: fig. 12).

TABLE 3.11. Correlation of stratigraphic terminology for the Plainview site[1]

Sellards et al. 1947	Holliday 1985b	Holliday 1990b	Holliday this volume
Dark, Sandy Soil	Unit 5	Unit 5B Unit 5A	Stratum 5B Stratum 5A
Massive, Compact Sandy Clay	Unit 4	Unit 4	Stratum 4s
[nr]	[nr]	Unit 3	Strata 3c & 3s
[nr]	[nr]	Unit 2 (top)	Stratum 2m
Basal Sand & Gravel	Unit 3 (sand) Unit 1 (gravel)	Unit 2	Stratum 1
[nr]	[nr]	Unit 1	Loamy mud filling bedrock channel
Panhandle Fm	Calcrete bedrock	Ogallala Fm Caprock Caliche	Ogallala Fm Caprock Caliche

[1] From Holliday (1995b: table 7A).   nr = Strata not recognized.

TABLE 3.12. Radiocarbon ages for the Paleoindian level and bracketing levels at the Plainview site

Site	^{14}C Age Years BP	Lab. No.	Material Dated & Remarks
	9,800±500	L-303	Fresh-water snail shell from bone level[1]
	7,100±160	O-171	"Organic portion of bones"[2]
	8,860±110	SMU-2341	Humates; stratum 2m at or overlying bone level[3]
	9,860±180	TX-3908	Bone apatite[4]
	10,200±400	TX-3907	Bone apatite[4]
	10,940±70	SMU-1359	Humates; near top of stratum 1m, below bone level[3]
	11,970±140	SMU-1376	Humates; near bottom of stratum 1m, below bone level[3]

[1] Broecker and Kulp (1957); originally reported as 9171±500 yrs BP by Krieger (1957).
[2] Brannon et al. (1957:149).
[3] Holliday (1995b).
[4] Speer (1990).

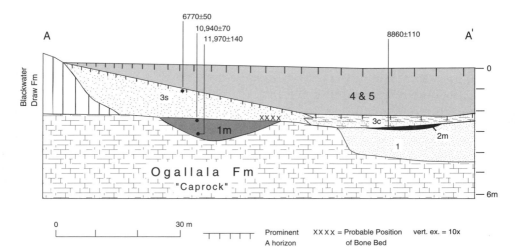

FIGURE 3.39. Geologic cross section A–A' (FIG. 3.37) of Running Water Draw in Pit 3 near the Plainview site, showing the location of radiocarbon samples and the interpolated stratigraphic position of the original Plainview bone bed (from Holliday 1995b:fig. 26B).

perhaps deposited in a cutoff meander. The age and stratigraphic position of stratum 1m suggest that final incision of the draw, which isolated the calcrete bench with its shallow channel, occurred after 11,000 years BP.

The principal facies of stratum 1 is a sand and gravel deposit up to 2.3 m thick that rests on the wide bedrock floor of the channel (FIG. 3.39). There also is a thin veneer (a few centimeters thick) of gravel across the calcrete bench. In most exposures the lower 50 cm of stratum 1 is a sandy gravel, although along the southwestern wall of Pit 2, which exposes both valley-margin and valley-axis facies, the gravel layer is only a few centimeters thick. The gravel usually is overlain by thick, bedded, medium sand. The Plainview bone bed, discussed below, was associated with stratum 1.

Stratum 2 is localized and only a few tens of centimeters thick, resting conformably on stratum 1. The layer is composed of dozens of thin, highly contorted, organic-rich mud lenses (2m) draped across stratum 1. A sample of these lenses from the upper 10 cm of 2m yielded a radiocarbon age of ca. 8900 years BP (Table 3.12).

Conformably overlying stratum 2 and resting on the bedrock bench is stratum 3 (FIG. 3.39). Along the valley axis, lacustrine carbonate (stratum 3c) buries stratum 2m. The sandy eolian facies (3s) is along the valley margin and buries the thin layer of stratum 1 and the bedrock bench.

The Plainview bone bed was "a mat of closely spaced, disarticulated bones and skeletons . . . of approximately 100 bison . . . in an area of about 500 square feet" and "an average thickness of scarcely a foot" (Sellards et al. 1947:934) (FIG. 3.40). At least 28 projectile points forming the type Plainview collection (FIG. 3.41) and 15 other lithic artifacts were recovered from the bone bed during and subsequent to the 1945 excavations; an unknown number of artifacts probably were removed by collectors (Speer 1990). Several of the points were reused as butchering tools (Holliday and Johnson 1996).

The bone bed originally was interpreted as being the result of a single-event stampede and kill (Sellards et al. 1947). The stampede hypothesis is plausible given the proximity of the bone bed to the valley wall and the steepness and relief of the wall. A Plainview bison jump is known from Bonfire Shelter in southwest Texas (Dibble and Lorrain 1968) (Chapter 4). Knudson (1983:27), in her study of Plainview lithic production, states that "There is a remarkable uniformity in raw materials and technique in

FIGURE 3.40. A segment of the Plainview bone bed jacketed by Sellards' crew, given to the Texas Tech Museum, and subsequently prepared. Note the densely packed, jumbled nature of the bone bed and the projectile point in place just right of center. Courtesy of the Lubbock Lake Landmark, Museum of Texas Tech University.

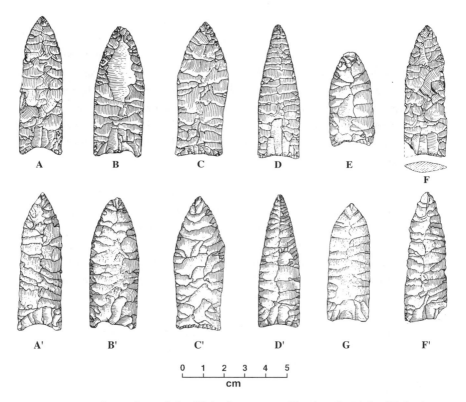

FIGURE 3.41. A portion of the Plainview type collection from the Plainview site, illustrating the wide range in artifact morphologies (modified from Sellards 1952: figs. 30, 31, 32). Drawn by Hal Story and reproduced courtesy of the Texas Memorial Museum, the University of Texas at Austin.

the Plainview collection, suggesting only a few individuals were involved in its production . . . perhaps only one and at the most two individuals made these tools." Such technological uniformity suggests contemporaneity among all of the artifacts and the kill, but such uniformity also would be likely if the same group repeatedly used the site as a kill. There is evidence indicating that the bone bed resulted from multiple kills, including the age structure of the bison, which suggests a kill in the fall and another in the spring (Johnson 1989), and varying stages of weathering on the bone (Holliday and Johnson 1996). Postdepositional mixing of the bone also is indicated (Guffee 1979; Holliday and Johnson 1996; Johnson 1989; Speer, pers. comm. 1980).

The stratigraphic relationship of the bone bed to the bedrock and to stratum 1 is an important geoarchaeological issue for dating the Plainview occupation. The bone bed was found on the quarry face along the south side of the draw (FIGS. 3.37, 3.38). Sellards et al. (1947:936) state that the fill associated with the bone "consists of a basal zone of cross-bedded sands and water-worn caliche gravels [i.e., stratum 1] from a few inches to 3.5 feet thick . . . , which contains the bison bone bed . . ." The relationship of the bone to the alluvium is clarified elsewhere in the original site report. "Over most of its area the bone bed rested directly on caliche bedrock, but near the upstream and downstream ends it was separated from bedrock by a few inches of the valley fill" (Sellards et al. 1947:931). Stratum 1 is very thin (<10 cm) throughout the area of and around Pit 1, based on descriptions from just east of the pit (Guffee 1979:41; Holliday 1985e, 1990a) (FIG. 3.37) and based on examination of the west wall of Pit 2 (FIG. 3.37) (Holliday 1990a).

Sellards et al. (1947:934) believed that the bones "accumulated in a shallow water hole or pond within a former channel" of the draw. "That the water was shallow is indicated by the thin layer of pond sediment . . . in the upper part [of the bone bed] and by the presence of abundant freshwater invertebrates . . . " An examination of blocks of bone and sediment removed by Sellards' team and recently excavated (Speer 1990) shows that part of the bone bed was in and on a deposit of grayish-brown (10YR 6/2, dry) sandy loam that was above the gravel. This sandy loam is distinctly different from the sand and gravel typical of stratum 1, although some gravel clasts and some pockets of fine sand are mixed in among the bone. The sandy loam is lithologically identical to the fill in the bedrock channel exposed on the west face of Pit 3. Therefore it is likely that the feature was associated with the same or a similar channel incised in the bedrock. The bone bed probably was draped across both the bedrock bench and across a channel fill. Some weathering of the bone bed is noted by Sellards et al. (1947:934) and E. Johnson (in Holliday and Johnson 1996), but otherwise the condition of the feature indicates burial by stratum 3 shortly after the kill or kills.

Dating the Plainview bone bed has proven difficult. The feature almost certainly is stratigraphically above the channel fill in the bedrock bench exposed in Pit 3. The upper channel fill dates to ca. 11,000 yrs BP (FIG. 3.39), so the bone bed is younger than that age. Shell and bone from the bone bed were submitted for radiocarbon dating in 1953, and additional bone was submitted in 1980 (Table 3.12). Evaluating the resulting ages is difficult, however, given the problems associated with radiocarbon dating of shell and bone, particularly in the early years of the method

(Taylor 1987), but they suggest that the feature may be ca. 10,000 years old (Chapter 5). The radiocarbon age of ca. 8900 yrs BP for stratum 2 probably is an upper limit on the age of the feature.

OTHER DRAW SITES

Paleoindian occupations associated with the draws are known from a number of localities in addition to the sites described above (FIG. 3.42), although the data are very sparse. Deflation of valley fill along upper Blackwater Draw exposed several sites near the Clovis gravel pit in addition to the Anderson Basin localities. These localities are associated with a white sand 1–2 m thick found along the south side of the draw (Unit B1 of Haynes 1975) (FIGS. 3.3, 3.43) (J. Warnica, pers. comm. 1994). Lenses of organic-rich muds locally are common in the sand. These sands are usually buried by younger red sands and stabilized by a well-developed soil (A–Bt profile). The archaeological debris is found where erosion breached the younger sands and soils and exposed the unconsolidated white sands to erosion. The white sands (and muds) rest on the Blackwater Draw Formation or late Pleistocene lake carbonate (stratum C of Holliday 1995b) (FIG. 3.43). At and near the Car Body site, Clovis artifacts and the remains of mammoths, camels, and horses were found at the base of the sand (Haynes 1975; J. Warnica, pers. comm. 1995) (FIGS. 3.3, 3.43). Hell Gap artifacts were found in the white sand at the Burns site (J. Warnica, pers. comm. 1995) (FIG. 3.3). The white sand probably is eolian, but its source is uncertain. Its setting within the draw and only in the draw suggests that it was deflated from the valley. The sand is identical in color and texture to Paleoindian-age alluvium and spring deposits reported in the draw (Haynes and Agogino 1966; Haynes 1975; Holliday 1995b); it probably was deflated from such deposits. Presence of the sand only along the south valley wall suggests that very localized factors played a role in its formation. Perhaps spring outlets were located along the south valley wall, discharging sand and water into the drainage. This would explain the attraction of the area to Paleoindians, as well as the source of the sand and the localized presence of mud layers.

The Seminole-Rose site in lower Seminole Draw (FIG. 3.42) yielded a collection of 24 lanceolate projectile points, probably Firstview, found among bison bones and burned rock (R. Rose, M. Collins, pers. comm. 1984; Kibler 1991: Appendix B). The bone and stone were exposed by deflation in a field and by erosion on a road bed. Coring by the author revealed that the valley fill was relatively thin. The lower 100 cm of the section is alluvial fine sand (stratum 1). Above the alluvium is a sandy marl

FIGURE 3.42. The distribution of reported Paleoindian sites in draws on the Southern High Plains.

(stratum 3c) up to 30 cm thick. There was no other valley fill except for modern dunes. The archaeological feature appeared to be eroding from the top of stratum 3. Test excavations failed to find intact archaeological deposits (M. Collins, pers. comm. 1990). The surface sediments throughout this reach of the draw are sandy, and the draw in the site area is relatively wide (400 m). Such a wide, sandy basin may have promoted deflation of the younger valley fill, thereby exposing the bone bed.

Other Paleoindian sites are reported from surface finds in or adjacent to draws. In Yellowhouse Draw, just below Lubbock Lake (FIGS. 1.3, 3.42), a variety of Paleoindian artifacts are reported in association with a buried terrace in the Canyon Lakes site (Johnson and Stafford 1976). Reported projectile point types include Clovis, Folsom, Midland, Agate Basin, Plainview, and Firstview. Bones of extinct bison and mammoths also were found in the area. On the southern Llano Estacado, Folsom and unfluted lanceolate styles were found on the surface at and near the Mustang Springs site in Mustang Draw (D. Meltzer, pers. comm. 1993) (FIGS. 1.3, 3.42). The Carley-Archer site is on lower McKenzie Draw, at its confluence with Mustang Draw (FIG. 3.42). A collection of Folsom, Midland, Plainview, and Rex Rodgers points (discussed below) was recovered among considerable lithic debris and burned rock (Carley 1987). The material was exposed by plowing and deflation of a sheet of wind-derived calcareous sand

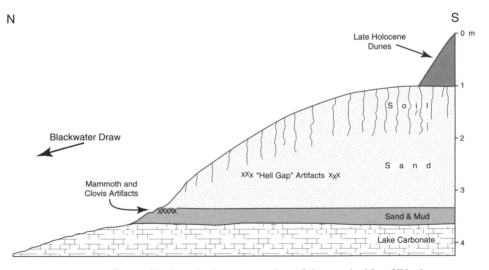

FIGURE 3.43. Generalized geologic cross section of the south side of Blackwater Draw in the area of the Car Body and Burns sites (FIG. 3.3), illustrating the stratigraphic relationships of Paleoindian finds.

TABLE 3.13. Paleoindian sites along draws reported by the High Plains Paleoecology Project[1]

Artifact Style	Site No.	Site Description & Location
Late Paleoindian[2]	LA 3692	Kill site on Blackwater Draw below Marks Beach
	LA 6205	Kill site on Blackwater Draw above Clovis site
	LA 6207	Kill site on Blackwater Draw above Clovis site
	LA 6250	Camp site on Yellowhouse Draw
	LA 6251	Camp site on Yellowhouse Draw above Lubbock Lake
	41GA28	Camp site on Seminole Draw
	41GA33	Camp site on Seminole Draw
	41GA39	Camp site on Seminole Draw
Folsom	LA 6205	Kill site on Blackwater Draw above Clovis site
	LA 6207	Kill site on Blackwater Draw above Clovis site
	LA 6246	Camp site on Yellowhouse Draw near confluence of N & S Forks
	LA 6248	Kill site on Blackwater Draw below Anderson Basin
	LA 6251	Camp site on Yellowhouse Draw above Lubbock Lake
	LA 6256	Camp site on Sulphur Draw near Brownfield Lake
Clovis	LA 6205	Kill site on Blackwater Draw above Clovis site
	LA 6207	Kill site on Blackwater Draw above Clovis site
	LA 6243	Kill site on Sulphur Springs Draw
	LA 6251	Camp site on Yellowhouse Draw above Lubbock Lake
	LA 6257	Kill site on Boone Draw

[1] Hester (1975a: table 13-1; exclusive of Anderson Basin, Clovis, Lubbock Lake, and Plainview) and Kibler (1991); see Appendix 1.
[2] Late Paleoindian = "Parallel Flaked Horizon" of Wendorf and Hester (1962) and Hester (1975a).

(similar to sediment that comprises lunettes, discussed below) up to 1 m thick on the uplands immediately adjacent to the draw.

The High Plains Paleoecology Project generated considerable data on surface collections of Paleoindian artifacts (Wendorf and Hester 1962; Hester 1975a; Hester and Grady 1977). Among sites associated with draws are the following artifact affiliations and site types (Table 3.13; FIG. 3.42):

two Clovis–Folsom–Late Paleoindian kill sites on Blackwater Draw above the Clovis site; a Clovis–Folsom–Late Paleoindian campsite on Yellowhouse Draw above Lubbock Lake; a Clovis kill site on upper Boone Draw and one on middle Sulphur Springs Draw; a Folsom kill site on Blackwater Draw below Anderson Basin; two Folsom campsites on Yellowhouse Draw below the confluence of the north and south forks; one Folsom campsite on lower Sulphur Draw near Brownfield Lake; one Late Paleoindian kill site on Blackwater Draw below Marks Beach; and one Late Paleoindian campsite on Yellowhouse Draw near the confluence of the two forks.

Playas

The lake basins of the Southern High Plains undoubtedly were attractive locations for Paleoindian peoples, especially the large present-day salinas (FIG. 1.2), which probably held fresh water as "pluvial lakes" at the end of the Pleistocene (Reeves 1965). The chronology of lake levels in the large lake basins and small playa basins is largely unknown, however. Sedimentological and geochronological data from several playa basins indicate that at least some of the depressions contained perennial or near-perennial lakes, ponds, or marshes in the late Pleistocene and early Holocene (Holliday et al. 1996).

Of the thousands of small playa basins in the area, however, only three are known to have Paleoindian archaeological material buried in the basin fill: Miami, Ryan, and San Jon (FIG. 1.3), which are the subject of this section. Archaeological material from all Paleoindian stages is reported from the surface around the margins of many basins, however, and several sites are reported from the lunettes that border some playas (discussed under dunes) (Wendorf and Hester 1962; Hester 1975a). No Paleoindian sites in stratigraphic context are reported from fills in salinas, however. Certainly such sites exist, as do many others in the small playas, but their discovery awaits increased visibility. Exposures of the fill in the ca. 25,000 playa basins and several dozen salinas are rare except along the margins of the plains (e.g., San Jon) or as a result of human activity (e.g., Miami and Ryan).

Two distinct types of lake sediment comprise the surface deposits of the playas (Holliday 1985a, 1995a; Holliday et al. 1996). The most common sediment is a clayey, dark gray, weakly calcareous mud. The layer has no formal lithostratigraphic designation but informally is called the Randall Clay based on the soil series mapped on county soil surveys. Radiocarbon ages show that these muds date to the late Pleistocene and Holocene (Holliday et al. 1996). The other type of sediment is a silty to loamy, light gray, highly calcareous deposit. The layer informally is called the Arch Loam, again based on the associated soil series mapped on county soil surveys. Locally, the Arch Loam occurs as a bench around the edges of playas, with the Randall Clay in the center inset against the Arch. Very limited age control suggests that these lake carbonates are late Pleistocene deposits (Holliday 1985a, 1995a; Holliday et al. 1996).

MIAMI

The Miami site is on the extreme northeast end of the Southern High Plains (FIG. 1.3). The site is on the flat, open surface of the Llano Estacado, but within 60 m of the heavily dissected terrain which marks the eastern margin of the plains (FIG. 3.44). When the site was discovered there was no obvious indication of it from topography or soils; bone simply was being exposed due to plowing in a flat field. The 1937 excavations showed that the site was a bone bed of mammoths in a small depression that filled with organic-rich silt (Sellards 1938, 1952) (FIG. 3.45). The bone bed was completely excavated (FIG. 2.5), and then the site was backfilled. As a result, the same conditions that greeted Sellards' crew also awaited a reinvestigation team in 1990: the only surface indication of the site was broken mammoth bone scattered across a flat field (FIGS. 3.44, 3.46). The following discussion of the site is based on the original excavation reports (Sellards 1938, 1952) and on the recent reinvestigation (Holliday et al. 1994) (Table 3.14).

The playa basin at Miami, inset into the Blackwater Draw Formation, was bowl-shaped, 23 m in diameter, and 1.6 m deep (FIG. 3.45). The fill in the basin mostly is silty loam varying in color from gray or grayish-brown to black. This sediment, which originally filled the basin to the level of the High Plains surface, generally is similar to the Randall Clay typical of most

TABLE 3.14. Correlation of stratigraphic terminology for the Miami site[1]

Sellards 1938, 1952	Holliday et al. 1994
"Silt similar to that below"[2]	[Removed in 1937 excavation]
"Loess stratum about 6 inches thick"[2]	Light Gray Silt
"Fine silt colored by organic matter ... [with] ... the appearance of a dark sandy clay"[2] "Fine silt"[3]	Very Dark Gray Silt Loam
"Red sandy clay bedrock"[4]	Blackwater Draw Fm

[1] From Holliday et al. (1994:table 1).   [3] Sellards (1952:18).
[2] Sellards (1938:1002).   [4] Sellards (1938:figs. 3, 5).

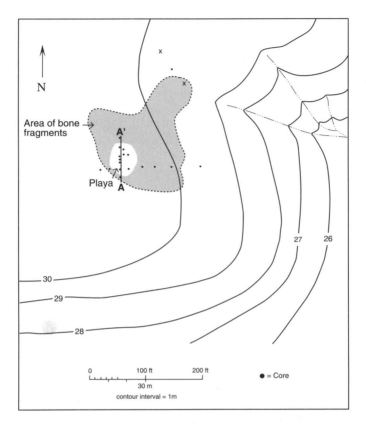

FIGURE 3.44. Map of the Miami site, showing the area of exposed bone scattered by plowing, the location of the filled playa, core locations, section A–A′ (FIG. 3.45), position of two flakes (x) found on the surface in 1990 (an end scraper found in 1990 was 150 m northeast of the playa), and the topographic breaks to the south and southeast (modified from Holliday et al. 1994:fig. 3).

playas in the region. This fine-grained, dark-colored fill probably resulted from slow accumulation of dust in a well-vegetated and moist basin. Within this fill is a gray silt "loess" layer. This deposit is >87% coarse silt, averages 10 cm thick, and occurs between 30 and 50 cm below surface in the center of the basin (FIGS. 2.5, 3.45). As Sellards observed, this layer probably is eolian in origin. There seems no other way to produce such a well-sorted and lithologically distinct layer. Today the uppermost 30–40 cm of fill in the depression is backdirt from the 1937 excavation. The contact between the backdirt and the black silt loam marks the level of the bone bed (FIG. 3.45). The basin started to fill ca. 13,700 yrs BP; the loess dates to

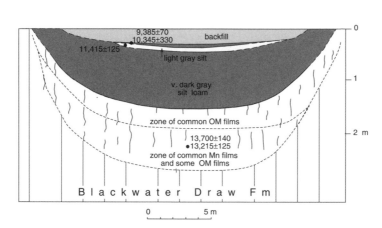

FIGURE 3.45. Geologic cross section of the Miami site playa (A–A' in FIG. 3.44) in 1990, showing the lithostratigraphy, pedostratigraphy, and position of radiocarbon samples (modified from Holliday et al. 1994: fig. 4). The bone bed was at the base of the backfill.

FIGURE 3.46. Coring in progress at the Miami site in 1990, looking northeast across the buried playa (compare with FIG. 2.5). The Giddings rig is at about the center of the filled basin. Note the reentrant draw beyond the vehicles (shown on the right side of FIG. 3.44).

TABLE 3.15. Radiocarbon ages from Paleoindian levels and bracketing levels at the Miami and Ryan sites

Site	^{14}C Age Years BP	Lab. No.	Material Dated & Remarks
Miami[1]			
	9385±70	AA-7084	Residue; playa fill at or above bone level
	10,345±330	AA-7085	Humates; playa fill at or above bone level
	11,415±415	AA-7086	Residue; loess layer below bone bed
	13,215±125	AA-7082	Humates; base of playa fill
	13,700±140	AA-7083	Residue; base of playa fill
Ryan[2]			
	9220±220	SMU-2448	Humates; playa fill below Plainview cache
	10,380±140	SMU-2446	Humates; playa fill below Plainview cache
	10,650±120	SMU-2447	Humates; playa fill below Plainview cache

[1]Holliday et al. (1994).   [2]Hartwell (1995).

ca. 11,400 yrs BP; and the bone bed probably dates to ca. 11,400–10,800 yrs BP (FIG. 3.45; Table 3.15). These radiocarbon ages fit well with the Clovis chronology known elsewhere (Haynes 1993; Holliday et al. 1994). The basin probably was completely filled relatively soon after Clovis time.

The bone bed was in playa fill 0–10 cm above the loess layer. The partial remains of five mammoths (*Mammuthus columbi*, three adults and two juveniles) (Sellards 1938; Saunders 1980) were recovered along with three Clovis projectile points and a nondiagnostic stone tool. The bone is heavily weathered, and there are no clear indications of human modification (Johnson and Shipman 1986; Johnson 1989; Holliday et al. 1994). Johnson (1989) suggests that part of the Miami site was on the surface adjacent to the playa and that it was destroyed by subsequent weathering because it was never buried. In 1990 a side scraper and two bifacial retouch flakes were found in the cultivated field outside the area of the original excavation (FIG. 3.44). Their association with the occupation is circumstantial and based largely on the apparent lack of later occupations in this locality.

The origins of the bone and stone assemblage are uncertain. Sellards felt the "most probable explanation" of this association of mammoths (and only mammoths) with human artifacts "seems to be that disease, starvation, or drought may have caused the death of some of the elephants and that others, enfeebled by disease or otherwise, may have been killed by early man" (Sellards 1938:1008, 1952:23). Saunders (1980) proposed that the bone assemblage represents the catastrophic death of a small matriarchal family group. Four scenarios for the origin of the site are offered by Holliday et al. (1994): a successful mammoth kill; an unsuccessful kill with wounded animals dying at the watering hole; opportunistic scavenging following natural deaths; a palimpsest of multiple deaths following both natural and human causes. Unfortunately, the extant data set provides no clear indication of the most likely scenario.

RYAN

Ryan's site is a small playa (ca. 12 m diameter, 60 cm deep) on the central Llano Estacado (FIG. 1.3). Ryan is similar to the Miami site in that it is a very small playa that completely filled, so that there is no indication of the basin from topographic maps, air photos, or soil surveys. The site was exposed by construction of a drainage ditch along a county road that removed almost one-half of the playa (FIG. 3.47). Subsequent erosion and the excavation of two potholes yielded a large collection of Paleoindian stone

FIGURE 3.47. Excavations in progress at Ryan's site in July 1988, looking southwest. The dark gray playa fill (P) exposed in the bar ditch (FIG. 3.48) is obvious on either side of the planks that cross the ditch. The location of the gully that exposed the artifacts is indicated by "G." The crew is working in the center of the remaining half of the playa.

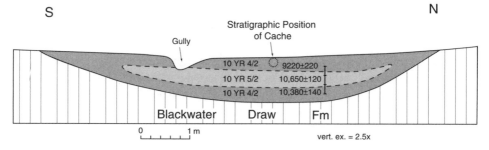

FIGURE 3.48. Geologic cross section of Ryan's site as exposed in the bar ditch, showing color variations due to soil formation, the location of the Plainview cache, and radiocarbon ages (^{14}C samples collected approximately 4 m behind—west of—bar ditch exposure).

tools (Johnson et al. 1987). Controlled excavations recovered additional Paleoindian material (Hartwell 1991, 1995).

The playa basin is inset into the Blackwater Draw Formation. The fill is dark gray loam to silty loam, similar to the fill in most playas of the area. There is some color variation in the fill, giving the appearance of stratification (FIG. 3.48), but this is due mostly to pedogenic translocation of calcium carbonate. Otherwise the only variation exhibited by the fill is higher content of sand at the bottom and margins of the paleobasin. The fill probably represents aggradation of fines from dust and slopewash in a marsh or pond.

The artifact inventory from the site includes 13 Plainview points, a reworked Clovis point, almost 50 bifaces, and numerous utilized flakes and blades (Hartwell 1991, 1995). The site originally was thought to be a single-component Plainview campsite (Johnson et al. 1987). Analysis of the artifacts and their spatial distribution, however, indicates that it was a Plainview cache (Hartwell 1991, 1995). Three radiocarbon ages from below the cache zone range from ca. 10,700 to 9200 yrs BP (FIG. 3.48; Table 3.15).

SAN JON

The San Jon site is in a setting somewhat similar to that at Miami: a playa basin within a few hundred meters of the High Plains escarpment (FIGS. 1.3, 3.49). The San Jon basin, however, is much larger and more obvious than Miami, and is heavily dissected by a canyon cut deep into the escarpment (FIGS. 2.6, 3.49). The playa fill containing the archaeological material is preserved in several peninsulas or promontories isolated between arroyo tributaries of the canyon (FIGS. 2.6, 3.49, 3.50). The geoarchaeological discussion is based on data from Roberts (1942), Judson (1953), Harbour (1975), Oldfield (1975), and field data collected by the writer (Hill et al. 1995) (Table 3.16).

The San Jon site is in a lake basin with a complex history of filling. The archaeological material is associated with late Quaternary sediment that filled a playa cut into Pleistocene deposits which filled an older, larger basin (FIG. 3.50). The sizes of the two basins are difficult to discern due to the drainage development through the site. Judging from a 7.5′ topographic map, the older, original basin was approximately 1 km wide (FIGS. 3.49, 3.50), although Judson (1953:10) estimates it as over 1.6 km. The older Pleistocene basin fill covered an area that probably was over 700 m in diameter. The younger basin with the archaeological deposits probably was about 360 m in diameter (FIG. 3.50). The late Quaternary sediments, up to 10 m thick, almost completely filled the younger basin before canyon

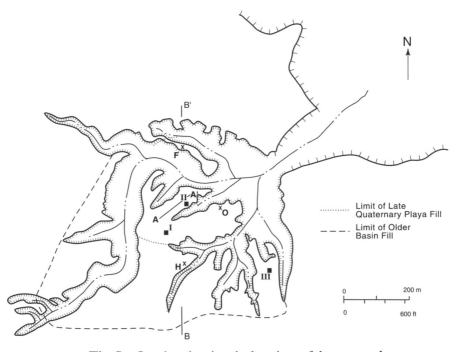

FIGURE 3.49. The San Jon site, showing the locations of the 1940 and 1941 excavation areas (H "Hibben dig," I–III are Roberts' excavations, F the Folsom find by Roberts' crew), the pollen profile sampled by Frank Oldfield (O), the location of sections A–A′ (FIG. 3.51) and B–B′ (FIG. 3.50), and the limits of the older basin fill and the late Quaternary playa fill (based on Judson 1953:fig. 4).

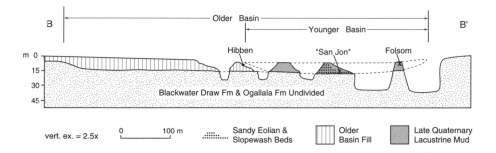

FIGURE 3.50. Generalized north-south cross section B–B' (FIG. 3.49) of the San Jon basin, showing the stratigraphic relationships of the older and younger basin fill and the archaeological finds (based on Judson 1953: fig. 7). Dashed lines indicate the inferred extent of the late Quaternary basin fill.

TABLE 3.16. Correlation of stratigraphic terminology for Area II of the San Jon site[1]

		Judson 1953	Hill et al. 1995	Holliday this volume
Sand Canyon Fm		[nr]	4s	4s
		Clayey-humic Alluvium	4si	4m
		Sandy Alluvium	3s	3s
		[nr]	3si	3m[2]
		Sandy Alluvium	2s	2s
San Jon Fm[3]	Zone 3	Green Sandy Clay	2si	2m
		Red Alluvium	1s	1s
		Green Sandy Clay	1si	1m
	Zone 1	Basal Sand or leached Ogallala Fm or White Sand	White Sand	White Sand

[1] From Hill et al. (1995).
[2] 3m (3si in Hill et al. 1995) is a relatively thin layer of silty clay within a relatively thick section of sandy sediment (2s and 3s) identified as the Sandy Alluvium of the Sand Canyon Formation by Judson (1953).
[3] Zone 2 is volcanic ash in discontinuous lenses.
nr = Facies not recognized by Judson (1953).

entrenchment. The following geoarchaeological discussion focuses on the late Quaternary sediments in the smaller, younger basin.

Three basic lithologies were identified in the playa fill. The oldest sediment in the basin is a light tan, clean sand, usually about 1 m thick (the "basal sand" or "leached Ogallala" of Judson 1953) (Table 3.16). Most of the sediment in the archaeologically significant fill is a light gray (sometimes greenish-gray) to dark gray mud, essentially identical to the Randall Clay soil series mapped in most playas. Toward the basin margins, especially to the west, southwest, and south, there are layers of reddish-brown, somewhat sandier loam and silty loam interbedded with the darker mud. Some of these sandier, redder layers are bedded, and other redder deposits are massive and homogeneous and have a higher content of fines. The redder facies of basin fill also exhibits pedogenic modification (Bw and Bt soil horizons), indicative of landscape stability and weathering prior to burial. The fill in the center of the basin essentially is a homogeneous accumulation of the gray mud, but toward the basin margin in the area of most of the Paleoindian excavations this deposit splits into four layers (1m–4m) (Table 3.16; FIGS. 3.50, 3.51). There also are four layers of the redder, sandy sediment (1s–4s) (Table 3.16; FIG. 3.51). The two lower layers are thickest near the basin margin and thin out toward the center of the basin.

The gray mud probably is lacustrine fill. The coarser, redder deposits include some alluvial sediments (from slopewash), indicated by up to 50 cm

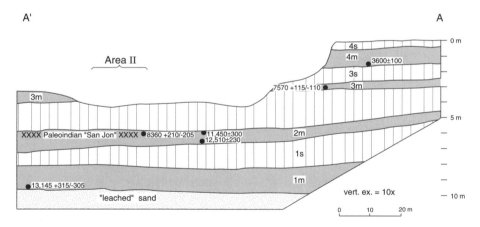

FIGURE 3.51. Geologic cross section A–A' (FIG. 3.49) through Area II at the San Jon site, illustrating the lithostratigraphy and the stratigraphic relationships of the radiocarbon samples and archaeological features (modified from Hill et al. 1995: fig. 3).

of laminated, graded beds, as noted by Judson, but also probably have a high content of eolian sediment. The eolian interpretation is based on the high content of fines (from dust), the position of these layers largely on the upwind side of the basin, and the thickness, which is at its maximum near the upwind basin margin and thins toward the center (downwind). Materials washed in should be thinnest upslope and thickest where the basin margin merges with the basin floor (i.e., where the slope of the basin flattens).

Three Paleoindian or possible Paleoindian occupation layers were investigated at San Jon. The most intensively studied is near the top of stratum 2m in Area II (FIGS. 3.49, 3.51). Roberts tested a bone bed consisting of butchered remains of extinct bison. At least five *Bison antiquus* were represented (Hill et al. 1995). A notable characteristic of some of the bone is that lower limb units were recovered articulated and in an upright position in the gray mud (Roberts 1942:plate 3.1; Hill et al. 1995:fig. 7). This situation suggested that animals were mired in mud, died, and subsequently were butchered. Data are not available to indicate whether the animals died

FIGURE 3.52. Paleoindian artifacts from the San Jon site: (A) Folsom point fragment; (B) the "type" San Jon point from the Area II bone bed; and (C) the lanceolate projectile point found on the surface at the "Hibben dig." Scale is in centimeters and millimeters.

naturally and then were scavenged or were purposely killed by hunters. A single projectile point was recovered from this feature: a lanceolate projectile point named "San Jon" by Roberts (1942:8) (Hill et al. 1995:fig. 8b; Knudson 1995:fig. 1e) (FIG. 3.52B).

Approximately 150 m from Area II "a portion of a true Folsom point was found weathering out of this same layer [upper 2m] in association with fragments of similarly fossilized bone" (Roberts 1942:8) (FIG. 3.52A) (Knudson 1995:fig. 1a). This area was not tested, and the Folsom artifact was not found in place. The precise lithostratigraphic relationship between Area II and the Folsom area is impossible to determine because of a wide and deep canyon that separates the two areas (FIGS. 3.49, 3.50).

The other possible Paleoindian feature was discovered in 1993 (Hill et al. 1995). It consists of extensive lithic debris and tools along with bone fragments eroding from stratum 2s on the Area II peninsula, directly above the San Jon bone bed (FIG. 3.51). The feature yielded two side-notched projectile points and the base of a lanceolate point. The two side-notched artifacts are similar in morphology to a variety of artifacts from the central and eastern United States considered to be very Late Paleoindian or Early Archaic. These styles include Kirk, from the eastern U.S. (O'Brien and Warren 1983; Justice 1987), Keithville and Palmer in far eastern Texas (Turner and Hester 1993:134, 166), and artifacts from the Logan Creek Complex on the central Plains dating from 8600 to 6300 yrs BP (Thies and Witty 1992:144–145). A Late Paleoindian affiliation for this feature is in keeping with the recovery of the broken lanceolate point and bracketing radiocarbon ages, discussed below.

The area of the 1940 "Hibben dig," separated from Area II by two deep arroyos (FIG. 3.49), yielded "slightly fossilized bones" (Judson 1953:25) from "an essentially modern species of bison, a much smaller animal than that of the lower layer [i.e., smaller than the bone in stratum 2m, Area II]" (Roberts 1942:9). Associated with this bone were several "Collateral or Eden Valley Yuma" points (only one of which is available for study, FIG. 3.52C; Knudson 1995:fig. 1d). No other data are available for this feature beyond the general remarks made by Roberts (1942). The finds from the "Hibben dig" have long been problematic. Roberts (1942), Judson (1953), and others (Wheat 1972:143; Wormington 1957:122–123) point out several inconsistencies concerning the stratigraphic relationship of the lanceolate points with modern bison. Reinvestigation of the area in 1993, 1994, and 1995 determined that the sediments exposed in the area of the "Hibben dig" are related to the older Pleistocene basin (Hill et al. 1995).

TABLE 3.17. Radiocarbon ages from Paleoindian levels and bracketing levels at the San Jon site

^{14}C Age Years BP	Lab. No.	Material Dated & Remarks
7300±800	A-713B	Humates; playa fill, top of Unit 3 of San Jon Fm, approx. level of "San Jon" bone bed[1]
9700±650	A-740A	Residue; playa fill 10′ above base of Unit 3 of San Jon Fm[1]
2670±380	A-712A	Residue; playa fill 20″ above base of Unit 3 of San Jon Fm[1]
4110±60	A-7865.1	Humates (AMS); bottom of stratum 3c[2]
7570+115/−110	A-7865	Residue; bottom of stratum 3m[2]
8360+210/−205	A-7864	Residue; top of stratum 2m[2]
8275±65	A-7438.1	Humates (AMS); top of stratum 2m[3]
11,450±300	A-7438	Residue; top of stratum 2m[3]
8640±65	A-7439.1	Humates (AMS); bottom of stratum 2m[3]
12,510±230	A-7439	Residue; bottom of stratum 2m[3]

[1] Haynes et al. (1967); Hester (1975b). Samples collected at pollen profile "I & III" of Oldfield (1975), 100 m east of Roberts' (1942) Area II, on same peninsula as Area I, but 180 m northeast of it (FIG. 3.49).
[2] Samples collected 10 m upslope from Area II.
[3] Hill et al. (1995).

TABLE 3.18. Paleoindian sites around playas reported by the High Plains Paleoecology Project[1]

Artifact Style	Site No.	Site Description & Location
Late Paleoindian[2]	LA 3960	Campsite on Rich Lake
Folsom	LA 3956	Campsite near Double Lakes salina
	LA 3958	Campsite on playa south of Sulphur Springs Draw
	LA 3960	Campsite on Rich Lake salina
	LA 6222	Kill site west of Lewiston Lake salina
	LA 6244	Campsite on playa near Sulphur Springs Draw
	LA 6254	Campsite on Brownfield Lake salina
	LA 6255	Campsite on Brownfield Lake salina
Clovis	None reported	

[1] Hester (1975a: table 13-1); see Appendix 1.
[2] Late Paleoindian = "Parallel Flaked Horizon" of Wendorf and Hester (1962) and Hester (1975a).

The bone and stone recovered from this area, therefore, must have been mixed and redeposited.

Only a few radiocarbon ages are available that bear on the Paleoindian occupations at San Jon (Table 3.17). Hester (1975b: 19–20) reports three ages from playa sediments collected from a section on the Area I peninsula 100 m east of Area II (Table 3.17; FIG. 3.49) (also reported by Haynes et al. 1967). The section contains 7.3 m of an essentially homogeneous deposit of the typical dark gray, clayey playa fill. The stratigraphic relationship between this section and Area II has not been determined. A sample taken 0.5 m below the top of the layer produced an age, on soil humates, of ca. 7300 yrs BP. Sediment 4 m below the surface yielded an organic residue age of ca. 9700 yrs BP. Organic residue from the base of the playa sediment was dated to ca. 2600 yrs BP. The upper and middle ages from this section seem to be the correct order of magnitude for dating the fill, but further evaluation awaits additional stratigraphic investigation. The lower age clearly is in error.

In Area II, radiocarbon ages are available from stratum 1m, the bottom and top of 2m, and the base of stratum 3m (FIG. 3.51; Table 3.17). The bottom of stratum 1m, which is the base of the late Quaternary lacustrine sediment, dates to ca. 13,150 yrs BP. The residue samples from stratum 2m provided the oldest ages for the layer, bracketing it between ca. 12,500 (bottom) and 11,500 (top) yrs BP. The upper age suggests that the San Jon bone bed from Area II is of Clovis age, but the radiocarbon sampling locality was upslope from the feature and just below an erosional disconformity. At the sampling site the stratigraphic equivalent to the San Jon level probably is missing. Another sample from the top of 2m, but within the feature area, yielded an age of ca. 8360 yrs BP, which is in line with the few ages for Late Paleoindian lanceolate styles from other sites in the region (Hofman 1989a; Johnson and Holliday 1981; Haynes 1995; see Chapter 5). A sample from the base of stratum 3m dates to ca. 7570 yrs BP, bracketing the newly discovered feature in stratum 2s between 8400 and 7600 yrs BP (Table 3.17; FIG. 3.51).

OTHER PLAYA SITES

Paleoindian sites around or on some playas and salinas are reported from several surface collections. Hester (1975a) identifies seven Folsom sites, including a kill site and two camps associated with small playas, two camps around Brownfield Lake salina, a camp near Double Lake salina, and one at Rich Lake salina (Table 3.18; FIG. 3.53). Hester (1975a) also reports one Late Paleoindian camp on Rich Lake (Table 3.18), and M. B. Collins (pers.

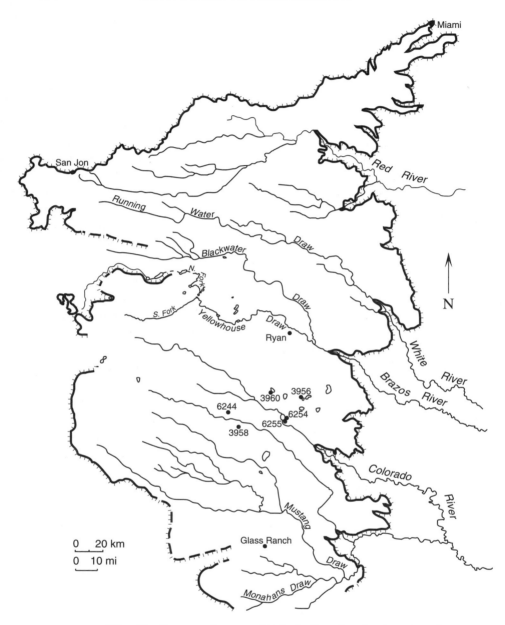

FIGURE 3.53. The distribution of reported Paleoindian sites in playas on the Southern High Plains. Other sites associated with playas include some dune localities (FIG. 3.61).

comm. 1983) recovered Plainview artifacts from the Glass Ranch salina (FIG. 3.53).

Some sites associated with dunes (discussed in the following section) were undoubtedly associated with playas as well. These sites include all lunette localities, probably Elida and Robertson, and possibly the Tatum site.

Dunes

The dunes of the Southern High Plains locally are rich in archaeological material, particularly Paleoindian remains (e.g., Fritz and Fritz 1940; Polyak and Williams 1986), but few sites are reported with *in situ* material or with well-exposed stratigraphy. Those few sites with such characteristics are in the sand dune fields; none are reported from lunettes. Of the sites discussed in this section only Milnesand and Ted Williamson yielded undisturbed features, and evidence presented below indicates that these bone beds pre-date the dunes. The other five dune sites yielded abundant archaeological material, but typically after deflation of the dunes. Fortunately, the artifacts were carefully recorded, many very soon after exposure, and the sites have well-exposed stratigraphy. The geoarchaeological contexts of the Paleoindian occupations could therefore be reconstructed.

The dunes of the region include three west-to-east-trending sand fields associated with reentrant valleys in the western escarpment (FIG. 1.2), and lunettes formed on the downwind side of some playas (Holliday 1995a). The reentrant valleys formed "ramps" from the floor of the Pecos Valley to the High Plains surface. On the northwest Llano Estacado is a linear, west-to-east-trending belt of dunes locally known as the "Sandhills" or the "Muleshoe Dunes," which follow the Portales Valley. On the west-central Llano, in the Simanola Valley, is a set of west-to-east-trending, anastomosing dune fields, here termed the "Lea-Yoakum Dunes." These dunes are an eastward extension of the Mescalero Dunes, which formed in the Pecos River valley adjacent to the High Plains escarpment. On the southwestern Llano Estacado, in the Winkler Valley, is a small dune field that is a northeastward extension of the Monahans Dunes and informally termed the "Andrews Dunes." Green (1961b) referred to the entire set of dunes as the Monahans. The Monahans Dunes proper are in the Pecos River valley east of and trending parallel to the river.

The dune fields probably originated as sand moved from the Pecos River valley up the reentrant valleys and onto the High Plains surface (Hawley et al. 1976; Holliday 1995a). Stratigraphic and geochronologic work in the dune fields has been limited. Notable exceptions are work in

the Monahans Dunes by Green (1961b), part of the High Plains Paleoecology Project, and soil-geomorphic studies by Gile (1979, 1985) in one
area of the Muleshoe Dunes. Typically the dunes rest on the Blackwater
Draw Formation, but locally lacustrine sediments are common below or
interfingering with the sands. In the Muleshoe Dunes, these lake deposits
probably are associated with ancient courses of Blackwater Draw (Holliday
1995b). Lake sediments under the western (New Mexico) portion of the
Lea-Yoakum Dunes are associated with a Pleistocene precursor of upper
Sulphur Draw (Holliday 1995b). In the Andrews Dunes, the lake sediments probably accumulated locally on the floor of the Winkler Valley or,
to the west, in Monument Draw. The available data suggest that the sands
accumulated in the late Quaternary, and that sand deposition probably occurred in several discrete episodes. Buried soils are common within the
dunes, and stratigraphic differentiation of sand layers usually is based on
pedologic characteristics (e.g., Gile 1979, 1985). The earliest phase of
eolian sand accumulation during the human occupation of the Llano Estacado occurred in Paleoindian times, between ca. 11,000 and 9000 yrs BP,
discussed below.

One other dune field of geoarchaeological significance, here referred
to as the "Crosby Dunes," is on the eastern edge of the Llano Estacado,
50 km east of Lubbock (FIG. 1.2). This dune field is enigmatic because
there is no obvious upwind source of the sand. The Blackwater Draw Formation in the immediate area is unusually sandy relative to adjacent areas,
and the immediate source of the sand is almost certainly this formation.
This observation begs the question, however, of the origin of the Pleistocene sands. No clues are forthcoming.

The stratigraphy and geochronology of lunettes associated with small
playas are known from several sites (Holliday 1985a, 1995a, unpub. data).
The lunettes generally are silty and highly calcareous and probably deflated
from calcareous lacustrine sediment (the Arch Loam soils discussed above).
Sandy layers also are found in the lunettes and suggest some deflation of
the Blackwater Draw Formation. Buried soils are common within lunettes
and provide excellent stratigraphic markers in the otherwise lithologically
similar layers of sediment (e.g., Holliday 1985a). The lunettes accreted
episodically during the late Quaternary, most probably starting to form before 16,000 yrs BP (Holliday 1995a, unpub. data). Limited age control suggests that generally the dunes were stable (and subjected to pedogenesis)
ca. 14,000 to 11,000 yrs BP, followed by episodic dune accretion between
11,000 and 7000 yrs BP (Holliday 1985a, 1995a, unpub. data).

ANDREWS DUNES SITES

Four important collections of Paleoindian artifacts came from blowouts in the Andrews Dunes, the southmost of the three major dune fields of the Southern High Plains (FIG. 1.2): Winkler-1, Shifting Sands, Bedford Ranch, and Wyche Ranch (FIG. 1.3). The artifacts were collected from the floors of the blowouts, but with sufficient documentation over prolonged periods that the stratigraphic provenience is clear. At Winkler-1 (Blaine 1968, 1971; pers. comm. 1994) and Shifting Sands (Amick and Rose 1990; Hofman et al. 1990; R. Rose, pers. comm. 1994) the artifacts were collected during or immediately after exposure and therefore were essentially *in situ*. These four sites are discussed together because of their similar settings, stratigraphies, and proximity to one another (FIGS. 1.3, 3.54).

The four sites provide a rough transect of the Andrews Dunes (FIG. 1.3). Winkler-1 is in the western end of the dunes and also is in Monument Draw, a narrow, dry drainage that crosses the mouth of the Winkler Valley and feeds into the Pecos River to the south. Shifting Sands is near the center of the dune field. Bedford Ranch is toward the south edge of the dunes and the Winkler Valley, and the Wyche Ranch site is on the extreme southeastern side of the dunes and near the eastern end of the dune system.

The Quaternary stratigraphy of the entire Monahans system was most extensively and intensively investigated by Green (1961b), and his stratigraphic nomenclature (Units I–IX) will be followed with a few exceptions

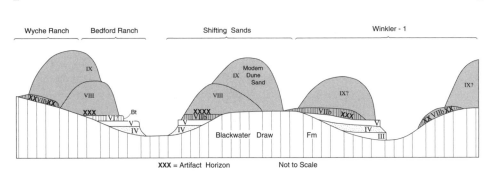

FIGURE 3.54. Schematic geologic cross section through the Andrews Dunes, illustrating the stratigraphic relationships of the occupation zones (xxx) and deposits among the Winkler-1, Shifting Sands, Bedford Ranch, and Wyche Ranch sites.

FIGURE 3.55A. The deflated landscape in one of the blowouts at Shifting Sands. The white lumps are eroded remnants of sandy marl (Unit III or Unit V). The Folsom level was just above the marl in dune sand modified by soil formation (the sand with a darker tone; indicated by arrow). Modern dunes make up the ridge in the middle distance.

FIGURE 3.55B. An outstanding example of clay bands in Unit VIII exposed at the Bedford Ranch site. Late Paleoindian artifacts were found eroding from these sands.

(Table 3.19). The Andrews Dunes extension of the Monahans system is underlain by the Blackwater Draw Formation (the Judkins Formation or Unit I of Green 1961b). Locally, the Blackwater Draw Formation is gleyed and has some coatings and concretions of secondary manganese, a phenomenon likely related to marshes that rested on top of the formation (discussed below). Above the Blackwater Draw Formation is paludal and eolian sediment that represents the late Quaternary stratigraphic record (Units II–IX) and contains the Paleoindian archaeological debris. Unit II is a "light gray or light tan unconsolidated eolian sand" observed only "at a few localities" (Green 1961b:26). Unit II is not apparent at the four sites discussed here.

At all observed exposures in the Andrews Dunes, the oldest fill above the Blackwater Draw Formation is sandy marl (FIG. 3.55A) interbedded with cleaner, less calcareous sand. Where complete, the sequence of marl and sand consists of a basal sandy marl (Unit III), a clean, weakly calcareous, tan sand (Unit IV), and another sandy marl (Unit V) (Table 3.19). The extent of the complete sequence is not indicated by Green (1961b), but in the recent investigations the III–IV–V package was observed only at Winkler-1 (Table 3.19). At Shifting Sands and Bedford Ranch the Blackwater Draw Formation was buried by a noncalcareous, tan sand that grades upward into a marl (FIG. 3.55A), suggesting correlation with Units IV and V, respectively. None of the three units (III, IV, V) was apparent at Wyche Ranch. The remains of late Pleistocene megafauna (e.g., *Bison antiquus, Mammuthus columbi, Equus* sp.) are common in Unit III at Winkler-1 and in Unit V at Shifting Sands and Bedford Ranch. Mastodont was found in Unit IV at Winkler-1 (J. Blaine, E. Johnson, pers. comm. 1994), the only find of this species reported for the Llano Estacado. Archaeological materials are not known from any of the three layers, however.

According to Green (1961b) the marls formed in depressions of varying size and are not continuous through the dune system. At Winkler-1 the deposits accumulated along the floor of Monument Draw and thin toward the margins of the drainage. The carbonate may be more or less continuous along the axis of the Winkler Valley, but it thins out and disappears against the valley margin at Bedford Ranch and is absent at Wyche Ranch. The marls likely were precipitated in shallow ponds and around seeps, as proposed by Green (1961b), and as indicated by the gleying in the underlying Blackwater Draw Formation. The Winkler Valley crosscuts the Ogallala Formation, which is the important aquifer of the region, and seeps and springs almost certainly were common along the valley. Historic seep-fed ponds in the dunes are described by Brune (1981:49, Andrews

TABLE 3.19. Stratigraphic correlation of Paleoindian archaeological sites in the Andrews Dunes

| | | | Holliday this volume | | |
Green 1962a	Lithology	Winkler-1	Shifting Sands	Bedford Ranch	Wyche Ranch
VIII	Sand w/prominent clay bands	[nr]	VIII	VIII	[nr]
VIIb	Sheet Sand w/ A & Bw horizon	VIIb "fossil dune"	VIIb	VIIb	VIIb
VIIa	Calcareous silt	[nr]	[nr]	[nr]	[nr]
VI	Gleyed sandy clay (Btg horizon?)	[nr]	[nr]	VI? (Bt horizon)	[nr]
V	Sandy Marl	V	V	V	[nr]
IV	Tan Sand	IV	IV	IV	[nr]
III	Sandy Marl	III	[nr]	[nr]	[nr]
II	Tan Sand	[nr]	[nr]	[nr]	[nr]
I (Judkins Fm)	Sandy Clay (Bt horizon)	Blackwater Draw Fm			

nr = Strata not recognized.

County site 7). The high sand content of the two marls, and the massive, well-sorted sand of Unit IV, are indicative of considerable eolian activity. The top of the Unit V marl locally was heavily eroded, probably by wind deflation, prior to burial by overlying sand. The erosion probably was linked to the subsequent phase of eolian sedimentation.

Overlying the Unit V marl at Winkler-1 and Shifting Sands, and resting unconformably on the Blackwater Draw Formation at Wyche Ranch, is a compact, reddish-brown, loamy sand, generally less than 1 m thick. An A-horizon is preserved at the top of this zone in some exposures. The color and consistence characteristics of the deposit likely represent formation of a Bw (or possibly a Bt) horizon. This stratum is the "fossil dune" of Blaine (1968). This deposit probably is Unit VIIb, described as including a "soil zone" or "paleosol" (Green 1961b:figs. 7,13) (Table 3.19).

Unit VIIa is a calcareous silt that Green (1961b) identified in only a few exposures. Based on his descriptions and field examination of sites that he reported, VIIa is sediment deflated from playa basins and forming small lunettes. Unit VIIa was not observed in any exposures in the Andrews Dunes. The deposit does not appear to be a significant component of the sand dune fields in the region.

Above VIIb at Shifting Sands and above the marl at Bedford Ranch is Unit VIII (Table 3.19). This deposit is a well-sorted eolian sand up to 2 m thick characterized by "clay bands" or "clay lamellae," which are thin (a few millimeters to a few centimeters thick), subhorizontal zones of clay (FIG. 3.55B). These "bands," common in well-sorted sands in a variety of environments, are reported from other dune fields in the region (Gile 1979) and are believed to be made of illuvial clay (Dijkerman et al. 1967; Gile 1979; Larsen and Schuldenrein 1990). Unit VIII, with dozens of reddish clay bands standing in contrast to the pale tan dune sand, forms striking exposures at Bedford Ranch and Shifting Sands (FIG. 3.55B). In the Bedford Ranch blowout, at the base of the Unit VIII sand and resting on the Unit V marl, is a Bt-horizon 15 cm thick that may represent a local facies of clay bands where clay illuviated in the lower sands of thinner sections (Table 3.19). Lower Unit VIII exhibits reduced colors (2.5Y 7/4) in some exposures at Shifting Sands. Green (1961b:30) reports "light greenish-gray argillaceous sands" (Unit VI) above the Unit V marl and below the Unit VIII sand at a few localities. This zone may be a gleyed facies of the Bt-horizon (i.e., a Btg-horizon).

Paleoindian artifacts in the Andrews Dunes are found in the sands overlying the Unit V marl. At Winkler-1, Unit VIIb yielded over 40 Midland points, along with other stone tools and debitage, and a single bone needle (Blaine 1968, 1971, 1991; Blaine and Wendorf 1972). This locality is one of the few "pure" Midland assemblages known. Shifting Sands produced an extensive "Folsom-Midland" collection (at least 150 points and point fragments; R. Rose, pers. comm. 1995) from Unit VIIb and lower VIII (Amick and Rose 1990; Hofman et al. 1990; R. Rose, pers. comm. 1994). Although a surface collection, the spatial patterning of artifact types, manufacturing debitage, and bone fragments indicates that one part of the site probably was a bison kill and initial processing area and other areas were used for further processing and short-term habitation (Hofman et al. 1990). The collection from Unit VIII at Bedford Ranch has not been studied, but projectile points largely are Late Paleoindian lanceolate styles, mostly Firstview. Midland and possible Folsom artifacts were found in VIIb at Wyche Ranch (R. Rose, pers. comm. 1994). Green (1961b:33) reports Folsom and unfluted lanceolate points from blowouts near Winkler-1, but could not associate the artifacts with his stratigraphic units.

The area of the present-day Andrews Dunes obviously was important to Paleoindians, but the reasons are not clear. There are no stratigraphic or sedimentologic clues to indicate attractions such as vegetation or water that would draw Paleoindians; the obvious lacustrine sediments pre-date the human occupation. Perhaps seepage continued in the area once humans arrived, but the associated deposits were diluted with eolian sand and subsequently deflated or otherwise obliterated by weathering due to the high permeability of the younger sand.

ELIDA

The Elida site is on the flat, open surface of the High Plains, exposed by deflation of a small sand dune field (covering approximately 0.75 km²) that is a segment of the larger Lea-Yoakum dune field (FIGS. 1.2, 1.3, 3.56). Archaeological material was acquired over a number of years of surface collecting (Warnica 1961; Hester 1962) (Table 3.20). No systematic excavations were carried out. The site is significant because it was a Folsom campsite, which is rare, and because it is a "pure" Folsom lithic collection (Hester 1962:92), i.e., a single-component collection.

The bedrock of the area is the Blackwater Draw Formation, which varies in thickness from <1 m to as much as 3 m. Overlying the Blackwater Draw Formation is a reddish dune sand with moderate to strong soil development (A–Bw to A–Bt profile) (FIG. 3.57). Deflation of the small dune field removed most of the red sand down to the Blackwater Draw Formation and, over large areas, through the uppermost Bt-horizon of the formation down to the upper Bk calcrete (FIG. 3.57). Archaeological material was collected from the deflated surface of the calcrete. The artifacts probably were worked into the upper Blackwater Draw Formation by faunal and floral mixing during and after occupation, and then exposed on top of the calcrete after deflation of the Bt-horizon.

The site is on the north-central side of the dune field, covering an area of about 0.3 km² (FIG. 3.56). Over 50 stone artifacts were collected, including 15 Folsom points and 3 unfluted points. About 150 m north of the

TABLE 3.20. Correlation of stratigraphic terminology for the Elida site

Warnica 1961 Hester 1962	Holliday this volume
Brown Sand (youngest fossil dune)	Dune Sand
Red Sandy Clay (earliest fossil dune)	Blackwater Draw Fm Bt-horizon
Caliche (Ogallala Fm)	Blackwater Draw Fm Bk-horizon

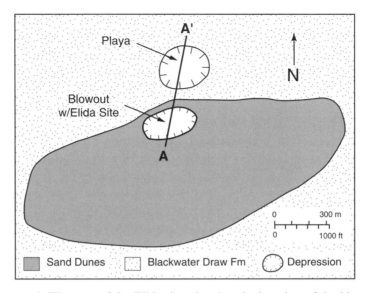

FIGURE 3.56. The area of the Elida site, showing the location of the blowout–collecting locale within the small dune field, the playa north of the collecting area, and section A–A' (FIG. 3.57).

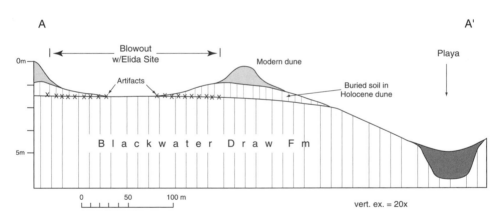

FIGURE 3.57. Geologic cross section A–A' (FIG. 3.56) of the Elida site from the blowout to the playa, illustrating the stratigraphic and geomorphic relationships of the occupation level, the dunes, and the playa basin.

occupation area is a small playa (200 m diameter $\times$ 5 m depth) (FIG. 3.56). Hester (1962:94) speculated that the camp was related to the playa. Almost certainly it was. The site is in the part of the dune field nearest the playa; the north boundary of the site is the north edge of wind deflation, suggesting that the site may continue north toward the playa.

MILNESAND AND TED WILLIAMSON

These two sites are similar in stratigraphy (FIG. 3.58) and archaeology, and are located only 550 m apart, and, therefore, are discussed together. The sites were exposed by deflation of two blowouts in the Lea-Yoakum Dunes (FIGS. 1.2, 1.3, 2.9) in the early 1950s and subsequently collected by the landowner and investigated by Sellards and Jim Warnica. A report on Milnesand was published (Sellards 1955a) (Table 3.21), but the only information on Williamson is from landowner Ted Williamson (pers. comm. 1985), who collected the site, Jim Warnica (pers. comm. 1985), who tested remnants of the site, and from Sellards' unpublished revision of his classic 1952 volume (Sellards n.d.b). Sellards (n.d.a) also made a few revisions of his original Milnesand paper. Bones from the Milnesand site, including sections of the bone bed preserved in plaster jackets, have also undergone some long-overdue analyses (Drake 1994; Hill et al. 1994). Reconstructing the stratigraphic and paleogeomorphic contexts of these two sites is difficult because there was relatively little deposition during or immediately after they were occupied and because the bone beds were completely destroyed by deflation and weathering following their exposure in the 1950s. Test excavations by J. Warnica in the 1960s and cores, trenches, and test

TABLE 3.21. Correlation of stratigraphic units at the Milnesand and Williamson sites

Milnesand	Milnesand	Williamson
Sellards 1955a	Holliday this volume	Holliday this volume
Yellow Sand	Historic Dune Sands	
[nr]	Sheet Sands (A-horizon)	Sheet Sands (Bw-horizon w/clay bands)
Reddish-Brown Sand	Blackwater Draw Fm (Bt-horizon)	
Caliche	Ogallala Fm Calcrete ("Ogallala Caprock caliche")	

nr = Strata not recognized.

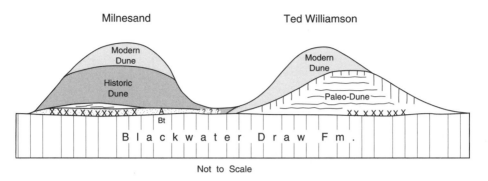

FIGURE 3.58. Schematic geologic cross section through the Milnesand and Ted Williamson sites, illustrating the stratigraphic relationships of the bone beds (xxx) and the dunes.

excavations by E. Johnson and the author in 1995 shed considerable light on the geoarchaeology of the Milnesand and Williamson sites, however.

The area with the two sites is described as "a broad, shallow, north-eastward-trending drainage way" (Sellards 1955a:337). Such a geomorphic feature is not apparent on topographic maps, but a smaller draw trending to the east-southeast is obvious on maps and in the field. The draw, 300 m north of the Milnesand site, probably is the upper end of Sulphur Draw, which largely is obscured by dunes and playas between Milnesand and the Texas state line (Holliday 1995b) (FIG. 1.2). As discussed below, the two sites probably were created in shallow depressions on top of the Blackwater Draw Formation adjacent to dunes rimming each depression. At some time after the sites were abandoned they were covered by sand sheets.

Both sites contained extensive beds of extinct *Bison antiquus* (FIG. 3.59). The Milnesand feature covered at least 300 m². The size of the Williamson bone bed is unknown except that it had an "approximate . . . width of 54 feet" (Sellards n.d.b). The present area covered by bone fragments at Williamson is roughly the same as that at Milnesand. The number of bison in each bone bed is uncertain. Bone recovery and curation during the Milnesand excavations were highly selective (Hill et al. 1994). The extant collections indicate that at least 33 bison were represented in the feature (Drake 1994; Hill et al. 1994). Over 90 whole and broken projectile points were recovered from the Milnesand bone bed (19 discussed and illustrated by Sellards 1955a, and about 75 collected by the landowner; Warnica and Williamson 1968). Most are the Milnesand variety and represent the type collection (FIG. 3.60), but a few are more similar to Plainview points

FIGURE 3.59. A segment of the bone bed at the Milnesand site exposed during Sellards' excavations in 1953. The photo illustrates the dense nature of the bone concentration and the thinness of sand that covered the feature historically (see also FIG. 2.9). Courtesy of the Texas Memorial Museum, the University of Texas at Austin.

(compare FIG. 3.60D and FIG. 3.41E) (Warnica and Williamson 1968; Wheat 1972:154). Bone was not recovered from the Williamson site, but about 150 Plainview points were found in and around the bone bed (Ted Williamson, pers. comm. 1985). One Milnesand point came from an adjacent camping area. At least one hearth was found in association with each bone bed (Sellards 1955a; Warnica and Williamson 1968; J. Warnica, pers. comm. 1985).

The bone beds at both sites rested on the Bt-horizon of the upper Blackwater Formation (Table 3.21; FIG. 3.58). The two features probably formed in microtopographic lows on the surface of the formation. The top of the Blackwater Draw Formation below the bone beds is 25–50 cm lower than the top of the formation surrounding and between both sites. The Blackwater Draw Formation in the Milnesand-Williamson area typically is 50–100 cm thick over the Ogallala Caprock Caliche. The upper half of the Blackwater Draw Formation has a deep reddish-brown Bt-horizon, a typical pedologic feature in the formation, but much of the lower half of the formation is an olive-green or greenish-gray gleyed zone (Btg-horizon). These gley colors, combined with the presence of dissolution pipes in the

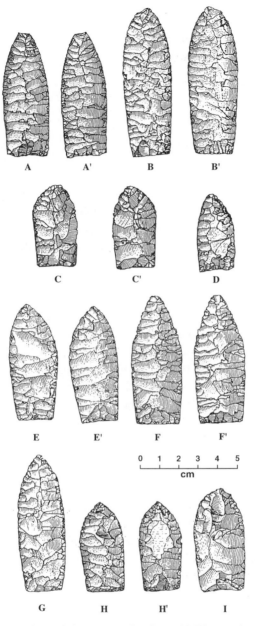

FIGURE 3.60. A portion of the type collection of Milnesand points recovered during Sellards' excavations, illustrating the variation in morphology (from Sellards 1955a:figs. 98, 99). Drawn by Hal Story and reproduced courtesy of the Texas Memorial Museum, the University of Texas at Austin, and by permission of the Society for American Archaeology, from *American Antiquity* 20(4), 1955.

Caprock Caliche, and manganese coatings in the Bt, all characteristic of the Blackwater Draw Formation in the Lea-Yoakum region, indicate that the groundwater once was very near the surface.

The Williamson site contains the best clues to the paleotopography of both localities during the Paleoindian occupation. On the east (downwind) side of the depression that contained the bone at Williamson is a paleodune up to 2.5 m thick (FIG. 3.58). The sand near the base of the dune probably was accumulating during the occupation, because bone and stone artifacts were found within the lower sand. That the dune is old also is suggested by evidence for long-term weathering in the form clay bands within the sand (i.e., the dune has been in place for much of the Holocene).

At Milnesand, sand that encased and covered the bone was part of an A-horizon (Table 3.21). This surficial soil zone probably formed by slow accretion of sand on the heavily vegetated surface of the Blackwater Draw Formation. The encasement of the bone by the sand suggests that the bone bed probably was created during development of the A-horizon. The vegetation interpretation is indicated by the darker color of the A-horizon (7.5YR 4/4), which is in contrast to the lighter color (10YR 6/4) of the dry, more sparsely vegetated modern surface. The dark color also indicates a relatively high original organic carbon content, considering the oxidizing environment of the horizon (porous, well-drained sediment; shallow burial). Accretionary development of the A-horizon (by slow accumulation of sand on a vegetated surface) is suggested by the absence of 5YR hues and low clay content. A-horizons formed syngenetically with the Bt-horizon of the Blackwater Draw Formation typically are reddish-brown and higher in fines (Holliday 1989a, 1990b).

Some occupation debris surrounding the Milnesand bone bed was in remnants of a paleo–sand sheet (<20 cm thick). This sand is distinguished from the younger (late Holocene, probably Historic) sands that surround and formerly buried the site by the presence of a thick (2.5 cm) band of illuvial clay, roughly comparable to the total clay accumulation in the clay bands of the paleodune at the Williamson site.

The reason why these two sites are located where they are is not obvious, but, as Sellards (1955a, n.d.a,b) believed, they probably were in shallow ponds or perhaps marshes. Sellards (1955a:337) interpreted the upper Bt-horizon of the Blackwater Draw Formation to be a pond deposit due to its clay content. The color, structure, and micromorphological features show that most of the characteristics of the horizon are pedogenic rather than depositional phenomena, but the evidence for a formerly high water table, combined with the paleotopography at both sites, and the evidence for a moist, heavily vegetated landscape at Milnesand suggest that ponds or marshes were once present. Determining when the water table was higher is not possible, but a reasonable hypothesis is that this condition obtained during the Milnesand-Plainview occupation and that the depressions at both sites intersected the water table, producing shallow ponds or marshes. The paleo–sand sheets adjacent to both sites may have aided in trapping or slowing the bison. How such large numbers of bison could come to grief in an area of such low relief is otherwise unknown.

OTHER DUNE SITES

Collections of Paleoindian artifacts are reported from many of the dunes of the Southern High Plains, but very few specific sites are recorded or reported, much less systematically studied. Most sites and collections are from the sand dune fields and include Folsom and various lanceolate styles (e.g., Fritz and Fritz 1940; Polyak and Williams 1986). Folsom and Midland artifacts were found in the dunes at the Midland site away from Monahans Draw, discussed above (Wendorf et al. 1955). Paleoindian sites also are common in the Muleshoe Dunes on the uplands adjacent to upper Blackwater Draw near the Clovis gravel pit, including the Bethel site and the Barber site (FIG. 3.3). Bethel is a blowout in the dunes that yielded a collection of Plainview artifacts (J. Warnica, pers. comm. 1994). Barber was visited by Sellards in the 1950s and noted by Sellards and Evans (1960) (J. Warnica, pers. comm. 1995), but they provided no details on the site. The locality yielded Folsom artifacts, including a Folsom point in a bison skeleton (J. Warnica, pers. comm. 1995).

In the Lea-Yoakum Dunes, about 8 km west of Milnesand, J. Warnica (pers. comm. 1994) collected Clovis, Folsom, Midland, and Milnesand artifacts from the "Ro-16" site (FIG. 3.61). The locality is a series of blowouts exposing a stratigraphy similar to the Elida site. Eolian sand up to 150 cm thick rests on the Blackwater Draw Formation. The lower 30 cm of sand is the cumulized A-horizon of the Blackwater Draw Formation. A well-expressed Bt-horizon formed in the upper sand (representing illuviation spanning most of the Holocene). The archaeology is from the lower half of the eolian sand, including the buried A-horizon and immediately overlying sand. The Paleoindian occupants apparently were utilizing the surface of the Blackwater Draw Formation prior to and in the early stages of eolian deposition. There are no geomorphic indicators (i.e., a playa or draw) in the immediate vicinity that hint at the reason the area was occupied.

The Tatum site also is in the Lea-Yoakum Dunes and was visited by Sellards (J. Warnica, pers. comm. 1995) (FIG. 3.61). Tatum, like the Barber

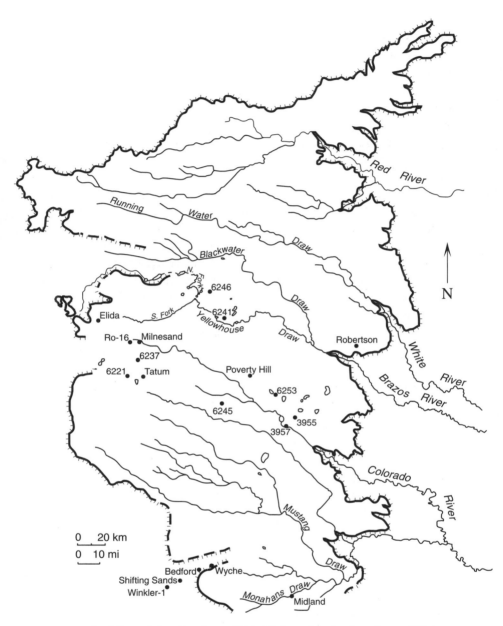

FIGURE 3.61. Map of the Southern High Plains with the locations of Paleo-indian sites in sand dune fields and lunettes. All lunette localities (Poverty Hill and the sites with LA numbers), Elida, Robertson, and possibly the Tatum site also are associated with playas (FIG. 3.53). The Ted Williamson site is immediately adjacent to the Milnesand site.

site, was mentioned by Sellards and Evans (1960), but they provided no archaeological or stratigraphic information except to note that Tatum was a Folsom site. Deflation of the dunes at Tatum exposed stone and bone artifacts, including four Folsom points (J. Warnica, pers. comm. 1995). The oldest deposits exposed at the site are late Pleistocene lake beds resting on the Caprock Caliche. Above the lake beds is a layer of eolian sandy clay loam 50 cm thick. The eolian deposit probably deflated from the lake beds, based on similarities in color and texture. The Folsom occupation was on top of this oldest eolian deposit. The site was covered by younger dunes, probably soon after the occupation. This interpretation is based on the degree of postoccupation pedogenesis, best expressed as illuvial clay bands. The zone of illuviation includes one unusually thick (5–10 cm) band of clay that encased the archaeological material.

The Crosby Dunes on the eastern Llano Estacado (FIG. 1.2) yielded thousands of Paleoindian artifacts, largely from blowouts (W. Parker, pers. comm. 1983; R. Walter, pers. comm. 1994). The largest collection, consisting of hundreds of points from the Robertson site (FIG. 3.61), includes most

TABLE 3.22. Paleoindian sites in lunettes reported by the High Plains Paleoecology Project[1]

Artifact Style	Site No.	Site Description & Location
Late Paleoindian[2]	LA 3955	Campsite on lunette near Mound Lake salina
	LA 6221	Kill site on lunette
	LA 6246	Campsite on lunette near Muleshoe National Wildlife Refuge
	LA 6253	Campsite on lunette near Rich Lake salina
Folsom	LA 3957	Campsite on lunette near Lost Draw
	LA 6221	Kill site on lunette
	LA 6237	Campsite on lunette south of Milnesand
	LA 6241	Campsite on lunette near Silver Lake salina
	LA 6245	Campsite on lunette between Sulphur Springs & Lost draws
	LA 6246	Campsite on lunette near Muleshoe National Wildlife Refuge
Clovis	LA 6221	Kill site on lunette

[1]Hester (1975a: table 13-1); see Appendix 1.
[2]Late Paleoindian = "Parallel Flaked Horizon" of Wendorf and Hester (1962) and Hester (1975a).

Paleoindian artifact styles known in the region: Clovis, Folsom, Plainview, Milnesand, Firstview, Rex Rodgers (see below), and constricted-stem variants. The site is a low sand dune adjacent to a small playa and near several other small lake basins.

Some Paleoindian sites are reported from lunettes, which also indicates an association with playas. A Clovis point was found in association with mammoths at Poverty Hill (Parker 1983; R. Walter, pers. comm. 1984) (FIG. 3.61). The site largely was destroyed by natural and artificial processes, but nevertheless documents Clovis activity on a lunette and adjacent to a playa. Eight additional Paleoindian sites are reported from lunettes on the central Llano Estacado (Hester 1975a; Hester and Grady 1977) (Table 3.22; FIG. 3.61). Four of the lunettes contained evidence of multiple Paleoindian occupations. Seven sites yielded Folsom artifacts, seven contained unfluted lanceolate points, and two produced Clovis artifacts.

Other Sites

Three Paleoindian sites off but near the Llano Estacado (FIGS. 1.1, 1.3) are pertinent to this discussion by virtue of chronologic or typological data. These sites will be summarized only briefly because (1) their settings are very different from those on the Llano Estacado and direct stratigraphic comparisons cannot be made, and (2) relatively little geoarchaeological data are available.

The Horace Rivers site is in the Canadian River valley, near the northeastern corner of the Southern High Plains (FIG. 1.1). The site is a Plainview campsite in a terrace of a minor tributary to the Canadian River (Mallouf 1994; Mandel 1994a). Horace Rivers is one of the very few Late Paleoindian campsites reported on the Great Plains. The occupation level is within the A-horizon of a soil formed in and buried by alluvium, now isolated by dissection of the terrace. A suite of radiocarbon ages on soil humates and charcoal from hearths dates the Plainview occupation of the site to 9300–9000 yrs BP (Table 3.23) (Mallouf 1994; Mandel 1994a).

The Rex Rodgers site (Speer 1978; Willey et al. 1978), now covered by MacKenzie Reservoir, was along Tule Creek, a tributary of the Red River, where the creek formed a deep reentrant canyon cut into the High Plains escarpment (FIG. 1.3). The site was a bison kill, with the remains of at least six *Bison antiquus* associated with five projectile points and other stone tools. Very little stratigraphic data are available for the site. The bone bed was on a terrace of Tule Creek inset against the bedrock of the canyon walls and underlain by sandy and gravelly alluvium considered to be of late

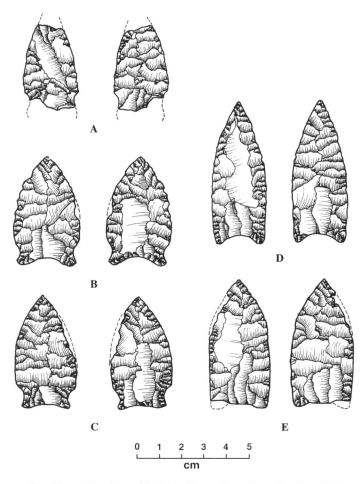

FIGURE 3.62. The collection of Paleoindian points from the Rex Rodgers site. Points D and E are similar to classic Plains lanceolate styles such as Plainview, but A, B, and C are very similar to southeastern styles such as San Patrice. Drawings from Hughes and Willey 1978, courtesy of Texas Historical Commission, Austin.

Pleistocene age. The kill apparently took place at the mouth of a small gully cut in the canyon wall when the floodplain of the creek was nearer the level of the terrace. Three of the projectile points, referred to as "Rex Rodgers," are side-notched and very similar to styles common in the southeastern United States (FIGS. 3.62A,B,C) (Willey et al. 1978:66) (discussed further in Chapter 5). The other two points are unfluted lanceolate styles similar to Clovis or Plainview (FIGS. 3.62D,E) (Willey et al. 1978:

TABLE 3.23. Radiocarbon ages from Paleoindian levels and bracketing levels at the Horace Rivers, Rex Rodgers, and Big Lake sites

Site	^{14}C Age Years BP	Lab. No.	Material Dated & Remarks
Horace Rivers [1]			
	9000±70	?	Charcoal
	9040±70	?	Charcoal
	9060±90	?	Charcoal
	9290±80	?	Charcoal
Rex Rodgers [2]			
	9120±80	SMU-274	Bone apatite
Big Lake [3]			
	7530±150	TX-6165	Bone apatite
	8375±435	GX-16474A	Bone apatite
	8130±120	TX-7117	Organic-rich sediment, fraction unknown

[1] Mallouf (1994); Mandel (1994a).
[2] Speer (1978).
[3] Turpin et al. (1992).

65–66). There seems little doubt that the bone bed represented a single kill and that the two artifact styles were used by a single group that executed the kill. A radiocarbon age of ca. 9400 yrs BP was determined on bone apatite from the extinct bison (Speer 1978:94) (Table 3.23).

Turpin et al. (1992) report a Paleoindian feature from Big Lake, a permanent lake ca. 40 km southeast of the Llano Estacado, on the Edwards Plateau (FIG. 1.1). The remains of at least nine extinct bison, along with two fragments of unfluted, lanceolate projectile points ("Scottsbluff or Milnesand," Turpin et al. 1992:45), were recovered from the lake sediments. The feature, dating to ca. 8100 yrs BP (Table 3.23), probably was a processing station.

CHAPTER FOUR

Regional Comparisons

Introduction

Comparisons of Paleoindian geoarchaeology and cultural chronology on the Southern High Plains with those of other areas is facilitated by the spatial and physiographic proximity of the region to other areas with extensive or well-known Paleoindian records or considerable geoarchaeological data for Paleoindian occupations. Beginning in the early 1980s a substantial geoarchaeological record emerged from the Rolling Plains to the east and the Edwards Plateau–Central Texas region to the south and southeast, both of which are contiguous with the Llano Estacado (FIGS. 1.1, 4.1). The Brazos and Colorado River systems, which head in the draws of the Llano Estacado, and the Canadian and Pecos systems, which bound it, pass through one or both of these regions (FIG. 4.1). The northern Great Plains of eastern Colorado, Wyoming, and western Nebraska (FIG. 4.1) contain one of the best-known Paleoindian records in North America. Paleoindian research in this region has historical roots similar to those of the Llano Estacado: such work has been more or less continuous since the 1930s, and geoarchaeological studies were an important component.

This chapter is a brief examination of Paleoindian geoarchaeology and cultural chronology in these physiographic regions that border or are physiographically related to the Southern High Plains. Conclusions regarding the cultural chronology and geoarchaeology are drawn in Chapter 5. This section is not an exhaustive review or detailed comparison, largely because there have been no systematic, region-wide studies of Paleoindian archaeology in these areas. Moreover, though some of these regions are well known for their Paleoindian archaeology and for long traditions of geoarchaeological research, there are only a few localities for which well-dated Paleoindian geoarchaeological records are available. The focus is on a few key studies with enough information available to make some comparisons with the Llano Estacado and to draw significant conclusions.

Edwards Plateau and Central Texas

The Edwards Plateau is an extensive physiographic region in Central Texas (FIG. 4.1) composed largely of horizontal beds of Cretaceous limestone. The northwestern end of the Edwards Plateau is generally flat and merges imperceptibly with the Southern High Plains, the limestone buried by the thinned edge of the Ogallala Formation. Dissection along the western, southern, southeastern, and eastern margins of the plateau produced areas of relatively high relief, locally including deep canyons (in the west) and broad alluvial valleys (in the east). Central Texas essentially is that part of the northeastern Edwards Plateau incised by the Colorado River system. The Edwards Plateau and Central Texas are regions of considerable and long-term archaeological interest, but the emphasis was largely on Archaic and later groups (e.g., Prewitt 1981). With a few exceptions, the Paleoindian chronology and the geoarchaeological characteristics of Paleoindian occupations have only recently begun to emerge.

Perhaps the best-known Paleoindian site on the Edwards Plateau, and one of the more spectacular Paleoindian sites in North America, is Bonfire

FIGURE 4.1. The Great Plains with the locations of all Paleoindian sites off the Southern High Plains mentioned in text and tables in Chapters 4 and 5, the location of selected cities (A Austin; Al Albuquerque; C Clovis; D Denver; DC Dodge City; L Lubbock; NP North Platte; OC Oklahoma City; R Rapid City), and principal physiographic features and provinces. Archaeological sites are numbered from north to south: 1 Mill Iron, 2 Agate Basin (including Sheaman and Brewster), 3 Betty Green, 4 Ray Long, 5 Lange-Ferguson, 6 Hell Gap, 7 Hudson-Meng, 8 Scottsbluff, 9 Clary Ranch, 10 Lindenmeier, 11 Johnson, 12 Nelson, 13 Frasca, 14 Nolan, 15 Lime Creek, Red Smoke, 16 Dent, 17 Powars, 18 Klein, 19 Frazier, 20 Jurgens, 21 5MR388, 22 Bijou Creek, 23 Fox, 24 Keenesburg, 25 Lamb Springs, 26 Hahn, 27 Claypool, 28 Selby, 29 Jones-Miller, 30 Dutton, 31 Wetzel, 32 Harrison, 33 Gettenger, 34 Olsen-Chubbock, 35 Folsom, 36 Nall, 37 Waugh, 38 Cooper, 39 Lipscomb, 40 Domebo, 41 Perry Ranch, 42 Lake Theo, 43 Pumpkin Creek, 44 Field Ranch, 45 Aubrey, 46 Lewisville, 47 George King, 48 Acton, 49 Horn, 50 Beidleman Ranch, 51 Adair-Steadman, 52 Lone Wolf Creek, 53 McLean, 54 Wilson-Leonard, 55 Loeve, 56 Levi, 57 Bonfire Shelter, 58 Baker Cave, 59 Devil's Mouth, 60 Kincaid Shelter, 61 Richard Beene.

South Dakota

Wyoming

Nebraska

NP

Kansas

Colorado

SOUTHERN ROCKY MTNS.

COLORADO PIEDMONT

RATON

VOLCANICS

HIGH PLAINS

ROLLING PLAINS

Oklahoma

OC

DC

New Mexico

Texas

EDWARDS PLATEAU

Gulf of Mexico

0   200 km

R

Cheyenne River

Missouri River

Niobrara River

N. Platte

S. Platte River

Republican

Smokey Hill River

Arkansas River

Cimarron

Canadian River

Red River

Brazos

Colorado

Pecos River

Devils R.

Rio Grande

Trinity River

1
2
3
4
5
6
7
8
9
10
11
12
13
14
15
16 17 18 19 20 21 22 23 24 25
26
27 28 29 30
31
32 33 34
35
36
37 38 39
40
41
42
43 44
45 46 47 48 49
50 51
52 53
54 55 56
57 58 59 60 61

Al
C
L
A
D
DC
OC

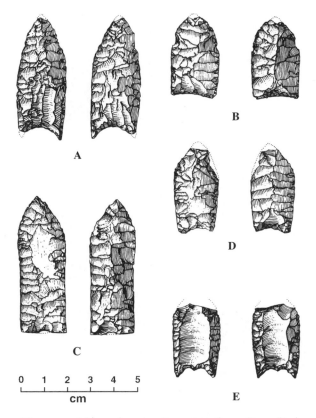

FIGURE 4.2. The assemblage of projectile points from Bone Bed 2 at Bonfire Shelter (from Dibble and Lorrain 1968:fig. 14), illustrating the wide range in morphology. Drawn by Hal Story and reproduced courtesy of the Texas Memorial Museum, the University of Texas at Austin.

Shelter, located on the southwestern edge of the Edwards Plateau about 200 km south of the Llano Estacado (Dibble and Lorrain 1968; Bement 1986) (FIGS. 1.1, 4.1). The site is a rockshelter along a canyon that drains into the Rio Grande. Bonfire Shelter was used as a bison jump by Paleo-indian and Archaic peoples. It is the oldest jump site known in the New World. The Paleoindian level contains three beds of bone from *Bison antiquus*. Each level was in direct contact with the adjacent bed, separable only because the middle layer was burned, indicating very close contemporaneity of each jump. The lowest component of the bone bed yielded a Folsom point and a fragment of a constricted-stem point (Dibble and Lorrain 1968:fig. 15a). Plainview or "Plainview-like" artifacts (Dibble and

TABLE 4.1. Radiocarbon ages for the Paleoindian levels and bracketing levels at Bonfire Shelter, Lake Theo, Pumpkin Creek, and the Lipscomb site

Site	^{14}C Age Years BP	Lab. No.	Material Dated & Remarks
Bonfire Shelter			
	9920±150	TX-657	Charcoal; uppermost of three bone beds[1]
	10,100±300	TX-658	Charcoal; uppermost of three bone beds[1]
	10,230±160	TX-153	Charcoal; uppermost of three bone beds[2]
	10,280±430	AA-346	Charcoal; uppermost of three bone beds[3]
Lake Theo			
	8010±100	TX-2880	Bone apatite; Folsom bone bed[4]
	9360±170	TX-2879	Bone apatite; Folsom bone bed[4]
	9420±85	SMU-856	Humates; top of buried A-horizon, above Plainview bone bed[5]
	9950±110	SMU-866	Humates; base of buried A-horizon, same level as Plainview bone bed; above Folsom bone bed[5]
	11,040±270	TX-4663	Humates?; top of first buried A-horizon below Folsom level[6]
	11,980±320	TX-4664	Humates?; base of first buried A-horizon below Folsom level[6]
Pumpkin Creek[7]			
	7030±190	TX-2190	Bone; fraction unknown
Lipscomb[8]			
	10,820±150	NZA-1092	Charcoal; colluvium in gully adjacent to bone bed

[1] Dibble (1970).
[2] Dibble and Lorrain (1968).
[3] Bement (1986).
[4] Harrison and Killen (1978); S. Valastro, pers. comm. (1994).
[5] Johnson et al. (1982).
[6] Caran and Baumgardner (1986).
[7] Saunders and Penman (1979).
[8] Hofman (1995); five ages are available from the site, but only this one is accepted as dating the feature.

Lorrain 1968:75) were recovered from upper components of the bone bed or from portions of the bone bed that were not stratified (FIGS. 4.2A–D). Charcoal from the upper component of the Paleoindian bone beds yielded four radiocarbon ages that range from ca. 10,300 to ca. 9900 yrs BP (Table 4.1) (Dibble 1970; Bement 1986).

The Devil's Mouth site and Baker Cave provide additional insights into Late Paleoindian chronology and subsistence. Devil's Mouth, south-

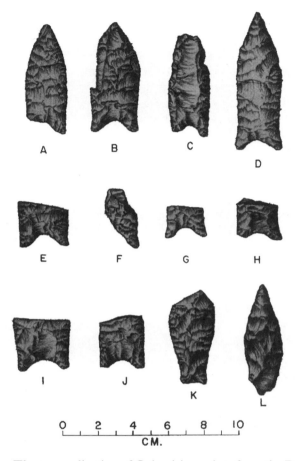

FIGURE 4.3. The type collection of Golondrina points from the Devil's Mouth site (from L. Johnson 1964:fig. 15). Drawn by Frank Wier. Courtesy of the Department of Anthropology, University of Texas at Austin.

east of Bonfire Shelter on the lower Devil's River (FIG. 4.1), yielded a variety of Late Paleoindian projectile points originally termed "Plainview Golondrina" (L. Johnson 1964) (FIG. 4.3). Subsequent technological analyses clearly show that this type is not related to Plainview, and it is now termed simply Golondrina (T. Hester 1977; Kelly 1982; Knudson 1983:165). Moreover, the style dates to ca. 9000 yrs BP (and continued to perhaps 8000 yrs BP) and seems to be most common in south Texas (T. Hester 1976, 1977, 1982; Thurmond 1990:FIG. 10). The technological and temporal distinctiveness of Golondrina versus Plainview is not completely resolved, however (e.g., Collins et al. 1993; Bousman et al. 1994; T. Hester

1994), further illustrating the typological problems inherent in simple comparisons of gross artifact morphology. Baker Cave, on a tributary of the Devil's River, provided secure dating of Golondrina at ca. 9000 yrs BP (Hester 1982). Moreover, Baker Cave and other stratified sites in the area show that the early Holocene was characterized by Paleoindian-style projectile points, and also present is evidence for an "Archaic" subsistence such as an increased focus on plant gathering, and processing and hunting of small and medium animals (Collins 1976; Hester 1982). Projectile points with more "Archaic" characteristics (e.g., "early Barbed," "early stemmed," and Baker) appear to overlap in time with Golondrina (Collins 1976; Hester 1982; Turner and Hester 1993).

Essentially no geoarchaeological data are available from the southwestern Edwards Plateau, but other forms of evidence hint at Paleoindian environments of the region. Aggradation of fine-grained sediment was the dominant geomorphic process on the lower Pecos and lower Devil's rivers in the early Holocene (Collins 1976; Patton and Dibble 1982). The Late Paleoindian inhabitants of the region apparently occupied these floodplain settings (Collins 1976). Pollen from several cave sites in the area, including Bonfire Shelter (Bryant and Shafer 1977; Bryant and Holloway 1985), show that during the period from ca. 14,000 to 10,000 yrs BP, pinyon-pine parklands were gradually replaced by expanding scrub grasslands. This trend is interpreted to represent cooler and more humid conditions of the late Pleistocene gradually changing to warmer and drier conditions. Bryant and Holloway (1985) suggest that the vegetation shift was due specifically to increasingly warmer summers. The trend in warming and drying continued into the middle Holocene. The vegetation data are supported by limited paleohydrologic information (Patton and Dibble 1982).

On the southeastern Edwards Plateau, a well-stratified and well-dated Paleoindian record is reported from the Wilson-Leonard site (FIG. 4.1). The site is in a fan deposited along a low-order tributary of the Brazos River. The occupations probably were associated with a spring that fed into the tributary. Among other notable finds, Wilson-Leonard yielded human remains dated to ca. 9500 yrs BP (Phelps et al. 1994). The stratified Paleoindian record contains some similarities to the High Plains sequence, but also several significant differences (Bousman et al. 1994; Collins, Bousman, Goldberg, Takac, Guy, Lanata, Stafford, and Holliday 1993; Collins, Bousman, Guy, and Kerr 1994; Goldberg et al. 1994). Technological and typological relationships, if any, between the Wilson-Leonard Paleoindian assemblages and those on the High Plains await analysis, however. A Clovis-age (>10,500 yrs BP) component was found in alluvial sand and

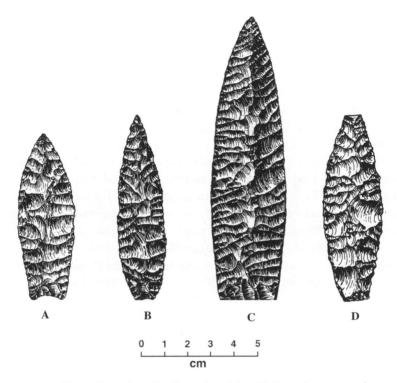

A   B   C   D

0   1   2   3   4   5
cm

FIGURE 4.4. Examples of projectile points identified as Angostura from archaeological sites in Texas (from Turner and Hester 1993:73, 74). Drawn by Kathy Roemer. Reproduced with permission of Ellen Sue Turner and Gulf Publishing Co.

gravel. Above is a Folsom-Midland level, dated at ca. 10,500 yrs BP, but represented only by a single Midland point and fragments of preforms with traits suggestive of Folsom technology. This zone was in fine-grained marsh deposits within an abandoned stream channel. The period ca. 10,000–9650 yrs BP is represented by soil formation, and archaeologically characterized by corner-notched "Wilson" points, which are similar to later Central Texas Archaic styles and the early Holocene "early barbed" and Baker styles of southwest Texas (Turner and Hester 1993). Above the Wilson level is a variety of unfluted lanceolate points similar to both Plainview and Golondrina styles but termed "St. Mary's Hall" (named for artifacts from the St. Mary's Hall site in San Antonio; T. Hester 1976, 1977) and dated to ca. 9700–8800 yrs BP.

The youngest lanceolate style at Wilson-Leonard is "Texas Angostura," dated to ca. 8800–8000. "Texas Angostura" is a very poorly defined category of constricted-stem, obliquely flaked, unfluted, sometimes leaf-shaped lanceolate points common in southern Texas, but reported throughout most of the state (Kelly 1983; Thurmond 1990:fig. 10; Turner and Hester 1993; Thoms 1993) (FIG. 4.4). The style was first named on the basis of a small, minimally described collection from the Ray Long site on the Northern High Plains (Hughes 1949; Wheeler 1954, 1995:372–450; Wormington 1957:138–141) (discussed below). The Angostura level at Wilson-Leonard, though characterized by Paleoindian-style projectile points, is otherwise similar to Early Archaic occupations, with a heavy reliance on plant gathering and processing, and on small and medium animals. This trait, Paleoindian-style artifacts with Archaic economic pursuits, appears to be characteristic of the early Holocene in Central Texas as well as southwestern Texas (Prewitt 1981; Collins et al. 1994).

Artifacts that may be related to the enigmatic "Texas Angostura" style have been found at several other sites in stratified contexts in or near Central Texas. Levi Rockshelter, on the edge of the Edwards Plateau near Austin (FIG. 4.1), yielded a large collection of projectile points first called "Plainview-Angostura" (Alexander 1963). Subsequent reviewers identified the artifacts as simply Angostura or Texas Angostura, but bearing no known relationship to Plainview (Kelly 1983; Turner and Hester 1993: 73–74). The dates on Angostura at Levi range from ca. 9300 to ca. 6800 yrs BP, but all are on shell in an area likely influenced by the hard-water effect.

Angostura points also were found off the Edwards Plateau on the Coastal Plain at the Loeve site and at the Richard Beene site. The Loeve site is in alluvium on the North San Gabriel River (Prewitt 1982) (FIG. 4.1). The Angostura zone, dated between ca. 9700 and ca. 6800 yrs BP, included extensive camping features in aggrading point-bar deposits. Prewitt (1982) interpreted the Angostura occupations as representing an Archaic subsistence. The Richard Beene site is along the Medina River (FIG. 4.1) and also buried in fine-grained alluvium (Thoms 1992; Thoms and Mandel 1992). A stratigraphic diagram of the site (Thoms and Mandel 1992:fig. 1) suggests that the river downcut between ca. 20,000 and 15,000 yrs BP, followed by episodic aggradation until the late Holocene. The Angostura occupation debris was found in a buried soil and in overlying fine-grained alluvium and dated ca. 8800 yrs BP (Thoms 1992).

Loeve and Richard Beene provide valuable data on geomorphic systems during early Holocene occupations but, along with Levi, only hint at the chronology of Texas Angostura finds. The morphologies of some of the artifacts in the various Angostura collections and the earlier radiocarbon ages on these collections suggest a relationship to Hell Gap, Agate Basin, and other constricted-stem styles of the High Plains (noted by Wheeler 1954, 1995:417; Wormington 1957:141; Thoms 1993:fig. 2), but this observation will remain only an hypothesis pending much more data and research.

Rockshelters such as Bonfire Shelter are common in the limestone throughout the Edwards Plateau (Collins 1991). Occupation debris of Holocene age (including Late Paleoindian features) is ubiquitous in these settings, but late Pleistocene features are rare (Dibble and Alexander 1971; Collins 1991) (discussed further in Chapter 5). One shelter site in Central Texas bears on the Paleoindian chronology of the Llano Estacado. Horn Shelter on the Brazos River (FIG. 4.1) has a stratified and dated Holocene archaeological sequence (Watt 1978; Redder 1985). Of particular interest is a zone containing "Brazos fishtail" points, an unfluted, expanding-stem artifact generally similar to the Rodgers point at the Rex Rodgers site (FIG. 3.62) (and more broadly, the San Patrice style; Turner and Hester 1993:181–182), and associated with charcoal ages of 9500–10,000 yrs BP. This same zone also produced a double burial that is about the same age as or older than the Wilson-Leonard interment (Watt 1978; Redder and Fox 1988; Young 1988).

One of the very few reported rockshelters with an essentially complete Paleoindian record is Kincaid Shelter, on the south-central Edwards Plateau (FIG. 4.1). Investigated in 1948 and 1953, the site was never fully reported. Paleoindian artifacts from the site include Clovis, Folsom, Plainview-like, Golondrina, and Texas Angostura points (Sellards 1952: 94; Hester et al. 1985; Collins et al. 1989). The remains of extinct bison, horses, and mammoths also were found in the Clovis-Folsom deposits (Hester et al. 1985; Collins et al. 1989). Little geoarchaeological or other paleoenvironmental data are available, however.

Although geoarchaeological data are relatively sparse for the Edwards Plateau–Central Texas region, some geomorphic trends are apparent in the stratigraphic records from the archaeological studies noted above, as well as stratigraphic and paleobotanical records for other areas of the eastern Edwards Plateau, the northern Edwards Plateau, and Central Texas (Blum 1989; Blum and Valastro 1992; Fredlund 1994; Nordt et al. 1994). Prior to ca. 10,500 yrs BP, competent streams flowed along the bottoms of channels that were deeply incised during the late Pleistocene. The subsequent stratigraphic record suggests lower-energy aggradation due to reduced stream discharge. This alluvial sequence is reported from both low-order tributaries such as the one occupied by Wilson-Leonard and main streams such as the Pedernales River. The latest Pleistocene vegetation was a woodland with some tall and short grasses. The assemblage changed in the early Holocene to one of fewer trees and expanded grasslands, with short grasses dominant.

Rolling Plains

The Rolling Plains of north Texas and west Oklahoma contrasts dramatically in geology and geomorphology with the High Plains directly to the west (FIGS. 1.1, 4.1). As the name implies, the Rolling Plains has more local relief. The topography is largely due to development of an integrated drainage system, which is absent on the High Plains. Some of the major drainages that cross the Rolling Plains are the Brazos, Trinity, Red, and Canadian systems (FIG. 4.1). Paleoindian artifacts are very common as surface finds on the Rolling Plains (Meltzer 1986; Largent et al. 1991), but relatively few *in situ* finds are reported.

The only well-documented, stratified Paleoindian site on the western Rolling Plains is Lake Theo, 10 km east of the High Plains escarpment (Harrison and Smith 1975; Harrison and Killen 1978) (FIGS. 1.3, 4.1). The site consists of two Paleoindian bone beds exposed in the eroded margins of a terrace of Holmes Creek. The creek heads in the High Plains escarpment and is a low-order tributary of the Red River. The bone beds are buried in fine-grained overbank alluvium (Unit 6) (Johnson et al. 1982). Soils buried immediately below this alluvium date to the terminal Pleistocene (Caran and Baumgardner 1986) (FIG. 4.5).

Both bone beds at Lake Theo consist of the butchered remains of *Bison antiquus*. The lower bone bed, near the top of the Unit 6 alluvium and just below an A-horizon formed in the deposits (FIG. 4.5), yielded several Folsom points. Harrison and Killen (1978, addendum) report radiocarbon ages of ca. 8000 and ca. 9400 yrs BP on bone apatite from the Folsom horizon (Table 4.1). The upper bone bed was in the lower half of the A-horizon developed in the alluvium (FIG. 4.5). Only a small portion of the feature was exposed during excavation, and it yielded no projectile points. Two Plainview points and a broken, heavily reworked, nondiagnostic projectile point were found within several meters of the upper bed, however, and at about the same elevation. A radiocarbon sample from the lower half of the A-horizon (i.e., the Plainview level) was dated to ca. 10,000 yrs BP (Johnson et al. 1982) (Table 4.1). A sample from the upper half of the A-horizon (i.e., collected from above the upper bone bed) dated to ca. 9400 yrs BP (Johnson et al. 1982) (Table 4.1). This soil was buried beneath three other dated stratigraphic units (Caran and Baumgardner 1986) (FIG. 4.5).

Neck (1987) proposed a paleoenvironmental reconstruction for Lake Theo, based on snail faunas. During the Paleoindian occupations, precipitation was distributed more evenly during the year and seasonal temperature contrasts were lower than today. Summer temperatures, in particular, were less extreme. Woodland vegetation also was more dense, but this may have been a local phenomenon related to a locally high water table and saturated soil.

On the Rolling Plains of far western Oklahoma two Folsom bone beds were investigated in the early 1990s. The Waugh site is in the Cimarron River basin (FIG. 4.1) on the uplands of a major drainage divide (Hofman et al. 1992; Hofman 1995). The site is near the base of sandy and silty fill in a large arroyo cut into Permian sandstone (Hofman and Carter 1991). Waugh includes a bone bed with the remains of at least 5 *Bison antiquus* and a nearby camping area probably related to the bone bed. Charcoal from the camp area yielded two radiocarbon ages of ca. 10,400 yrs BP (Hofman 1995). The Cooper site is adjacent to the floodplain of the North Canadian

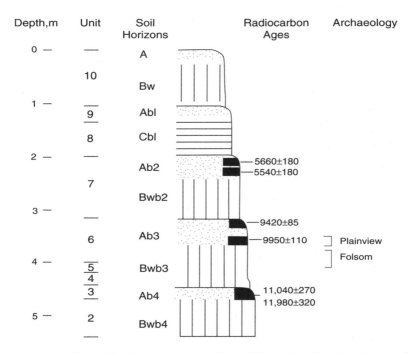

FIGURE 4.5. Generalized section at the Lake Theo site, showing the stratigraphic relationships of geologic units, soils, radiocarbon ages, and Paleoindian occupation levels (based on Johnson et al. 1982: fig. 4). The two oldest radiocarbon ages are from Caran and Baumgardner (1986).

River (Beaver River) (FIG. 4.1) (Bement 1994, 1995; Carter and Bement 1995). The locality is in the head of an arroyo cut into Permian bedrock and draining into the North Canadian. Three bone beds, one above the other, with the remains of a total of 40 *Bison antiquus*, were found at the site, and all are associated with Folsom occupations. A date of 10,050±210 yrs BP was secured on sediments below the lowest bone bed (Carter and Bement 1995).

Three buried Paleoindian sites were reported from the Abilene area: Beidleman Ranch, Adair-Steadman, and McLean (FIG. 4.1). The Beidleman Ranch site was in a small, filled lake basin on the Permian redbed uplands of the Brazos River system (Suhm 1960). The site yielded two unfluted, lanceolate projectile points (Plainview?) in association with extinct bison. The site is the only reported Paleoindian locality on the Rolling Plains associated with a lake. Adair-Steadman is on a high terrace of the Clear Fork of the Brazos River (Tunnell 1977). The site, in the edge of a dune field that blankets the terrace, produced a spectacular collection of Folsom manufacturing debris. Eolian sand apparently buried the site shortly after it was abandoned. The McLean site produced a Clovis point in association with mammoths buried under 3 m of alluvium along Mulberry Creek (Bryan and Ray 1938; Ray and Bryan 1938; Ray 1942). Little else is known about the site, but it provides some evidence for deep incision prior to the Clovis occupation and then aggradation following the Clovis period.

West of Abilene is the Lone Wolf Creek site, in a tributary of the Colorado River. Little is known of the site. It was excavated by Harold Cook in 1925 (Cook 1927; Figgins 1927), the last locality he investigated before digging at Folsom. The Lone Wolf Creek site was a bed of extinct bison buried under alluvium. During excavation of blocks removed from the site three projectile points were found. Wormington (1957:100) identified one of the points as Milnesand and another as Plainview (the third artifact was lost). Examination of the artifacts suggests that they are the same style (Johnson and Holliday 1980) and may be Milnesand or possibly Firstview. Lone Wolf Creek, therefore, may be the only other known Milnesand locality. The site may also be a bison jump. Photographs of the excavations and field investigation by the author and D. J. Meltzer show that the feature was at the base of a vertical sandstone bluff 5–8 m high.

On the central Rolling Plains of southwestern Oklahoma, Saunders and Penman (1979) reported the Perry Ranch site (FIG. 4.1). The site was in an arroyo cut into a bedrock knoll on the floodplain of a small creek. The original work plus a reinvestigation by Hofman and Todd (1996) show that the site was a small bison kill (MNI=2) in an arroyo cut in Permian bedrock. The site was originally reported as a Plainview bison kill, based on recovery of two projectile points and fragmentary bone. A sample of bone yielded an age of ca. 7030 yrs BP (Table 4.1). Johnson and Holliday (1980) suggested that the site was a Golondrina locality, based on artifact morphology and the radiocarbon age. The more recent work by Hofman and Todd (1996) shows that the artifacts probably are Plainview, fitting easily into the type collection, and that the radiocarbon age was in error due to considerable weathering of the bone. Bone recovered during the reinvestigation was too weathered for AMS radiocarbon dating.

The Domebo and Aubrey sites are deeply buried localities on the eastern margin of the Rolling Plains (FIG. 4.1). The Domebo site is in a tributary canyon of the Washita River in southwestern Oklahoma (Leonhardy 1966) (FIG. 4.1). The tributary was deeply incised in the late Pleistocene, then occupied, and subsequently alluviated with >10 m of valley fill. At the base of the fill three Clovis points were found in association with the remains of a mammoth (Leonhardy 1966). The bone bed itself was in alluvial sand and overlain by a marsh soil, together comprising the "lower member of the Domebo Formation" (Albritton 1966). The Clovis level was dated to ca. 11,000 yrs BP, and the marsh soil, which included tree stumps, is slightly younger (Albritton 1966; Stafford et al. 1987; Hofman 1988). Geological, paleontological, and paleobotanical data suggest that the local environment was a humid woodland within the canyon, surrounded by an upland grassland. The data also suggest significantly weaker seasonal contrasts during Clovis times, relative to today, with overall greater effective precipitation.

The Aubrey site (Ferring 1990b, 1994; Humphrey and Ferring 1994) is on the Elm Fork of the Trinity River in north-central Texas. The valley entrenched >15,000 yrs BP, then began to fill with pond, marsh, and colluvial deposits (15,000−11,200 yrs BP). Aubrey contains a Clovis occupation dated to ca. 11,200 yrs BP and buried by 6−8 m of floodplain sediments. The site, adjacent to a spring-fed pond, includes both a bison kill area and a rare Clovis camp. Stratigraphic and isotopic data suggest that before and during the Clovis occupation the area was a cool, dry grassland. From post-Clovis time into the early Holocene, a time of rapid alluviation, the environment was somewhat more humid.

The vegetation reconstructions for Domebo and Aubrey are similar, but the climatic reconstructions are at odds. The environmental reconstruction for Clovis time at Domebo, which is closer to the Southern High

Plains, is more similar to that for Clovis time on the Southern High Plains (Chapter 5). Interdisciplinary reinvestigation of Domebo clearly is warranted. The work at Domebo tended to focus on the Clovis level, but the site holds great potential for a late Quaternary environmental record. Moreover, Hofman (1988) presents evidence that the lower member of the Domebo Formation may be a relatively widespread unit in tributary canyons of the Washita and Canadian rivers in western Oklahoma. Several sites are reported with paludal soils, including *in situ* tree stumps, and Paleoindian artifacts, all dating between 12,000 and 9000 yrs BP. The region may hold an exceptional region-wide record documenting Paleoindian environmental history.

Five noteworthy Paleoindian sites are reported from high and old landscapes of the eastern Rolling Plains. The Lewisville site is a well-known and controversial locality on a high terrace of the Trinity River, below the Aubrey site (FIG. 4.1). Lewisville was a Clovis camp (Crook and Harris 1957; Stanford 1983; but also see Ferring 1990b:49), which is rare indeed, but the site generated years of controversy following publication of radiocarbon ages of >37,000 yrs BP (Crook and Harris 1957, 1961; Krieger 1964:45; Stanford 1983:70). The issue of the dating was laid to rest following a reinvestigation of the site and the discovery that the Clovis occupants used old lignite for the hearths (Stanford 1983:70). The Acton site is a large near-surface locality on a high terrace of the Brazos River (Blaine et al. 1968) (FIG. 4.1). Acton produced an extensive collection of stone artifacts, including Plainview, Cody/Firstview, Golondrina, and Dalton/San Patrice artifacts.

Paleoindian sites on old, stable upland surfaces of the eastern Rolling Plains include Pumpkin Creek in south-central Oklahoma, and the Field Ranch and George King sites in north-central Texas (FIG. 4.1). The Pumpkin Creek site probably was a lithic workshop and perhaps a retooling site, and also probably a quarry where chert gravels were mined (Wyckoff and Taylor 1971). The large artifact collection includes Plainview, Cody, and "Dalton-like," as well as Early Archaic, styles (Wyckoff and Taylor 1971; J. Hofman, pers. comm. 1995). Surface collection and some testing at Field Ranch, on a high divide of the Trinity River, produced Clovis, Folsom, and Plainview artifacts (Jensen 1968). The geologic situation is unclear, but the suggestion of "clay weathering out of bedrock" (Jensen 1968:134) indicates the presence of authigenic clay and that the site is associated with an old, stable surface. Similarly, George King is on a high divide, buried by dunes (Ferring 1995). The site yielded Cody and Dalton artifacts from the top of a well-expressed soil and below Holocene eolian sand. The setting and soils indicate that the site was a stable surface in the late Pleistocene and through most of the Holocene.

The data from the archaeological sites described above, as well as information from regional stratigraphic studies on the Rolling Plains (Ferring 1990a, 1994; Blum and Valastro 1992; Blum et al. 1992), suggest a geomorphic history very similar to that described for the Edwards Plateau and Central Texas. The streams were subjected to deep incision late in the Pleistocene (just prior to the Clovis occupation), and then they slowly aggraded well into the Holocene. Paleoindian archaeological sites, therefore, are found deeply buried in alluvium or they are exposed at the surface on old, high terraces or on bedrock uplands.

Central and Northern Great Plains

The Great Plains north of the Llano Estacado to Wyoming contains a remarkable number of well-known or historically important Paleoindian sites as well as many lesser-known but nevertheless significant localities (Wormington 1957; Stephenson 1965; Cassells 1983; Frison 1991a). These sites, combined with the record from the southern Great Plains, provide the basis for many classical (and perhaps erroneous) views of Paleoindian archaeology in North America (Meltzer and Smith 1986; Meltzer 1993). Some comparisons of selected northern Plains sites therefore are warranted in view of the physiographic and historical relationships between northern Plains Paleoindian sites and those on the Llano Estacado.

For the purposes of this discussion the central Great Plains includes the Central High Plains (the High Plains between the Canadian and Arkansas rivers) and the Raton section, and the northern Great Plains includes the Northern High Plains (the High Plains north of the Arkansas River) and the Colorado Piedmont (FIG. 4.1).

The High Plains north of the Canadian River is, like the Llano Estacado, underlain by extensive Cenozoic alluvial and eolian deposits along with locally significant accumulations of volcanic sediments. Several well-developed, integrated stream systems cross the region, such as the Cimarron, Arkansas, and South Platte rivers (FIG. 4.1), providing more local relief than is apparent on the Llano Estacado. The uplands between the drainages are quite level, however. Also like the Llano Estacado, the uplands contain numerous playa basins and several extensive dune fields.

The Central High Plains is separated from the Rocky Mountains by the Raton volcanic field, and the Northern High Plains is separated from the mountains by the Colorado Piedmont (Hunt 1974). The Raton volcanic field is a plateau composed largely of upper Cenozoic basalt flows, heavily dissected by the upper Cimarron drainage, that covered the High Plains surface. The Colorado Piedmont is both a topographic and structural basin, with a relationship to the Northern High Plains somewhat similar to that of the Pecos River to the Llano Estacado (Hunt 1974; Colton 1978; Wayne et al. 1991). The Piedmont was once covered by Cenozoic sediments, but erosion by the South Platte and Arkansas rivers and their tributaries throughout the late Cenozoic removed most of the Cenozoic cover and cut into Mesozoic rocks.

The Central High Plains has remarkably few reported Paleoindian sites given the numbers and notoriety of such sites to the north and south. One important locality is the Lipscomb site, on the eroded southern margin of the Central High Plains, just north of the Canadian River and north of the northeastern corner of the Llano Estacado (FIGS. 1.1, 4.1). The site is along Sand Creek, a low-order tributary of the North Canadian River, which is one of several drainage systems that eroded westward into the High Plains. The Lipscomb site rests on an erosional bench now being dissected by a wide gully cutting back from the creek (FIG. 4.6). The bench is cut on pedogenically modified eolian fines of the Ogallala Formation.

Lipscomb is a Folsom site consisting of a bed of *Bison antiquus* bone. The early investigations at the site were reported only in preliminary form (Barbour and Schultz 1941; Schultz 1943). Renewed investigations at the site and reexamination of data from the earlier work provide considerable

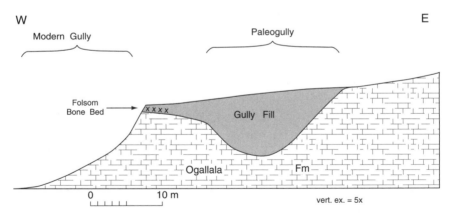

FIGURE 4.6. Geologic cross section of the Lipscomb site, illustrating the relationship of the Folsom level to the paleolandscape, the gully fill, and the present landscape.

new information (Hofman and Todd 1990; Hofman et al. 1989). The bone bed, exposed in the gully now cutting into the bench (FIG. 4.6), represents more than 50 bison and yielded over 40 Folsom artifacts. The bone bed is dated to ca. 10,800 yrs BP on the basis of a small charcoal sample (Hofman 1995). The bench on which the site rests originally was interpreted as a terrace of Sand Creek (Schultz 1943). Both the gully and the now-flat surface around the site are very young geomorphic features, however, and are not alluvial landforms created directly by Sand Creek. Subsurface exploration and geoarchaeological investigation show that the bone bed formed along the west side of a deep arroyo once graded to and draining into Sand Creek (FIG. 4.6). The arroyo filled during the early Holocene, producing the broad, level surface around the site. The recent gullying then cut into this level surface on the west side of the bone bed, and the resulting topography resembles a terrace.

The Nall site, on the High Plains surface of the western Oklahoma Panhandle, produced a large and varied collection of Paleoindian artifacts (Baker et al. 1957) (FIG. 4.1). The site is in a dune field just south of the North Canadian River (Beaver River) (Eifler and Fay 1984) and is one of the many localities exposed by wind erosion during the 1930s drought (Baker et al. 1957). The site is known exclusively from surface collections, but the occupations almost certainly were associated with a small playa covered by recent dunes (Baker et al. 1957:2). Over 200 projectile points considered Paleoindian were found at the site and classified as "Clovis (2), Folsom (1), Plainview (174), Meserve (10), Milnesand (11), and Angostura (8)" (Baker et al. 1957:2). The typological affiliations of the unfluted points are difficult to assess independently, and no artifacts were found in a stratigraphic context, but the single publication on the site clearly indicates that the locality produced a noteworthy collection of parallel-sided and constricted-stem Paleoindian lanceolates. Clovis, Midland, Plainview, and various Late Paleoindian lanceolates are also reported in surface collections from nearby deflating uplands (Lintz 1978; White 1987).

The Raton volcanic field contains probably the most historically important Paleoindian site on the continent—the Folsom type site (FIG. 4.1). The locality was a *Bison antiquus* kill in a small arroyo. The results of the excavations (1926–1928) never were fully described or published, and therefore little of substance is known about the site. The bone bed, with the remains of at least 28 individuals (L. Todd and J. Hofman, pers. comm. 1995), was in fine-grained sediment that filled a channel cut before the Folsom occupation (Anderson and Haynes 1979). Lack of evidence for weathering in the fill below the bone suggests that the channel cutting occurred not long before the occupation. Dating of charcoal from the bone level yielded an average age of ca. 10,900 yrs BP (Haynes, Beukens, Jull, and Davis 1992).

Several sites on the Northern High Plains are germane to the discussion of Paleoindians on the Llano Estacado: Olsen-Chubbock, Dutton and Selby, Jones-Miller, Lime Creek, and Claypool (FIG. 4.1). Olsen-Chubbock represented the trapping of a group of *Bison antiquus* in an arroyo cut into the High Plains surface (Wheat 1972). The arroyo apparently filled rapidly after the kill, based on the degree of preservation of the bone and the degree of soil development in the arroyo fill. Wheat (1967) originally classified the substantial projectile point collection as Eden and Scottsbluff, part of the Cody Complex. Closer examination of the Olsen-Chubbock collection and other "Cody" collections from the region led Wheat (1972) to conclude that there are distinctive typological and technological differences between the classic Cody Complex materials of the northern Plains and the Late Paleoindian lanceolate styles of the southern Plains, although gross morphological similarities are apparent. Wheat (1972) proposed the term "Firstview" in lieu of Eden and Scottsbluff for the Olsen-Chubbock materials, and "Firstview Complex" in lieu of "Cody Complex" for this southern Plains tradition, based on systematic morphometric and technological analysis. Dating the type Firstview collection has proven difficult, however. Only a single radiocarbon age is available from the Olsen-Chubbock site: 10,150±500 yrs BP obtained on bone. This radiocarbon assay is problematic because it is a single age and was determined on questionable material (Haynes 1967, 1968; Taylor 1987).

The Dutton and Selby sites are both in small, shallow playa basins on the High Plains of northeastern Colorado (Stanford 1979; Bannan 1980; Graham 1981; Reider 1990) (FIG. 4.1). Both basins are inset into late Pleistocene Peoria Loess and are filled with reworked loess interbedded with lacustrine sediments (Bannan 1980; Reider 1990). The two sites produced fractured and polished bones of extinct megafauna (*Mammuthus columbi, Equus* sp., *Camelops hesternus, Bison antiquus,* and *Platygonus compressus*), with modifications suggesting the possibility of pre-Clovis features (Stanford 1979). The pre-Clovis bone was in redeposited loess buried below clayey lacustrine sediments and has a complex taphonomic history. The question of human associations with this bone remains unresolved. Above the lake deposits was another layer of redeposited loess. In the Dutton site a Clovis occupation was found on top of this loess, possibly at a disconformity, and at the base of a younger layer of redeposited loess. Dark gray, clayey soils with evidence of iron reduction (Btg-horizon) formed in the redeposited loess above and below the Clovis occupation. The color, texture, and mineralogy of the soils suggest formation under water-logged conditions on the playa floor (Bannan 1980; Reider 1990). Indeed, these soils resemble the dark gray Randall Clay of the playas on the Southern High Plains (Chapter 3). Graham (1981), in a study of the pre-Clovis fauna, reconstructed a prairie habitat, but also identified a trend toward increasingly moist conditions about the time of the Clovis occupation. The significance of the disconformity at about the Clovis level has not been addressed, but the shift from marshy, poorly drained conditions in the soil below the Clovis level to eolian sedimentation following the Clovis occupation suggests a change in the environmental trend and development of drier conditions in post-Clovis time.

Northeast of Dutton and Selby is the Jones–Miller site, an extensive bison kill on a terrace of the Arikaree River, a tributary of the Republican River (Stanford 1978) (FIG. 4.1). The site represents multiple kills of *Bison antiquus* (totaling almost 300 individuals) by Hell Gap hunters. The kills, dated to about 10,000 yrs BP (Reider 1990:343), took place in a shallow draw that once drained into a tributary of the Arikaree River (Albanese 1977). Exactly how the animals were trapped is unknown, but Stanford (1978:96) speculates that snowdrifts may have repeatedly buried the draw, allowing hunters to trap bison there.

Farther down the Republican River system, along a tributary in southwestern Nebraska, is the Lime Creek site (Schultz and Frankforter 1948; Schultz et al. 1948; Davis 1953, 1962) (FIG. 4.1). There, three Paleoindian occupation zones were recovered beneath >12 m of loess and overbank fines. The cultural debris was associated with the A-horizons of weakly developed soils within stratified silt deposits. The stratigraphy of the occupation zones, though not described in detail, is very suggestive of a floodplain with Fluvent soils or of a colluvial setting. Most of the artifacts came from the lowest (Zone I) and highest (Zone III) occupation levels. The relatively small artifact collection is difficult to place typologically. Davis (1962:78–83) considered the Zone I artifacts to be Scottsbluff and Milnesand, but both Wheat (1972:144) and Knudson (1983:172) considered the small assemblage to be related to the Firstview ("San Jon") or Cody traditions. The Zone III assemblage was classed as Plainview, Milnesand, and "untyped obliquely-flaked fragment" (Davis 1962:83–86). Davis (1953) also reported Plainview from a similar stratigraphic setting at the neighboring Red Smoke site. Knudson (1983:172) emphatically rejects the Plainview association for both localities. The obliquely flaked fragment almost certainly is related to the Frederick–James Allen–Angostura continuum (Wheat 1972:144; Frison 1991a:74), and the rest of the assemblage probably is Frederick as well (Wheat 1972:144). The only dating of Lime Creek is a radiocarbon age on charcoal of ca. 9520 yrs BP (average of two runs; Libby 1952:82), but it was determined using the solid-carbon method, which often produced questionable ages (Taylor 1987:82, 168). Regardless of the specific typological affiliations, Lime Creek and neighboring sites seem to represent successive Late Paleoindian occupations (ca. 10,000–8000 yrs BP) in an aggrading alluvial setting.

The geoarchaeological characteristics of Lime Creek and vicinity reflect sedimentological and geomorphological trends documented for many drainages cut into the eastern High Plains of Kansas and Nebraska. Throughout much of the region the early Holocene was characterized by intermittent deposition of fine-grained alluvium alternating with pedogenesis, producing Fluvent soil-sediment packages. These alluvial settings include: the South Loup River, Nebraska (May 1989); the Kansas River, Kansas (Johnson and Logan 1990:276); and the Pawnee River, Kansas (Mandel 1992, 1994b, 1995) (FIG. 4.1). Not all valleys conform to this pattern, however, including: low-order tributaries of the Pawnee River (Mandel 1992, 1994b, 1995) and the Smokey Hill River, Kansas (Mandel 1992, 1995) (FIG. 4.1). The alluvial geoarchaeology of the late Pleistocene (earlier Paleoindian period) is poorly known from this region, but many of the valleys apparently were undergoing downcutting sometime between 15,000 and 10,000 yrs BP (Martin 1993; May et al. 1995:fig. 3). In summary, the stratigraphic and geomorphic records from the valleys of the eastern High Plains in Nebraska and Kansas show that Paleoindian occupations in alluvial systems were deeply buried beneath alluvium, were preserved as surface sites on Pleistocene terraces, or were destroyed by late Pleistocene entrenchment (Brown and Logan 1987; Johnson and Logan 1990; Mandel 1992, 1994b, 1995).

The dune fields of northeastern Colorado are known to produce extensive collections of Paleoindian artifacts. Indeed, one of the first systematic attempts to classify Paleoindian projectile points in North America was based on large collections from these dunes (Renaud 1931, 1932). Very few finds in the dunes have any stratigraphic contexts, however. One of these few is the Claypool site (Dick and Mountain 1960; Malde 1960) (FIG. 4.1), on the edge of dunes that stretch northeastward into Nebraska. Claypool yielded an extensive collection of classic Cody Complex artifacts found in a blowout in the dunes and in the dunes themselves. The basal stratum exposed in the blowout is a sandy marl that yielded both mammoths and a Clovis point. Above the marl is a sand sheet that contained the Cody

Complex artifacts. A soil formed in the sand subsequent to the occupation, but the morphology of the soil is unclear. Malde (1960:239) describes an A–B–C profile, with the B-horizon "columnar jointed and enriched in clay and oxides . . . ," suggesting that the B-horizon is argillic (or at least a Bt-horizon). Reider (1990), however, describes only an A–C profile. This apparent variability in soil morphology may be real, due to topographic variation across the original sand sheet and local deflation of the soil. The investigators, both quite clear in their descriptions, but working 20 years apart, may have seen different facies of the soil due to expansion of the blow-out during the intervening decades. Reinvestigation of the site by Stanford and Albanese (1975; along with Reider) demonstrated that the Cody Complex artifacts were redeposited, probably during accumulation of the sand sheet. The site nevertheless documents the presence of a Paleoindian site near a small paleo–lake basin, both of which were buried by eolian sand.

Late Quaternary eolian deposits are ubiquitous on the uplands of the High Plains in Kansas and Nebraska, but relatively little eolian deposition was coincident with Paleoindian occupation. In the Sand Hills region of Nebraska, sand deposition ended before 11,500 yrs BP, and marshy conditions obtained in many depressions until the middle Holocene (May et al. 1995). The marshes undoubtedly attracted Paleoindians, resulting in the surface collections reported from the region (Barbour and Schultz 1936; Myers 1987, 1995). South of the Sand Hills, deposition of Peoria Loess ended at the close of the Pleistocene, possibly by ca. 12,000 yrs BP. Pedogenesis in the Peoria Loess (formation of the Brady soil) occurred during some part of the Paleoindian occupation of the region, although the dating is unclear. Martin (1993) believes that the soil formed in the silt until at least ca. 10,500 yrs BP, whereas Feng, Johnson, Lu, and Ward (1994), Feng, Johnson, Sprowl, and Lu (1994), and Pye et al. (1995) present evidence that dates pedogenesis from 10,500 until 8500 yrs BP, implying that eolian deposition did not end until 10,500 yrs BP. In any case, stability of upland landscapes probably was the norm throughout Kansas and Nebraska during much if not most of Paleoindian times. Depending on the validity of the dating, Late Paleoindian occupations may have been coincident with subsequent, localized accumulation of the Bignell Loess (Martin 1993). Paleoindian sites on the uplands may occur, therefore, in the upper Peoria Loess, in the Brady soil, or in the Bignell Loess, though few are reported.

The Colorado Piedmont contains an unusually high number of important Paleoindian sites (Holliday 1987b; McFaul et al. 1994), most along the South Platte River between Denver and the Nebraska border (FIG. 4.1).

The sites near the river are on, within, or otherwise associated with the Kersey Terrace (known as the Broadway Terrace near Denver), a prominent fill terrace composed of late Pleistocene sediments (correlated with the last full glacial and early postglacial events in the nearby Rocky Mountains) and abandoned early in the Holocene (Bryan and Ray 1940; Hunt 1954; Machette 1975, 1977; Holliday 1987b; Madole 1991; McFaul et al. 1994). Clovis artifacts and mammoths were found in Kersey alluvium at the Dent site, probably the first reported association of fluted points and mammoths (Figgins 1933; Wormington 1957; Cassells 1983), the Klein site (Holliday 1987b; Zier et al. 1993; McFaul et al. 1994), in other unnamed alluvial localities (Wheat 1979; Holliday 1987b), and in eolian sand along the valley margin at the Fox site (McFaul et al. 1994). The Clovis occupation apparently was coincident with the final stages of late Pleistocene alluviation of the South Platte and the beginning stages of eolian sedimentation on the uplands. Folsom artifacts were found in eolian sand along the valley margin at the Powars site (Roberts 1937) and the Fowler-Parrish site (Agogino and Parrish 1971), demonstrating that eolian sedimentation continued during at least part of the Folsom occupation. The dunes at the Powars site also rest directly on the Kersey Terrace, providing a firm cutoff date for alluviation (i.e., by Folsom time).

Two Late Paleoindian sites on the Kersey Terrace, Frazier and Jurgens, were excavated in the 1970s. The Frazier site, investigated by Malde (1984) and briefly described by Wormington (1984), contained butchered *Bison antiquus* associated with Agate Basin projectile points (ca. 10,500–9500 yrs BP). The Jurgens site contained butchered *Bison antiquus* as well as evidence for camping, and yielded Kersey projectile points, a Late Paleoindian stemmed-lanceolate style in the Cody-Firstview tradition (Wheat 1979; Frison 1991a). Jurgens is the youngest of the Paleoindian sites in the area, dated to ca. 9100 yrs BP. Occupations at both sites rested on a gleyed soil formed in the Kersey alluvium, and both occupations were buried by eolian sand (Malde 1984; Holliday 1987b; McFaul et al. 1994). This geologic situation indicates that the occupations may have been associated with poorly drained conditions on the floodplain and shows that eolian sedimentation continued into the early Holocene, possibly contemporaneous with incision of the Kersey alluvium and formation of the terrace.

In the southern Colorado Piedmont, south of Denver, another important Paleoindian locality was found at the Lamb Springs site (Stanford et al. 1981; Rancier et al. 1982; Fisher 1992) (FIG. 4.1). Two bone beds of extinct fauna were investigated at the site. Both were found below the spring head itself, in channels filled with sheetwash alluvium. Soils formed in the alluvium filling the channels are indicative of saturated or boggy conditions. The lower bone bed is of pre-Clovis or Clovis age and contained extinct megafauna (*Mammuthus, Bison, Equus,* and *Glossotherium*), but whether humans were involved in creation or modification of the feature remains uncertain (Fisher 1992). The upper bone bed contains the remains of approximately two dozen extinct bison. Its origins as a cultural feature are indicated by the presence of Cody Complex artifacts dated to ca. 8900 yrs BP (Rancier et al. 1982).

Other Sites on the Great Plains

Four sites on the Great Plains north of the South Platte River, Hell Gap, Ray Long, Mill Iron, and Lindenmeier (FIG. 4.1), have little physiographic relationship to sites on the Southern High Plains and are clearly quite distant, but their collections and chronology contribute to the discussion of Paleoindian cultural chronology (Chapter 5). The Hell Gap site is in a narrow valley in southeastern Wyoming (Irwin-Williams et al. 1973). The site contains one of the most complete Paleoindian sequences reported for the northern Great Plains, from pre-Folsom to terminal Paleoindian. Below the Folsom level were unfluted projectile points superficially similar to Plainview and termed "Goshen." The status of Goshen as a valid Paleoindian assemblage remained unclear for several decades until another Goshen site, Mill Iron, was found in Montana (discussed below). A Midland occupation was identified at Hell Gap, radiocarbon dated to ca. 10,700–10,400 yrs BP and stratigraphically slightly younger than the Folsom level.

The Ray Long site is in southwest South Dakota, along a tributary of the Cheyenne River just north of the northern edge of the High Plains (FIG. 4.1). The site yielded essentially no geoarchaeological data, but a few remarks and photos in Wheeler (1995) indicate that it was in an aggrading alluvial setting during occupation. The site had an important bearing on Plains Paleoindian projectile point typology because it is the type site for the Angostura style (Wheeler 1954, 1995). The Angostura point has long been a problematic style in Plains archaeology, especially in Texas (noted above) because (1) the final report on the excavations and descriptions of the type collection (Wheeler 1995) was not published until over 40 years after the field work and (2) the style is poorly dated on the northern Plains. Angostura is an unfluted, lanceolate, constricted-stem style with some striking morphological similarities to Agate Basin, but unlike Agate Basin has distinct oblique-parallel flaking (Wheeler 1995:417). Angostura may be a younger stylistic tradition than Agate Basin. Frison (1991a:74) groups Angostura with the Frederick and James Allen artifact traditions of the Late Paleoindian stage. A radiocarbon age of 9380±500 yrs BP from charcoal was published for Angostura (M-370; Crane 1956), but the assay was based on the solid-carbon method of dating and therefore must be suspect (Taylor 1987:82, 168). Test excavations at Ray Long in 1984 yielded evidence of multiple occupations dating ca. 11,000–9000 yrs BP (Banks et al. 1995), but which levels yielded the type Angostura collection is unknown.

The introduction of the Angostura style into archaeological classification in Texas apparently was based on comparison of only the most general attributes of the type (in part because the type collection was unpublished). Wheeler (1995:418) is emphatic on this point: "In their brief description of 'Angostura points' in Texas, Suhm, Krieger, and Jelks (1954: 402 and Plate 80) pay so little heed to the salient attributes of the Angostura type that in their hands it becomes simply a gallimaufry of lanceolate points having a narrow convex, straight, or slightly concave, thinned base." Like Plainview, Angostura became another catchall category.

Significant new information on the Goshen Complex came from the Mill Iron site, a bison-kill and camp-processing site in southeastern Montana (Frison 1991b, 1993) (FIG. 4.1). Goshen dates to late Clovis or early Folsom time and exhibits technological traits suggesting that it is a precursor to Folsom. Goshen also exhibits morphological and possibly technological traits similar to Plainview (Haynes 1993) and has sometimes been mistakenly classified as such.

To conclude this chapter, a comment is in order on the famous Lindenmeier site. Lindenmeier is in a low-order tributary of the Cache La Poudre River, which joins the South Platte near the Klein and Powars sites (Bryan and Ray 1940; Haynes and Agogino 1960; Wilmsen and Roberts 1978) (FIG. 4.1). The site is in a small valley on the physiographic boundary of the northern Colorado Piedmont and the High Plains. Lindenmeier is best known as a Folsom locality, containing evidence of extensive, multiple Folsom campsites, which are dated to ca. 10,700 yrs BP (Haynes and Agogino 1960; Haynes, Beukens, Jull, and Davis 1992). The site also contains stratified post-Folsom Paleoindian occupations yielding Alberta and Cody artifacts (Wilmsen and Roberts 1978; Haynes, Beukens, Jull, and Davis 1992), but very little is known about these features. All of the Paleoindian occupations were associated with a slowly aggrading "wet meadow" landscape and periodic, extensive slopewash accumulation (Haynes and Agogino 1960:9; Wilmsen and Roberts 1978; Holliday, unpub. data).

CHAPTER FIVE

Discussion and Conclusions

Introduction

The Southern High Plains has a remarkable record of buried, well-stratified Paleoindian sites. Archaeological and geoscientific investigations at these localities during the past 60-plus years provide a wealth of data concerning artifact typology, technology, and chronology, site setting and stratigraphy, Paleoindian hunting practices and subsistence, regional and local paleoenvironments in the terminal Pleistocene and early Holocene, and environmental changes throughout this time. The focus of this volume is on several of these issues. This final chapter includes my perspective on the Paleoindian cultural chronology (an artifact chronology, in fact) (FIG. 5.1), based on the historical record of Paleoindian research (Chapter 2), cultural chronologies proposed by others (especially Hofman 1989a), and the stratigraphy and geochronology of individual sites (Chapter 3). Complementing the cultural chronology is an overview of Paleoindian environments and environmental change, based on the geologic record from the sites (Chapter 3), geoscientific data from other localities, and data from paleontological, paleobotanical, and isotope studies. Some comments and speculations also are offered regarding Paleoindian chronologies and environments throughout the southern and central Great Plains.

Cultural Chronology and Paleoenvironments

The Paleoindian cultural chronology of the Southern High Plains, as elsewhere in North America, largely is an artifact chronology focusing on the typology of projectile points (e.g., Wormington 1957). Frison (1993:7) suggests that this emphasis on typology is because "little else of substance" is known about this period. Frison may be overstating the case (for example, much is known about Paleoindian stone-tool technology and butchering), but his point is clear: geographic and temporal relationships between Paleoindian sites and assemblages are most often based on apparent similarities or differences in artifact styles. Such emphasis on projectile point typology has resulted in considerable confusion, however, because this emphasis has not been matched by clear definitions of types, which are rare or nonexistent, or by concomitant technological and functional analyses, and comparisons of types, which also are very rare, or by consideration of site function, raw material type and availability, and artifact life histories (Judge 1974; Knudson 1983; Frison and Todd 1987; Bamforth 1991; Hofman 1992).

The first Paleoindian chronology for the Southern High Plains and one of the first for North America was proposed by Sellards (1952) and refined by Sellards and Evans (1960). The cultural sequence, from oldest to youngest, was established as: the Llano Complex (characterized by Clovis points and mammoth remains); the Folsom Complex (characterized by Folsom points and extinct bison); the Plainview Complex (characterized by Plainview points and extinct bison); and the Portales Complex (characterized by a collection of unfluted lanceolate points from the Clovis site, including types believed similar to Eden, Scottsbluff, and San Jon, in association with extinct bison; Sellards 1952:72–74). This sequence largely was based on the stratified archaeological record at Clovis and radiocarbon dating at Lubbock Lake and Plainview. The stratigraphic relationship of Clovis, Folsom, and the unfluted lanceolate types of the Portales Complex was based on the work at Clovis. The relationship of Plainview to the other complexes was somewhat problematic because little Plainview material was found at Clovis. Krieger (1947), in his description and discussion of the Plainview collection, proposed that the style is intermediate between Folsom and the later lanceolate styles based on characteristics of Plainview shared with both of the other styles. Subsequent radiocarbon dating of bone from Lubbock Lake believed to be of Folsom age and dating of shell from the Plainview bone bed tended to confirm that Plainview post-dated Folsom.

The basic sequence of Clovis–Folsom–unfluted lanceolates essentially was upheld on the Great Plains in succeeding decades, and only recently has evidence emerged in the northern Great Plains suggesting a more complex temporal relationship between the fluted assemblages and the unfluted styles (Frison 1993; Haynes 1993). On the Southern High Plains, however, the basic sequence still is valid, though temporal overlap in artifact styles is now apparent, as discussed below (FIG. 5.1), and the initial radiocarbon

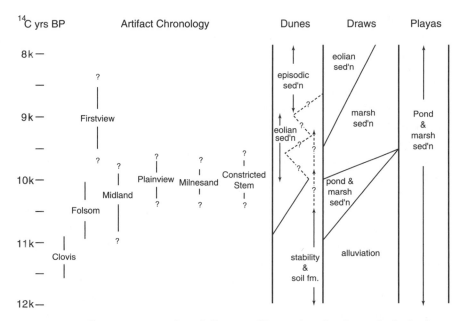

FIGURE 5.1. Summary geocultural diagram, illustrating the chronological relationships of artifact styles and geologic events throughout Paleoindian time on the Southern High Plains.

dating from Lubbock Lake and Plainview is questionable if not invalid (Johnson and Holliday 1980; Holliday and Johnson 1986). The Clovis-Folsom relationship remains straightforward. Since Sellards' and Evans' work, most of the refinements in the sequence dealt with sorting out the chronological and technological relationships of the various unfluted lanceolate styles.

A tree-ring calibrated chronology for Paleoindian occupations throughout the Plains shows that the "absolute" ages are ca. 2000 years older than the uncalibrated ages (Eighmy and LaBelle 1996). The calibration does not significantly alter the sequence of Paleoindian traditions, with one exception. The revised chronology suggests a substantial overlap in Clovis and Folsom ages. The overlap may be real, but stratigraphic data repeatedly show that Folsom followed Clovis. The calibration chronology is based on radiocarbon ages from throughout the Plains. Geographically defined subsets of the data might illuminate chronological subtleties.

Pre-Clovis occupations are proposed for many parts of the Americas (e.g., Bryan 1986), but there is essentially no evidence for occupation on the Llano Estacado prior to Clovis times. The single possibility is the butchered bison bone in the buried terrace at Lubbock Lake (Johnson 1991). The feature probably is >11,100 yrs BP, but whether it is early Clovis or pre-Clovis is unknown.

CLOVIS

Unequivocal Clovis occupations are documented at the Clovis type site and at the Miami site, and strongly hinted at at Poverty Hill (FIG. 5.2). A Clovis-age occupation also is known from Lubbock Lake. Clovis artifacts also are reported from surface collections at the Car Body, Ro-16, and Robertson sites, and from 14 additional sites reported by Hester (1975a: table 13-1) (see Appendix 1), 6 of which are more than just isolated finds (Tables 3.13, 3.18, 3.22; FIG. 5.2). Four radiocarbon ages are available from the Clovis site and range from ca. 11,600 to ca. 10,800 yrs BP (Haynes 1993: table 1; Johnson and Holliday 1996), but Haynes (1993:226) favors a date of ca. 11,000 years for the occupation. Dating at Miami brackets the Clovis level between ca. 11,400 and 10,500 yrs BP. The Lubbock Lake feature dates to ca. 11,100 yrs BP. The Clovis occupation of the Llano Estacado therefore is bracketed between 11,400 and 10,800 yrs BP, and probably was confined to a shorter interval (perhaps 11,200–10,900), based on radiometric dating in neighboring regions (Haynes 1992). This age range fits well with the beginning of the Folsom occupation (10,800 yrs BP). The chronostratigraphic and lithostratigraphic "fit" between Clovis and Folsom on the Southern High Plains is best seen at the Clovis type site.

The environment during the Clovis period probably was the most equable of any time during the human occupation of the Southern High Plains. Shortly before the Clovis occupation, the region may have been a cool-dry grassland or savanna, based on limited data from pollen (Hall and Valastro 1995), stable-carbon isotopes (FIG. 5.3), and the presence of eolian silt at the Miami site (Holliday et al. 1994). By Clovis times the region was still cool, but possibly wetter than in preceding millennia. All of the draws contained permanent, relatively high-energy streams. Upland settings, including both playa basins and areas of present-day dune fields, commonly had ponds or marshes (Reeves 1965; Holliday 1995a,b; Holliday et al. 1996). Pedological, paleontological, and isotopic data indicate that during the Clovis occupation the region probably was a grassland (perhaps a savanna) subjected to lower seasonal extremes relative to today, and, therefore, effective moisture was higher (Dalquest 1986; Graham 1987; Holliday 1987a, 1990b, 1995b; Johnson 1991; Dalquest and Schultz 1992).

Butzer (1991:148–149) speculated that "most of the Great Plains" probably was not suitable for occupation in the late Pleistocene (>12,000

FIGURE 5.2. The distribution of Clovis sites on the Southern High Plains.

yrs BP), because resources were neither abundant nor predictable and because environmental hazards were a major threat. While environments of
the northern Great Plains may have been harsh, especially in winter, they
likely were suitable for descendants of the Beringian colonists. Moreover,
the environment of the Southern High Plains during the Clovis occupation probably was near ideal for hunters and gatherers. Water was abundant, with perennial streams in all draws, fed by runoff and, probably more
importantly, by springs, and many lake basins contained permanent fresh
water (FIG. 5.1). Game, including megafauna and smaller animals, was varied and likely abundant (Johnson 1986a, 1991). By the end of the Clovis
occupation, however, most of the megafauna was gone. At Lubbock Lake,
for example, the Pleistocene varieties of bison, elephant, horse, camel,
bear, and armadillo were present at 11,100 yrs BP, but only the bison is
present in overlying deposits associated with the Folsom occupation and
dated to 10,800 yrs BP (Johnson 1987c).

Haynes (1991, 1993) proposes that the Southern High Plains was subjected to drought during the Clovis occupation and that megafauna extinctions at the end of the Pleistocene were linked to the drought. The data are
from localities throughout the southwestern U.S., but the principal site on
the Llano Estacado is Clovis. Erosional disconformities in Unit B at Clovis
are interpreted as deflation surfaces resulting from drought, and Unit D is
interpreted as being the result of increased spring discharge due to increased effective precipitation following the drought. Alternately, the disconformities in Unit B at Clovis may represent alluvial cut-and-fill sequences, perhaps related to fluctuations in the spring discharge that filled
the Clovis paleobasin. Clovis artifacts may have been associated with eolian sands at the Car Body site, on the south side of Blackwater Draw just
south of the Clovis site (FIG. 3.3), and Clovis-age eolian sedimentation was
also hypothesized for Lubbock Lake (Holliday 1985b), but alluvial sand
was abundant in both Blackwater Draw and Yellowhouse Draw at the time.
Localized eolian reworking of the sand undoubtedly took place, but there
are no indications that such reworking had any regional environmental
significance.

There is no other evidence for a regional, Clovis-age drought from
dunes, draws, or playas (Holliday 1995a,b). The layer of loess below the
Clovis bone bed at the Miami site also is cited as evidence for a Clovis
drought, but this eolian deposit is separated from the occupation level by
lacustrine sediment (Holliday et al. 1994). At Miami, therefore, the megafauna survived under more moist conditions following an arid interval. A
pre-Clovis arid interval and more moist Clovis period also are indicated at

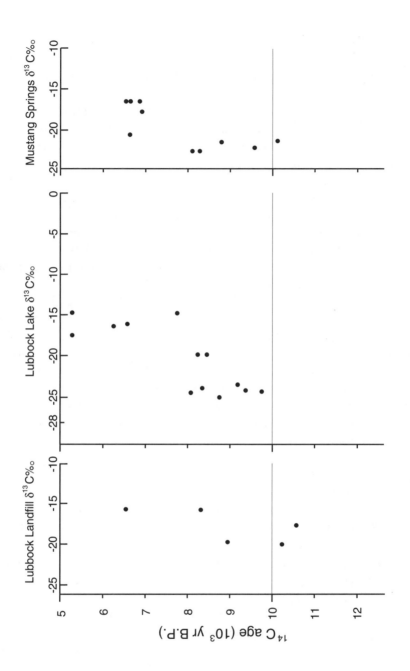

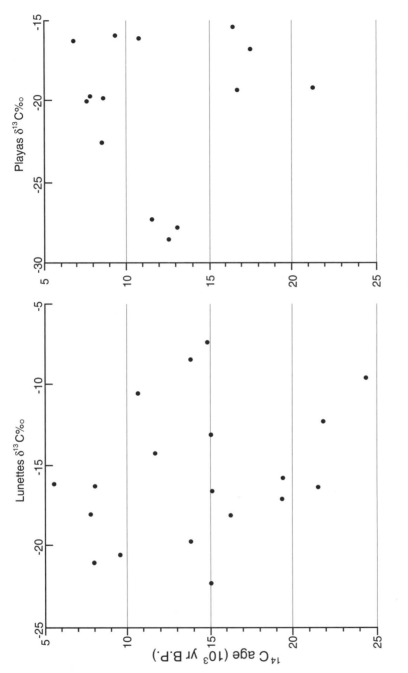

FIGURE 5.3. Stable-carbon isotopes from buried A-horizons in lunettes and from organic-rich mud in playa fill.

San Jon. Limited isotopic data from lunette soils (FIG. 5.3) hint at a warming trend that began before the Clovis occupation, but this isotopic shift toward heavier values culminated during the Folsom occupation. The few isotope values from playa sediments indicate that vegetation in these settings also underwent a dramatic change to warm-season grasses at the close of the Pleistocene, but a change that began in or after Clovis time.

FOLSOM

Three sites on the Llano Estacado, Anderson Basin #2, Clovis, and Lubbock Lake, yielded *in situ* Folsom remains (FIG. 5.4). Folsom artifacts also were found on the surface, but in reasonable stratigraphic contexts, at San Jon, Elida, Ro-16, Shifting Sands, Wyche Ranch, Midland, and Tatum (FIG. 5.4). Hester (1975a:table 13-1) (see Appendix 1) reports an additional 29 Folsom sites based on surface collections, 19 of which are more than isolated finds (Tables 3.13, 3.18, 3.22; FIG. 5.4). Adjacent to the High Plains, Folsom features were excavated at Lake Theo, Lipscomb, Waugh, and Cooper (FIG. 4.1). The bone bed at Bonfire Shelter (FIG. 4.1) also yielded a single Folsom artifact. The Folsom occupation of the Llano Estacado is reasonably well dated. Two of the radiocarbon ages from Lubbock Lake are on samples from a Folsom bone bed excavated by Sellards (Holliday, Johnson, Haas, and Stuckenrath 1983, 1985). The other Folsom ages from Lubbock Lake and all from Clovis are from strata known to contain Folsom features but came from features that produced no diagnostic artifacts. Four ages are available from Unit D at Clovis and range from 10,500 to 10,200 yrs BP (with relatively large standard deviations). Twelve ages from stratum 2d at Lubbock Lake bracket the Folsom occupation between 10,800 and 10,200 yrs BP. The Folsom features at Lipscomb and Waugh are dated between 10,900 and 10,200 yrs BP. At both Lake Theo and Bonfire Shelter, the Folsom bone beds are >10,000 yrs BP. The age range for the Folsom occupation of the Southern High Plains, therefore, is 10,800–10,200 yrs BP.

The environment of the region during the Folsom occupation was broadly similar to that of Clovis—a savanna under relatively cooler and wetter conditions owing to reduced seasonality—although the changes affecting the globe at the close of the Pleistocene also were influencing the Llano Estacado (Johnson 1986a, 1987b; Graham 1987) (FIG. 5.1). Early in the Folsom occupation, perennial streams still existed in some reaches of the draws, but extensive freshwater ponds producing diatomaceous muds also began to appear where discharge declined. Water levels in these lakes and ponds fluctuated; the water was centimeters to meters deep or it was at

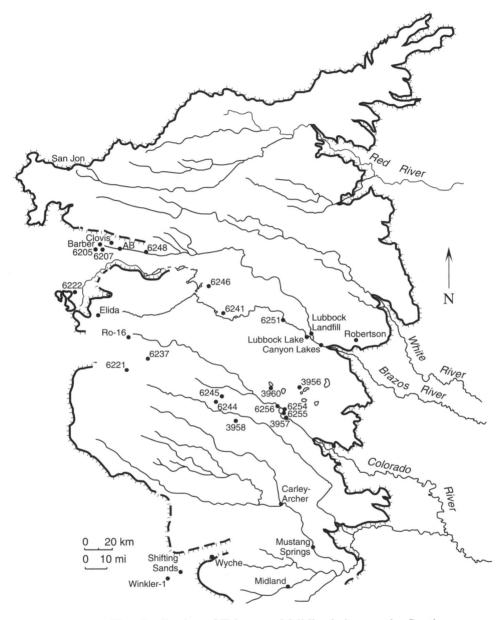

FIGURE 5.4. The distribution of Folsom and Midland sites on the Southern High Plains.

or below the surface, exposing the floor of the draw. By the end of Folsom times, however, many of the streams ceased to flow, and the diatomite lakes evolved into muddy marshes. The playas and salinas continued to have seasonal if not perennial fresh water (Holliday et al. 1996), although details of lake level histories and water chemistry are lacking.

The transition from flowing water to standing water and marshy conditions represents a dramatic hydrologic change in the draws. The widespread decrease in water in the draws was the result of decrease in regional effective precipitation from the late Pleistocene to the early Holocene. This decrease affected both runoff and spring discharge. Paleontological data (Johnson 1986a, 1987b; Graham 1987) document this environmental change as well as sedimentologic and stratigraphic information (Holliday 1995b).

Folsom occupants at Clovis, Ro-16, Shifting Sands, Wyche Ranch, Midland, and possibly Tatum, Elida, and Carley-Archer also experienced the first significant period of eolian deposition during the human occupation of the Llano Estacado. The stratigraphic manifestation of these sediments, as localized sand sheets (some in lowland settings or depressions) heavily modified by pedogenesis, suggests that the sand accumulated in well-vegetated sites. This situation in turn suggests that regional drying was affecting the landscape by reducing vegetation cover and allowing the surface to be deflated, at least in the sandier western and southwestern areas of the Llano Estacado. Lowland areas were still sufficiently moist enough to support vegetation, however, which trapped some of the deflated sand.

Warming during the Folsom occupation also is indicated by carbon isotopes from lunettes and playas (FIG. 5.3). The few data points for this time show a dramatic shift toward heavier values, a change that began earlier (before the Clovis occupation) in the well-drained, exposed setting of lunettes. Warming and drying during the Folsom occupation mark the initial stages of the environmental conditions that characterized much of the early and middle Holocene.

Haynes (1975, 1995) interprets the Folsom-age lacustrine and paludal deposits at the Clovis site as marking an increase in spring discharge due to increase in effective moisture over the preceding Clovis period, which was marked by a hypothesized drought. Damming by dunes is the only mechanism proposed that would impound the water (C. V. Haynes, pers. comm. 1994). However, the Clovis-age deposits primarily are alluvial and indicative of water flowing out of the spring-fed basin. An increase in discharge likely would prevent formation of a dam or quickly destroy one. Formation of eolian dunes during increased effective precipitation also seems unlikely. An alternative interpretation is that the shift from alluvial deposition to lacustrine deposition (and damming by eolian sediment) reflects a decrease in spring discharge resulting from an overall decline in effective precipitation (Holliday 1995b). A trend toward a relatively warmer and drier environment from Clovis to Folsom time is strongly suggested by data from draws (Holliday 1995b), eolian strata (noted above), and isotopes (FIG. 5.3). Eolian sedimentation at Clovis, clearly documented, combined with declining spring discharge, could have effectively impounded water in the basin.

The results of the High Plains Paleoecology Project were used to propose that the Southern High Plains was under a cold, wet boreal forest at the close of the Pleistocene, particularly during the Folsom occupation (e.g., Wendorf 1970). The data now available from stratigraphy, sedimentology, pedology, paleontology, paleobotany, and isotopes support an interpretation more closely approximating that of Wendorf and Hester (1962: 159) (and Antevs 1954, before them), who proposed that the terminal Pleistocene environment "consisted of a savanna grassland with abundant ponds and streams" and trees along the escarpments to the north and west. Eolian strata and isotopes further suggest that at the close of the Pleistocene the region may have been subjected to conditions warmer and drier than previously suspected.

LATE PALEOINDIAN

There are more sites on the Llano Estacado with unfluted Paleoindian styles (66) than the total of known Clovis (20) and Folsom sites (43) in the region, based on the data presented in Chapter 3 and the survey information presented by Hester (1975a: table 13-1) (see Appendix 1) and Kibler (1991) (FIG. 5.5). However, the age and typological relationships of the various unfluted, lanceolate Paleoindian projectile point styles historically have been much less clear than those of the fluted styles. These relationships among the unfluted lanceolate styles are becoming more apparent in the northern Great Plains, where large artifact assemblages from many well-dated sites have undergone relatively intense analyses (Frison 1991a,b, 1993). On the Southern High Plains, however, the stratigraphic, radiometric, and typological relationships of the unfluted, Paleoindian artifact traditions remain confused, although some order is emerging. There are three issues of particular significance in this regard: (1) the dating of the Midland style and its relationship to Folsom; (2) the age relationships of other unfluted styles, especially Plainview, to Folsom; and (3) the age and

FIGURE 5.5. The distribution of Late Paleoindian sites (those with unfluted, lanceolate projectile points exclusive of Midland) on the Southern High Plains.

typological relationships of Plainview and other unfluted, lanceolate Paleo-indian point styles, including those of the "Portales Complex."

Among the unfluted lanceolate styles, the one most often linked directly to fluted points on the basis of morphology and technology is the Midland point. This style is similar to Folsom, except lacking flutes. Since excavations at the type Midland site (Wendorf and others 1955; Wendorf and Krieger 1959) there has been considerable debate over the relationship of Midland to Folsom (e.g., Agogino 1969; Judge 1970; Amick 1995). Following the initial field work at the site the points were referred to simply as "unfluted Folsom" (Wendorf et al. 1955:49). The term "Midland point" was proposed following subsequent excavations at the Midland site (Wendorf and Krieger 1959), but only as a typological category. The relationship of Folsom to Midland was unknown (Wendorf and Krieger 1959:67). The distinction between Midland and Folsom took on added significance with evidence that the Midland skeleton was contemporaneous with Midland points and that both were substantially older than Folsom. The idea that Midland substantially pre-dated Folsom was not long-lived, although Krieger (1964:table 3) associated the site with Clovis occupations, but without elaboration. Presumably he viewed Midland as a predecessor to Folsom.

Subsequent debates on Midland versus Folsom implicitly or explicitly accepted the two as essentially contemporaneous and focused on the cultural and technological relationship of the styles. The argument essentially is whether Midland is "fully contemporary with Folsom and . . . part of the same technological system" (Hofman et al. 1990:240) or whether "Midland points represent a distinct and separate complex . . . [and] a different cultural group perhaps closely related to Folsom in time, technology, and economic orientation" (Hofman et al. 1990:243) (see also Blaine 1968, 1971, 1991; Judge 1970; Irwin 1971). The proposition that Midland points simply are Folsom points too thin to be fluted no longer is considered valid (Hofman et al. 1990). The two types have yet to be found in place together in stratified contexts on the Southern High Plains, however, and to date, the collection from Winkler-1 (Blaine 1968, 1991) is the only "pure" Midland assemblage reported. Hofman et al. (1990:243) further note that Shifting Sands initially yielded a "pure" Midland assemblage, but further collection as the blowout enlarged produced Folsom artifacts. The stratigraphic subtleties of the Folsom-Midland occupations at Shifting Sands and Winkler-1 in the Andrews Dunes have yet to be established, however. As noted in Chapter 3, the Midland stratum at Winkler-1 may be equivalent to or older than the Folsom layer at Shifting Sands.

Many archaeologists note the presence of unfluted points in Folsom assemblages throughout the Great Plains (Bamforth 1991; Frison 1991a: 50–51, 1993; Hofman 1992). Irwin-Williams et al. (1973) report Midland points from the Hell Gap site on the northern Plains of Wyoming, and their data suggest that the Midland style persisted after Folsom. Hell Gap is the only site to yield purported Midland points from a dated, stratified context. This site is far outside of the core area of Midland sites on the southern Llano Estacado, however, and the artifact sample is small and unstudied, and the typological categorization questionable (Frison 1993). Frison (1993:12) also notes that some of the Midland points from Hell Gap could fit the unfluted Folsom category and others resemble Goshen points. Despite the presence of unfluted points in Folsom assemblages in the central and western United States, Midland appears to be most common on the southern Llano Estacado (FIG. 54; Hofman 1989a:38, 1992:212; Amick 1995).

There have been few systematic attempts to compare the Midland– unfluted Folsom assemblages to Folsom materials, but several authors have suggested some plausible relationships. At a regional scale, Bamforth (1991) suggested that the presence of both unfluted (Midland) and fluted Folsom points may reflect the presence of flint-knappers with varying degrees of skill in executing a flute. This argument is supported by the observation that in Folsom communal bison kills, if only the most skilled knappers prepare the projectiles, then few unfluted points should be found. This is in fact the case in the few communal Folsom kills reported from the Plains.

Hofman (1992:212) proposed that on the Southern High Plains the lack of fluting on Midland points may be a matter of resource conservation. The area of highest concentration of Midland sites, in the vicinity of the type site on the southwestern Llano Estacado, is farther from the stone resources favored by Folsom tool makers (Alibates agate and Edwards Formation cherts; Appendix 2) than any other on the Southern High Plains. In an area far from preferred supplies the elimination of the fluting step makes Midland production less risky. This explanation is attractive because it explains both the geographic distribution of Midland and the lack of fluting. Matters of skill and risk in the production of flutes are related, and therefore the Bamforth and Hofman hypotheses are complementary. Amick (1995) tested Hofman's hypothesis by comparing various geographic, raw material, and technological attributes of Folsom and Midland. The results essentially support Hofman's idea. Amick (1995:34) concludes that "Midland points are most often made from Edwards chert and associated with the Southern Plains. . . . Midland points may reflect a special case of Folsom point manufacture that allows a more conservative use of tool stone." Furthermore, "Midland technology may simply represent a strategy used by Folsom groups for conserving tool stone under conditions of high mobility and logistical land use on the Southern Plains" (p. 35).

Midland also may represent the transition from fluted styles to the classic unfluted lanceolate points, specifically Plainview (Hofman et al. 1990). There are some technological similarities between the two styles (Knudson 1983) and apparently some overlap in age between Folsom and Plainview (and therefore between Midland and Plainview), discussed below. Two of the unfluted lanceolate points from Bonfire Shelter (FIGS. 4.2A,C), in the bone bed producing a Folsom point, are very similar to one of the type Midland specimens (FIG. 3.36B) (Dibble and Lorrain 1968:36).

In summary, Midland appears to be essentially contemporaneous with Folsom, and there is some evidence that it also slightly pre-dates and slightly post-dates Folsom. Folsom and Midland both may have evolved from the Clovis tradition, with the Midland style and technology evolving into Plainview and the fluted point styles becoming an evolutionary dead end. The similarities between Midland and Folsom, Midland and Goshen, and Midland and Plainview raise another possibility: perhaps Goshen, Midland, and Plainview represent technological and morphological traditions that paralleled, were directly related to, and continued beyond Clovis-Folsom.

The Plainview style was the first unfluted Paleoindian point type to be formally described and proposed based on a sizeable collection (by Krieger 1947) (the San Jon "type" was based on a single artifact; Roberts 1942). Through the years, however, Plainview became a catchall term for lanceolate, concave-base projectile points (Wheat 1972; Knudson 1983; Johnson and Holliday 1980). This confusion in part stems from the wide morphological variability in the type collection, which is not unusual for projectile point collections from kill sites, owing to "technological restraints and point reworking" (Hofman 1989a:39–40). But much of the confusion also stems from type categorization based on offhand gross morphological features rather than careful comparisons of morphology, technological attributes, and age relationships. Knudson's (1983) study of the Plainview collection remains one of the few systematic, technological investigations of Late Paleoindian lanceolate styles.

Plainview assemblages were found in place on the Llano Estacado at the Plainview type site, Lubbock Lake, Williamson, and Ryan, and off the Llano Estacado at Horace Rivers, Lake Theo, and Bonfire Shelter, and possibly at Rex Rodgers. Projectile points with Plainview affinities also are reported in collections from Anderson Basin #2, Bethel, Clovis, Carley-Archer, Milnesand, Mustang Springs, and Ro-16. Krieger (1947), when describing the type collection, and Sellards and Evans (1960) correctly believed Plainview to immediately post-date Folsom; it may also overlap late Folsom time. Some questions continue to be raised about the dating of Plainview (e.g., Haynes 1993), but in fact Plainview has the best stratigraphic and radiocarbon age control of any nonfluted artifact style on the Llano Estacado. Plainview artifacts were stratigraphically above Folsom at Lubbock Lake (Johnson and Holliday 1980) and Lake Theo (Harrison and Killen 1978), and probably were above Folsom at the Clovis site (Hester 1972). The type Midland collection contains at least one artifact (FIG. 3.36B) quite similar to the type Plainview assemblage (FIG. 3.41). Off of the Llano Estacado, at Bonfire Shelter, Plainview essentially is contemporaneous with Folsom.

The Plainview assemblages at Lubbock Lake and Lake Theo date to ca. 10,000 yrs BP, but date to 10,300 yrs BP or older at Bonfire Shelter. At Ryan, the Plainview cache was above radiocarbon samples dating between 10,600 and 9200 yrs BP. The younger age could be contaminated due to proximity to the surface of the playa fill, but it could also be a reliable age. Artifacts morphologically similar to Plainview from other sites in the region generally are younger than 10,000 yrs BP. The Rex Rodgers assemblage probably is between 10,000 and 9600 yrs BP (discussed below). The Horace Rivers artifacts date between 9300 and 9000 yrs BP.

Five radiocarbon ages are available for the type Plainview collection (Table 3.12). The ages determined in the 1950s are rejected because of the problems with dating shell and bone in the early years of the radiocarbon method (Taylor 1987). The two ages on bone fit in well with the other Plainview ages, although radiocarbon ages on bone apatite are questionable (Hassan et al. 1977; Taylor 1992). The age of ca. 8900 for stratum 2 at the site, stratigraphically equivalent to or above the original bone bed, provides an upper limiting age. An age assessment of 10,000 yrs BP seems most likely given the observation that the Bonfire artifacts represent "the same major technological and stylistic subsystems as Plainview" (Knudson 1983:165). The dating from Ryan and Horace Rivers, however, may hint that Plainview, or at least the general Plainview morphological style, persisted long after 10,000 yrs BP.

Unequivocal Plainview artifacts have not been reported from dated contexts outside of the localities noted above. Elsewhere on the Great Plains, however, artifacts displaying very similar morphologies indicate that the basic Plainview-like shape (lanceolate, unfluted, parallel [or collateral?] flaking, concave base, and parallel sides) was the longest-lived of any among Paleoindian assemblages. Similarities to the Clovis-age Goshen style are noted by Frison (1993) and are emphatically stated by Haynes (1993: 225). The basic shape, therefore, dates to at least 11,000 yrs BP (Chapter 4) on the northern Great Plains. At the Wilson-Leonard site on the Edwards Plateau (Chapter 4), a general style initially linked to Plainview (Collins et al. 1993), but now termed "St. Mary's Hall" (Bousman et al. 1994), is dated to ca. 9700–8800, correlating with the Plainview-like artifacts at Horace Rivers and possibly with the Plainview material at Ryan. The Golondrina style, which also has gross morphological similarities to Plainview, fits into this time range as well (T. Hester 1994). In summary, this basic morphological style appears during the Clovis-Folsom transition, during late Folsom and early post-Folsom time, and again around 9000 yrs BP.

Wheat (1972) grouped Plainview into his proposed "Firstview Complex," a post-Folsom, southern Plains Paleoindian assemblage (discussed further below) viewed as a temporal equivalent to the Cody Complex of the northern Plains. Most Cody sites date between 9500 and 8000 yrs BP, however, generally younger than most Plainview sites (as noted above). Wheat's original dating of Firstview placed it at around 10,000 yrs BP, based on a single and probably erroneous date from the type locality (the Olsen-Chubbock site). Bamforth (1991:317–318) also identifies several key morphological and technological characteristics of Cody and Firstview missing in Plainview (stemming and evidence for a complex, multistage reduction strategy).

The artifact collection from Rex Rodgers further illustrates the unresolved typological issues involving Plainview and other styles. Three of the five projectile points from the bone bed are "side-hollowed" styles referred to as "Rodgers side-hollowed" points (Willey et al. 1978:67). This style, never before reported from *in situ* contexts on the High Plains, has striking morphological similarities to various southeastern styles such as Dalton and San Patrice (Willey et al. 1978:66–67; Ensor 1986; Hofman 1989a). The other two points from Rex Rodgers are unfluted, lanceolate artifacts with gross morphological similarities to Plainview (Willey et al. 1978:65–66). These typological comparisons are admittedly based on gross morphology, but done so in the absence of systematic technological analysis or other data.

The dating of the Rex Rodgers feature is not firm, but comparisons with similar artifact styles suggest some general age relationships. Bone apatite from the Rex Rodgers site was dated to 9400 yrs BP (Table 3.23), but, as noted, bone apatite can yield inaccurate results. Speer (1986) also indicates that the age may be a minimum estimate. At Horn Shelter in Central Texas (Chapter 4) the "Brazos fishtail" point, generally similar to the Rodgers point, is associated with charcoal ages between 9500 and 10,000 yrs BP (Watt 1978; Redder 1985). In the southeastern United States, the Dalton and probably the San Patrice styles date between 10,500 and 9900 yrs BP and possibly are as late as ca. 9600 yrs BP (Goodyear 1982, 1991; Ensor 1986; Wyckoff 1989; see also L. Johnson 1989:13–26). These data suggest that the Rex Rodgers site and the Rodgers side-hollow style date to at least ca. 9600 yrs BP and possibly to 10,000 yrs BP. Explaining the association of two such otherwise geographically distinct point styles has proven difficult (Willey et al. 1978:66–67). As Hofman (1989a:40) observes, "The variety of projectile points recovered at Rex Rodgers further illustrates the problems, incompleteness, and limitations of our available typological framework for Paleo-Indian assemblage studies in the Southern Plains region."

The age, typological, and technological relationships of most other post-Folsom lanceolate styles on the Southern High Plains are considerably less clear than those of Clovis, Folsom, and Plainview. These styles include various types identified as San Jon, Agate Basin, Milnesand, Firstview, Eden, and Scottsbluff. Several investigators suggest that the San Jon and Agate Basin styles share some contemporaneity with Folsom. At the San Jon site there is some evidence for the chronological association of a Folsom point and the single San Jon type specimen (Roberts 1942:8; Judson 1953), but direct stratigraphic correlation is impossible due to the deep and wide arroyos separating the San Jon and Folsom find sites (Chapter 3).

Artifacts referred to as "Agate Basin" are reported from the Clovis site, but this categorization is based on general morphological characteristics (long, narrow, parallel-flaked with a constricted stem and straight to slightly convex base) and not on a systematic comparison with the type Agate Basin collection from Wyoming. Haynes and Agogino (1966:819) suggest that these "Agate Basin" types share a "late contemporaneity" with Folsom, based on their work around the spring conduits. Other "Agate Basin" material at Clovis came from lower Unit E (Hester 1972:59), likely dating to ca. 10,000 yrs BP.

Other constricted-stem styles appear to be generally contemporaneous with "Agate Basin." At Lubbock Lake a collection of projectile points broadly similar in morphology to Agate Basin is dated to ca. 10,000 yrs BP (Holliday and Johnson 1984). Several artifacts from the Paleoindian bone bed at Bonfire Shelter, also dated to ca. 10,000 yrs BP, appear to be constricted-stem points (Dibble and Lorrain 1968:figs. 15A,B,C), but may also be knives (D. Dibble, pers. comm. 1983). The dating of the constricted-stem lanceolates at Clovis, Lubbock Lake, and Bonfire is similar to the dates on Agate Basin occupations in the northern Plains (Frison and Stanford 1982:178–180; Frison 1991a:table 2.2). The poorly defined "Texas Angostura" style is another constricted-stem point reported from some collections (e.g., the Robertson site; inventory on file at the Crosby County Pioneer Museum). Age control for this style likewise is poor, but the style seems to post-date Plainview–Agate Basin time. Artifacts referred to as Angostura date to 8800–8000 yrs BP at the Wilson-Leonard site in Central Texas (Bousman et al. 1994) and to ca. 8800 yrs BP on the western Edwards Plateau (Turner and Hester 1993:73) (Chapter 4).

The Milnesand type, another constricted-stem style, was found in good archaeological contexts only at the type Milnesand and the Williamson sites. The Milnesand and Williamson sites yielded the largest collections of Milnesand and Plainview points, respectively, known in the region, and the Milnesand type collection is the only sizeable assemblage of this type reported. Of the 100 or so points from each site, there are several similar to Plainview from the Milnesand collection and several similar to Milnesand from the Williamson collection, suggesting that Milnesand is contemporaneous with Plainview. The proximity and similarity of the two sites also suggest a temporal relationship, as do the similarities in the "lithic production subsystem" (Knudson 1983:165; see also Bamforth 1991:317–319). This apparent contemporaneity, the morphological and technological similarities between Milnesand and the constricted-stem artifacts from Lubbock Lake (Holliday and Johnson 1984; R. Knudson, pers. comm. 1988), and the similarities between Milnesand and at least some of the artifacts from the Plainview level at Bonfire Shelter (FIG. 4.2D; Dibble and Lorrain 1968:36, figs. 15A,B,C) indicate that Milnesand dates to ca. 10,000 yrs BP.

A variety of unfluted lanceolate styles formed part of the "Portales Complex" (Sellards 1952:72–74), the first post-Folsom Paleoindian assemblage formally described for the Llano Estacado. This collection and the defined complex are the source of considerable typological confusion and exemplify the long-standing problems of Late Paleoindian typology. For example, Sellards (1952:74) describes the type Portales collection to include artifacts similar to Eden, Scottsbluff, Plainview, and San Jon types, and Hester (1972:37, 136–137) describes Milnesand, Eden, Scottsbluff, Angostura, and Plainview types. Agogino and Rovner (1969), Hester (1972), and Hofman (1989a), among others, suspect that the Portales

Complex is a mix of assemblages. These suspicions were confirmed by the work of Johnson (1986b; Johnson and Holliday 1996), who demonstrated that the bone bed producing the assemblage was indeed churned and probably was a mixture of at least two bone beds. The "Portales Complex" therefore no longer is valid.

Full reevaluation of the type "Portales Complex" assemblage is not possible because provenience and stratigraphic data are inadequate, but reexamination of the type Portales collection and investigations of unmixed, dated assemblages at other sites are beginning to resolve some of the typological and chronological confusion over the Late Paleoindian artifact styles included in the type collection. The Plainview and Milnesand styles were discussed above. Classification of other points in the "Portales Complex" such as Eden and Scottsbluff (e.g., Sellards 1952; Hester 1972) raises several typological issues. The Eden and Scottsbluff styles typify the Cody Complex, the classic Late Paleoindian tradition of the northern Plains (e.g., Frison 1991a). As noted by Knudson (1983:1), however, "Sites assigned to the Cody Complex have a vast distribution, from Wisconsin to Alberta to Texas, over a 3,000-year period . . . , suggesting a rather unusual post-Pleistocene cultural stability." Moreover, "the Cody complex . . . is a complicated archaeological construct having multiple interpretations" (Hofman 1989a:42), and "there are few detailed published reports of the sites and assemblages assigned to Cody, and many comparative generalizations have been based on preliminary comments and hearsay" (Knudson 1983:1).

The problems in assigning southern Plains Paleoindian assemblages to the Cody Complex led both Knudson (1983) and Wheat (1972) to reexamine the "Cody" collections from the region. They both conclude that there are distinctive typological and technological differences between the northern and southern Plains Late Paleoindian lanceolate styles, although gross morphological similarities persist (Knudson 1970, 1983; Wheat 1972). Wheat (1972) proposed the term "Firstview" in lieu of Eden and Scottsbluff for the Portales Complex materials, and "Firstview Complex" in lieu of "Portales Complex" or "Cody Complex," based on systematic morphometric and technological analysis (Chapter 4). Bamforth (1991) presented an alternative approach, suggesting that Eden-Scottsbluff and Firstview–San Jon are northern and southern variants, respectively, of Cody, because the differences between these sets of projectile point styles are minor (see also Bradley and Frison 1987). Subsequent research indicated that the San Jon style (represented by the single type specimen as well as artifacts in the

Portales collection) simply is the result of reworking the Firstview style (Wheat 1976).

Wheat's approach to Late Paleoindian artifact typology is criticized by some (Bonnichsen and Keyser 1982; Bradley and Frison 1987:225; Hofman 1989a), but the basic conclusions of Wheat and Knudson cannot be ignored: there seem to be some subtle but nevertheless distinct technological differences between southern and northern Plains Late Paleoindian assemblages. The morphological similarities between the northern and southern assemblages are obvious, but identification of the southern Plains material as "Cody Complex" may obscure or overlook significant cultural and temporal regionalization. A typology other than Cody Complex for the southern assemblages therefore seems prudent, and Firstview is used here.

Firstview assemblages are reported only from a few sites on the Southern High Plains: Clovis, Lubbock Lake, the single point at San Jon, and surface collections at Seminole-Rose, Bedford Ranch, and also in extensive surface collections from the Seminole-Rose area (Polyak and Williams 1986; Kibler 1991). The "type" Portales Complex collection at the Clovis site came from a bone bed in upper Unit E. Johnson (1986b) excavated several blocks of the bone bed removed by Sellards' crew. Sediment samples collected during excavation of the blocks were dated to ca. 8700 yrs BP and ca. 8900 yrs BP (Johnson and Holliday 1996; Table 3.2). Haynes (1995) notes Cody Complex features throughout Unit E, dating 10,000–8500 yrs BP, and Cody Complex artifacts in lower Unit F, between 8500 and 8000 yrs BP. Many if not all of these features probably can be considered Firstview. Even if they are not all Firstview, however, these assemblages are indicative of another long-lived Late Paleoindian morphological tradition. At Lubbock Lake, Firstview artifacts are found in stratum 2m, which dates from 10,000 to 8500 yrs BP. Only one feature with clear Firstview associations was studied and is dated to about 8500 yrs BP (Johnson and Holliday 1981).

The environment during the Late Paleoindian occupation (<10,000 yrs BP) was one of continued change as the relatively cooler, wetter conditions of the late Pleistocene evolved into warmer and drier ones (FIG. 5.1). Water flow ceased completely in the draws early in the Holocene, and alkaline marshes became common along the valleys. Freshwater marshes were available in scattered localities, but lakes and ponds essentially were nonexistent along the draws. By the end of the early Holocene hard-water, alkaline marshes and localized desiccation typified the draws. These hydrologic changes probably resulted both from warming of water and from reduction in effective precipitation, which decreased spring and seep discharge (Holliday 1985d, 1995b; Winsborough 1988, 1995). Variations in local depositional environments probably are related to the site-specific characteristics and history of groundwater changes. Playa basins probably had seasonal water, although slopewash and eolian sediments dating to the early Holocene are noted at San Jon. Little paleoenvironmental data are available for these settings, however. Wind deflation of the High Plains surface and deposition of eolian sediments in draws and as sand sheets and dunes became increasingly common phenomena during the Late Paleoindian occupation. The environmental changes from Early to Late Paleoindian times were not unidirectional. Marsh muds and buried soils intercalated with early Holocene eolian deposits both in draws and dunes (and the San Jon playa) document fluctuations in local environments. Stable-carbon isotopes from lunettes and playas (FIG. 5.3) also indicate that in the early Holocene there were shifts back and forth between cool-season and warm-season grasses. More broadly, the presence of eolian strata combined with the isotope data suggests that the environment during the Late Paleoindian occupation shifted between wetter-cooler and warmer-drier, continuing a trend that began in earlier Paleoindian times.

Other proxy indicators (Holliday 1989b, 1995b; Johnson 1986a, 1987a, 1991) and climate models (Kutzbach 1987; COHMAP Members 1988) indicate that during Late Paleoindian times temperatures were warming or were at least warmer in the summers and effective precipitation was declining. Vegetation on the uplands probably was short-grass prairie, reflecting a continuation of the late Pleistocene prairie (Bozarth 1995; Holliday 1995b). Evidence for regional wind deflation suggests that there were periods of desiccation and reduced vegetative cover on the uplands. Culmination of the environmental changes experienced by the Paleoindians came in the form of aridity and probable drought in the middle Holocene (Johnson and Holliday 1986; Holliday 1989b, 1995a,b; Meltzer and Collins 1987; Meltzer 1991), long after the Paleoindians disappeared from the Plains.

Establishing the "end" of the Paleoindian occupation of the Southern High Plains or the timing of the Paleoindian-Archaic transition is essentially impossible given the current data base. The Archaic on the southern Plains (which also includes the Rolling Plains of Texas and Oklahoma and, by some definitions, an even broader region; Hofman 1989a) is typified by a variety of notched and stemmed projectile points, grinding equipment for processing plants, roasting ovens, rock-lined hearths, and modern animal species (Johnson and Holliday 1986; Hofman 1989a:45). There are no sites on the Llano Estacado or in nearby areas that yielded an artifact sequence illustrating the Paleoindian-Archaic transition, however. Indeed, there are no known sites with a stratified cultural sequence spanning the period from 8000 to 6000 yrs BP, although Clovis, Lubbock Lake, and Mustang Springs have potential. The youngest dated archaeological features with Paleoindian artifacts are those from the base of Unit F at the Clovis site dating between 8500 and 8000 yrs BP. Just beyond the southern edge of the Llano Estacado, two broken, unfluted lanceolate projectile points associated with *Bison antiquus* are dated to ca. 8100 yrs BP (Turpin et al. 1992). Based on these rough indicators, the end of the Paleoindian stage tentatively is placed at 8000 yrs BP.

Paleoindian Sites and Assemblages on the Southern High Plains

The Paleoindian record of the Southern High Plains is one of the best known and most intensely studied of any area in North America except for the northern Plains of Colorado, Nebraska, and Wyoming (Frison 1991a). The reasons for this notoriety are partly historical and partly geological. As discussed in Chapters 1 and 2, the region has long been the scene of interdisciplinary Paleoindian research because of the fortuitous discovery of sites such as Clovis, Lubbock Lake, and Midland, and the activities and interests of such individuals as E. B. Howard, E. H. Sellards, James Warnica, Fred Wendorf, and Eileen Johnson. Geologically, Paleoindian sites are well preserved and often geoculturally stratified because two of the more attractive site settings—draws and playas—also were slowly aggrading settings during the span of human occupation. Erosion of these sediments was minimal during this time. Slow aggradation effectively sealed and preserved the sites. In the dune fields most Paleoindian sites pre-date the accumulation of sand, and thus they, too, were buried, although they often were reexposed and deflated.

The geologic conditions that help to preserve archaeological sites on the Llano Estacado also help to hide them. Almost all of the buried sites were discovered as a result of human disturbance. Most sites exposed by natural agents are those in dunes, which are relatively easy to erode. Otherwise, the draws and playas undergo little erosion except along the margins of the Llano Estacado (e.g., San Jon). The relatively slow rate of natural exposure probably helps to explain the relatively slow rate of discovery of Paleoindian sites. Most of the investigated Paleoindian sites were found and first studied in the first 30 years of the 60-year history of such research. This first 30-year period was marked by two episodes (1930s and 1950s) of extreme drought and soil erosion, which led to discovery of many of the sites (Anderson Basin, Milnesand, Williamson, Elida, Midland). This also was a time of relatively intense searches for Paleoindian sites (by Sellards and by the members of the High Plains Paleoecology Project).

SITE SETTINGS

Sufficient geoarchaeological data are available from the sites discussed in Chapter 3 and from the survey data of Hester (1975a:table 13-1) (see Appendix 1) to offer some observations on site settings, general trends in occupation density, and archaeological diversity. Most sites, not surprisingly, are located in or near water sources (draws and playas), as noted by Hester (1975a:249–250). Besides their obvious importance as a resource, these settings also favor the preservation of sites. Indeed, the sites most likely preferred for sequential occupation—those with a good supply of water available for centuries if not millennia—also are those sites whose sedimentological settings favor preservation of the occupation debris (e.g., the pond and marsh deposits at Clovis and Lubbock Lake).

Kill sites and butchering locales are most commonly preserved in draws and playas, but camps are uncommon in these settings. Hester (1975a:249) notes that based on site survey information "campsites tend to . . . overlook either a stream channel [draw] or a pond [playa], at a distance of several hundred yards to a mile." These data on the frequency of campsites in draws and playas versus those on the uplands strongly indicate that most Paleoindian campsites are indeed on uplands and further suggest that discovery of such sites in buried contexts will be rare. Data from sites with multiple, buried Paleoindian features—Clovis and Lubbock Lake—support the results of the survey data. Among the scores of Paleoindian features reported from these two sites, only one camp (feature FA6-3 at Lubbock Lake; Johnson and Holliday 1981) is in a lowland setting. Paleoindian camping debris is known from uplands at both sites, however (e.g., Boldurian 1990).

The relative lack of reported sites buried in playa sediments is surprising given the ubiquity of playas on the Llano Estacado (there are about 25,000) and the likelihood that some if not most had permanent water in the late Pleistocene. Site visibility may again play a role in this situation. Except for rare instances where natural erosion cuts into a playa (e.g., San Jon), exposure of sites buried in playas will be only by artificial disturbance (e.g., Miami and Ryan). Playas have been filling more or less constantly throughout the Holocene. Exposure of Paleoindian sites buried in playa fill, therefore, will require relatively deep disturbance except in the case of very small, shallow playas. Statistical data are not available on the number of disturbed playas, but examination of topographic maps, soil surveys and other air photos, and ground surveys indicates that only a very small percentage of playas (ca. 1%) are subjected to the kinds of disturbance that would expose deeply buried features.

The lack of reported sites in lunettes also is surprising considering the apparent attraction of uplands (relative to lowlands) for campsites. These landforms should have been very attractive settings for occupation because they offered excellent visibility, access to water, and well-drained sites. No sites in these settings are formally reported beyond the 11 (including finds of isolated points) listed by Hester (1975a:table 13-1) and Poverty Hill. Visibility may be one reason these sites are underreported. Sites in these settings probably were exposed for a long time before burial, if they were buried at all. They would be heavily disturbed and probably contained few large objects such as bone. Bone, in any case, would not preserve well due to exposure and the highly alkaline nature of the sediments.

The dichotomy in the landscape settings of specific types of features (kills in lowlands, camps on uplands) probably is a function of both Paleoindian activities and feature preservation and visibility. Water sources in lowlands will attract game, and topographic and perhaps vegetation conditions in valleys and basins facilitate kills. Lowlands probably were not attractive settings for camps, except perhaps for a specific function such as plant processing (e.g., Bamforth 1985, on the Paleoindian camp at Lubbock Lake), due to lack of visibility and fear of frightening game. Upland areas provided a view of the surrounding countryside as well as of the draw or playa, ready access to water, game, and perhaps a variety of plants, and better drainage (and comfort), and would not be as likely to inhibit game from entering the lowlands. Kill and butchering sites, however, may have been common on uplands, but the obvious evidence of a kill or butchering site—bones—will not be preserved for 8000 to 12,000 years unless buried, which is not likely. Milnesand, Ted Williamson, and Shifting Sands were upland kills, and they were preserved largely because they were buried by dunes. Eolian sedimentation is the only mechanism likely to bury upland sites, and such activity was localized in dune fields and lunettes.

The visibility of and interest in bone beds versus camping debris may also contribute to the lack of data on camping sites in lowlands. For example, only a small portion of Paleoindian-age deposits at Lubbock Lake have been explored, and virtually all of those explorations focused on valley-axis pond and marsh deposits. Moreover, the excavations tended to focus on features obvious in the exposures of the old reservoir (i.e., bone beds). At Clovis, early workers were interested in firm associations of artifacts with Pleistocene fauna (i.e., bone beds, not likely to be associated with camps), and later investigators worked under chaotic conditions, with limited amounts of time, to excavate only the most obvious or spectacular features (again, bone beds, which are not typically associated with camps).

Kill sites are perhaps the best known and certainly most visible of Paleoindian sites on the Llano Estacado, as elsewhere on the Plains, but in contrast to the northern Great Plains, very little evidence is available to indicate that hunters used topography to trap or kill animals. The Plainview site presents the best, though not conclusive, evidence for a drive, containing a large mass of bone near the base of a steep and deep valley wall. There are hints that the bison at Milnesand and Williamson were trapped against sand dunes fringing shallow depressions. In part, this absence of evidence for use of topography in hunting may be fortuitous; the sites or the evidence was not preserved or has yet to be discovered. The opportunities for employing the landscape as a hunting tool certainly existed. Most of the draws were relatively deeply incised and locally had valley walls steep enough to impede large ungulates, and most of the saline-lake basins have steep walls. Sand dunes were also beginning to form by post-Folsom times. Any of these settings would have made efficient traps. However, the relatively low relief of the Llano Estacado may have reduced the opportunity and therefore the frequency of use of landforms for trapping or jumping. For example, arroyos, common off the Llano Estacado and apparently favored settings for kills (discussed below), are relatively uncommon landforms on the Southern High Plains. Short and often shallow arroyos form along the margins of draws and playas, but the classic long, steep-walled, deep, and rapidly aggrading arroyos so typical of many semiarid regions are and probably were rare on the Llano Estacado. All other regions of the Plains are much more heavily dissected owing to the presence of throughflowing streams with extensive drainage networks and higher local and regional relief. These alluviated terrains undoubtedly provided many more opportunities to use the landscape for trapping large game.

Stafford (1981) proposed that Paleoindian sites may be common along deeply entrenched, highly sinuous meanders of draws because these curved reaches provided easy access to the valley bottoms (due to gently sloping valley walls) and because springs, ponds, and marshes may be commonly associated with meanders. These conclusions are based mostly on geoarchaeological studies in lower Yellowhouse Draw at and below Lubbock

TABLE 5.1. Association of Paleoindian sites (surface and *in situ*) with deeply entrenched, highly sinuous meanders and with springs in draws of the Southern High Plains[1]

Sites[2]	Meander Neck	Water[3]	Multiple Occupations
Anderson Basin[4]		X	X
Clovis		X	X
Lubbock Lake	X	X	X
Lubbock Landfill		X	
Marks Beach		X	
Midland			
Mustang Springs		X	X
Plainview		X	
Seminole-Rose	X		
LA 3692		X	
LA 6205			X
LA 6207			X
LA 6243			
LA 6246		X	
LA 6248			
LA 6250			
LA 6251		X	X
LA 6256		X	
LA 6257			
41GA28	X		
41GA33	X		
41GA39			

[1] Historic springs are documented for Texas portion only (Brune 1981; Holliday 1995b). Springs at Clovis are based on geologic interpretations (Haynes and Agogino 1966; Green 1992).
[2] Named sites are discussed in Chapter 3; LA sites are from Hester (1975a: table 13-1; exclusive of the named sites and isolated finds); GA sites are from Kibler (1991, 1992).
[3] Sites with evidence for historic or prehistoric springs or other evidence of permanent water during Paleoindian occupation.
[4] Anderson Basin #2 produced Paleoindian occupation debris, but Anderson Basin #1 did not (Howard 1935a; Hester 1975b).

Lake. Kibler (1991, 1992) attempted a test of some of Stafford's proposals for site locations, though only via surface survey on lower Seminole Draw (FIG. 3.42). Three of four Paleoindian sites, including the Seminole-Rose site, were located near deeply entrenched meanders (Table 5.1). However, none of the other Paleoindian sites discussed in Chapter 3, except Lubbock Lake, or reported by Hester (1975a: table 13-1) is directly associated with deeply entrenched meanders (Table 5.1). Most sites are near meanders, however, because most of the draws have meandering valleys; straight reaches are rare (Holliday 1995b). Topography probably did not influence site selection along the draws, because almost all valley walls were easily traversed by humans, even when valley floors were deepest. Furthermore, there is no known relationship between meanders and springs (Holliday 1995b).

A more likely contributing factor to site location within or along draws, as well as regionally, noted above and by others (Hester 1975a; Kibler 1991, 1992), was the presence of permanent water. Of the sites discussed in Chapter 3 and identified by Hester (1975a: table 13-1) and Kibler (1991), exactly half are located at or near sites of historic or prehistoric springs or other evidence of perennial water during Paleoindian times (Table 5.1). Moreover, most sites (five out of seven) with evidence for multiple or long-term occupation are, not surprisingly, associated with localities with evidence of perennial (spring-fed) water. The two sites with the longest and most complete Paleoindian records, Clovis and Lubbock Lake, are the best examples.

The distribution and location of Paleoindian sites in the sand dune fields of the Llano Estacado are much more difficult to understand than the relationship of sites to draws and playas. The dunes of today were not present when Paleoindians inhabited the region, so the present landscape of the dune fields does not afford the same topographic clues to site location as do the playas and draws. And the dunes effectively bury most of the evidence of whatever features may have attracted the early occupants of the region. At Elida the nearby playa probably was attractive, but for the other known sites there are almost no clues as to the reasons the locations were chosen. At most of the sites there is evidence of surface water at some time in the geologic past (the Unit III and V marls below the Andrews Dunes and the gleying of the Blackwater Draw Formation below the Milnesand and Williamson sites, along with their microtopographic settings), but there is very little evidence for the availability of water during the Paleoindian occupations. The open landscapes of the dune field settings prior to dune construction, and the sandy nature of the soils buried below the dunes, may have contributed to destruction, by deflation, of water-lain deposits that may have been associated with the sites. The well-drained nature of the soils also could have contributed to oxidation of any organic-rich sediments that formed in wet settings.

SITE DENSITIES

Hester (1975a:256) proposes that Paleoindian populations increased from Clovis through Late Paleoindian times, based on site survey information. At Clovis, which had the most Paleoindian features reported for the Llano Estacado, Hester (1972:166) specifically identifies the Folsom occupation as the most intensive (based on artifact density in the "Brown Sand Wedge," which probably is early Folsom age), followed by Clovis, and then Late Paleoindian. Both of these observations raise several important issues of feature visibility, feature preservation, and occupation intensity. Comparison of Clovis versus Folsom occupation intensity based on data from the draws is difficult because of the very different depositional environments associated with each occupation. The draws (including the Clovis paleobasin) were relatively high-energy alluvial environments during Clovis times. Disconformities are common in the alluvium (Haynes 1995; Holliday 1995b), the result of cut-and-fill cycles or possibly deflation, indicating that some, if not substantial, portions of the Clovis record are missing. In contrast, the post-Clovis depositional environments are aggradational, with essentially no evidence of substantial erosion. The record of Folsom and later Paleoindian occupations therefore should be relatively complete. Unless the Clovis occupation was substantially heavier than the post-Clovis occupation, the draw settings should have fewer Clovis features because fewer are preserved.

Other measures of relative Paleoindian population fluctuations or occupation intensity are available from several different data sets: the High Plains Paleoecology Project (HPPP) (Hester 1975a:table 13-1) (Tables 3.13, 3.18, 3.22) (see Appendix 1); a survey on lower Seminole Draw (in the area of the Seminole-Rose site, FIG. 3.42) by Kibler (1991, 1992); and the inventory of sites discussed in Chapter 3. The three data sets are not easy to compare, however, because the HPPP set groups all sites with unfluted Paleoindian projectiles under "parallel flaked horizon." This group of unfluted points almost certainly includes artifact styles that overlap in time with Folsom (e.g., Midland, Plainview, and the constricted-stem styles).

Before examining the various data sets, component-frequency (components defined as artifact assemblages per site) and feature-frequency (features defined as assemblage-specific activity areas per site) per cultural complex must be normalized on the basis of length of occupation. The radiocarbon record indicates that the Clovis occupation spanned the period 11,200–10,900 yrs BP, a 300-year duration. The Folsom and Midland occupations, at most, occurred between 10,900 and 10,000 yrs BP, a 900-year duration. Duration of the Late Paleoindian styles, in contrast, varies depending on how the assemblages are defined and grouped, as illustrated in the following discussion.

Only the most general indication of component frequency is apparent when collapsing the data generated in Chapter 3 with the HPPP and Kibler collections (Table 5.2). The "parallel flaked horizon" includes all unfluted, lanceolate points, which could date to any time from 10,900 to 8000 yrs BP, spanning 2900 years. The resulting trend is the reverse of that proposed by Hester (1975a:256): highest frequency of sites is Clovis (6.7/century), followed by Folsom (4.8/century), and parallel-flaked styles (2.3/century), some of which overlap with Folsom.

A somewhat different trend in occupation frequency appears upon closer examination of the site-inventory data discussed in Chapter 3 (Table 5.3), providing more detail on frequency of specific artifact styles. The unfluted contemporaries of Folsom that also post-date the fluted style (Plainview and the constricted-stem styles) at most date between 10,500 and 9500 yrs BP (1000-year duration). The miscellaneous Late Paleoindian styles that probably did not overlap with Folsom probably began ca. 10,000 yrs BP and likely ran to 8000 yrs BP, a 2000-year duration. On this basis Folsom-Midland and sites in this age range represent peak occupation intensity (2.8 sites/century). Clovis and the unfluted late-Folsom/early-post-Folsom groups were somewhat less common than Folsom (2.3 sites/century and 1.8 sites/century, respectively), and the miscellaneous Late Paleoindian occupants were substantially less common (0.4 sites/century).

Another approach to occupation frequency or density is provided by subdividing the site-inventory data from Chapter 3 into frequency of individual features per century (Table 5.4). The resulting data yield a trend similar to that generated by the HPPP site inventory: peak feature frequency for the Clovis occupation (6.0 features/century), followed by Folsom-Midland (2.9) and the unfluted late-Folsom/early-post-Folsom groups (1.5), and Late Paleoindian with the lowest feature frequency (0.8 features/century).

The trend in component- or feature-frequency from Folsom to Late Paleoindian is the same in all comparisons (a clear decline through time), but the frequency or density of Clovis occupations based on the data in Tables 5.2–5.4 appears equivocal. Clovis, from the combined HPPP–Chapter 3 data (Table 5.2) and from *in situ* features (Table 5.4), has the highest frequency of individual Paleoindian artifact styles, but site

TABLE 5.2. Paleoindian site frequency

Artifact Style	AB	Ba	Be	Bu	BR	CB	CA	CL	Clo	Eli	LLk	Mia	Mil	Mid	Mu	Plv	R16	Ro	Ry	SJ	SR	Sem	SS	Ta	Wil	Win	Wy	HPPP[2]	TOTAL	Per Century
Unfluted Lanceolate	X	X	X		X	X	X			X		X	X	X	X	X	X	X	X	X	X	3			X	X		44	66	2.3
Folsom	X	X	X				X			X	X	X		X			X	X		X			X	X			X	29	43	4.8
Clovis							X		X			X				X	X	X										14	20	6.7

[1] Sites with diagnostic artifacts. Key: AB = Anderson Basin 2; Ba = Barber; Be = Bethel; Bu = Burns; BR = Bedford Ranch; CB = Car Body; CA = Carley-Archer; CL = Canyon Lakes; Clo = Clovis; Eli = Elida; LLk = Lubbock Lake; Mia = Miami; Mid = Midland; Mil = Milnesand; Mu = Mustang Springs; Plv = Plainview; Pv = Poverty Hill; R16 = Ro-16; Ro = Robertson; Ry = Ryan; SJ = San Jon; SR = Seminole-Rose (41GA11 in Kibler 1991); Sem = Seminole Draw (41GA28,33,39; Kibler 1991); SS = Shifting Sands; Ta = Tatum; Wil = Williamson; Win = Winkler-1; Wy = Wyche Ranch; HPPP = High Plains Paleoecology Project.

[2] HPPP = Number of sites listed by Hester (1975b: table 13-1) less sites listed here (Anderson Basin, Clovis, Elida, Lubbock Lake, Milnesand, and Plainview) and not including 11 sites off of the Llano Estacado to the east (see Appendix 1).

TABLE 5.3. Paleoindian component frequency

Artifact Style	AB	Ba	Be	Bu	BR	CB	CA	CL	Clo	Eli	LLk	LLf	MB	Mia	Mid	Mil	Mu	Plv	Pv	R16	Ro	Ry	SJ	SR	SS	Ta	Wil	Win	Wy	SUBTOTAL	TOTAL	Per Century
Misc Late Paleoindian[2]							X	X	X	X										X	X		X	X						8	8	0.4
Plainview age									X				X																	2		
Plainview	X		X			X	X		X					X	X			X		X						X				10	18	1.8
Constricted-stem "Milnesand"[3]																X				X										2		
Constricted-stem "Agate Basin"[4]			X				X	X													X									4		
Midland or Unfluted Folsom					X	X								X		X				X	X							X	X	8		
Folsom age											X	X																		2		
Folsom	X	X			X	X	X	X	X					X		X		X		X	X			X		X		X		15	25	2.8
Clovis age									X																					1		
Clovis								X							X				X	X			X						X	6	7	2.3

[1] Key: AB = Anderson Basin 2; Ba = Barber; Be = Bethel; Bu = Burns; BR = Bedford Ranch; CB = Car Body; CA = Carley-Archer; CL = Canyon Lakes; Clo = Clovis; Eli = Elida; LLk = Lubbock Lake; LLf = Lubbock Landfill; MB = Marks Beach; Mia = Miami; Mid = Midland; Mil = Milnesand; Mu = Mustang Springs; Plv = Plainview; Pv = Poverty Hill; R16 = Ro-16; Ro = Robertson; Ry = Ryan; SJ = San Jon; SR = Seminole-Rose (41GA11 in Kibler 1991); SS = Shifting Sands; Ta = Tatum; Wil = Williamson; Win = Winkler-1; Wy = Wyche Ranch.

[2] Misc Late Paleoindian includes Firstview, San Jon, Eden, Scottsbluff.

[3] "Milnesand" refers only to points described as Milnesand.

[4] "Agate Basin" refers to artifacts identified as Agate Basin and to other constricted-stem points.

TABLE 5.4. Paleoindian feature frequency

Features[1]/Site[2]

Artifact Style	AB	Ba	Be	Bu	BR	CB	Clo[3]	Eli	LLk	LLf	MB	Mia	Mid	Mil	Plv	Pv	Ry	SJ	SR	SS	Ta	Wil	Win	Wy	SUBTOTAL	TOTAL	Per Century
Misc Late Paleoindian[4]	1					5		7											2	1						16	0.8
Plainview age						4					1														5		
Plainview			1			1					1			1	1						1				6		
Constricted-stem "Milnesand"[5]										1				1			1									14	1.4
Constricted-stem "Agate Basin"[6]			1			1																			2		
Midland or Unfluted Folsom													1										1	1	3		
Folsom age			1									1					1								4		
Folsom		1	1			9		2					2					1				1			17	24	2.4
Clovis age						2																			2		
Clovis					1	12						1				1									15	17	6

[1] Sites yielding single-component surface collections (Bethel, Burns, Bedford Ranch, Elida, Poverty Hill, Tatum, Winkler-1, Wyche) are assigned one feature. Sites producing multicomponent surface collections (Carley-Archer, Canyon Lakes, Mustand Springs, Ro-16, Robertson) are not considered in this tabulation.

[2] Key: AB = Anderson Basin 2; Ba = Barber; Be = Bethel; Bu = Burns; BR = Bedford Ranch; CB = Car Body; Clo = Clovis; Eli = Elida; LLk = Lubbock Lake; LLf = Lubbock Landfill; MB = Marks Beach; Mia = Miami; Mid = Midland; Mil = Milnesand; Plv = Plainview; Pv = Poverty Hill; Ry = Ryan; SJ = San Jon; SR = Seminole-Rose; SS = Shifting Sands; Ta = Tatum; Wil = Williamson; Win = Winkler; Wy = Wyche.

[3] Clovis = minimum number of features.

[4] Misc Late Paleoindian includes Firstview, San Jon, Eden, Scottsbluff.

[5] "Milnesand" refers only to points referred to as Milnesand.

[6] "Agate Basin" refers to artifacts identified as Agate Basin and to other constricted-stem points.

frequency based on the Chapter 3 data (Table 5.3) shows Clovis lower than Folsom. The dichotomy in Clovis occupation frequency may be due to geographical and sampling factors. The high number of HPPP Clovis sites produces the high frequency of sites/century in Table 5.2. Most of the HPPP Clovis sites are along the western Llano Estacado, in and near the Clovis type site (FIG. 5.2), in contrast to sites associated with later artifact traditions, scattered more or less evenly across the central Llano Estacado (FIGS. 5.4, 5.5). Furthermore, most of the *in situ* Clovis features (12 out of 15) were found at the Clovis site (Table 5.4). These data suggest that Clovis occupations were most intense on the west-central Llano Estacado, whereas subsequent Paleoindian activity was much broader.

Data on the distribution and frequency of Clovis and Folsom points from throughout Texas are available in two surveys (Meltzer 1986; Meltzer and Bever 1995; Largent et al. 1991; Largent 1995). Comparing the data sets in terms of artifact frequency is difficult, however, because different methods of data collection were employed in each survey. Data on Clovis finds, in addition to published material, were actively collected using forms easily available to local collectors (Meltzer 1986; Meltzer and Bever 1995). The Folsom data, in contrast, were gathered largely from the literature (Largent 1995; Largent et al. 1991). A larger Clovis inventory might therefore be expected.

The component- and feature-frequencies plus the paleoenvironmental reconstructions lead to several very broad observations. During the Clovis occupation the environmental diversity was high (there were many sources of water and a wide variety of game and plants), but at a regional scale site density was low. Assuming Clovis to be the first occupants of the Llano Estacado, then a low site density is reasonable. Meltzer and Bever (1995) suggest that the low density of Clovis sites relative to later Paleoindian occupations may be a function of adaptations: Clovis groups may not have participated "in the highly structured spatial behavior that [produced] sites. As highly mobile hunter-gatherers, whose movements were virtually unrestricted across the very thinly inhabited and relatively rich late Pleistocene landscape, Clovis groups were not forced to use the same localities repeatedly, and hence would not necessarily build up a visible archaeological record at any one" (Meltzer and Bever 1995:62) (see also Kelley and Todd 1988).

During the Folsom occupation and into the early post-Folsom, the environmental diversity still was reasonably high and the site density was at its highest. Artifact diversity also was very high at this time, with a wide variety of artifact styles being manufactured, largely between 10,500 and 9500 yrs BP (FIG. 5.1). The environments of the Southern High Plains from Clovis time to ca. 10,000 yrs BP were quite hospitable for hunters and gatherers, conditions which could allow populations to grow (and increase site densities) and to evolve, experiment with, and diversify their tool kits and artifact styles (e.g., Knudson 1983, 1988). As populations and site densities increased throughout the southern Great Plains in the last millennia of the Pleistocene there was an increased likelihood of exchange of ideas regarding artifact manufacture and morphology. This could have resulted in increasing diversity in technologies and styles as site density peaked at ca. 10,000 yrs BP. Kelley and Todd (1988:240) further argue that "As populations became more packed [and as climate became more continental] . . . trade . . . could have been used as a way to cope with resource fluctuations." They also see this tendency reflected in the stylistic evolution of artifacts from types with broad geographic continuity (Clovis) to more regionally restricted styles (unfluted Late Paleoindian lanceolates).

After 10,000 yrs BP and especially after 9000 yrs BP, site density, environmental diversity, and artifact diversity declined (FIG. 5.1). This was a time of increasing seasonality and the beginning of Holocene warming and drying. Water sources became scarce, at least in the draws, and wind erosion became common, especially in the sandier regions of the western and southwestern Llano Estacado. The wind erosion probably was the result of decline in vegetation density as effective moisture decreased (Holliday 1989b, 1995b). The apparently rapid onset of drier and warmer conditions (perhaps first experienced during Folsom time?) coincided with and likely resulted in decline of site density. Greiser (1985:121–122) and L. Johnson (1989:53–54) suggest that environmental conditions in the early Holocene throughout the Great Plains drove many Late Paleoindians into neighboring, more hospitable, settings. L. Johnson (1989) in particular proposed that the appearance of "Plains" Late Paleoindian artifacts (i.e., the classic unfluted lanceolate styles) in the woodlands of the eastern Rolling Plains and farther east was due to periodic movement off the High Plains in response to drought. This model can be seen as a variation on the Kelley and Todd (1988) hypothesis of increased trade by Late Paleoindians in response to environmental stress. Evidence for drying of the High Plains during the Late Paleoindian times is now abundant, which offers some support for both Greiser's and L. Johnson's models. What is less clear is whether the "Plains" Late Paleoindian styles truly evolved on the High Plains and were "interlopers in the eastern Woodlands" (L. Johnson 1989).

These models offer hypotheses that could be tested with better age control on unfluted lanceolate styles in the Central Lowlands.

STYLISTIC DIVERSITY

Stylistic diversity among projectile points, including the Clovis and Folsom types, but especially common in the unfluted types, is a recurrent pattern of the Paleoindian archaeology on the Southern High Plains. This trait is noted by many investigators (e.g., Knudson 1983, 1988; Hofman 1989a, 1992) and historically is the source of much of the typological confusion. A number of factors probably are responsible for this diversity. Stylistic experimentation (Knudson 1983, 1988) and contacts with other regions such as the Southeast (Knudson 1988) probably played a role. The relatively low-stress environment probably afforded the time to experiment, and the striking morphological similarities in artifact styles between the Plains and Southeast are clearly suggestive of some sort of communication.

Other factors may also be involved in producing the wide variety of Paleoindian artifact styles in the region, however. Many of the styles likely were multipurpose artifacts used both as projectiles and knives, probably hafted knives (Wheat 1972; Judge 1974; Johnson and Holliday 1981, 1987b). These varying uses increased the likelihood of breakage and especially reworking. Conservation of tools, indicated by repeated reworking and "exhaustion," also probably was related to the relative paucity of lithic resources (Johnson and Holliday 1981, 1987b). There are essentially no large sources of high-quality stone for flaking in the interior of the region. Materials suitable for the manufacture of stone tools are relatively localized and found only along the periphery of the Llano Estacado, if not farther afield, as discussed in Chapter 1 and Appendix 2. Hofman (1992) expands on this theme by considering how an artifact assemblage might change in appearance depending on the number of retooling events and the frequency of visits to a quarry. His study focuses on Folsom assemblages, but could apply to any assemblage of hunting tools.

> If Folsom groups could not plan the specific time when a kill would occur, they had to maintain a tool kit flexible enough to make a kill, and had to retool at any time or at any distance from a quarry source. After several kill-butchery-retooling events, and a quarry visit and restocking effort, the assemblage appearance changed dramatically as expended or lost stone tools were replaced by a transported and curated stone supply. (Hofman 1992:198–199)

> If the functional assemblage . . . changed in composition and appearance depending on its position in a quarry and retooling cycle, then the

assemblage that was lost and discarded at a kill-processing event and that which is available to be sampled in the archaeological record could differ substantially from place to place, even if the assemblages were used by the same group. (Hofman 1992:208)

Regional Geoarchaeological Comparisons

Paleoindian research in regions bordering or near the Southern High Plains (Chapter 4) provides enough data to compare artifact chronologies and to make initial interregional comparisons of late Pleistocene and early Holocene landscape evolution and environmental changes. Some data also are available for limited observations on site settings and occupation intensities across portions of the Great Plains.

CULTURAL CHRONOLOGY

The Central and Northern High Plains have perhaps the best-dated, stratified Paleoindian sequence in North America (e.g., Frison 1991a; Haynes 1992, 1993; Haynes, Beukens, Jull, and Davis 1992). Analysis of all uncalibrated radiocarbon ages from Clovis sites (including some localities off the Great Plains) dates the Clovis occupation from 11,200 to 10,900 yrs BP (Haynes 1992:364). The Folsom occupation is dated between 10,900 and 10,200 yrs BP (Haynes 1992:364). The Clovis-Folsom chronology for the Southern High Plains is very similar to this regional chronology.

The chronologies for other artifact types are more difficult to compare because of apparent regionalization of styles and technologies. But several observations can be offered. Unequivocal Plainview artifacts are not known from the central and northern Great Plains. The Goshen style has some striking morphological similarities to Plainview, but may be as much as 1000 years older. Constricted-stem styles on the central and northern Plains, such as Agate Basin and Hell Gap, have generally the same age range as the constricted-stem artifacts from the Llano Estacado, although the latter have generally poor age control. Agate Basin overlaps with Folsom, dating 10,500–10,000 yrs BP (similar to the stratigraphic relationship of Agate Basin and Folsom at the Clovis site), and Hell Gap is ca. 10,000 yrs BP and perhaps a little younger (Frison 1991a:57–62). The Cody Complex dates ca. 9200–8800 (Frison 1991a:66), which is similar to the age range of Firstview, the southern stylistic equivalent of Cody.

Paleoindian artifact chronologies for regions off the High Plains are very poorly known, although stratified sites such as Wilson-Leonard are providing substantial new data. The basic Clovis–Folsom–unfluted lanceolate sequence seems to hold for the Edwards Plateau and Rolling Plains, but the chronological (much less typological) relationships among the unfluted styles remain bewildering. Artifacts generally similar in morphology to Plainview (such as St. Mary's Hall) and to Firstview-Cody are found in the area but may not necessarily be related to the High Plains equivalents technologically or chronologically. Artifact styles such as Golondrina and Texas Angostura appear to be characteristic of the Late Paleoindian occupation of Central Texas, but are comparatively rare on the High Plains. These styles may be Paleoindian artifacts only in a technological and morphological sense; emerging data suggest that Golondrina and Angostura, and probably other unfluted lanceolate styles, are associated with an Archaic subsistence (Collins 1976; Prewitt 1981; T. Hester 1982; Collins et al. 1994). Moreover, the early Holocene artifact sequence east of the High Plains is complicated by the appearance of "Archaic-style" points with stemmed and notched triangular blades contemporaneous with many of the unfluted lanceolate styles (Collins 1976; Prewitt 1981; Wyckoff 1984; Turner and Hester 1993; Collins et al. 1994).

GEOARCHAEOLOGICAL AND PALEOENVIRONMENTAL COMPARISONS

Among the paleoenvironmental comparisons that can be made among the regions discussed, one of the most striking similarities is the evidence for deep incision of drainages shortly before the Clovis occupation. Although not well-dated, the evidence for downcutting is apparent at all spatial scales, from low-order tributaries (Wilson-Leonard site, Domebo site, Folsom site, and the draws of the Llano Estacado) to master streams (the Colorado, Brazos, Trinity, Kansas, and South Loup rivers, and segments of the Medina and North San Gabriel rivers). In all of these settings, Clovis-age deposits are the first to post-date the incision.

Very broadly, various proxy indicators and climate models show that in the late Pleistocene the Great Plains was subjected to lower seasonal extremes relative to today, and, therefore, effective moisture was higher (Dalquest 1986; Graham 1987; Holliday 1987a, 1995b; Johnson 1986a, 1987a; Dalquest and Schultz 1992; Hall and Valastro 1995; Neck 1995). The notable pre-Clovis incision may be providing details on environmental changes within the last few millennia of the late Pleistocene, reflecting an increase in effective precipitation on already well-vegetated surfaces (grasslands on the High Plains, western Rolling Plains, and western Edwards Plateau; woodlands on the eastern Edwards Plateau, eastern Rolling Plains, and in Central Texas). There is some evidence for a shift from relatively dry to more humid conditions (cool-dry grassland to cool-humid grassland) from pre-Clovis to Clovis times, based on data from the Southern High Plains (discussed above), vertebrates from the Dutton and Selby sites, and dune construction in northeastern Colorado (Madole 1995). Such an increase in effective precipitation likely would produce higher runoff and discharge, but little increase in sediment yield. These conditions in many semiarid settings result in channel incision (Knox 1983; Bull 1991). Increases in effective precipitation may not directly influence runoff and discharge in a significant way on the Southern High Plains due to the very small catchment areas of the draws. Springs fed by groundwater, however, probably had a significant effect on stream discharge and the hydrology of the draws, and groundwater levels and spring discharge are significantly affected by changes in precipitation in the region (Cronin 1964; Fallin et al. 1987; Ashworth 1991; Ashworth et al. 1991). Increased precipitation and resulting increased spring discharge would increase flow in the valleys without increasing sediment yield, likely resulting in incision.

A notable exception to the drainages affected by pre-Clovis incision is the South Platte River. There, the last phase of incision prior to the Clovis occupation probably occurred before the last full glacial stage in the Front Range of the Rocky Mountains, i.e., >20,000 yrs BP (Machette 1977; Madole 1986, 1991). In contrast to the Clovis occupation in other regions of the Plains, that of the South Platte is coincident with the waning phases of alluviation that began during or immediately after full glacial conditions (Holliday 1987b; McFaul et al. 1994; Madole 1991). The influence of glacial events in the Rockies on the alluvial history of the South Platte produced a significantly different stratigraphic and geomorphic record compared to the nonglaciated drainages of the Plains.

Regardless of the specific timing of the late Pleistocene incision, the Clovis occupation in the regions discussed is coincident with alluviation of valleys. Stream deposits for this period typically are gravelly and the coarsest of any time during the human occupation of the Great Plains. This sedimentological characteristic in turn suggests that streams were at their highest energies and highest discharges at any time of the past 11,000 or so years. Eolian deposits also accumulated in Clovis times along the flanks of the South Platte (Fox site; see also Madole 1995). Given that many streams carried sandy and gravelly loads in Clovis time, the appearance of dunes probably is related to high sediment supply in the streams.

Valley sedimentation continued in post-Clovis times, but the deposits typically are finer-grained (representing lower energy conditions) relative to Clovis, and more local stratigraphic variability is apparent. As noted above, the draws of the Llano Estacado had conditions varying from competent streams to alkaline marshes during Folsom times, but in post-Folsom times most reaches were marshy. Elsewhere, the post-Clovis depositional environment in streams, valleys, and creeks varied: some aggraded with fine-grained alluvial deposits, locally containing multiple, weakly developed Fluvent-like soils (Richard Beene, Loeve, Lake Theo, Lipscomb, Aubrey, and Lime Creek; lower Pecos, lower Devil's, Pawnee, Kansas, and South Loup rivers); others accumulated paludal sediments or marshy soils (Wilson-Leonard, Domebo and neighboring areas, Lindenmeier, and Hell Gap); and yet other localities experienced alluvial stability with soil formation, followed by downcutting and Late Paleoindian eolian sedimentation (Kersey Terrace of the South Platte).

Most data on upland (i.e., out of draws and stream valleys) Paleoindian geoarchaeology are from the High Plains, with some additional data from the Rolling Plains. Lacustrine sedimentation apparently was common during Clovis times in both playas (San Jon, Miami, Dutton, and Selby) and in depressions now buried by dune fields (Winkler-1, Shifting Sands, and Bedford Ranch in the Andrews Dunes, Claypool in the Wray Dunes, and several other sites in dunes of northeastern Colorado noted by Madole 1995). Eolian sedimentation then became relatively widespread during the Folsom occupation (western Llano Estacado) and especially in post-Folsom time (throughout the High Plains and locally on the Rolling Plains), although playa basins locally maintained ponds or marshes and attracted Late Paleoindian peoples (San Jon, Ryan, Big Lake, Beidleman Ranch). The High Plains apparently was drying out from Clovis to Late Paleoindian time. This is perhaps most evident when comparing the geoarchaeology of the Andrews Dunes with that of the Claypool site. Both areas are underlain by late Pleistocene (Clovis?) lacustrine carbonates, and covered by sand sheets containing post-Clovis Paleoindian materials. Nonarchaeological sites in dunes of northeastern Colorado exhibit a similar stratigraphy (Madole 1995).

Some significant regional trends clearly are apparent in landscape evolution during the Paleoindian occupation of the Great Plains, a point first explicitly made at a regional scale in a classic geoarchaeological study by Haynes (1968; building on the work of Bryan 1941a,b). Considerable regional variation also is notable, however. The beginning and end of Paleoindian times seem marked by similar geomorphic trends. Widespread downcutting in late pre-Clovis time was followed by relatively high-energy alluviation during the Clovis occupation. Late Paleoindian (post-Folsom) time is characterized in many areas by eolian deposits in both lowlands and uplands, especially after ca. 9000 yrs BP on the High Plains.

Such regional similarities in geomorphic and depositional processes suggest regional (subcontinental-scale) similarities in environmental changes. In contrast, the local variability in Folsom and early post-Folsom geologic events suggests more local environmental variability.

Consideration of local versus regional environmental changes results in a very cautious approach to geologic and environmental correlations between different physiographic regions and among varying depositional environments. For example, comparisons of the Southern High Plains with the Colorado Piedmont and Northern High Plains are complicated by: (1) the limited number of external environmental variables such as throughflowing streams on the Southern High Plains; (2) proximity of the Piedmont and northern Plains to the Rocky Mountains; and (3) the impact of glacial and interglacial events in the mountains on streams far out on the Plains. Moreover, local environmental variability hampers local correlations. On the Southern High Plains this problem is well illustrated in the microstratigraphy of the draws (Holliday 1995b). The draws contain a generally similar lithostratigraphic sequence, but local variability in the presence or absence and termination of spring discharge produced considerable chronostratigraphic variability. On the northern Plains, the problem is exemplified by attempts at correlating the Lindenmeier site, in a small, seasonally dry tributary near the mountain front, with the mainstream (and glaciated) South Platte River (Wilmsen and Roberts 1978; Holliday 1987b). Given the variations in local geomorphic and hydrologic responses to environmental changes in small tributaries, particularly in drier environments, depositional and erosional cycles may well be out-of-phase and otherwise have no relationship with those in the larger drainages (Bull 1991).

SITE SETTINGS AND OCCUPATION INTENSITIES

Throughout the Great Plains, as on the Llano Estacado, the locations of most Paleoindian sites seem to be controlled by the presence of water, not surprisingly. Such settings certainly attracted both humans and game animals. For this reason, and as noted by others (Haynes 1968; Albanese 1977; Reider 1990), many Paleoindian sites off the Llano Estacado (as well as those on the Llano, discussed above and in Chapter 3), including both kills and camps, are associated with springs (Lamb Springs, Aubrey, and possibly Wilson-Leonard) or marshy settings or other indicators of a high water table and damp soil conditions (Lindenmeier, Dutton and Selby, Domebo, Wilson-Leonard, and possibly Hell Gap).

Many kill sites are found near waterways varying in size from draws and arroyos to master streams. Fluvial settings on the Great Plains but off the Llano Estacado served as effective means of trapping animals, usually bison, for kills. These kinds of sites are most commonly associated with ar-royos (Frison 1991a:156–186), which, for reasons noted earlier, are and probably were more common off the Llano Estacado. Paleoarroyos and pa-leobasins containing Paleoindian bison bone beds are found in upland set-tings such as Lipscomb, Waugh, Perry Ranch, Beidleman Ranch, Olsen-Chubbock, and possibly at Folsom (Frison 1991a:159) and Lamb Springs. Hofman (1995:422) proposes that the frequent occurrence of bison kills in upland settings may be related to "a pattern of bison-intercept hunting that involved monitoring of herd movements along . . . divides." Paleoindian bison-kill sites in lowland paleoarroyos, where the cuts drain directly into large streams, include Cooper (Bement 1995; Carter and Bement 1995) and possibly Rex Rodgers (Willey et al. 1978:60). Active streams and floodplains likely attracted animals that could then be trapped in nearby arroyos. Use of arroyos in hunting mammoths is hinted at at Domebo, Dent (Brunswig and Fisher 1993), and Lamb Springs.

Bison-kill sites on floodplains provide little evidence of any topographic means of trapping the animals (e.g., Frazier, Jurgens, Jones-Miller, and Lake Theo). The Jurgens, Frazier, and Jones-Miller bone beds are associ-ated with shallow swales, however, and Stanford (1978:96) proposes that bison may have been trapped in snowdrifts that buried shallow depressions.

Watercourses were obviously attractive to game and probably were a good setting to hunt animals, but the strong relationship between water-ways and bone beds may be more apparent than real. Kill sites (expressed as bone beds) have relatively high visibility in the archaeological record, so they are more likely to be spotted when exposed by erosion. Watercourses also are prone to disturbance and exposure of sites, which also may provide a biased view of site preferences. Running water focuses on these drain-ages, which, combined with the geomorphic relief typical along creeks and valleys, can accelerate erosion and further expose sites. High concentra-tion of Historic Anglo-American activity along waterways also may result in discovery of more sites in these settings, either by accident (disturbance or accelerated erosion) or due to the relatively high concentration of ar-chaeological surveys in such areas.

Jump sites are rare on the High Plains or Rolling Plains. Off of the Llano Estacado, a spectacular exception is Bonfire Shelter, which probably was used at least three times by Paleoindians. The Lone Wolf Creek site may have been a jump as well.

The relative absence of reported archaeological sites buried in playa fill is as remarkable on the Central and Northern High Plains as it is on the Southern High Plains. Playa fills, because they typically are related to water, should contain abundant archaeological material. Only three Paleoindian sites are reported from such settings, and two were found during artificial disturbance (Dutton and Selby). The other locality (Nall) was found by deflation of a sand dune field and erosion of the top of older lake beds. The occupation at Claypool, also exposed by deflation of dunes, may be associated with a very small, extinct playa as well. As on the Llano Estacado, the seeming lack of Paleoindian sites in playas of the central and northern Plains may reflect the rarity of deep disturbance of playa fills.

Also similar to the Southern High Plains is the high incidence of Paleoindian materials found in sand dune fields on the Central and Northern High Plains (Nall and Claypool and other sites in the dunes of northeastern Colorado) and on the Rolling Plains (Adair-Steadman) (Hofman 1989a: 160, 161), and the association of these sites with buried lake or marsh beds (Claypool and Nall). In these regions as well as on the Llano Estacado, the dunes largely post-date the Paleoindian occupations, which seem to be associated with lake or marsh beds buried by the dunes. Some eolian deposition was coincident with Folsom and Late Paleoindian times, however, and disturbance of the more extensive younger dunes led to erosion of the older dunes and exposure of the sites.

Rockshelters are relatively uncommon geomorphic features in many parts of the Great Plains owing to characteristics of regional bedrock and topography. The Edwards Plateau at the southern end of the Great Plains is the outstanding exception to this general characteristic. The absence of evidence for Paleoindian occupations older than ca. 10,000 yrs BP in Texas rockshelters is the subject of some debate and may be a geoarchaeological and perhaps paleoenvironmental issue. Some argue that the increased frequency of Late Paleoindian and especially post-Paleoindian cultural debris in rockshelters reflects an increased cultural preference for rockshelters in the Holocene (e.g., Thomas 1978; Prewitt 1981). This interpretation is challenged by Collins (1991), who argues that older archaeological deposits may be obscured due to the natural evolution and degradation of rockshelters, based on data from limestone shelters in France as well as Texas. Moreover, rates of sedimentation in Texas rockshelters due to degradation (mostly from roof spall) probably were more rapid in the late Pleistocene than in the Holocene due to environmental changes (Collins 1991). Earlier Paleoindian ($>$10,000 yrs BP) archaeological debris, therefore, is more likely to be deeply buried and less concentrated than younger occupation zones. The apparent increase in occupation frequency beginning at ca. 10,000 yrs BP therefore may mark a significant environmental change rather than indicating a characteristic of habitation preference.

SITE FREQUENCY AND OCCUPATION INTENSITIES

The collection and presentation of data on site and feature frequency for regions of the Great Plains outside of the Llano Estacado (comparable to the data presented above for the Llano Estacado) are far beyond the purpose or scope of this volume, but some published data for areas on or near the Plains provide an opportunity to make a few comparisons. For the Rolling Plains east of the Llano Estacado, Hofman (1989a) presents a comprehensive overview of Paleoindian archaeology as part of a broader discussion of archaeology in the south-central United States. Three maps (Hofman 1989a:figs. 9, 10, 11), and addition of the Aubrey, Waugh, Cooper, Field Ranch, George King, Beidleman Ranch, and Acton sites, provide some indication of occupation frequency for Clovis, Folsom, and Late Paleoindian components (Table 5.5). Calculating site frequency per century is based on durations of the artifact traditions presented for Table 5.2 (300 years for Clovis, 900 years for Folsom, and 2900 years for Late Paleoindian unfluted lanceolates). The results of the comparison suggest that peak occupation intensity was by Clovis peoples, in contrast to the trend on the Llano Estacado if Folsom and Midland are grouped together (Table 5.5). Inventories of Clovis and Folsom points in Texas suggest a similar trend on the Rolling Plains ("North Central Texas" and the "Lower Plains" in Largent 1995; Largent et al. 1991; Meltzer 1986; Meltzer and Bever 1995), but as noted above, differences in methods of data collection in these two surveys make comparisons very difficult.

Thurmond (1990:Table 4) tabulated data for Late Paleoindian sites on the Rolling Plains. These data were not incorporated into Table 5.5, because Thurmond dealt expressly with Late Paleoindian sites and did not gather information on earlier occupations. His data are enlightening, however, because they suggest a decrease in site frequency during Late Paleoindian occupations through the early Holocene. Plainview sites are considerably more common (n=14) than later Firstview-Cody (n=3) sites (Thurmond 1990:figs. 9, 10), a trend in site frequency very similar to the component frequency presented for the Southern High Plains (Table 5.3).

Assessing early Holocene component frequency and occupation intensity based on the occurrence of lanceolate projectile points may be misleading, however. As noted above, east of the High Plains in Texas and Oklahoma, post-Folsom artifact styles include more triangular, notched, classically "Archaic" projectile points. This situation raises the possibility

TABLE 5.5. Paleoindian component frequency on the Rolling Plains compared with the Southern High Plains

Artifact Style	Rolling Plains Sites		Southern High Plains Sites[1]	
	No.	Per Century	No.	Per Century
Late Paleoindian	9[2]	0.3	26[3]	1.0
Folsom	7[4]	0.8	17(25)[5]	1.9(2.8)
Clovis	5[6]	1.7	7	2.3

[1] From Table 5.3.
[2] Acton, Beidleman Ranch, Field Ranch, George King, Lake Theo, Lone Wolf Creek, Perry Ranch, Pumpkin Creek, Rex Rodgers.
[3] Constricted-stem styles, Plainview, and Miscellaneous Late Paleoindian.
[4] Adair-Steadman, Field Ranch, Cedar Creek, Cooper, Lake Theo, Waugh, Winters.
[5] Folsom only = 17; Folsom + Midland = 25.
[6] Aubrey, Domebo, Field Ranch, Lewisville, McLean.

that early post-Folsom occupations (early Holocene, Paleoindian-age) are not being recognized as such because sites producing these poorly dated, notched, triangular artifacts are considered to be Archaic (i.e., middle Holocene). This consideration raises a broader, more fundamental issue. As Paleoindian hunters and gatherers settled into the area east of the High Plains, they may have discovered that their Plains-adapted subsistence was not as well suited for the more humid, more heavily vegetated, rolling landscape. Folsom and post-Folsom bison hunters may have tended to concentrate their efforts on the High Plains while their contemporaries to the east began to adopt what we see as an Archaic lifestyle.

More generally, the data tabulated for Paleoindian sites on and east of the Southern High Plains (Tables 5.2, 5.5) clearly show that many more are known on the High Plains than on the Rolling Plains. This pattern also appears in various surveys of Clovis, Folsom, and Late Paleoindian sites (Meltzer 1986; Meltzer and Bever 1995; Largent 1995; Largent et al. 1991; Thurmond 1990). The dearth of sites on the Rolling Plains is attributed to lack of artifact collectors (Meltzer 1986) and concentration of resources along ecotonal boundaries (i.e., along the western and eastern margins of the Rolling Plains) (Thurmond 1990). The apparent concentration of Paleoindian sites along the western and eastern margins (clearly evident in FIG. 4.1) may indeed reflect settlement patterns, but the pattern may be due to presence of a specific resource—fresh water—rather than the more general, intrinsic attractiveness of ecotones. Historically, potable water was abundant in springs along the western Rolling Plains (Brune 1981), issuing from the Ogallala Aquifer along the eastern escarpment of the High Plains. Springs and flowing water are and were abundant throughout most of the rest of the Texas Rolling Plains, but most of the water is very high in dissolved salts and probably has been since the Tertiary owing to salt dissolution in the Permian bedrock beneath the High Plains and Rolling Plains (Gustavson et al. 1980; T. C. Gustavson, pers. comm. 1995). Salt concentration decreases to the east and potability increases. A logical conclusion is that concentrations of archaeological sites on the Rolling Plains are related to the drinkability of the water, which is highest on the western and eastern margins.

The low concentration of reported Paleoindian sites on the Rolling Plains also may be due to factors of site visibility and site preservation: rates of erosion in the region are relatively high: the area includes several large, closely spaced, well-integrated drainage systems (the Red, Brazos, and Colorado rivers) with dense drainage networks; the area has relatively high relief; and it has relatively easily eroded rock and soils. More specifically, geoarchaeologists working in the region (e.g., Ferring 1990a, 1994; Blum and Valastro 1992; Blum et al. 1992) show that when the first Paleoindians arrived in the area, most drainages were deeply incised. As first proposed by Meltzer (1986), subsequent Paleoindian-age landscapes were heavily eroded or buried (in alluvium, such as McLean, Lake Theo, and Aubrey, or under upland sand sheets, such as Adair-Steadman), resulting in very low site visibility (Blum et al. 1992). Most known sites are preserved on uplands (on bedrock or on high terraces).

The central Rio Grande valley yielded sufficient data to make further comparisons of Paleoindian occupation intensity as indicated by component frequency (Judge 1973). The area is distinctly different from the Great Plains in physiography (due to much higher relief and tectonic activity), but is used for comparison because: (1) it is in reasonable proximity to the Southern High Plains (FIG. 4.1), (2) it produced a comprehensive data set on Paleoindian sites (Judge 1973); and (3) climatically, the region is broadly comparable. The study conducted by Judge (1973) focused on the central Rio Grande valley centered on Albuquerque, New Mexico (FIG. 4.1). This work is one of the few published regional surveys designed expressly to look at the distribution of Paleoindian sites as a function of the landscape. The survey focused on the floodplain, terraces, and arroyo systems of the Rio Grande and did not deal with the mountains that bound the study area. The sites and localities found during the survey were categorized as Clovis, Folsom, Belen, or Cody based on projectile point types. "Belen" was a tentative artifact classification "most closely related to the Plainview/

Midland/Milnesand" artifact styles (Judge 1973:71, 321–322). Duration of the typologies follows that used for Tables 5.3 and 5.4: Clovis is 300 years; Folsom is 900 years; Belen (as equivalent to Midland, Plainview, and Milnesand; 10,900–9500 yrs BP) is 1400 years; and Cody is 2000 years. The resulting tabulation (Table 5.6) is very similar to the results for the Southern High Plains, with a small Clovis presence, very high Folsom site frequency, and a lower post-Folsom (and Midland?) site density. These data suggest that the peak Paleoindian occupation of the middle Rio Grande valley, as of the Southern High Plains, came during Folsom time.

The Northern High Plains and Colorado Piedmont, as noted in Chapter 4, have some of the highest frequencies of reported and investigated Paleoindian sites in North America (e.g., Frison 1991a) and provide a good contrast and comparison with the southern Plains. The Paleoindian archaeology of the region and the neighboring Wyoming Basin has been subjected to exceptionally intense scrutiny by Frison (1991a), and it probably has the best-dated and most complete Paleoindian record in North America. The cultural chronology is broadly similar to that on the Southern High Plains, though the detail provided by Frison (1991a), unavailable for the Southern High Plains, produces an inexact comparison. Typological groupings and durations of artifact styles for the Plains Paleoindian groups (from Frison 1991a and Haynes 1992) include: Clovis (300 years); Folsom-Midland (900 years); constricted-stem (Agate Basin, Hell Gap; 10,500–9500 yrs BP = 1000 years); Alberta-Cody and parallel-oblique (Frederick, Lusk, Angostura; 9500–8000 yrs BP = 1500 years). In the comparison (Tables 5.7 and 5.8), data from the Southern High Plains and Rolling Plains are lumped together to better standardize the comparison with the northern Plains. A more exact comparison would be provided if data on

TABLE 5.6. Paleoindian component frequency in the Rio Grande Valley compared with the Southern High Plains

	Rio Grande Valley Sites[1]		Southern High Plains Sites[2]	
Artifact Style	No.	Per Century	No.	Per Century
Late Paleoindian[3]	9	0.5	8	0.4
Belen[4]	13	0.9	26	1.9
Folsom	29	3.2	23	2.4
Clovis	2	0.7	6	2.0

[1] From Judge (1973).   [3] Cody-Firstview.
[2] From Table 5.3.   [4] Midland, constricted-stem styles, and Plainview.

TABLE 5.7. Paleoindian component frequency on the Northern High Plains and Colorado Piedmont[1]

Artifact Assemblage	Duration 14C Years BP	Sites	Sites Per Century
Alberta–Cody and parallel-oblique[2]	1500 yrs 9.5k–8k	26	1.7
Constricted-stem[3]	1000 yrs 10.5k–9.5k	8	0.8
Folsom–Midland[4]	900 yrs 10.9k–10k	11	1.2
Clovis[5]	300 yrs 11.2k–10.9k	10	3.3

[1] Based on data in Cassells (1983:37–71), Greiser (1985:tables 4, 6, 7, 9, 11), and Frison (1991a:39–79).
[2] Alberta (Hell Gap, Hudson-Meng); Cody (Bijou Creek, Claypool, Frasca, Gettenger, Hahn, Harrison, Hell Gap, Jurgens, Lamb Springs, Lime Creek, Lindenmeier, Nelson, Nolan, Olsen-Chubbock, Scottsbluff, Wetzel, 5MR338); Frederick (Clary Ranch, Hell Gap, Lime Creek, Red Smoke); Lusk (Betty Greene, Hell Gap); Angostura (Ray Long).
[3] Agate Basin (Agate Basin, Brewster, Frazier, Hell Gap, Keenesburg); Hell Gap (Hell Gap, Jones-Miller, Keenesburg).
[4] Agate Basin, Bijou Creek, Brewster, Fowler-Parrish, Hahn, Hell Gap, Johnson, Lindenmeier, Nolan, Powars, 5MR338.
[5] Bijou Creek, Claypool, Dent, Dutton, Fox, Hahn, Klein, Lange-Ferguson, Sheaman, 5MR338.

TABLE 5.8. Paleoindian component frequency on the southern Plains[1]

Artifact Assemblage	Duration 14C Years BP	Sites	Sites Per Century
Miscellaneous Late Paleoindian	2000 yrs 10k–8k	9	0.5
Plainview and "Constricted-Stem"	1000 yrs 10.5k–9.5k	22	2.2
Folsom–Midland	900 yrs 10.9k–10k	32	3.6
Clovis	300 yrs 11.2k–10.9k	12	4.0

[1] From Tables 5.3 and 5.5.

Paleoindian occupations were available for the Pecos Valley, just east of the Llano Estacado, but such literature is not generally available.

The component frequency data from the northern Plains (Table 5.7) provide a striking contrast to the component frequency data for the southern Plains (Table 5.8). The frequencies in the north are almost exactly the opposite of the trends in the south; Clovis sites have the highest frequency, followed by a decline that bottoms with Agate Basin–Hell Gap sites and then increases with Alberta-Cody and other Late Paleoindian sites. On the northern Plains, the Folsom-Midland and Agate Basin–Hell Gap occupations overlapped between ca. 10,500 and 10,000 yrs BP, so another approach to the data is to combine it, yielding 19 sites over a 1400-year span (ca. 10,900–9500 yrs BP), or a frequency of 1.4 sites per century. In either case, the data suggest a decline in occupation frequency following Clovis and an increase during Alberta-Cody/Late Paleoindian time.

Additional data show that the increase in component frequency on the northern Plains in the early Holocene record is even more dramatic than indicated in Table 5.7. In the chronology of the Wyoming Basin and neighboring areas, Frison (1991a:67–71) notes the development of a distinct dichotomy in artifact styles and subsistence beginning ca. 10,000 yrs BP. One group continued to practice a classically Paleoindian "open plains, part-time bison hunting way of life, whereas the other favored a more hunting and gathering subsistence in foothill and mountain slope areas and were more Archaic in terms of subsistence strategies" (Frison 1991a:67). The artifact styles represented by the plains, bison-hunting groups include late Agate Basin and Hell Gap and all other post-Folsom lanceolate styles. This divergence in subsistence is attributed to the onset of drying conditions that characterized the early Holocene. The data for site frequency in the early Holocene on the northern Plains include only sites of the plains, bison-hunting groups. Addition of early Holocene sites from the foothills and mountains would produce an early Holocene site frequency higher than the Folsom-Midland and constricted-stem styles.

Accounting for the dramatic difference in component frequencies between the northern Plains and southern Plains is difficult. The issue is unresolvable given the present data base, but three broad hypotheses can be posed to explain the dichotomy in the trends: (1) sample bias by archaeologists in one or both regions; (2) sample bias due to site formation processes in one or both regions; or (3) the trends reflect real differences in the frequency of components during Paleoindian times. There is no obvious evidence for sample bias. In the data base used for the regional comparisons, there are about the same number of reported Paleoindian sites on the

northern Plains (n=36) as on the southern Plains (n=39). And there is no
reason why in one area sites with one particular assemblage (e.g., Folsom
occupations) should be preferentially recognized and reported over another. Most of the site discoveries in both regions were due to isolated, fortuitous finds over a period of some decades. Only a few localities were
found due to basin surveys or CRM work (Canyon Lakes and Lubbock
Landfill in the south; Lime Creek and Red Smoke in the north).

Sample bias due to the effects of site formation processes probably is
not a factor either. Both areas underwent broadly similar geomorphic evolution during the Paleoindian occupation, as discussed above. The northern region has been subjected to more fluvial erosion, but there is no obvious difference between the regions that could account for sample bias,
such as extensive erosion or burial during specific time intervals or of particular components.

In the absence of evidence for some sort of artificial or natural sample
bias, the remaining explanation for the differences in trends in site
frequency between the Southern and Northern High Plains—that the
samples reflect real differences in Paleoindian site density or occupation
frequency—seems plausible. This tentative conclusion, of course, raises
several broader issues: what do the site frequencies represent? and why are
the site frequencies different in the two areas? A tempting conclusion is
that the site frequencies are a direct reflection of population densities, but
there is no way of substantiating this proposal. But even as a simple indicator of site density a comparison of the trends between regions could be
instructive.

So what could account for the inverse relationship in site densities in
Paleoindian times between the Southern High Plains and Northern High
Plains? Unfortunately there are no answers at this writing. As discussed
in the concluding section of this chapter (below), the environment of the
Southern High Plains was conducive to the expansion of human populations until Late Paleoindian times, when warming and drying conditions
may have reduced occupation intensity. The trends in site density for the
region reflect the environmental trend. For the Northern High Plains, however, no comprehensive stratigraphic, paleontological, or paleobotanical
data sets exist to compare with the archaeological record. Of particular interest in the component-frequency data is the apparent drop in site visibility during Folsom and Agate Basin occupations. No explanation is yet
available in the geoarchaeological record (Chapter 4), which is generally
similar to that of the Southern High Plains, nor in the regional stratigraphic record, which indicates landscape stability and soil formation

(Brady soil) during much of Paleoindian time (Martin 1993; Feng, Johnson, Lu, and Ward 1994; Feng, Johnson, Sprowl, and Lu 1994). The paleontological and paleobotanical records for the period of Paleoindian occupation on the greater northern Plains are notably weak or nonexistent (e.g., Barnosky et al. 1987; Davis 1987; Fredlund and Jaumann 1987; Semken and Falk 1987; Thompson et al. 1993; Elias 1995b).

Conclusions

The above scenarios probably are a gross oversimplification of the Paleoindian cultural and environmental history of the Southern High Plains and neighboring regions, but this largely is because the archaeological record provides only an incomplete perspective on Paleoindian cultures. Nevertheless, the data provide several reasonable working hypotheses regarding the Paleoindian cultural chronology, occupation intensity, and environments on the Llano Estacado. The principal subdivisions of Paleoindian occupation are Clovis (11,200–10,900 yrs BP), Folsom (10,900–10,000 yrs BP), and Late Paleoindian (10,000–8000 yrs BP). These subdivisions are based on the duration of artifact styles. The Clovis period is represented only by Clovis points, but the Folsom period is represented by both Folsom and Midland points, with some evidence that Midland appeared before Folsom. Late Paleoindian includes a variety of unfluted, lanceolate styles including Plainview, Milnesand and other constricted-stem styles (such as Agate Basin), and Firstview. Plainview and particularly some of the constricted-stem styles may overlap with Folsom, appearing as early as 10,500 yrs BP. Firstview appeared possibly as early as 10,000 yrs BP, but was most common ca. 9000 to 8000 yrs BP.

On the Llano Estacado, late Folsom and early post-Folsom time, roughly 10,000±500 yrs BP, represents the convergence of the peak site density, feature frequency, artifact variation, and environmental or at least landscape diversity (FIG. 5.1). There are more sites and features from this time than from any other during the Paleoindian occupation of the region and probably more than from the early and middle Arachic (i.e., more sites and features than at any other time between 11,200 and 5000 yrs BP). Artifact styles include Folsom, Midland, Plainview, Milnesand and other constricted-stem types, and possibly Firstview. In the draws streams, ponds, and marshes coexisted. The playas remained wet and probably shifted between lake and marsh settings. On the uplands sand sheets and possibly sand dunes were beginning to accumulate in some settings. Megafauna were not as diverse at this time, roughly a thousand years after the late Pleistocene extinctions, but other kinds of fauna were abundant and varied. The peak in site density and artifact stylistic diversity coincides with the final phase of a period of environmental diversity and relative hospitality in the last millennia of the Pleistocene and early centuries of the Holocene in the region. The equable environment probably allowed for the apparent flowering of the Paleoindian occupation, but the precise causal mechanisms are unknown.

Elsewhere on the Great Plains, trends in artifact styles and paleoenvironments are generally comparable to those on the Llano Estacado. In particular, the time around 10,000 yrs BP seems regionally significant. Geoarchaeologically (and of paleoenvironmental significance), eolian deposition became more widespread on the High Plains after ca. 10,000 yrs BP, and there may have been a distinct shift in the rate of cave sedimentation on the Edwards Plateau after this time (Collins 1991). On the northern Plains and in the Wyoming Basin, 10,000 yrs BP also apparently marked the appearance of a dichotomy in landscape utilization and subsistence (plains groups and foothills-mountain groups). Site densities in the central Rio Grande valley west of the Llano Estacado are essentially identical to those on the Llano Estacado. The single biggest difference noted throughout the Great Plains, other than physiographic contrasts, is in density of Paleoindian sites on the Northern High Plains compared to the Southern High Plains. The trends are essentially the inverse of one another.

The changes in stratigraphy, sedimentation, and soil formation at and after ca. 10,000 yrs BP (but which probably began as early as 11,000 yrs BP) on the Llano Estacado and in other parts of the Great Plains, and reported changes in plant and animal communities throughout the region at this time, almost certainly had direct or indirect links to climate changes that characterized the late Pleistocene and early Holocene (i.e., occurring around the oxygen isotope stage 2-1 boundary). In particular, the decline in density of Paleoindian sites after ca. 9500 yrs BP probably is linked to the regional drying that characterized the early Holocene.

Testing these hypotheses of cultural chronology, variation in occupation density and artifact diversity, the timing and nature of environmental changes, and the relationship between the Paleoindian artifact and geoarchaeological records and paleoenvironments, of course requires additional archaeological and paleoenvironmental data. Several fundamental kinds of information are especially important: good chronological control on the archaeological record, especially artifact assemblages, and on environmental changes; and morphological, technological, and chronological data on the various artifact styles and related comparative studies of the various styles. Lack of clear age and stylistic relationships among the known Paleo-indian artifact styles is the most persistent problem in Paleoindian studies.

Better understanding of the Paleoindian record on the Southern High Plains requires continued work at known sites, discovery of new sites with *in situ* and, ideally, stratified occupations, systematic surveys, and research on existing collections. Sites such as San Jon, Clovis, and Lubbock Lake are known to have considerable archaeological materials still in place. Continued geoscientific research at the known localities is providing critical new information. Although many undiscovered sites must exist, their discovery awaits fortuitous exposure. Discovery of more sites could easily result from surveys designed to locate Paleoindian sites, from surveys for cultural resource management, and from inventories of private artifact collections. Hester (1975a) developed a very informative and useful data set based on interviews with collectors.

Perhaps the most fruitful line of inquiry for future investigation is study of collections recovered from earlier work. The artifact analyses of Wheat (1972), Knudson (1983), and Hofman (1992; Hofman et al. 1989), the excavation of blocks by Johnson (1986b; Johnson and Holliday 1996) and Drake (1994), and the examination of long-unstudied bone collections (especially for taphonomic analyses) by Saunders and Daeschler (1994), Hill et al. (1994), and Johnson (1987d, 1989; Johnson and Holliday 1996), for example, demonstrate the sorts of new data and insights that can be gained from such work. Investigation of blocks recovered from some sites can provide significant lithologic and chronologic data (e.g., Johnson and Holliday 1996), and taphonomic studies of bone assemblages show that considerable caution is required when interpreting "kills" based simply on the co-occurrence of projectile points and bone (e.g., Holliday et al. 1994; Saunders and Daeschler 1994). The vast and accessible collections of materials from High Plains Paleoindian sites are a greatly underutilized resource, and they await many an indoor field season.

Site Settings and Stratigraphic Descriptions

This section presents basic location information and stratigraphic data for the Paleoindian sites investigated by the author and discussed in Chapter 3. A few sites reported by local informants and yielding important collections also are included, but are not described stratigraphically. Collections reported by Hester (1975a:table 13-1) as part of the High Plains Paleoecology Project are also discussed. The stratigraphic descriptions are primarily for those layers containing or with the potential for containing Paleoindian archaeology. Some older units are described briefly to provide a geologic context. The descriptions are based on the most recent references unless otherwise noted. "Key References" are given if available, but also focus only on the Paleoindian research. For those sites with a long history of research, the citations are not exhaustive; more complete lists of pertinent work are in Chapters 2 and 3.

The stratigraphic descriptions follow standard terminology (AGI 1982; Birkeland 1984; Birkeland et al. 1991; Soil Survey Division Staff 1993). Colors (Munsell notation) are given dry and moist (m). For deposits with significant pedogenic modification colors are given for maximum expression of the B-horizon. Lithofacies nomenclature includes terms common in either geology or pedology, but not both; in particular "mud" and "loam" are used in accordance with conventions of the respective disciplines and are not interchangeable (Holliday 1995b). These terms are used for convenience and brevity. A mud is a deposit containing mostly silt and clay (after Bates and Jackson 1980). Late Quaternary muds on the Southern High Plains typically are stained dark gray or black by organic matter (Holliday 1995b). A loam is a deposit with more or less equal amounts of sand, silt, and clay (Soil Survey Division Staff 1993).

Sites with Stratigraphic Descriptions

Anderson Basin #1 (Roosevelt Co., New Mexico; 34°14′N 103°13′W)
Anderson Basin #2 (Roosevelt Co., New Mexico; 34°14′N 103°12′W)

These sites are ca. 1 km apart in blowouts of the Muleshoe Dunes on the north side of Blackwater Draw, downstream from the Clovis site (FIGS. 1.3, 3.3). AB1 covers a roughly rectangular area of ca. 400,000 m². Deflation removed valley fill down to the Blackwater Draw Formation in many areas. AB2 is a blowout covering a roughly ovoid area of ca. 130,000 m². Valley fill was removed locally down to Pleistocene lake carbonates. The western half of the site was destroyed by installation of center-pivot irrigation sometime in the 1980s.

Key References: Howard 1935a; Hester 1975b; Haynes 1975.

Stratigraphic Descriptions: Haynes 1975; and Holliday 1995b (sections Bw-58 and Bw-71). Stratigraphic nomenclature follows Holliday 1995b. For stratigraphic correlations see Table 3.1.

Anderson Basin #1 (Bw-71 of Holliday 1995b)

STRATUM 3C Sandy marl up to 18 cm thick, white to light gray (10YR 8/2 7/2m), with common limonite stains.

STRATUM 2S OR 3S Sand 70 cm thick, light gray to dark grayish-brown (10YR 6/2 4/2m, 7/2 6/2m) with Ag-horizon in upper 10 cm (10YR 6/2 4/2m); faint bedding; common limonite stains; clear, irregular lower boundary.

STRATUM 2M Mud 15–20 cm thick, dark grayish-brown (10YR 4/2 3/1m); very hard; common vertical cracks 3–8 mm wide filled with sand; black peaty mud 0–5 cm thick at base; abrupt, irregular lower boundary.

STRATUM 1 Sand up to 45 cm thick, white to light gray (10YR 7/1 5/2m, 7/2 5/2m, 8/1 6/2m); locally indurated, bedded and/or contorted; thin discontinuous lenses of mud in upper 4 cm; clear, irregular lower boundary.

BLACKWATER DRAW FM Mottled, yellowish-red and gleyed (10YR 8/2 6/2m; 5YR 5/6 5/6m) Btg-horizon.

Anderson Basin #2 (Bw-58 of Holliday 1995b)

STRATUM 3 Sandy marl up to 50 cm thick, light gray (10YR 7/1 5/1m, 7/2 5/2m), with zones of organic matter accumulation (10YR 5/1 3/1m, 6/3 8/1m), probable A-horizons; clear, wavy lower boundary.

STRATUM 2S OR 3S Sand 33 cm thick, grayish-brown (10YR 5/2 7/1m), with localized staining by organic matter (10YR 7/1 8/1m); abrupt, irregular lower boundary.

STRATUM 2D Interbedded diatomite and diatomaceous mud, light gray to gray (10YR 5/1 3/1m, 7/1 5/1m); 10–20 cm thick, locally missing; Folsom artifacts found within this zone and unfluted lanceolate (possibly Plainview) projectile points on top; abrupt, irregular lower boundary.

STRATUM 1 Sand 83 cm thick, light gray (10YR 7/2 5/1m) with gray A-horizon (10YR 6/1 3/1m) in upper 33 cm; bones of mammoths, horses, and bison common; abrupt, irregular lower boundary.

STRATUM B Indurated lacustrine carbonate; white (10YR 8/1 8/2m).

Bedford Ranch (Andrews Co., Texas; 32°06′N 102°50′W)

Bedford Ranch is a series of small blowouts near the southern edge of the west-central Andrews Dunes (FIGS. 1.2, 1.3). Late Paleoindian projectile points (including Firstview) were collected from the deflation basins along with debitage and burned rock. No formal publications on the archaeology are available. Stratigraphic terminology follows Green (1961b).

UNIT VIIb Sand, light yellowish-brown to very pale brown (10YR 6/4 5/4m, 8/3 6/4m), 1–2 m thick; 25–30 prominent brownish-yellow (10YR 6/6 4/6m) clay bands, 5–15 mm thick; Late Paleoindian artifacts locally common; clear lower boundary.

UNIT VI Sandy clay, Btg-horizon, light yellowish-brown to dark brown (10YR 6/4 5/4m, 10YR 3/3 2/2m); up to 15 cm thick; illuvial clay throughout but faint discontinuous clay bands locally apparent; bone (bison?) locally common; abrupt lower boundary.

UNIT V Sandy marl, white (10YR 8/1 6/2m, 7/3m), up to 15 cm thick; bone (bison?) locally common; clear lower boundary.

UNIT IV Sand, white to pale yellow (2.5Y 7/4 7/2m, 5Y 8/2 6/2m, 10YR 8/2 6/3m) Cg-horizon; typically 50 cm thick, locally up to 260 cm; abrupt lower boundary.

UNIT I Blackwater Draw Fm; mottled, reduced Btg-horizon, strong brown to brownish-yellow to light yellowish-brown (7.5YR 4/6m, 10YR 6/6 5/4m, 7/2 7/1m, 2.5Y 6/4m).

Car Body (Roosevelt Co., New Mexico; 34°14′N 103°17′W)

The Car Body site (also the "Model-T" site of Haynes 1975) is a deep, roughly rectangular blowout of ca. 60,000 m² along the south side of Blackwater Draw (FIGS. 1.3, 3.3). Wind deflation excavated a steep-walled depression up to 5 m deep, exposing late Quaternary valley fill. Clovis and Folsom artifacts and bone from mammoths, horses, and camels were collected in and near the site (Haynes 1975; J. Warnica, pers. comm. 1995). The site is not published except for a brief discussion and description of the stratigraphy by Haynes (1975). For stratigraphic correlations see Table 3.3 and Holliday (1995b).

STRATUM C Sand, white to light yellowish-brown (10YR 8/2 6/2m, 10YR 6/4 5/4m) up to 3 m thick; prominent brown (7.5YR 5/4 3/4m) A–Bt soil formed in upper 100 cm; A-horizon 20 cm thick locally apparent below Bt; interbedded sand and organic-rich clay in lower 50 cm; bedded zone with mammoths and Clovis artifacts exposed at the surface toward draw, where rest of unit is missing (never deposited?); abrupt lower boundary.

STRATUM B Marl; white (10YR 8/1, 2.5Y 7/2m); typically 100 cm thick over olive sand (10YR 8/1, 2.5Y 6/2).

Clovis (Roosevelt Co., New Mexico; 34°17′N 103°20′W)

The Clovis site, also known as Blackwater Draw Locality 1, is in a small basin on the north edge of the Muleshoe Dunes, 2 km north of and draining into Blackwater Draw (FIGS. 1.3, 3.3, 3.6). Mining destroyed much of the site; a large pit now occupies most of the topographic basin that originally marked the site (FIG. 3.7). Remnants of the basin fill are exposed along the margins of the pit, and extensive deposits remain in the "outlet channel" that connected the basin with the draw proper (FIGS. 3.6, 3.7).

Key References: Hester 1972; Stevens 1973 (on the history of research); Boldurian 1990; Stanford et al. 1990 (on the history of research); Howard 1935a,b; Antevs 1935, 1949; Cotter 1937, 1938; Sellards 1952; Green 1962a, 1963; Haynes and Agogino 1966; Haynes 1975, 1995; Haynes et al. 1992.

Stratigraphic Descriptions: Howard 1935a; Antevs 1935, 1949; Sellards 1952; Haynes and Agogino 1966; Haynes 1975, 1995; Holliday 1985e. Only a generalized description is presented below (largely representing the South Bank) because of the considerable data provided by Haynes 1975, 1995. For stratigraphic correlations see Table 3.3.

UNIT E Organic-rich silt and fine sand (locally a cumulic A-horizon) with sandy basin-margin facies, locally including sandy facies of Units D and F; bison bones and Late Paleoindian artifacts locally common.

UNIT D Diatomaceous earth, locally including mud or diatomite; sands and coarser deposits (1) occur locally below the diatomaceous earth and interface with upper Unit C, (2) occur as valley-margin facies to the diatomaceous earth, and (3) bury the diatomaceous earth; bison bone, Folsom artifacts, and Agate Basin artifacts are locally common.

UNIT C Sand, locally with organic-rich loamy sand interbeds; discontinuous and locally interfacing with lower Unit D; mammoth and bison bones and Clovis artifacts locally common; Unit C probably is several different sand or sandy units between Units B and D.

UNIT B Sand with coarse basin-margin facies; muddy interbeds locally common; bones of mammoths, horses, and other Rancholabrean fauna locally common; Clovis artifacts in upper portion of unit (intrusive); abrupt lower boundary.

UNIT A Blackwater Draw Fm; multiple, welded Bt–Bk soils (2.5YR 7/2 6/2m, 5YR 5/6 5/4m) interbedded with lacustrine carbonate (10YR 8/2 8/3m).

Elida (Roosevelt Co., New Mexico; 33°48′N 103°32′W)

Elida is in a large, deflated portion of a small sand dune field (covering approximately 0.75 km²) that is a segment of the larger Lea-Yoakum dune field (FIGS. 1.2, 1.3, 3.56). A large assemblage of Folsom artifacts was acquired over a number of years of surface collecting. No systematic excavations were conducted.

Key References: Warnica 1961; Hester 1962.

COVER SAND Sand, yellowish-red to reddish-brown (5YR 4/6 4/4m), up to 2 m thick; A–Bt (5YR 4/6 3/4m) soil formed in upper half of unit; abrupt lower boundary.

BLACKWATER DRAW FM Sandy clay loam, Bt–Bk soil, yellowish-red (5YR 4/6 4/4m); Folsom artifacts in Bt-horizon (via bioturbation from surface?).

Lubbock Lake (Lubbock Co., Texas; 33°37′N 101°54′W)

Lubbock Lake is an archaeological site occupying a meandering, 2 km reach of Yellowhouse Draw on the northwestern edge of the city of Lubbock (FIGS. 1.3, 3.20). The site was discovered in 1936, following excavation of a U-shaped reservoir on the inside of one of the meanders (FIGS. 2.7, 3.20). The reservoir construction cut through the late Quaternary valley fill, yielding abundant archaeological debris.

Key References: Black 1974 (including a history of investigations); Holliday and Johnson 1986; Johnson and Holliday 1987a (on the history of investigations); Sellards 1952; Green 1962b; Black 1974; Johnson and

Holliday 1980, 1981; Stafford 1981; Holliday, Johnson, Haas, and Stuckenrath 1983, 1985; Holliday 1985b,d; Holliday and Allen 1987; Johnson 1987a.

Stratigraphic Descriptions: Stafford 1981; Holliday 1985b. Description below is generalized from Holliday 1985b. For stratigraphic correlations see Table 3.5.

STRATA 2M & 2S *2m* (valley-axis facies): gray mud (10YR 5/1 3/1m) 30–80 cm thick; bison bone beds and Late Paleoindian artifacts locally common; Ag–Cg soil profile developed in upper 30–50 cm; *2s* (valley-margin facies): sandy loam up to 2 m thick; pale brown to gray (10YR 6/3 3/1m, 2.5YR 7/2 5/2m); abrupt lower boundary for both facies.

STRATA 2D & 2S *2d* (valley-axis facies): white diatomite (10YR 8/1) interbedded with gray diatomaceous mud (10YR 5/1 2/1m), 30–100 cm thick; bison bone beds and Folsom artifacts locally common; *2s* (valley-margin facies): pale brown to gray sandy loam up to 2 m thick (10YR 6/3 3/1m, 2.5YR 7/2 5/2m); abrupt lower boundary for both facies.

STRATUM 1 Gravel, sand, and some clay, very pale brown (10YR 7/3 8/2 6/2m), locally gleyed (2.5Y 7/2 4/2m, 6/2 5/2m); up to 2 m thick; cross-bedding and cut-and-fill sequences common; bones of mammoths, horses, bison, and camels locally common; abrupt lower boundary.

BLANCO FM Pliocene lacustrine carbonate.

Lubbock Landfill (Lubbock Co., Texas; 33°41'N 101°52'W)

The landfill is along an S-shaped series of deep, entrenched meanders of lower Blackwater Draw (FIGS. 1.3, 3.30). The site was exposed in a deep pit (the "Wind Pit") on the eastern end of the meander belt (FIG. 3.30).

Key Reference: Brown 1993.

STRATUM 3C Marl, light gray (10YR 7/1 3/2m), up to 100 cm thick; light brownish-gray (10YR 6/2 4/1m) A-horizon in upper 60 cm; clear lower boundary.

STRATUM 2M Mud, gray (10YR 5/1 6/2 3/1m), up to 1.5 m thick, interbedded with sand lenses up to 10 cm thick; lowest mud layer (2m1) has Ag–Cg soil in upper 10 cm in association with bison bone and Paleoindian artifacts; abrupt lower boundary.

STRATUM 2D Diatomite, white (10YR 8/1), interbedded with light brownish-gray diatomaceous mud (10YR 6/2 3/1m), 25 cm thick; interbeds of sand and organic-rich clay occur as channel-fill facies; abrupt lower boundary.

STRATUM 1   Sand, very pale brown to white (10YR 7/3 8/2 6/2m), up to 1.5 m thick with some lenses of gravel (<10 cm thick) and interbeds of organic-rich mud 1–10 mm thick; crossbedding and cut-and-fill sequences common; few bones of mammoths and bison; abrupt lower boundary.

BLANCO FM   Pliocene lacustrine carbonate.

Marks Beach (Lamb Co., Texas; 34°08′N 102°24′W)

Marks Beach is in an east-to-west-flowing reach of middle Blackwater Draw, the only such segment identified for any draw on the Llano Estacado (Holliday 1995b) (FIGS. 1.3, 3.32). The site is near the south edge of the Muleshoe Dunes and is part of a larger locality known as Gibson Ranch (FIG. 3.32). Marks Beach is exposed along the north side of the draw in an elliptical blowout in the valley fill covering ca. 175 m × 80 m (FIG. 3.32). Excavations on the floor of the deflation basin yielded *Bison antiquus* and flint flakes. Some recent testing has not been reported.

Key References: Honea 1980; Holliday 1995b. For stratigraphic correlations see Table 3.8.

Stratigraphic Descriptions: Honea 1980; Holliday 1995b. Description below is generalized from Holliday 1995b.

STRATA 3C & 3S   *3c* (valley-axis facies): sandy marl, gray to light gray (10YR 6/1 7/1 4/1m), 1–2 m thick; *3s* (valley axis and valley margin): sand, gray to light gray (10YR 6/1 4/1m, 7/2 5/2m), with few organic-rich interbeds 0.5–3.0 cm thick; bison bones and archaeological debris locally common; clear to abrupt lower boundary for both facies.

STRATA 2D & 2S   *2d* (valley-axis facies): interbedded gray diatomite (10YR 6/1 4/1m), gray mud (10YR 5/1 3/1m), and pale brown sand (10YR 6/3 3/1m) ca. 100 cm thick; some bison bones; *2s* (valley-margin facies): pale brown sand (10YR 6/3 3/1m) with few, thin interbeds of diatomite and mud, 2–4 m thick; bison bones and archaeological debris locally common; clear to abrupt lower boundary for both facies.

STRATUM 1   Sand, light gray (10YR 7/1 3/1m), at least 200 cm thick.

Miami (Roberts Co., Texas; 35°45′N 100°41′W)

The Miami site is in a small (23 m diameter), filled playa basin on the open High Plains surface, but within 60 m of the heavily dissected eastern margin (FIGS. 1.3, 3.44, 3.46). Excavations yielded mammoth bone in association with Clovis points.

Key References: Sellards 1938, 1952; Saunders 1980; Johnson 1989; Holliday et al. 1994.

Stratigraphic Descriptions: Sellards 1938; Holliday et al. 1994. Description below is generalized from Holliday et al. 1994.

UPPER MUD Mostly removed by excavations, but otherwise gray mud (10YR 6/1 4/1m) up to 40 cm thick; mammoths with Clovis artifacts at base of unit; abrupt lower boundary.

LOESS Silt, light brownish-gray (10YR 6/2 4/2m), ca. 10 cm thick; abrupt lower boundary.

LOWER MUD Mud, dark gray to gray (10YR 4/1 5/1 3/1m), up to 114 cm thick; clear lower boundary.

BLACKWATER DRAW FM Bt-horizon stained by organic matter, dark grayish-brown to light brownish-gray (10YR 4/2 3/2m, 6/2 4/2m); Mn patches common.

Midland (Midland Co., Texas; 31°53′N 102°07′W)

The Midland site, also known as the Scharbauer site or Scharbauer Ranch site, is located in a narrow bend of Monahans Draw, adjacent to and partially buried by a dune field (FIGS. 1.3, 3.34). The site was exposed by deflation of the dune sediments along the draw (Locality 1) and away from it (Locality 3 West). The site is best known for yielding human remains that may be early Holocene in age or older. The site is the type locality for the Midland point, and it also yielded Folsom artifacts and the remains of extinct vertebrates.

Key References: Wendorf et al. 1955; Sellards 1955b; Wendorf and Krieger 1959; Holliday 1995b. Stratigraphic description based on Holliday 1995b. For stratigraphic correlations see Table 3.9.

Stratigraphic Descriptions: Wendorf et al. 1955; Holliday 1995b. Description below is generalized from Holliday 1995b.

Locality 1 (Mn-5 of Holliday 1995b)

STRATUM 4S Sand, strong brown to reddish-yellow (7.5YR 5/6 4/6m, 6/6 5/4m, 5/6m), 90 cm thick; A–Bw soil formed throughout unit; clear lower boundary.

MIXED ZONE 3S & 4S Sand, mottled very pale brown and light brown (10YR 7/3 6/3m, 7.5YR 6/4 5/4m), 26 cm thick; clear lower boundary.

STRATUM 3S Sand, locally heavily mottled pink, yellowish-brown, and brownish-yellow (7.5YR 7/4 6/4m, 6/6m, 10YR 5/6 4/3m, 6/8 6/6m), up to 100 cm thick; fragments of lake carbonate common; bones of bison, horse, and antelope, and Midland artifacts locally common; rare human bone recovered; clear lower boundary.

STRATUM 1 Sand, pinkish-white to pink (7.5YR 8/2 7/4), at least 100 cm thick; bones of mammoths, camels, horses, wolves, and antelope locally common.

Locality 3W (Mn-19 of Holliday 1995b)

UPPER RED SAND Sand, yellowish-brown to brownish-yellow (5YR 5/8 4/6m, 6/8 4/8m), 165 cm thick; A–Bw–Bt soil profile formed throughout unit (few clay bands in Bt); Folsom artifacts locally common at base; clear lower boundary.

LOWER RED SAND Sand, yellowish-red to reddish-yellow (5YR 5/8 4/6m, 6/8 4/8m), at least 170 cm thick; A–Bt–Bw soil profile formed throughout unit.

Milnesand (Roosevelt Co., New Mexico; 33°41′N 103°18′W)

Ted Williamson (Roosevelt Co., New Mexico; 33°41′N 103°18′W)

These sites are in a segment of the Lea-Yoakum Dunes, near a narrow, shallow reach of Sulphur Draw (FIGS. 1.2, 1.3). Both sites were in small blowouts, exposing dense beds of *Bison antiquus* bone in association with large assemblages of Milnesand points (Milnesand; the type site) and Plainview points (Ted Williamson site). No reports were published on the work at Ted Williamson.

Key References: Sellards 1955a; Johnson et al. 1986; Hill et al. 1994. For stratigraphic correlations see Table 3.21.

Milnesand

HISTORIC (?) DUNE SAND Sand up to 1 m thick; light yellowish-brown (10YR 6/4 4/4m); A-horizon locally preserved in upper 40 cm; abrupt lower boundary.

SAND SHEET Sand up to 20 cm thick; light yellowish-brown (10YR 6/4 4/4m); few discontinuous clay bands up to 25 mm thick; this sand unit probably encased the bone bed; abrupt lower boundary.

BLACKWATER DRAW FM Sandy clay Bt-horizon, yellowish-red (5YR 5/6 4/4m), with gley mottling (Btg) (10YR 6/4, 8/2, 7/3 6/4m); A-horizon (7.5YR 5/6 4/6m, 5/4 4/4m) up to 10 cm thick locally preserved at top of unit (and probably formed contemporaneously with initial sand sheet deposition), associated with bison bone bed and Milnesand artifacts.

Ted Williamson

HISTORIC (?) DUNE SAND Sand up to 150 cm thick; pale brown to strong brown (10YR 7/4, 7.5YR 4/4m, 7.5YR 5/6 4/6m); loose, single grain; bedding obscured by rooting; clear, smooth lower boundary.

SAND SHEET Sand up to 230 cm thick; strong brown A–Bw soil (7.5YR 5/6 4/6m, 4/4m) formed throughout the unit; up to 6 strong brown clay bands (7.5YR 5/6 4/6m) 2–3 mm thick locally prominent in lower half of unit in and near center of dune; some Plainview artifacts encased in lower half of unit; abrupt lower boundary.

BLACKWATER DRAW FM Sandy clay Bt-horizon, yellowish-red (5YR 4/6m) with gley mottling (Btg) (10YR 6/4 6/3m); bison bone bed with Plainview artifacts rested on top of this unit.

Plainview (Hale Co., Texas; 34°11′N 101°43′W)

The well-known Plainview site is in a broad, curving reach of Running Water Draw in the city of Plainview, Texas (FIG. 3.37). The site, discovered during quarrying along the south margin of the draw, consisted of an extensive bone bed of *Bison antiquus* associated with the type Plainview assemblage. The pit that exposed the bone bed (Pit 1, FIG. 3.37) was filled by 1980.

Key References: Speer 1990 (for a history of investigations); Sellards et al. 1947; Holliday 1990a, 1995b. For stratigraphic correlations see Table 3.11.

Stratigraphic Descriptions: Sellards et al. 1947; Holliday 1985e, 1995b. Description below is generalized from Holliday 1995b, but is not from excavation area.

STRATA 3C & 3S *3c* (valley-axis facies): marl, white (10YR 8/1 7/2m), up to 40 cm thick; *3s* (valley-margin facies): loam, pale brown (10YR 6/3 5/3m), up to 100 cm thick; A–Bw profile formed throughout unit; gradual lower boundary.

STRATUM 2M Mud, dark brown (10YR 4/3 3/3m), up to 20 cm thick; discontinuous and locally convoluted and interbedded with stratum 1; abrupt lower boundary.

STRATUM 1 Sand and gravel, very pale brown to white (10YR 7/3 6/2m, 8/2 6/2m, 2.5Y 6/2 5/2m), up to 140 cm thick; discontinuous lenses of reduced sandy clay; bison bone with Plainview type collection was on top of this unit where it thinned out over a bedrock (Ogallala Formation) bench; abrupt lower boundary.

OGALLALA FM Massive, silicified, pisolitic Stage VI calcrete.

Ro-16 (Roosevelt Co., New Mexico; 33°37'N 103°25'W)

The site is exposed in a series of small deflation basins and gullies cut in a segment of the Lea-Yoakum Dunes (FIGS. 1.2, 3.61). Clovis, Folsom, Midland, and Milnesand artifacts were collected from the floors of the eroded areas. No reports were published.

COVER SAND Sand, yellowish-red (5YR 5/6 4/6m), up to 150 cm thick; yellowish-red (5YR 4/6 4/6m) A–Bt soil formed in upper 30 cm; artifacts locally common in lower 50 cm; abrupt lower boundary.

BLACKWATER DRAW FM Sandy clay loam, red (2.5YR 4/6 5/6m) Bt-horizon.

Ryan (Lubbock Co., Texas; 33°40'N 102°05'W)

The Ryan site is a small playa (12 m diameter) completely filled with lake sediments. The site was exposed in a small road cut along the south margin of a broad (2–3 km) basin that contains Yellowhouse Draw (FIG. 1.3). A large collection of Plainview points, bifaces, and other stone artifacts were found.

Key References: Johnson et al. 1987; Hartwell 1991, 1995.
Stratigraphic Description: Holliday, unpublished field notes.

PLAYA FILL Mud, dark grayish-brown (10YR 4/2 3/3m), up to 60 cm thick; cache of Plainview artifacts found in upper half of unit; abrupt lower boundary.

BLACKWATER DRAW FM Mottled strong brown, dark brown, and yellowish-red (7.5YR 4/6m, 3/2m, 5YR 4/8m) Btg-horizon.

San Jon (Quay Co., New Mexico; 34°58'N 103°21'W)

The San Jon site is a playa basin within a few hundred meters of the northwestern High Plains escarpment (FIGS. 1.3, 3.49). The basin is heavily dissected by a canyon cut deep into the escarpment (FIGS. 2.6, 3.49). The playa fill containing the archaeological material is preserved in several peninsulas or promontories isolated between arroyo tributaries of the canyon (FIGS. 2.6, 3.49, 3.50). The bone bed with the "type" San Jon point and *Bison antiquus* bone is in Area 2, location of the stratigraphic description.

Key References: Roberts 1942; Judson 1953; Harbour 1975; Oldfield 1975; Hill et al. 1995. For stratigraphic correlations see Table 3.16.

Stratigraphic Descriptions: Judson 1953. Description below is from Holliday, unpublished field notes.

3M Mud, dark brown (7.5YR 4/2 3/2m), up to 50 cm thick; ABt-horizon; clear lower boundary.

2S Sandy loam, brown (7.5YR 5/4 3/4m), 150–250 cm thick; lower half is interbedded sandy loam and mud; upper half more homogeneous with Bt-horizon; lithic debris and some bone common; clear lower boundary.

2M Mud, dark brown (7.5YR 4/2 3/2m), 50–200 cm thick; Bt-horizon; bison bone bed with "San Jon" artifacts at top of unit; clear lower boundary.

Shifting Sands (Winkler Co., Texas; 32°03′N 102°57′W)

Shifting Sands is a series of large blowouts in the middle of the west-central Andrews Dunes (FIGS. 1.2, 1.3). A Folsom-Midland assemblage, including projectile points and other tools, debitage, bone, and burned rock, was collected from the floors of the deflation basins.

Key References: Amick and Rose 1990; Hofman et al. 1990. Stratigraphic terminology follows Green (1961b).

UNIT VIIb Sand, very pale brown (10YR 7/4 5/4m), 70 cm thick, locally thicker; 10–20 prominent brownish-yellow (10YR 6/6 4/6m) clay bands, 5–25 mm thick; localized gleying of sand (2.5Y 7/4 6/4m) and clay bands (2.5Y 6/4) in lower 10–20 cm; bison bone and Folsom and Midland artifacts locally common; below clay band zone locally is sand with light yellowish-brown Bw-horizon (10YR 6/4 5/3m); clear lower boundary.

UNIT V Sandy marl, white (10YR 8/1 7/3m), 10–15 cm thick; bone (bison?) locally common; clear lower boundary.

UNIT IV Sand, white (10YR 8/2 7/2m), locally a light yellowish-brown to brownish-yellow Cg-horizon (2.5Y 6/4m, 7.5YR 6/8); typically 50 cm thick, locally up to 120 cm thick; abrupt lower boundary.

UNIT I Blackwater Draw Fm; mottled, reduced brownish-yellow Btg-horizon (10YR 6/6 5/4m).

Tatum (Lea Co., New Mexico; 33°28′N 103°28′W)

The Tatum site is a deflation basin in the Lea-Yoakum Dunes (FIGS. 1.2, 1.3). Wind erosion yielded a collection of Folsom artifacts. The site was mentioned in passing by Sellards and Evans (1960), but otherwise was never reported.

UPPER SAND Sand, light yellowish-brown (10YR 6/4 5/4m), 3–5 m thick; prominent dark brown (7.5YR 3/4m) clay band 5–10 cm thick at base of unit with Folsom artifacts locally common; clear lower boundary.

LOWER SAND Compact, resistant sand up to 50 cm thick with prominent color zonation, upper 10–15 cm pale brown (10YR 6/3 5/2m), middle 10–15 cm very pale brown (10YR 7/4 5/3m), and lower 20–30 cm very pale brown (10YR 7/3 6/3m); common, very irregular clay bands 1–5 mm throughout unit; clear lower boundary.

LAKE BEDS Sandy clay, gleyed with upper 35 cm light gray (2.5Y 7/2 6/2m) with abundant gastropods and few 1–5 mm clay bands from overlying unit, then light brownish-gray zone (2.5Y 6/2 5/2m) (A-horizon?), and lower 50 cm light gray (2.5Y 7/2 6/2m); abrupt lower boundary.

OGALLALA FM Silicified calcrete.

Winkler-1 (Lea Co., New Mexico; 32°02′N 103°01′W)

This site is exposed in a linear series of blowouts (totaling >500 m length) along Monument Draw in the northwestern end of the Andrews Dunes (FIGS. 1.2, 1.3). An extensive Midland assemblage was recovered during careful collecting for over 30 years. The site has not been fully reported.

Key Reference: Blaine 1968. Stratigraphic terminology follows Green (1961b).

UNIT VIIb Sand, brown (7.5YR 5/4 4/4m), generally 30–50 cm thick, locally thicker; A–Bw soil horizon formed throughout unit (A-horizon typically is missing); Midland artifacts locally common; abrupt lower boundary.

UNIT V Sandy marl, pinkish-white (7.5YR 8/2, 10YR 6/4m), up to 10 cm thick; horizontal and vertical carbonate tubules common; clear lower boundary.

UNIT IV Sand, pink (7.5YR 7/4 5/4m), 30–40 cm thick; mastodont teeth recovered from this unit; abrupt lower boundary.

UNIT III Sandy marl, white (10YR 8/2 7/3m), typically 10–20 cm thick, thicker toward valley margin; remains of mammoths, bison, and horses locally common; clear lower boundary.

UNIT I Blackwater Draw Fm; mottled, reduced Btg-horizon, reddish-yellow, brownish-yellow, light gray, light yellowish-brown, and pale yellow (7.5YR 6/6 4/6m, 10YR 6/6 5/4m, 7/2 7/1m, 2.5Y 6/4m, 5Y 7/3 6/3m).

Wyche Ranch (Andrews Co., Texas; 32°08′N 102°40′W)

The Wyche Ranch site is a small blowout along the south edge of the central Andrews Dunes (FIGS. 1.2, 1.3). Midland and possible Folsom artifacts were found in the deflation basin. No formal report is available. Stratigraphic terminology follows Green (1961b).

UNIT VIIb? Sand, brownish-yellow (7.5YR 6/6 4/6m), 50 cm thick; buried Btw-horizon; Midland artifacts locally common; abrupt lower boundary.

UNIT I Blackwater Draw Fm; strong brown Bt-horizon (7.5YR 5/6 4/6m).

Sites without Stratigraphic Descriptions

Barber (Roosevelt Co., New Mexico)

The Barber site is known only from a brief reference by Sellards and Evans (1960). The site probably was a Folsom locality visited by James Warnica and E. H. Sellards in the Muleshoe Dunes, ca. 15 km west of the Clovis site (J. Warnica, pers. comm. 1995; Texas Memorial Museum accession records, site 1263) (FIG. 3.3).

Bethel (Roosevelt Co., New Mexico; 34°17′N 103°27′W)

The Bethel site is a blowout in the Muleshoe Dunes on the south side of Blackwater Draw (FIG. 3.3). The site yielded a collection of Plainview artifacts (J. Warnica, pers. comm. 1994). The site is not published.

Burns (Roosevelt Co., New Mexico; 34°15′N 103°23′W)

The Burns site is an elongate blowout of ca. 45,000 m² in the Muleshoe Dunes on the south side of Blackwater Draw (FIGS. 1.3, 3.3). The site produced several constricted-stem ("Hell Gap") projectile points (J. Warnica, M. Burns, pers. comm. 1995). The site is not published.

Carley-Archer (Martin Co., Texas; 32°26′N 102°07′W)

Carley-Archer is at the confluence of Mustang Draw and McKenzie Draw (FIG. 3.42). The site is a dense scatter of lithic artifacts deflating from a thin sand sheet on the uplands immediately adjacent to the draw. The site produced mostly Folsom-Midland material (D. Carley, pers. comm. 1986). Site data are unpublished.

Seminole-Rose (Gaines Co., Texas; 32°32′N 102°20′W)

This site is along a broad, deeply incised reach of Seminole Draw (FIG. 3.42)

(Holliday 1995b). The valley fill is in a relatively narrow channel cut into the floor of the much wider valley. Eolian sand is draped across the draw. The site, an extensive bed of bone from extinct *Bison antiquus* associated with Firstview projectile points, was exposed by road construction on the floor of the draw. No reports were published.

Sites Recorded by the High Plains Paleoecology Project

Hester (1975a:table 13-1) lists and describes, in tabular form, 80 Paleo-indian sites for the southern Plains, 69 of which are on the Southern High Plains. These data are used in the tabulation and discussion of site settings in Chapters 3 and 5 (Tables 3.13, 3.18, 3.22, 5.1), and in the tabulation and discussion of site frequencies in Chapter 5 (Tables 5.2, 5.5). Sites discussed individually in Chapter 3 and listed by Hester (1975a:table 13-1) were not included in the tabulations in Chapters 3 and 5 (Anderson Basin #1, LA6211; Anderson Basin #2, LA6212; Clovis, LA3324; Elida, LA6225; Lubbock Lake, LA6242; Milnesand, LA6209; Plainview, LA6240). The tabulations of site settings do not include sites described by Hester (1975a:table 13-1) as "isolated points." The tabulations of site frequencies do include the sites that yielded isolated points.

Lithic Resources of the Southern High Plains

The lithostratigraphy of the Southern High Plains is well known from diverse studies (e.g., Sellards et al. 1933; Nicholson 1960; Kelley and Trauger 1972; Frenzel et al. 1988; Banks 1990), including geologic mapping at a scale of 1:250,000 (the *Geologic Atlas of Texas* series of the University of Texas Bureau of Economic Geology). The following discussion is organized on the basis of lithostratigraphic units (formations and members of sedimentary rocks) grouped by geologic time (oldest to youngest rocks). The focus of the discussion is on the primary units producing raw materials well known on the Southern High Plains: Alibates agate, Tecovas jasper, Dakota quartzite, Edwards chert, and Ogallala chert and quartzite (FIG. A2.1). Quaternary gravel sources and volcanic and metamorphic rocks are discussed at the end. Other lesser-known sources beyond the immediate boundaries of the Llano Estacado (within ca. 300 km) or those with unclear but potential archaeological connections to the region are listed in Table A2.1. Rock terminology follows Luedtke (1992) (see also Church 1994).

Permian: Quartermaster Formation, Alibates Dolomite

The Quartermaster Formation (Upper Permian) and older Permian redbeds crop out at the surface of the Rolling Plains east of the Llano Estacado and along the eastern, northeastern, and northern escarpment of the region (FIG. A2.1). The Quartermaster is the oldest unit near the Llano Estacado containing suitable material for stone tools. The redbeds consist of silty, evenly bedded, locally massive shales; sandy, well-indurated siltstone; and silty, fine-grained sandstone. Gypsum and dolomite beds are locally common but discontinuous.

The Alibates Dolomite Lentil, in the upper Quartermaster, has been mapped along the northern Llano Estacado, primarily in the Canadian River drainage. The unit, parts of which were altered to agate, is found near the top of the Quartermaster Formation (Gould 1907; Patton 1923: 36–47; Eifler 1969), although Nicholson (1960:fig. 45) shows it as a separate unit, underlying the Quartermaster.

The Alibates Dolomite produces one of the best-known raw materials in North America for the manufacture of stone tools, the Alibates agate (Bryan 1950; Schaeffer 1958). Alibates agate is the only material in the Quartermaster Formation suitable for manufacturing tools. This multicolored material, occurring as lenses and nodules, is the result of silicification of the dolomite (Gould 1907; Bowers 1975; Banks 1990). The best-known

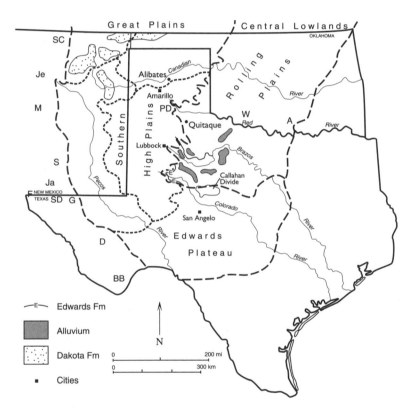

FIGURE A2.1. Distribution of principal stone-tool resources around the Southern High Plains, with locations of selected cities. Mountain areas with significant stone resources are indicated with letters (A Arbuckle Mtns; F Franklin Mtns; BB Big Bend; D Davis Mtns; G Guadalupe Mtns; Ja Jarilla Mtns; Je Jemez Mtns; M Manzano Mtns; PD Palo Duro; S Sacramento Mtns; SC Sangre de Cristo; SD Sierra Diablo; W Wichita Mtns).

TABLE A2.1. Sedimentary rock units with knappable materials of limited extent and/or unknown archaeological significance[1]

Formation	Age	Location[2]	Lithology	Reference
Gravel	Quaternary	Pecos River valley	various	Thomas 1972; Frye et al. 1982; Shelley 1993
		north-central New Mexico	chert[3]	Banks 1990:67–70
		central Rio Grande valley[4]	chert	Banks 1990:78
		Big Bend	various	Banks 1990:87
Blanco	Plio-Pleistocene	Southern High Plains[5]	silicified calcrete	Holliday and Welty 1981
Antlers Sand	Cretaceous	eastern Southern High Plains	quartzite, jasper, flint, petrified wood[6]	Holliday and Welty 1981
Madera	Permian	Sangre de Cristo Mtns, Manzano Mtns, NM; northeastern NM	chert	Banks 1990:72, 78, 89
		Guadalupe Mtns, Sierra Diablo Mtns	chert	Banks 1990:82–83
Markley Conglomerate		southeastern Rolling Plains	chert, quartzite	Banks 1990:110–114
Chico Ridge Member	Pennsylvanian	eastern Rolling Plains	chert	Banks 1990:110
	Mississippian	Sangre de Cristo Mtns, NM	chert	Banks 1990:71–72
	Late Paleozoic	Franklin Mtns, Sacramento Mtns, Jarillas Mtns, TX & NM	chert[7]	Harbour 1972; Banks 1990:80–82
	Late Paleozoic	Big Bend, Davis Mtns, TX	chert, petrified wood	Banks 1990:83–87
Caballos	Devonian	Big Bend	chert, novaculite	McBride and Thomson 1970

TABLE A2.1. *Continued*

Formation	Age	Location[2]	Lithology	Reference
	Early to Middle Paleozoic	Wichita Mtns, Arbuckle Mtns, OK	chert	Banks 1990:102–109
	Early to Middle Paleozoic	Big Bend, Davis Mtns, TX	chert, petrified wood	Banks 1990:83–87
	Precambrian to Middle Paleozoic	Franklin Mtns, Sacramento Mtns, Jarillas Mtns, TX & NM	chert	Harbour 1972; Banks 1990:80–82

[1] Within 300 km of the margin of the Southern High Plains.
[2] FIG. A2.1.
[3] Including redeposited Pedernal chert.
[4] "Palomas gravel."
[5] Scattered, localized outcrops in the central part of the region.

[6] Observed outcrops yielded only pebble clasts; availability of cobbles is unknown.
[7] Including a likely equivalent to the Madera Formation.

outcrops are in Alibates National Monument (FIG. A2.1). Other outcrops are found on both sides of the Canadian River northeast of Amarillo (Gould 1907; Patton 1923; Etchieson et al. 1978; Banks 1990). The colors in the agate occur mainly in bands, but also as mottles (Patton 1923; Banks 1990). Most colors are blues (5PB 5/2, 7/2), purples (5PB 4/2, 10R 4/2), reds (10R 4/6, 4/3, 5R 4/6, 5/6, 2.5YR 6/6), white (10YR 8/1, 5Y 8/1, N9), and various impure whites (7.5YR 8/2, 10R 8/1, 5B 9/1) (Banks 1990: 127–129). Other colors noted by Banks (1990:127–129) include browns (5YR 7/3, 3/2, 2/1, 10YR 4/3), blues (5PB 7/2), and yellows (10YR 6/6, 5Y 7/2).

Triassic: Dockum Group, Tecovas Formation

The Dockum Group (Upper Triassic) forms the lower portion of the Llano Estacado escarpment. Because the unit was deposited in a large northwest-southeast-trending basin (McGowan et al. 1979), outcrops occur only along the northwestern, eastern, and southeastern Llano Estacado, with beds generally becoming thicker from north to south. Along the northern and northeastern Llano Estacado, the Dockum often is subdivided into the Tecovas and Trujillo formations.

The Tecovas Formation, the oldest unit within the Dockum, is composed of a basal conglomerate with discontinuous chert lenses and overlying varicolored shales. The Trujillo Formation consists of red, interbedded sandy conglomerates, conglomeratic sandstones, and shales. To the south, the Dockum consists of a complex sequence of conglomerates; fine- to coarse-grained, red, indurated sandstones; reddish-brown sandy clays; and varicolored sandy shales. Discontinuous chert lenses occur throughout the unit (McGowan et al. 1979).

Several different kinds of knappable materials are available from the Dockum Group. Most common are the pebble and cobble conglomerates, particularly notable in the lower Dockum. In outcrops along the eastern escarpment between the Red and Brazos rivers (FIG. A2.1), dominant lithologies are coarse- to medium-grained, light-colored quartzites and red jaspers (Holliday and Welty 1981). Other materials include flint and light, glassy, fine-grained, tan and light- to medium-gray cherts. Similar lithologies are reported from a variety of areas (McGowan et al. 1979), and outcrops appear to be quite common along the eastern escarpment. Outcrops with cobbles were not observed, however (Holliday and Welty 1981). Some probably are available, and presumably lithologies would be similar.

Artifacts made of jasper from the Tecovas Formation of the lower Dockum Group are common in many archaeological sites in the area. The material is known locally as Tecovas or Quitaque jasper (after the best-known outcrop near the town of Quitaque) (FIG. A2.1). Other reported outcrops are in Palo Duro Canyon (Etchieson et al. 1978; McGowan et al. 1979) and along the Canadian River valley northwest of Amarillo (Holliday and Welty 1981) (FIG. A2.1). The material usually occurs as lenses. Colors typically are reds (5R 4/2, 4/6, 6/2, 10R 5/2, 4/8), browns (10R 4/6, 6/8, 10YR 4/6, 6/6), and purples (5RP 4/2, 6/2, 5P 6/2), with mottles of gray (10YR 6/2, 7/1, 5GY 4/1), yellow (10YR 6/8, 5Y 7/2), and white (5YR 8/2, N8) locally common (Banks 1990: 129–131). A quartzite coarser-grained than the jasper and freer of flaws but otherwise similar in appearance (Tecovas quartzite) also is found in the Tecovas Formation (Etchieson et al. 1978; Banks 1990:93–94).

Tecovas jasper can be confused with Alibates agate, particularly if the specimens are small, such as flakes (Green and Kelley 1960; Katz and Katz 1976). Banding has been used as an indicator of Alibates agate, but it also can be mottled. Alibates agate often has faint suggestions of other colors within the red, whereas Tecovas jasper usually has an even red color. Tecovas jasper also tends to have more tiny quartz vugs than Alibates agate. Alibates agate and Tecovas jasper also can be distinguished with relative confidence using low magnifications (10–20 ×) (Holliday and Welty 1981). Alibates agate tends to have a more vitreous, waxy luster, and frequently it is possible to see a short distance into the stone. Tecovas jasper, on the other hand, is opaque, and bluish-white quartz vugs are apparent. Banks (1990:93) also notes that the major distinction between Tecovas and Alibates is that "the Tecovas rarely, if ever, occurs in knappable pieces as large as the Alibates" (>7 or 8 cm).

A lateral equivalent to the Tecovas Formation is found in northeastern New Mexico. This unit is the Baldy Hill Formation, which produces a chert very similar to Alibates, and is sometimes referred to as "false Alibates" (Banks 1990:89).

Cretaceous: Dakota Formation

The Dakota Formation is an extensive sedimentary rock, dominantly sandstone, found throughout the Plains from New Mexico to the Dakotas. "The Dakota Formation . . . is the principal source for many of the better quartzites" on the Great Plains (Banks 1990:89). Outcrops in the Pecos River valley along the northwest escarpment of the Llano Estacado and extending into northeastern New Mexico (FIG. A2.1) probably supplied this quartzite for the Southern High Plains (Hester 1975a; Willey and Hughes 1978; Banks 1990:89–90, 94). Particularly high-quality Dakota quartzite is reported from the western Oklahoma Panhandle and from southeastern Colorado (Banks 1990:89–90). The Dakota quartzite has been described as "metamorphosed sandstone" (Willey and Hughes 1978:47), but this description is misleading because it is not a metamorphic rock. The material is a silica-cemented sandstone more properly termed Dakota orthoquartzite (Holliday and Welty 1981). The quartzite is coarse-grained and varies from reds to browns, causing some problems in differentiating it from Tecovas quartzite.

Cretaceous: Edwards Formation

The Edwards Limestone is a Lower Cretaceous deposit found along the east-central and southeast Llano Estacado. Along the margins of the High Plains the Edwards consists of fine- to medium-grained limestone with occasional chert lenses (Brand 1953; Meade et al. 1974; Banks 1990). Localized outcrops of light gray to tan cherts are known from the Edwards Limestone along the southeast escarpment of the Llano Estacado (FIG. A2.1) (Holliday and Welty 1981). This particular material probably does not account for the high percentages of similar chert in local archaeological sites. Hester (1972; 1975a) reports outcrops of chert in the Edwards Limestone in the San Angelo area, and Harrison and Killen (1978) mention an outcrop northeast of San Angelo (FIG. A2.1). The well-known, high-quality cherts of the Edwards Formation become more plentiful southeast of the Southern High Plains, in the direction of or on the Edwards Plateau (Banks 1990:60–61; Frederick and Ringstaff 1994), including outcrops on outliers of the Plateau such as the Callahan Divide (FIG. A2.1) (Banks 1990:109–110).

Tertiary: Ogallala Formation

The Ogallala Formation (Miocene-Pliocene) is the most ubiquitous rock unit of the High Plains, cropping out nearly continuously along the eastern, northern, and western escarpments of the Llano Estacado. The Ogallala consists of gravel, sand, silt, and clay (Reeves 1972; Hawley et al. 1976; Frye et al. 1982; Winkler 1987; Gustavson and Winkler 1988; Caran 1991). Along the northern Llano Estacado, Patton (1923) identified a basal gravel, termed the Potter Formation or Potter gravel (Hood 1978), lithologically different from the basal gravel common in the Ogallala to the south.

Along the eastern escarpment of the study area, gravel of the Ogallala Formation produces abundant and varied material for making stone tools (Holliday and Welty 1981). The Ogallala Formation in New Mexico also contains gravel composed of crystalline rocks (Frye et al. 1982). Quartzites are the most common knappable lithology in the Ogallala, and include light-colored, medium- to coarse-grained quartzites, dark gray to black, medium-grained quartzites, and a distinctive and ubiquitous purple quartzite. Ogallala gravel also includes red, brown, and yellow jaspers, medium- to dark-gray and dark-blue chert, and flint. The Potter Formation of the lower Ogallala produces a chert often referred to as "Potter chert" (Holliday and Welty 1981). The material is a dense, gray to brown, silica-cemented, very fine-grained siltstone. Other materials found in the Potter gravels are purple quartzite, some jasper, chert, petrified (silicified) wood, and various quartzites referred to as Potter quartzite (Etchieson et al. 1977; Hood 1978; Holliday and Welty 1981).

A very well-developed, strongly indurated calcrete formed at the top of the Ogallala Formation, the ledge-forming "Ogallala Caprock." The unit developed by soil forming processes in the upper Ogallala. On the southern Llano Estacado, where the Ogallala thins and the Edwards Limestone forms the surface outcrop, caliche formed in the latter. The Ogallala calcrete often is silicified and occasionally opalized. The calcrete locally provides marginal- to high-quality raw materials for stone-tool manufacture (Holliday and Welty 1981). The silicified calcrete, typically of poor quality, can be used for tools. Despite its poor workability the material is common in some archaeological sites (e.g., Johnson and Holliday 1981), particularly where outcrops are nearby. In some areas, the silicification process has gone so far as to produce an opalized caliche (Holliday and Welty 1981). The opal is of fairly good quality, and flakes of the material are common in archaeological sites in the area (e.g., Hughes and Willey 1978).

Upper Cenozoic: Seymour Gravels and Other Alluvial Deposits

An important source of rock for making tools is gravel derived from the deposits described above. Such deposits locally are extremely rich in knappable material such as chert and quartzite. The Seymour Formation (Pleistocene) occurs as a mantle of gravel on high surfaces across the Rolling Plains 140 to 160 km east of the Llano Estacado (Hood 1978). The deposit consists of gravels apparently derived from the Ogallala Formation, including the Potter gravels, and from the siliceous conglomerates in the Dockum Group (Hood 1978; Banks 1990:95–96). Nearer the eastern margin of the Southern High Plains, massive gravels of chert and quartzite, with evidence of quarrying, are found on terraces of the upper Brazos River and its tributaries (Boyd et al. 1990; Clifford 1994; Clifford and Hicks 1994). Farther to the southeast, gravel derived from the Edwards Formation of the Callahan Divide yields "a regionally significant source of high quality chert . . . second only to the Alibates" (Banks 1990:109). The Alibates itself produces archaeologically significant gravel along the Canadian River valley in western Oklahoma (Wyckoff 1993).

Volcanic and Metamorphic Sources

Artifacts made of rocks produced by volcanic and metamorphic processes are reported from a few sites on the Llano Estacado. Most of the source areas are probably in New Mexico, the nearest occurrence of volcanism and metamorphism. Paleoindian artifacts made of obsidian were found at Lubbock Lake and Clovis, and their source area determined to be an outcrop in the Jemez Mountains (Johnson et al. 1985). Obsidian and related deposits in the Jemez area have been subjected to considerable study, particularly using various analytical methods (Baugh and Nelson 1987; Banks 1990: 69–70). Volcanic rocks in the Jemez area also produce one of the best-known cherts in the region, Pedernal chert, which formed in the Abiquiu Tuff (Miocene) (Banks 1990:67).

The principal metamorphic rocks used for manufacture of stone tools are quartzites, as noted above. All metaquartzite sources are gravel; no known *in situ* metaquartzites are known in the region. The only other known metamorphic rock sought by Paleoindians on the Southern High Plains is red ocher, an impure form of hematite. Red ocher is very common in Paleoindian contexts in North America (Roper 1991; Tankersly et al. 1995), but rare on the Southern High Plains. The only reported occurrence is at Lubbock Lake (Johnson and Holliday 1985). The source is unknown. Ocher outcrops and quarries are known in the Llano Uplift area of Central Texas (G. D. Hall, pers. comm. 1995). Otherwise, the nearest potential outcrops are in the eastern mountains of New Mexico.

References Cited

AGI (American Geological Institute). 1982. *AGI Data Sheets*. Falls Church, Va.: American Geological Institute.

Agogino, George A. 1968. Archeological excavations at Blackwater Draw Locality No. 1, New Mexico, 1963–1964. *National Geographic Society Research Reports for Research and Exploration in 1963*: 1–7.

———. 1969. The Midland Complex: Is it valid? *American Anthropologist* 71: 1117–1118.

Agogino, George A., and Al Parrish. 1971. The Fowler-Parrish site: A Folsom campsite in eastern Colorado. *Plains Anthropologist* 16: 111–114.

Agogino, George A., and Irwin Rovner. 1969. Preliminary report of a stratified post-Folsom sequence at Blackwater Draw Locality no. 1. *American Antiquity* 34: 175–176.

Agogino, George A., David K. Patterson, and Deborah E. Patterson. 1976. Blackwater Draw Locality No. 1, South Bank: Report for the summer of 1974. *Plains Anthropologist* 21: 213–223.

Albanese, John P. 1977. Paleotopography and Paleoindian sites in Wyoming and Colorado. In *Paleoindian Lifeways*, ed. Eileen Johnson, 28–47. Lubbock: *Museum Journal* (West Texas Museum Association) 17.

Albritton, Claude C., Jr. 1966. Stratigraphy of the Domebo site. In *Domebo: A Paleo-Indian Mammoth Kill in the Prairie-Plains*, ed. Frank C. Leonhardy, 10–13. Lawton, Okla.: Contributions of the Museum of the Great Plains 1.

———. 1985. Presentation of the Archaeological Geology Division Award to C. Vance Haynes, Jr. *Geological Society of America Bulletin* 96: 1198–1199.

Albritton, Claude C., Jr., and Kirk Bryan. 1939. Quaternary stratigraphy in the Davis Mountains, Trans-Pecos Texas. *Bulletin of the Geological Society of America* 50: 1423–1474.

Alexander, Herbert L. 1963. The Levi site: A Paleo-Indian campsite in Central Texas. *American Antiquity* 28: 510–528.

———. 1978. The legalistic approach to Early Man studies. In *Early Man in America from a Circum-Pacific Perspective*, ed. Alan L. Bryan, 20–22. Calgary: University of Alberta, Department of Anthropology, Occasional Papers 1.

Amick, Daniel S. 1995. Patterns of technological variation among Folsom and Midland projectile points in the American Southwest. *Plains Anthropologist* 40:23–38.

Amick, Daniel S., and Richard O. Rose. 1990. Dimensioning Folsom variability: lessons from the Shifting Sands site. *Transactions of the Twenty-fifth Regional Archeological Symposium for Southeastern New Mexico and Western Texas*, 1–24.

Anderson, Adrienne B., and C. Vance Haynes, Jr. 1979. How old is Capulin Mountain?: Correlation between Capulin Mountain volcanic flows and the Folsom type site, northeastern New Mexico. In *Proceedings of the First Conference on Scientific Research in the National Parks*, vol. II, ed. R. M. Linn, 893–899. Washington, D.C.: National Park Service Transactions and Proceedings Series, no. 5.

Antevs, Ernst. 1935. The occurrence of flints and extinct animals in pluvial deposits near Clovis, New Mexico, part III: Age of Clovis lake beds. *Proceedings of the Philadelphia Academy of Natural Sciences* 87:304–311.

———. 1949. Geology of the Clovis sites. In *Ancient Man in North America*, by H. M. Wormington, 185–192. Denver: Denver Museum of Natural History.

———. 1954. Climate of New Mexico during the last glacio-pluvial. *Journal of Geology* 62:182–191.

Ashworth, J. B. 1991. Water-level changes in the High Plains Aquifer of Texas, 1980–1990. Austin: Texas Water Development Board Hydrologic Atlas 1.

Ashworth, J. B., P. Christian, and T. C. Waterreus. 1991. Evaluation of groundwater resources in the Southern High Plains of Texas. Austin: *Texas Water Development Board Report* 330.

Baker, William E., Glen L. Evans, and T. N. Campbell. 1957. The Nall site: Evidence of Early Man in the Oklahoma Panhandle. *Bulletin of the Oklahoma Anthropological Society* 5:1–20.

Bamforth, Douglas B. 1985. The technological organization of Paleo-Indian small-group bison hunters on the Llano Estacado. *Plains Anthropologist* 30:243–258.

———. 1991. Flintknapping skill, communal hunting, and Paleoindian projectile point typology. *Plains Anthropologist* 36:309–322.

Banks, Kimball M., L. Adrien Hannus, and R. Peter Winham. 1995. Foreword: Three reservoirs 40 years later. In *Archeological Investigations in Three Reservoir Areas in South Dakota and Wyoming, Part 1: Angostura Reservoir*, by R. P. Wheeler. Lincoln, Nebr.: Reprints in Anthropology 46.

Banks, Larry D. 1990. *From Mountain Peaks to Alligator Stomachs: A Review of Lithic Sources in the Trans-Mississippi South, the Southern Plains, and Adjacent Southwest*. Norman: Oklahoma Anthropological Society Memoir 4.

Bannan, David B. 1980. Stratigraphy and sedimentology of late Quaternary sediments in the High Plains depressions of Yuma and Kit Carson counties, Colorado. Master's thesis, University of California, Davis.

Barbour, Erwin Hinckley, and C. Bertrand Schultz. 1936. Palaeontologic and geologic consideration of Early Man in Nebraska. *Bulletin of the University of Nebraska State Museum* 1:431–449.

———. 1941. The Lipscomb Bison quarry, Lipscomb County, Texas. *Bulletin of the University of Nebraska State Museum* 2(7):67–68.

Barnosky, Cathy W., Eric C. Grimm, and H. E. Wright, Jr. 1987. Towards a Post-glacial history of the northern Great Plains: A review of the paleoecologic problems. *Annals of Carnegie Museum* 56:259–273.

Bates, R. L., and J. A. Jackson, eds. 1980. *Glossary of Geology*, 2d ed. Falls Church, Va.: American Geological Institute.

Baugh, Timothy G., and F. W. Nelson. 1987. New Mexico obsidian sources and exchange on the Southern Plains. *Journal of Field Archaeology* 14:313–329.

Becker, B. 1993. An 11,000-year German oak and pine dendrochronology for radiocarbon calibration. *Radiocarbon* 35:201–213.

Bement, Leland C. 1986. Excavation of the late Pleistocene deposits of Bonfire Shelter, Val Verde County, Texas. Austin: University of Texas at Austin, Texas Archeological Survey, Archeology Series 1.

———. 1994. The Cooper site: A stratified Paleoindian bison kill in northwest Oklahoma. *Current Research in the Pleistocene* 11:7–9.

———. 1995. The retooling index, seasonality, and the Folsom-age Cooper bison kill. *Current Research in the Pleistocene* 12:61–62.

Birkeland, Peter W. 1984. *Soils and Geomorphology*. New York: Oxford University Press.

Birkeland, Peter W., Michael N. Machette, and Kathleen M. Haller. 1991. Soils as a tool for applied Quaternary geology. *Utah Geological and Mineral Survey, Miscellaneous Publication* 91-3.

Black, Craig C., ed. 1974. *History and Prehistory of the Lubbock Lake Site*. Lubbock: *Museum Journal* (West Texas Museum Association) 15.

Blaine, Jay C. 1968. Preliminary report of an Early Man site in West Texas. *Transactions of the Third Regional Archaeological Symposium for Southeastern New Mexico and Western Texas*, 1–11.

———. 1971. Midland points. In *Guide to Certain American Indian Projectile Points*, by Robert E. Bell, 62–63. Norman: Oklahoma Anthropological Society Special Bulletin 4.

———. 1991. The Folsom-Midland controversy. *Transactions of the Twenty-seventh Regional Archaeological Symposium for Southeastern New Mexico and Western Texas*, 1.

Blaine, Jay C., and Fred Wendorf. 1972. A bone needle from a Midland site. *Plains Anthropologist* 17:50–51.

Blaine, Jay C., R. K. Harris, Wilson W. Crook, Jr., and Joel T. Shiner. 1968. The Acton site, Hood County, Texas. *Bulletin of the Texas Archeological Society* 39:45–94.

Blair, W. F. 1950. The biotic provinces of Texas. *Texas Journal of Science* 2:93–117.

Blum, Michael D. 1989. Quaternary stratigraphy of the Pedernales River. In *Geomorphology, Quaternary Stratigraphy, and Paleoecology of Central Texas*, ed. Michael D. Blum, James F. Petersen, and Richard S. Toomey III, 1–26. Friends of the Pleistocene, South Central Cell Field Trip Guidebook.

Blum, Michael D., and Salvatore S. Valastro, Jr. 1992. Quaternary stratigraphy and geoarchaeology of the Colorado and Concho Rivers, West Texas. *Geoarchaeology* 7:419–448.

Blum, Michael D., James T. Abbott, and Salvatore S. Valastro, Jr. 1992. Evolution of landscapes on the Double Mountain Fork of the Brazos River, West Texas: Implications for preservation and visibility of the archaeological record. *Geoarchaeology* 7:339–370.

Blum, Michael D., Richard S. Toomey III, and Salvatore S. Valastro, Jr. 1994. Fluvial response to late Quaternary climatic and environmental change, Edwards Plateau, Texas. *Palaeogeography, Palaeoclimatology, Palaeoecology* 108:1–21.

Boldurian, Anthony. 1990. *Lithic Technology at the Mitchell Locality of Blackwater Draw*. Lincoln, Nebr.: Plains Anthropologist Memoir 24.

Bolton, Herbert E. [1949] 1990. *Coronado, Knight of Pueblos and Plains*. Albuquerque: University of New Mexico Press.

Bonnichsen, B. Robson, and James D. Keyser. 1982. Three small points: A Cody Complex problem. *Plains Anthropologist* 27:137–144.

Bousman, C. Britt, Anne Kerr, and Paige Hake. 1994. Early Holocene archeology at the Wilson-Leonard site. 52nd Plains Anthropological Conference Abstracts, 35–36.

Bowers, R. L. 1975. Petrography and petrogenesis of the Alibates dolomite and chert (Permian), northern Panhandle of Texas. Master's thesis, University of Texas at Arlington.

Boyd, Douglas K., William A. Bryan, and Colin M. Garvey. 1990. Investigations at first-priority sites. In *Phase II Investigations at Prehistoric and Rock Art Sites, Justiceburg Reservoir, Garza and Kent Counties, Texas*, by Douglas K. Boyd, James T. Abbott, William A. Bryan, Colin M. Garvey, Steve A. Tomka, and Ross C. Fields, 63–158. Austin: Prewitt and Associates Report of Investigations 71.

Bozarth, Steven. 1995. Fossil biosilicates. In *Stratigraphy and Paleoenvironments of Late Quaternary Valley Fills on the Southern High Plains*, by Vance T. Holliday, 47–50. Boulder, Colo.: Geological Society of America Memoir 186.

Bradley, Bruce A., and George C. Frison. 1987. Projectile points and specialized bifaces from the Horner site. In *The Horner site: The Type Site of the Cody Cultural Complex*, ed. George C. Frison and Lawrence C. Todd, 199–231. Orlando, Fla.: Academic Press.

Brand, John P. 1953. *Cretaceous of Llano Estacado of Texas*. Austin: University of Texas at Austin, Bureau of Economic Geology Report of Investigations 20.

Brannon, H. R., Jr., A. C. Daughtry, D. Perry, L. H. Simmons, W. W. Whitaker, and Milton Williams. 1957. Humble Oil radiocarbon dates I. *Science* 125: 147–150.

Broecker, W. S., and J. L. Kulp. 1957. Lamont natural radiocarbon measurements IV. *Science* 126:1324–1334.

Brown, David O., ed. 1993. *Archeological Investigations at the City of Lubbock Landfill, Lubbock County, Texas.* Austin: Hicks and Co., Inc., Archeology Series 22.

Brown, Kenneth L., and Brad Logan. 1987. The distribution of Paleoindian sites in Kansas. In *Quaternary Environments of Kansas,* ed. William C. Johnson, 189–195. Lawrence: Kansas Geological Survey, Guidebook Series 5.

Brune, Gunnar. 1981. *Springs of Texas,* vol. 1. Fort Worth: Branch-Smith, Inc.

Brunswig, Robert H., Jr., and Daniel C. Fisher. 1993. Research on the Dent mammoth site. *Current Research in the Pleistocene* 10:63–65.

Bryan, Alan Lyle, ed. 1986. *New Evidence for the Pleistocene Peopling of the Americas.* Orono: Center for the Study of Early Man, University of Maine.

Bryan, Kirk. 1941a. Geologic antiquity of man in America. *Science* 93:505–514.

———. 1941b. Pre-Columbian agriculture in the Southwest as conditioned by periods of alluviation. *Annals of the Association of American Geographers* 31: 219–242.

———. 1950. *Flint Quarries.* Cambridge, Mass.: Peabody Museum Papers 17.

Bryan, Kirk, and Cyrus N. Ray. 1938. Long channelled point found in alluvium beside bones of *Elephas columbi. Bulletin of the Texas Archeological and Paleontological Society* 10:263–268.

Bryan, Kirk, and Louis Ray. 1940. *Geologic Antiquity of the Lindenmeier Site in Colorado.* Washington, D.C.: Smithsonian Miscellaneous Collections 99.

Bryant, Vaughn M., Jr., and Stephen A. Hall. 1993. Archaeological palynology in the United States: A critique. *American Antiquity* 58:277–286.

Bryant, Vaughn M., Jr., and Richard G. Holloway. 1983. The role of palynology in archaeology. *Advances in Archaeological Method and Theory* 6:191–224.

———. 1985. A late-Quaternary paleoenvironmental record of Texas: An overview of the pollen evidence. In *Pollen Records of Late Quaternary North American Sediments,* ed. Vaughn M. Bryant, Jr., and Richard G. Holloway, 39–70. Dallas: American Association of Stratigraphic Palynologists Foundation.

Bryant, Vaughn M., Jr., and James Schoenwetter. 1987. Pollen records from the Lubbock Lake site. In *Lubbock Lake: Late Quaternary Studies on the Southern High Plains,* ed. Eileen Johnson, 36–40. College Station: Texas A&M University Press.

Bryant, Vaughn M., Jr., and Harry J. Shafer. 1977. The Late Quaternary Paleoenvironment of Texas: A Model for the Archaeologist. *Bulletin of the Texas Archeological Society* 48:1–25.

Bryant, Vaughn M., Jr., Richard G. Holloway, John G. Jones, and David L. Carlson. 1994. Pollen preservation in alkaline soils of the American Southwest.

In *Sedimentation of Organic Particles,* ed. Alfred Traverse, 47–58. New York: Cambridge University Press.

Buchanan, Briggs, Luc Litwinionek, J. Kent Hicks, and Marcus Hamilton. 1995. Renewed investigations of the Milnesand and Ted Williamson Paleoindian sites. 53rd Plains Anthropological Conference Abstracts, 64.

Bull, William B. 1991. *Geomorphic Responses to Climatic Change.* New York: Oxford University Press.

Butzer, Karl W. 1971. *Environment and Archaeology,* 2d ed. Chicago: Aldine.

———. 1991. An Old World perspective on potential mid-Wisconsinan settlement of the Americas. In *The First Americans: Search and Research,* ed. Thomas D. Dillehay and David J. Meltzer, 137–156. Boca Raton, Fla.: CRC Press.

Campbell, C. A., E. A. Paul, D. A. Rennie, and K. J. McCallum. 1967. Factors affecting the accuracy of the carbon-dating method in soil humus studies. *Soil Science* 104:81–85.

Caran, S. Christopher. 1991. Cenozoic stratigraphy, southern Great Plains area. In *Quaternary Nonglacial Geology: Conterminous U.S.,* ed. Roger B. Morrison, plate 5. Boulder, Colo.: Geological Society of America, Centennial Volume K-2.

Caran, S. Christopher, and Robert Baumgardner, Jr. 1986. Summary of radiocarbon analyses, western Rolling Plains of Texas. In *Geomorphology and Quaternary Stratigraphy of the Rolling Plains, Texas Panhandle,* ed. Thomas C. Gustavson, 90–97. Austin: University of Texas at Austin, Bureau of Economic Geology Guidebook 22.

———. 1990. Quaternary stratigraphy and paleoenvironments of the Texas Rolling Plains. *Geological Society of America Bulletin* 102:768–785.

Carley, Denny. 1987. A preliminary evaluation of the potential significance of the Carley-Archer site, 41MT6, Mustang Draw, Martin County, Texas. Report submitted to the Texas Historical Commission, Austin, Texas.

Carr, John T. 1967. *The Climate and Physiography of Texas.* Austin: Texas Water Development Board Report 53.

Carter, Brian J., and Leland C. Bement. 1995. Soil investigations at the Cooper site. *Current Research in the Pleistocene* 12:109–111.

Cassells, E. Steve. 1983. *The Archaeology of Colorado.* Boulder, Colo.: Johnson Publishing.

Church, Tim, with contributions by Julie E. Francis and Cherie E. Haury. 1994. *Lithic Resource Studies: A Sourcebook for Archaeologists. Lithic Technology* Special Publication 3, Department of Anthropology, University of Tulsa.

Clarke, W. T., Jr. 1938. The occurrence of flints and extinct animals in pluvial deposits near Clovis, New Mexico, part VII: The Pleistocene mollusks from the Clovis gravel pit and vicinity. *Proceedings of the Philadelphia Academy of Natural Sciences* 90:119–121.

Clifford, Brian Elliott. 1994. Lithic analysis methodology and research design. In *Archaeological Survey along the Mobil ESTE CO₂ Pipeline Corridor from*

Denver City to Clairemont, Texas, ed. Eileen Johnson, 103–107. Lubbock: Lubbock Lake Landmark Quaternary Research Center Series 6, Museum of Texas Tech University.

Clifford, Brian Elliott, and J. Kent Hicks. 1994. Lithic analysis. In *Archaeological Survey along the Mobil ESTE CO₂ Pipeline Corridor from Denver City to Clairemont, Texas,* ed. Eileen Johnson, 109–163. Lubbock: Lubbock Lake Landmark Quaternary Research Center Series 6, Museum of Texas Tech University.

Clisby, K. H., and P. B. Sears. 1956. San Augustin Plains—Pleistocene climatic changes. *Science* 124:537–539.

COHMAP Members. 1988. Climatic changes of the last 18,000 years: Observations and model simulations. *Science* 241:1043–1052.

Collins, Michael B. 1971. A review of Llano Estacado archaeology and ethnohistory. *Plains Anthropologist* 16:82–104.

———. 1976. Terminal Pleistocene cultural adaptations in southern Texas. In *Habitats Humains Antérieurs a L'Holocène en Amérique,* ed. James B. Griffin, 102–135. Nice, France: IXe Congrès, Union Internationale des Sciences Préhistoriques et Protohistoriques.

———. 1991. Rockshelters and the early archaeological record in the Americas. In *The First Americans: Search and Research,* ed. Thomas D. Dillehay and David J. Meltzer, 157–182. Boca Raton, Fla.: CRC Press.

Collins, Michael B., C. B. Bousman, P. Goldberg, P. R. Takac, J. C. Guy, J. L. Lanata, T. W. Stafford, and V. T. Holliday. 1993. The Paleoindian sequence at the Wilson-Leonard site, Texas. *Current Research in the Pleistocene* 10:10–12.

Collins, Michael B., C. B. Bousman, J. C. Guy, and A. C. Kerr. 1994. Pleistocene archeology at the Wilson-Leonard site. 52nd Plains Anthropological Conference Abstracts, 43.

Collins, Michael B., Glen L. Evans, Thomas N. Campbell, Melissa C. Winans, and Charles E. Mear. 1989. Clovis occupation at Kincaid shelter, Texas. *Current Research in the Pleistocene* 6:3–4.

Colton, R. B. 1978. Geologic map of the Boulder–Fort Collins–Greeley Area, Colorado. U.S. Geological Survey Map I-855-G.

Cook, Harold J. 1927. New Geological and Paleontological Evidence Bearing on the Antiquity of Mankind in America. *Natural History* 27:240–247.

Cotter, John L. 1937. The occurrence of flints and extinct animals in pluvial deposits near Clovis, New Mexico, part IV: Report on excavation at the gravel pit, 1936. *Proceedings of the Philadelphia Academy of Natural Sciences* 90:2–16.

———. 1938. The occurrence of flints and extinct animals in pluvial deposits near Clovis, New Mexico, part VI: Report on the field season of 1937. *Proceedings of the Philadelphia Academy of Natural Sciences* 90:113–117.

———. 1991. Update on Natchez Man. *American Antiquity* 56:36–39.

Crane, H. R. 1956. University of Michigan radiocarbon dates I. *Science* 124:664–672.

Cronin, J. G. 1964. A summary of the occurrence and development of ground water in the Southern High Plains of Texas. *U.S. Geological Survey Water-Supply Paper* 1693.

Crook, Wilson W., and R. K. Harris. 1957. Hearths and artifacts of Early Man near Lewisville, Texas, and associated faunal material. *Bulletin of the Texas Archeological Society* 28:7–97.

———. 1961. Significance of a new radiocarbon date from the Lewisville site. *Bulletin of the Texas Archeological Society* 32:327–330.

Dalquest, Walter W. 1986. Vertebrate fossils from a strath terrace of Quitaque Creek, Motley County, Texas. In *Geomorphology and Quaternary Stratigraphy of the Rolling Plains, Texas Panhandle*, ed. Thomas C. Gustavson, 58–59. Austin: University of Texas at Austin, Bureau of Economic Geology Guidebook 22.

Dalquest, Walter W., and Gerald E. Schultz. 1992. *Ice Age Mammals of Northwestern Texas*. Wichita Falls, Tex.: Midwestern State University Press.

Davis, E. Mott. 1953. Recent data from two Paleo-Indian sites on Medicine Creek, Nebraska. *American Antiquity* 18:380–386.

———. 1962. *Archeology of the Lime Creek Site in Southwestern Nebraska*. Special Publication of the University of Nebraska State Museum 3.

Davis, Leo Carson. 1987. Late Pleistocene/Holocene environmental changes in the central Great Plains of the United States: The mammalian record. In *Late Quaternary Mammalian Biogeography and Environments of the Great Plains and Prairies*, ed. Russell W. Graham, Holmes A. Semken, Jr., and Mary Ann Graham, 88–143. Springfield: Illinois State Museum Scientific Papers 22.

Dibble, David S. 1970. On the significance of additional radiocarbon dates from Bonfire Shelter, Texas. *Plains Anthropologist* 15(50):251–254.

Dibble, David S., and Robert K. Alexander. 1971. The archeology of Texas caves. In *Natural History of Texas Caves*, ed. Ernest L. Lundelius, Jr., and Bob H. Slaughter, 133–148. Dallas: Gulf Natural History.

Dibble, David S., and Dessamae Lorrain. 1968. *Bonfire Shelter: A Stratified Bison Kill Site, Val Verde County, Texas*. Austin: Texas Memorial Museum Miscellaneous Papers 1.

Dick, Herbert W., and Bert Mountain. 1960. The Claypool site: A Cody Complex site in northeastern Colorado. *American Antiquity* 26:223–235.

Dijkerman, J. C., M. C. Kline, and G. W. Olson. 1967. Properties and genesis of textural subsoil lamellae. *Soil Science* 104:7–16.

Dittert, A. E. 1957. Salvage excavations at Blackwater No. 1 Locality near Portales, New Mexico. *Museum of New Mexico, Highway Salvage Archaeology* 3:1–9.

Drake, Douglas. 1994. The Milnesand site—40 years later. 52nd Plains Anthropological Conference Abstracts, 46–47.

Drake, Robert J. 1975. Fossil nonmarine molluscs. In *Late Pleistocene Environments of the Southern High Plains*, ed. Fred Wendorf and James J. Hester, 201–246. Taos, N.Mex.: Publication of the Fort Burgwin Research Center, no. 9.

Eifler, G. K. 1969. *Geologic Atlas of Texas, Amarillo Sheet*, 1:250,000. Austin: University of Texas at Austin, Bureau of Economic Geology.

Eifler, G. K., and R. O. Fay. 1984. *Geologic Atlas of Texas, Dalhart Sheet*, 1:250,000. Austin: University of Texas at Austin, Bureau of Economic Geology.

Eighmy, Jeffrey L., and Jason M. LaBelle. 1996. Radiocarbon dating of twenty-seven Plains complexes and phases. *Plains Anthropologist* 41:53–69.

Elias, Scott A. 1995a. Fossil insects. In *Stratigraphy and Paleoenvironments of Late Quaternary Valley Fills on the Southern High Plains*, by Vance T. Holliday, 50–52. Boulder, Colo.: Geological Society of America Memoir 186.

———. 1995b. A paleoenvironmental setting for early Paleoindians in western North America. In *Ancient Peoples and Landscapes*, ed. Eileen Johnson, 255–272. Lubbock: Museum of Texas Tech University.

Elias, Scott A., and Eileen Johnson. 1988. Pilot study of fossil beetles at the Lubbock Lake Landmark. *Current Research in the Pleistocene* 5:57–59.

Ensor, H. Blaine. 1986. San Patrice and Dalton affinities on the central and western Gulf Coastal Plain. *Bulletin of the Texas Archeological Society* 57:69–81.

Etchieson, Gerald M., Roberta D. Speer, and Jack T. Hughes. 1977. An archeological survey of certain tracts in and near Caprock Canyons State Park in eastern Briscoe County, Texas. Canyon: Archeological Research Laboratory, Killgore Research Center, West Texas State University.

———. 1978. Archeological investigations in the Truscott Reservoir Area, King and Knox Counties, Texas. Canyon: Archeological Research Laboratory, Killgore Research Center, West Texas State University.

Evans, Glen L. 1949. Upper Cenozoic of the High Plains. In *Cenozoic Geology of the Llano Estacado and Rio Grande Valley*, 1–22. West Texas Geological Society Guidebook 2.

———. 1951. Prehistoric wells in eastern New Mexico. *American Antiquity* 17:1–8.

———. 1986. E. H. Sellards' contributions to Paleoindian studies. In *Guidebook to the Archaeological Geology of Classic Paleoindian Sites of the Southern High Plains, Texas and New Mexico*, ed. Vance T. Holliday, 7–18. Guidebook for the 1986 Annual Meeting of the Geological Society of America. College Station: Department of Geography, Texas A&M University.

———. 1995. Grayson E. Meade, 1912–1995. *Society of Vertebrate Paleontology News Bulletin* 164:50–54.

Evans, Glen L., and Grayson E. Meade. 1945. Quaternary of the Texas High Plains. *University of Texas Publication* 4401:485–507.

Fairbridge, Rhodes W. 1983. The Pleistocene-Holocene boundary. *Quaternary Science Reviews* 1:215–244.

Fallin, J. A., P. Nordstrom, and J. B. Ashworth. 1987. 1986 water level rises and recharge patterns in the Southern High Plains aquifer of Texas. *Symposium on the Quaternary Blackwater Draw and Tertiary Ogallala formations, Program with Abstracts*, 10. Austin: University of Texas at Austin, Bureau of Economic Geology.

Farrand, William R. 1990. Origins of Quaternary-Pleistocene-Holocene stratigraphic terminology. In *Establishment of a Geologic Framework for Paleoanthropology*, ed. Leo F. Laporte, 15–22. Geological Society of America Special Paper 242.

Feng, Zhao-Dong, William C. Johnson, Yanchou Lu, and Phillip A. Ward III. 1994. Climatic signals from loess-soil sequences in the central Great Plains, USA. *Palaeogeography, Palaeoclimatology, Palaeoecology* 110:345–358.

Feng, Zhao-Dong, William C. Johnson, D. R. Sprowl, and Yanchou Lu. 1994. Loess accumulation and soil formation in Central Kansas, United States, during the past 400,000 years. *Earth Surface Processes and Landforms* 19:55–67.

Fenneman, Nevin M. 1931. *Physiography of Western United States*. New York: McGraw-Hill Book Company.

Ferguson, W. Keene. 1981. *History of the Bureau of Economic Geology, 1909–1960*. Austin: University of Texas at Austin, Bureau of Economic Geology.

Ferring, C. Reid. 1989. Presentation of the Archaeological Geology Division Award to Claude C. Albritton, Jr. *Geological Society of America Bulletin* 101:991–992.

———. 1990a. Archaeological geology of the Southern Plains. In *Archaeological Geology of North America*, ed. Norman Lasca and Jack Donahue, 253–266. Boulder, Colo.: Geological Society of America, Centennial Special Volume 4.

———. 1990b. Late Quaternary geology and geoarchaeology of the upper Trinity River drainage basin, Texas. Boulder, Colo.: Geological Society of America Guidebook, Field Trip 11.

———. 1994. The role of geoarchaeology in Paleoindian research. In *Method and Theory for Investigating the Peopling of the Americas*, ed. Robson Bonnichsen and D. Gentry Steele, 57–72. Corvallis, Oreg.: Center for the Study of the First Americans.

———. 1995. Middle Holocene environments, geology, and archaeology in the Southern Plains. In *Archaeological Geology of the Archaic Period in North America*, ed. E. Arthur Bettis III, 21–25. Boulder, Colo.: Geological Society of America Special Paper 297.

Figgins, Jesse D. 1927. The antiquity of man in America. *Natural History* 27:229–239.

———. 1933. A further contribution to the antiquity of man in America. *Proceedings of the Colorado Museum of Natural History* 12(2):4–10.

Fisher, John W., Jr. 1992. Observations on the Late Pleistocene bone assemblage from the Lamb Spring site, Colorado. In *Ice Age Hunters of the Rockies*, ed. Dennis J. Stanford and Jane S. Day, 51–81. Denver: Denver Museum of Natural History and University Press of Colorado.

Frederick, Charles D., and Christopher Ringstaff. 1994. Lithic resources at Fort Hood: Further investigations. In *Archeological Investigations on 571 Prehistoric Sites at Fort Hood, Bell and Coryell Counties, Texas*, ed. W. N. Trierweiler,

125–181. Austin: Mariah Assoc., Inc., U.S. Army Fort Hood, Archeological Resource Management Series Research Report 31.

Fredlund, Glen G. 1994. The phytolith record at the Wilson-Leonard site. 52nd Plains Anthropological Conference Abstracts, 50.

Fredlund, Glen G., and Pater J. Jaumann. 1987. Late Quaternary palynological and paleobotanical records from the central Great Plains. In *Quaternary Environments of Kansas,* ed. William C. Johnson, 167–178. Lawrence: Kansas Geological Survey, Guidebook Series 5.

Frenzel, H. N., and others. 1988. The Permian Basin region. In *Sedimentary Cover—North American Craton: U.S.,* ed. L. L. Sloss, 261–306. Boulder, Colo.: Geological Society of America, Centennial Volume D-2.

Frison, George C. 1991a. *Prehistoric Hunters of the High Plains,* 2d ed. San Diego: Academic Press.

———. 1991b. The Goshen Paleoindian complex: New data for Paleoindian research. In *Clovis: Origins and Adaptations,* ed. Robson Bonnichsen and Karen L. Turnmire, 133–151. Orono, Maine: Center for the Study of the First Americans.

———. 1993. The North American Paleoindian: A wealth of new data but still much to learn. In *Prehistory and Human Ecology of the Western Prairies and Northern Plains,* ed. Joseph A. Tiffany, 5–16. Lincoln, Nebr.: Plains Anthropologist Memoir 27.

Frison, George C., and Dennis J. Stanford. 1982. *The Agate Basin Site.* San Diego: Academic Press.

Frison, George C., and Lawrence C. Todd. 1987. *The Horner Site: The Type Site of the Cody Cultural Complex.* Orlando, Fla.: Academic Press.

Fritz, W. C., and Bernice Fritz. 1940. Evidence of the Folsom culture in the sand dunes of western Texas. *Bulletin of the Texas Archeological and Paleontological Society* 12:217–222.

Frye, John C., A. Byron Leonard, and H. D. Glass. 1982. Western extent of Ogallala Formation in New Mexico. *New Mexico Bureau of Mines and Mineral Resources Circular* 175.

Gile, Leland H. 1979. Holocene soils in eolian sediments of Bailey County, Texas. *Soil Science Society of America Journal* 43:994–1003.

———. 1985. *The Sandhills Project Soil Monograph.* Las Cruces: New Mexico State University, Rio Grande Historical Collections.

Godfrey-Smith, D. I., J. Kronfeld, A. Strull, and J. M. D'Auria. 1993. Obsidian provenancing and magmatic fractionation in central Oregon. *Geoarchaeology* 8:385–394.

Goldberg, Paul, Gene Mear, Vance T. Holliday, and Barbara Winsborough. 1994. Geology of the Wilson-Leonard site. 52nd Plains Anthropological Conference Abstracts, 52.

Goodyear, Albert C. 1982. The chronological position of the Dalton horizon in the southeastern United States. *American Antiquity* 47:382–395.

————. 1991. *The Early Holocene Occupation of the Southeast United States: A Geoarchaeological Summary.* Columbia: University of South Carolina, South Carolina Institute of Archaeology and Anthropology.

Gould, Charles N. 1907. The geology and ground water resources of the western portion of the Panhandle of Texas. *U.S. Geological Survey Water Supply and Irrigation Paper* 191:1–70.

Graham, Russell W. 1981. Preliminary report on late Pleistocene vertebrates from the Selby and Dutton archaeological/paleontological sites, Yuma County, Colorado. *University of Wyoming Contributions to Geology* 20:33–56.

————. 1987. Late Quaternary mammalian faunas and paleoenvironments of the southwestern plains of the United States. In *Late Quaternary Mammalian Biogeography and Environments of the Great Plains and Prairies,* ed. Russell W. Graham, Holmes A. Semken, Jr., and Mary Ann Graham, 24–86. Springfield: Illinois State Museum Scientific Papers 22.

Green, F. Earl. ms. Unpublished manuscript on file at the Museum of Texas Tech University, Lubbock.

————. 1961a. Geologic environment of pollen bearing sediments. In *Paleoecology of the Llano Estacado,* ed. Fred Wendorf, 48–58. Santa Fe: Museum of New Mexico Press, Publication of the Fort Burgwin Research Center, no. 1.

————. 1961b. The Monahans Dunes area. In *Paleoecology of the Llano Estacado,* ed. Fred Wendorf, 22–47. Santa Fe: Museum of New Mexico Press, Publication of the Fort Burgwin Research Center, no. 1.

————. 1962a. Additional notes on prehistoric wells at the Clovis site. *American Antiquity* 28:230–234.

————. 1962b. The Lubbock Reservoir site. *Museum Journal* (West Texas Museum Association) 6:83–123.

————. 1963. The Clovis blades: An important addition to the Llano complex. *American Antiquity* 29:145–165.

————. 1992. Comments on the report of a worked mammoth tusk from the Clovis site. *American Antiquity* 57:331–337.

Green, F. Earl, and Jane Holden Kelley. 1960. Comments on Alibates flint. *American Antiquity* 25:413–414.

Greiser, Sally Thompson. 1985. *Predictive Models of Hunter-Gatherer Subsistence and Settlement Strategies on the Central High Plains.* Lincoln, Nebr.: Plains Anthropologist Memoir 20.

Guffee, Eddie. 1979. *The Plainview Site: Relocation and Archeological Investigation of a Late Paleo-Indian Kill in Hale County, Texas.* Plainview, Tex.: Wayland Baptist College Archeological Research Laboratory.

Gustavson, Thomas C., and Robert J. Finley. 1985. *Late Cenozoic Geomorphic Evolution of the Texas Panhandle and Northeastern New Mexico.* Austin: University of Texas at Austin, Bureau of Economic Geology Report of Investigations 148.

Gustavson, Thomas C., and Dale A. Winkler. 1988. Depositional facies of the

Miocene-Pliocene Ogallala Formation, northwestern Texas and eastern New Mexico. *Geology* 16:203–206.

Gustavson, T[homas]. C., R. W. Baumgardner, Jr., S. C. Caran, V. T. Holliday, H. H. Mehnert, J. M. O'Neill, and C. C. Reeves, Jr. 1990. Quaternary geology of the southern Great Plains and an adjacent segment of the Rolling Plains. In *Quaternary Nonglacial Geology: Conterminous U.S.*, ed. R. B. Morrison, 477–501. Boulder, Colo.: Geological Society of America, Centennial Volume K-2.

Gustavson, Thomas C., Robert J. Finley, and Kathy A. McGillis. 1980. *Regional Dissolution of Permian Salt in the Anadarko, Dalhart, and Palo Duro Basins of the Texas Panhandle.* Austin: University of Texas at Austin, Bureau of Economic Geology Report of Investigations 106.

Gustavson, Thomas C., Vance T. Holliday, and Susan D. Hovorka. 1995. *Origin and Development of Playa Basins, Sources of Recharge to the Ogallala Aquifer, Southern High Plains, Texas and New Mexico.* Austin: University of Texas at Austin, Bureau of Economic Geology Report of Investigations 229.

Haas, Herbert, Vance T. Holliday, and Robert Stuckenrath. 1986. Dating of Holocene stratigraphy with soluble and insoluble organic fractions at the Lubbock Lake archaeological site, Texas: An ideal case study. *Radiocarbon* 28:473–485.

Hafsten, Ulf. 1961. Pleistocene development of vegetation and climate in the Southern High Plains as evidenced by pollen analysis. In *Paleoecology of the Llano Estacado*, ed. Fred Wendorf, 59–91. Santa Fe: Museum of New Mexico Press, Publication of the Fort Burgwin Research Center, no. 1.

———. 1964. A standard pollen diagram for the southern High Plains, USA, covering the period back to the early Wisconsin glaciation. *6th International Quaternary Congress, Warsaw, 1961, Report* 2:407–420.

Hageman, B. P. 1972. Reports of the International Quaternary Association Subcommission on the study of the Holocene, Bulletin 6.

Hall, Stephen A. 1981. Deteriorated pollen grains and the interpretation of Quaternary pollen diagrams. *Review of Paleobotany and Palynology* 32:193–206.

———. 1995. Pollen. In *Stratigraphy and Paleoenvironments of Late Quaternary Valley Fills on the Southern High Plains*, by Vance T. Holliday, 53–54. Boulder, Colo.: Geological Society of America Memoir 186.

Hall, Stephen A., and Salvatore Valastro. 1995. Grassland vegetation in the Southern Great Plains during the last glacial maximum. *Quaternary Research* 44:237–245.

Hammond, A. P., K. M. Goh, P. J. Tonkin, and M. R. Manning. 1991. Chemical pretreatments for improving the radiocarbon dates of peats and organic silts in a gley podzol environment: Grahams terrace, North Westland. *New Zealand Journal of Geology and Geophysics* 34:191–194.

Harbour, Jerry. 1975. General stratigraphy. In *Late Pleistocene Environments of the Southern High Plains*, ed. Fred Wendorf and James J. Hester, 33–55. Taos, N.Mex.: Publication of the Fort Burgwin Research Center, no. 9.

Golondrina typology. 52nd Plains Anthropological Conference Abstracts, 56.

Hester, Thomas R., Glen L. Evans, Frank Asaro, Fred Stross, T. N. Campbell, and Helen Michel. 1985. Trace element analysis of an obsidian Paleo-indian projectile point from Kincaid rockshelter, Texas. *Bulletin of the Texas Archeological Society* 56:143–153.

Hill, Matthew E., Jr., Jack L. Hofman, Matthew G. Hill, and Douglas Drake. 1994. The Paleoindian bison bonebed at the Milnesand Site, New Mexico. Paper presented at the Annual Meeting of the Society for American Archaeology, Anaheim.

Hill, Matthew G., Vance T. Holliday, and Dennis J. Stanford. 1995. A further evaluation of the San Jon site, New Mexico. *Plains Anthropologist* 40:369–390.

Hofman, Jack L. 1988. Dating the lower member of the Domebo Formation in western Oklahoma. *Current Research in the Pleistocene* 5:86–88.

———. 1989a. Prehistoric culture history—Hunters and gatherers in the Southern Great Plains. In *From Clovis to Comanchero: Archeological Overview of the Southern Great Plains*, ed. Jack L. Hofman et al., 25–60. Fayetteville: Arkansas Archeological Survey Research Series 35.

———. 1989b. Land of sun, wind, and grass. In *From Clovis to Comanchero: Archeological Overview of the Southern Great Plains*, ed. Jack L. Hofman et al., 5–14. Fayetteville: Arkansas Archeological Survey Research Series 35.

———. 1991. Folsom land use: Projectile point variability as a key to mobility. In *Raw Material Economies among Prehistoric Hunter-Gatherers*, ed. A. Montet-White and S. Holen, 336–355. Lawrence: University of Kansas Publications in Anthropology 19.

———. 1992. Recognition and interpretation of Folsom technological variability on the Southern High Plains. In *Ice Age Hunters of the Rockies*, ed. Dennis J. Stanford and Jane S. Day, 193–224. Denver: Denver Museum of Natural History and University Press of Colorado.

———. 1995. Dating Folsom occupations on the Southern High Plains: The Lipscomb and Waugh sites. *Journal of Field Archaeology* 22:421–437.

Hofman, Jack L., and Brian J. Carter. 1991. The Waugh site: A Folsom-bison association in northwestern Oklahoma. In *A Prehistory of the Plains Border Region*, ed. B. J. Carter and A. Ward III, 24–37. Stillwater: Oklahoma State University, Agronomy Department, South-Central Friends of the Pleistocene Guidebook.

Hofman, Jack L., and Lawrence C. Todd. 1990. The Lipscomb bison quarry: 50 years of research. *Transactions of the Twenty-fifth Regional Archeological Symposium for Southeastern New Mexico and Western Texas*, 43–58.

———. 1996. Reinvestigation of the Perry Ranch Plainview bison bonebed, southwestern Oklahoma. Plains Anthropologist Memoir, in press.

Hofman, Jack L., Daniel S. Amick, and Richard O. Rose. 1990. Shifting Sands: A Folsom-Midland assemblage from a campsite in western Texas. *Plains Anthropologist* 35:221–253.

Hofman, Jack L., Brian J. Carter, and Matthew Hill. 1992. Folsom occupation at the Waugh site in northwestern Oklahoma. *Current Research in the Pleistocene* 9:22–25.

Hofman, Jack L., Lawrence C. Todd, C. Bertrand Schultz, and William Hendy. 1989. The Lipscomb bison quarry: Continuing investigation at a Folsom kill-butchery site on the Southern Plains. *Bulletin of the Texas Archeological Society* 60:149–189.

Hohn, Matthew H. 1975. The diatoms. In *Late Pleistocene Environments of the Southern High Plains,* ed. Fred Wendorf and James J. Hester, 197–200. Taos, N.Mex.: Publication of the Fort Burgwin Research Center, no. 9.

Hohn, Matthew H., and Joan Hellerman. 1961. The diatoms. In *Paleoecology of the Llano Estacado,* ed. Fred Wendorf, 98–104. Santa Fe: Museum of New Mexico Press, Publication of the Fort Burgwin Research Center, no. 1.

Holliday, Vance T. 1985a. Holocene soil-geomorphological relations in a semi-arid environment: The Southern High Plains of Texas. In *Soils and Quaternary Landscape Evolution,* ed. John Boardman, 325–357. New York: John Wiley and Sons.

———. 1985b. Archaeological geology of the Lubbock Lake site, Southern High Plains of Texas. *Geological Society of America Bulletin* 96:1483–1492.

———. 1985c. Morphology of late Holocene soils at the Lubbock Lake site, Texas. *Soil Science Society of America Journal* 49:938–946.

———. 1985d. Early Holocene soils at the Lubbock Lake archaeological site, Texas. *Catena* 12:61–78.

———. 1985e. New data on the stratigraphy and pedology of the Clovis and Plainview sites, Southern High Plains. *Quaternary Research* 23:388–402.

———. 1987a. Re-examination of late-Pleistocene boreal forest reconstructions for the Southern High Plains. *Quaternary Research* 28:238–244.

———. 1987b. Geoarchaeology and late Quaternary geomorphology of the middle South Platte River, northeastern Colorado. *Geoarchaeology* 2:317–329.

———. 1988a. Mt. Blanco revisited: Soil-geomorphic implications for the ages of the upper Cenozoic Blanco and Blackwater Draw Formations. *Geology* 16:505–508.

———. 1988b. Genesis of late Holocene soils at the Lubbock Lake archaeological site, Texas. *Annals of the Association of American Geographers* 78:594–610.

———. 1989a. The Blackwater Draw Formation (Quaternary): A 1.4-plus m.y. record of eolian sedimentation and soil formation on the Southern High Plains. *Geological Society of America Bulletin* 101:1598–1607.

———. 1989b. Middle Holocene drought on the Southern High Plains. *Quaternary Research* 31:74–82.

———. 1990a. Late Quaternary stratigraphy of the Plainview site and middle Running Water Draw. *Guidebook to the Quaternary History of the Llano Estacado,* ed. Vance T. Holliday and Eileen Johnson, 93–104. Lubbock, Tex.: Lubbock Lake Landmark Quaternary Research Series 2.

————. 1990b. Soils and landscape evolution of eolian plains: The Southern High Plains of Texas and New Mexico. In *Soils and Landscape Evolution,* ed. Peter L. K. Knuepfer and Leslie D. McFadden. *Geomorphology* 3:489–515.

————. 1995a. Late Quaternary stratigraphy of the Southern High Plains. In *Ancient Peoples and Landscapes,* ed. Eileen Johnson, 289–313. Lubbock: Museum of Texas Tech University.

————. 1995b. *Stratigraphy and Paleoenvironments of Late Quaternary Valley Fills on the Southern High Plains.* Boulder, Colo.: Geological Society of America Memoir 186.

Holliday, Vance T., and B. L. Allen. 1987. Geology and soils. In *Lubbock Lake: Late Quaternary Studies on the Southern High Plains,* ed. Eileen Johnson, 14–21. College Station: Texas A&M University Press.

Holliday, Vance T., and Adrienne B. Anderson. 1993. "Paleoindian," "Clovis" and "Folsom": A brief etymology. *Current Research in the Pleistocene* 10:79–81.

Holliday, Vance T., and Thomas C. Gustavson. 1991. Quaternary stratigraphy and soils of the Southern High Plains. In *Quaternary Nonglacial Geology: Conterminous U.S.,* ed. Roger B. Morrison, 479–484. Boulder, Colo.: Geological Society of America, Centennial Volume K-2.

Holliday, Vance T., and Eileen Johnson. 1981. An update on the Plainview occupation at the Lubbock Lake Site. *Plains Anthropologist* 26:251–253.

————. 1984. The Lubbock Lake 1983 Season. *Current Research* (Center for the Study of Early Man) 1:11–13.

————. 1986. Re-evaluation of the first radiocarbon age for the Folsom culture. *American Antiquity* 51:332–338.

————. 1996. Geoarchaeology and Paleoindian archaeology of the Llano Estacado: A Glen Evans retrospective. In *Tribute to Glen Evans,* ed. C. E. Mear and M. B. Collins. Austin: Texas Memorial Museum, in press.

Holliday, Vance T., and David J. Meltzer. 1996. Geoarchaeology of the Midland (Paleoindian) site. *American Antiquity* 61:755–771.

Holliday, Vance T., and Curtis Welty. 1981. Lithic tool resources of the eastern Llano Estacado. *Bulletin of the Texas Archeological Society* 52:201–214.

Holliday, Vance T., C. Vance Haynes, Jr., Jack L. Hofman, and David J. Meltzer. 1994. Geoarchaeology and geochronology of the Miami (Clovis) site, Southern High Plains of Texas. *Quaternary Research* 41:234–244.

Holliday, Vance T., Susan D. Hovorka, and Thomas C. Gustavson. 1996. Lithostratigraphy and geochronology of fills in small playa basins on the Southern High Plains. *Geological Society of America Bulletin* 108:953–965.

Holliday, Vance T., Eileen Johnson, Herbert Haas, and Robert Stuckenrath. 1983. Radiocarbon ages from the Lubbock Lake site, 1950–1980: Framework for cultural and ecological change on the Southern High Plains. *Plains Anthropologist* 28:165–182.

————. 1985. Radiocarbon ages from the Lubbock Lake site, 1981–1984. *Plains Anthropologist* 30:277–291.

Holliday, Vance T., Eileen Johnson, Stephen A. Hall, and Vaughn M. Bryant, Jr. 1985. Re-evaluation of the Lubbock Subpluvial. *Current Research in the Pleistocene* 2:119–121.

Honea, Kenneth. 1980. The Marks Beach site, stratified Paleoindian site, Lamb County, Texas. *Bulletin of the Texas Archeological Society* 51:243–269, 329.

Hood, Charles N. 1978. Analysis of the Seymour Gravels. In *Archeological Investigations in the Truscott Reservoir Area, King and Knox Counties, Texas*, ed. Gerald M. Etchieson, Roberta D. Speer, and Jack T. Hughes, 379–386. Canyon: West Texas State University, Killgore Research Center, Archeological Research Laboratory.

Howard, E. B. 1935a. Evidence of Early Man in North America. *Museum Journal, University of Pennsylvania Museum* 24:61–175.

———. 1935b. The occurrence of flints and extinct animals in fluvial deposits near Clovis, New Mexico, part 1: Introduction. *Proceedings of the Academy of Natural Sciences of Philadelphia* 87:299–303.

———. 1943. The Finley site: Discovery of Yuma points, *in situ*, near Eden, Wyoming. *American Antiquity* 8:224–234.

Hrdlicka, Ales. 1918. *Recent Discoveries Attributed to Early Man in America.* Bureau of American Ethnology Bulletin 66.

Huffington, R. M., and C. C. Albritton, Jr. 1941. Quaternary sands on the Southern High Plains of western Texas. *American Journal of Science* 239:325–338.

Hughes, Jack T. 1949. Investigations in western South Dakota and northwestern Wyoming. *American Antiquity* 14:266–277.

Hughes, Jack T., and Patrick S. Willey. 1978. *Archeology at MacKenzie Reservoir.* Austin: Texas Historical Commission, Archeological Survey Report 24.

Humphrey, John D., and C. Reid Ferring. 1994. Stable isotopic evidence for latest Pleistocene and Holocene climatic change in north-central Texas. *Quaternary Research* 41:200–213.

Hunt, Charles B. 1954. Pleistocene and Recent deposits in the Denver Area, Colorado. *U.S. Geological Survey Bulletin* 996-C:91–140.

———. 1974. *Natural Regions of the United States and Canada.* San Francisco: W. H. Freeman and Co.

Irwin, Henry T. 1971. Developments in Early Man studies in western North America, 1960–1970. *Arctic Anthropology* 8:42–67.

Irwin-Williams, Cynthia, Henry Irwin, George Agogino, and C. Vance Haynes. 1973. Hell Gap: Paleo-Indian occupation on the High Plains. *Plains Anthropologist* 18:40–53.

Jacobs, Peter M. 1995. Appendix B: Laboratory methods and data. *Stratigraphy and Paleoenvironments of Late Quaternary Valley Fills on the Southern High Plains*, by Vance T. Holliday, GSA data repository 9541. Boulder, Colo.: Geological Society of America Memoir 186.

Jennings, Jesse D. 1955. The archeology of the Plains: An assessment. Salt Lake

City: University of Utah, Department of Anthropology, and the National Park Service.

———. 1983. Origins. In *Ancient North Americans,* ed. Jesse D. Jennings, 23–67. San Francisco: W. H. Freeman and Co.

———. 1989. *Prehistory of North America,* 3d ed. Mountain View, Calif.: Mayfield Publishing Co.

Jensen, Harald P., Jr. 1968. Report on excavations at the Field Ranch site (X41CO-10), Cooke County, Texas. *Bulletin of the Texas Archeological Society* 39: 133–146.

Johnson, Charles A., II, and Thomas W. Stafford. 1976. *Report of 1975 of the Archaeological Survey Investigation of the Canyon Lakes Project, Yellowhouse Canyon, Lubbock, Texas.* Report submitted to the Texas Antiquities Committee and City of Lubbock.

Johnson, Eileen, ed. 1977. *Paleoindian Lifeways.* Lubbock: *Museum Journal* (West Texas Museum Association) 17.

Johnson, Eileen. 1986a. Late Pleistocene and early Holocene paleoenvironments on the Southern High Plains (USA). *Geographie Physique et Quaternaire* 40: 249–261.

———. 1986b. The 1949 bone bed from the carbonaceous unit at Blackwater Draw Locality #1. *Current Research in the Pleistocene* 3:7–9.

———, ed. 1987a. *Lubbock Lake: Late Quaternary Studies on the Southern High Plains.* College Station: Texas A&M University Press.

———. 1987b. Paleoenvironmental overview. In *Lubbock Lake: Late Quaternary Studies on the Southern High Plains,* ed. Eileen Johnson, 90–99. College Station: Texas A&M University Press.

———. 1987c. Vertebrate remains. In *Lubbock Lake: Late Quaternary Studies on the Southern High Plains,* ed. Eileen Johnson, 49–89. College Station: Texas A&M University Press.

———. 1987d. Cultural activities and interactions. In *Lubbock Lake: Late Quaternary Studies on the Southern High Plains,* ed. Eileen Johnson, 120–158. College Station: Texas A&M University Press.

———. 1989. Human-modified bones from early Southern Plains sites. In *Bone Modification,* ed. Robson Bonnichsen and Marcella Sorg, 431–471. Orono, Maine: Center for the Study of the First Americans.

———. 1991. Late Pleistocene cultural occupation on the Southern Plains. In *Clovis: Origins and Adaptations,* ed. Robson Bonnichsen and Karen L. Turnmire, 215–236. Orono, Maine: Center for the Study of the First Americans.

———. 1993. Paleoecologic and taphonomic assessment of 41LU87 based on the 1992 test excavations. In *Archeological Investigations at the City of Lubbock Landfill, Lubbock County, Texas,* ed. David O. Brown, 74–98. Austin: Hicks and Co., Inc., Archeology Series 22.

———. 1994. An appraisal of the taphonomy and paleoecology of the Lubbock

Landfill site, Southern High Plains of Texas. *Current Research in the Pleisto-cene* 11:68–70.

———, ed. 1995a. *Ancient Peoples and Landscapes.* Lubbock: Museum of Texas Tech University.

———. 1995b. Site formation and disturbance processes at Lubbock Lake (Southern High Plains, U.S.A.) during the terminal Pleistocene. In *Ancient Peoples and Landscapes,* ed. Eileen Johnson, 315–340. Lubbock: Museum of Texas Tech University.

Johnson, Eileen, and Vance T. Holliday. 1980. A Plainview kill/butchering locale on the Llano Estacado—The Lubbock Lake site. *Plains Anthropologist* 25: 89–111.

———. 1981. Late Paleoindian Activity at the Lubbock Lake Site. *Plains Anthro-pologist* 26:173–193.

———. 1985. Paleoindian investigations at Lubbock Lake: The 1984 season. *Current Research in the Pleistocene* 2:21–23.

———. 1986. The Archaic record at Lubbock Lake. In *Current Trends in South-ern Plains Archaeology,* ed. Timothy G. Baugh, 7–54. Lincoln, Nebr.: Plains Anthropologist Memoir 21.

———. 1987a. Introduction. In *Lubbock Lake: Late Quaternary Studies on the Southern High Plains,* ed. Eileen Johnson, 3–13. College Station: Texas A&M University Press.

———. 1987b. Lubbock Lake artifact assemblages. In *Lubbock Lake: Late Quater-nary Studies on the Southern High Plains,* ed. Eileen Johnson, 100–119. Col-lege Station: Texas A&M University Press.

———. 1989. Lubbock Lake: Late Quaternary cultural and environmental change on the Southern High Plains, USA. *Journal of Quaternary Science* 4:145–165.

———. 1996. Analysis of Paleoindian bone beds at the Clovis site: New data from old excavations. *Plains Anthropologist,* in press.

Johnson, Eileen, and Pat Shipman. 1986. Scanning electron microscope studies of bone modification. *Current Research in the Pleistocene* 3:47–48.

Johnson, Eileen, Vance T. Holliday, Frank Asaro, Fred Stross, and Helen Michel. 1985. Trace element analysis of Paleoindian obsidian artifacts from the Southern High Plains. *Current Research in the Pleistocene* 2:51–53.

Johnson, Eileen, Vance T. Holliday, and Raymond Neck. 1982. Lake Theo: Late Quaternary paleoenvironmental data and new Plainview (Paleoindian) date. *North American Archaeologist* 3:113–137.

Johnson, Eileen, Vance T. Holliday, Ronald W. Ralph, Ruthann Knudson, and Sonny Lupton. 1987. Ryan's site: A Plainview occupation on the Southern High Plains, Texas. *Current Research in the Pleistocene* 4:17–18.

Johnson, Eileen, Vance T. Holliday, James Warnica, and Ted Williamson. 1986. The Milnesand and Ted Williamson Paleoindian sites, east-central New Mexico. *Current Research in the Pleistocene* 3:9–11.

Johnson, LeRoy, Jr. 1964. *The Devil's Mouth Site: A Stratified Campsite at Amistad*

Reservoir, Val Verde County, Texas. Austin: University of Texas at Austin, Department of Anthropology Archaeology Series 6.

————. 1989. *Great Plains Interlopers in the Eastern Woodlands during Late Paleo-Indian Times.* Austin: Texas Historical Commission, Office of the State Archeologist Report 36.

Johnson, William C., and Brad Logan. 1990. Geoarchaeology of the Kansas River Basin, central Great Plains. In *Archaeological Geology of North America,* ed. Norman P. Lasca and Jack Donahue, 267–299. Boulder, Colo.: Geological Society of America, Centennial Special Volume 4.

Judge, W. James. 1970. Systems Analysis and the Folsom-Midland Question. *Southwestern Journal of Anthropology* 26:40–51.

————. 1973. *Paleoindian Occupation of the Central Rio Grande Valley in New Mexico.* Albuquerque: University of New Mexico Press.

————. 1974. Projectile point form and function in Late Paleo-Indian period assemblages. In *History and Prehistory of the Lubbock Lake Site,* ed. Craig C. Black, 123–132. Lubbock: *Museum Journal* (West Texas Museum Association) 15.

Judson, Sheldon. 1950. Depressions on the northern portion of the Southern High Plains of Eastern New Mexico. *Bulletin of the Geological Society of America* 61:253–274.

————. 1953. *Geology of the San Jon Site, Eastern New Mexico.* Washington, D.C.: Smithsonian Miscellaneous Collection 121.

Justice, Noel D. 1987. *Stone Age Spear and Arrow Points of the Midcontinental and Eastern United States.* Bloomington and Indianapolis: Indiana University Press.

Kaczor, Michael John. 1978. A Correlative Study of the West Texas Museum Excavations at the Lubbock Lake Site, 1959–61: An Example of Applied Museum Collection Management Techniques within a Research Analysis Design. Master's thesis, Texas Tech University, Lubbock.

Katz, Susanna, and Paul R. Katz. 1976. *Archeological Investigations in Lower Tule Canyon, Briscoe County, Texas.* Austin: Texas Historical Commission, Archeological Survey Report 16.

Kelley, J. Charles, T. N. Campbell, and Donald J. Lehmer. 1940. *The Association of Archaeological Materials with Geological Deposits in the Big Bend Region of Texas.* Alpine: West Texas Historical and Scientific Society Publication 10 (Sul Ross State Teachers College Bulletin 21).

Kelley, Jane Holden. 1964. Comments on the archaeology of the Llano Estacado. *Bulletin of the Texas Archeological Society* 35:1–18.

————. 1974. A brief resume of artifacts collected at the Lubbock Lake site prior to 1961. In *History and Prehistory of the Lubbock Lake Site,* ed. Craig C. Black, 15–42. Lubbock: *Museum Journal* (West Texas Museum Association) 15.

Kelley, Robert L., and Lawrence C. Todd. 1988. Coming into the country: Early Paleoindian hunting and mobility. *American Antiquity* 53:231–244.

Kelley, Vincent, and Frederick D. Trauger, eds. 1972. *Guidebook for East-Central New Mexico.* Socorro: New Mexico Geological Society Guidebook 24.

Kelly, E. F., C. Yonker, and B. Marino. 1993. Stable carbon isotope composition of paleosols: An application to Holocene. In *Climate Change in Continental Isotopic Records,* ed. P. K. Swart et al., 233–239. Geophysical Monographs 78.

Kelly, Thomas C. 1982. Criteria for classification of Plainview and Golondrina projectile points. *La Tierra: Journal of the South Texas Archaeological Association* 9:2–25.

————. 1983. The Brom-Cooper Paleo-Indian collection from McMullen County, Texas. *La Tierra: Journal of the South Texas Archaeological Association* 10: 17–40.

Kibler, Karl W. 1991. Surface distributions of sites and survey strategies for draws on the southern Llano Estacado. Master's thesis, University of Texas at Austin.

————. 1992. Surface distributions of aboriginal sites on the southern Llano Estacado. *Transactions of the Twenty-eighth Regional Archeological Symposium for Southeastern New Mexico and Western Texas,* 26–48.

Knox, James C. 1983. Responses of river systems to Holocene climates. In *Late-Quaternary Environments of the United States, v. 2: The Holocene,* ed. H. E. Wright, Jr., 26–41. Minneapolis: University of Minnesota Press.

Knudson, Ruthann. 1970. Continuities in cultural development, 10,000–6,000 years ago. Yellowstone Park, Mont.: AMQUA Abstracts, 77.

————. 1983. *Organizational Variability in Late Paleo-Indian Assemblages.* Pullman: Washington State University, Laboratory of Anthropology, Reports of Investigations 60.

————. 1988. Plains Paleoindian systematics. Paper presented at the Society for American Archaeology annual meeting, Phoenix.

————. 1995. The San Jon points and Paleoindian typology. *Plains Anthropologist* 40:391–397.

Kreutzer, Lee A. 1988. Megafaunal butchering at Lubbock Lake, Texas: A taphonomic reanalysis. *Quaternary Research* 30:221–231.

Krieger, Alex D. 1947. Artifacts from the Plainview bison bed. *Bulletin of the Geological Society of America* 58:938–952.

————. 1950. Notes and news: Early Man. *American Antiquity* 16:181–182.

————. 1957. Notes and news: Early Man. *American Antiquity* 22:321–323.

————. 1964. Early Man in the New World. In *Prehistoric Man in the New World,* ed. Jesse D. Jennings and Edward Norbeck, 23–81. Chicago: University of Chicago Press.

Kutzbach, John E. 1987. Model simulations of the climatic patterns during the deglaciation of North America. In *North America and Adjacent Oceans during the Last Deglaciation,* ed. William F. Ruddiman and H. E. Wright, Jr., 425–446. Boulder, Colo.: Geological Society of America, The Geology of North America, vol. K-3.

Largent, Floyd B., Jr. 1995. Some new additions to the Texas Folsom point database. *Plains Anthropologist* 40:69–71.

Largent, Floyd B., Jr., Michael R. Waters, and David L. Carlson. 1991. The spatiotemporal distribution and characteristics of Folsom projectile points in Texas. *Plains Anthropologist* 36:323–341.

Larsen, Curtis E., and Joseph Schuldenrein. 1990. Depositional history of an archaeologically dated floodplain, Haw River, North Carolina. In *Archaeological Geology of North America*, ed. Norman P. Lasca and Jack Donahue, 161–181. Boulder, Colo.: Geological Society of America, Centennial Special Volume 4.

Leonhardy, Frank C., ed. 1966. *Domebo: A Paleo-Indian Mammoth Kill in the Prairie-Plains*. Lawton, Okla.: Contributions of the Museum of the Great Plains 1.

Libby, Willard. 1952. *Radiocarbon Dating*. Chicago: University of Chicago Press.

Lintz, Christopher R. 1978. The Johnson-Cline site (34TX40): An upland dune site in the Oklahoma Panhandle. *Bulletin of the Oklahoma Anthropological Society* 27:111–140.

Lohman, K. E. 1935. Diatoms from Quaternary lake beds near Clovis, New Mexico. *Journal of Paleontology* 9:455–459.

Lotspeich, F. B., and M. E. Everhart. 1962. Climate and vegetation as soil forming factors on the Llano Estacado. *Journal of Range Management* 15:134–141.

Luedtke, Barbara E. 1992. *An Archaeologist's Guide to Chert and Flint*. Los Angeles: University of California, Los Angeles, Institute of Archaeology, Archaeological Research Tools 7.

Lundelius, Ernest L., Jr. 1972. Vertebrate remains from the Gray Sand. In *Blackwater Locality no. 1: A Stratified Early Man Site in Eastern New Mexico*, by James J. Hester, 148–163. Taos, N.Mex.: Publication of the Fort Burgwin Research Center, no. 8.

McBride, E. F., and A. Thomson. 1970. *Caballos Novaculite, Marathon Region, Texas*. Geological Society of America Special Paper 122.

MacCurdy, George Grant, ed. 1937. *Early Man*. Philadelphia: J. B. Lippincott Co.

McFaul, Michael, K. L. Traugh, G. D. Smith, and W. Doering. 1994. Geoarchaeologic analysis of South Platte River terraces: Kersey, Colorado. *Geoarchaeology* 9:345–374.

McGowan, J. H., G. E. Granaton, and S. J. Seni. 1979. *Depositional Framework of the Lower Dockum Group (Triassic), Texas Panhandle*. Austin: University of Texas at Austin, Bureau of Economic Geology Report of Investigations 97.

Machette, Michael N. 1975. The Quaternary geology of the Lafayette Quadrangle, Colorado. Master's thesis, University of Colorado, Boulder.

———. 1977. *Geologic Map of the Lafayette Quadrangle, Adams, Boulder, and Jefferson Counties, Colorado*, 1:24,000. U.S. Geological Survey Quadrangle Map GQ-1392.

McKinney, Curtis R. 1992. Midland Woman: The Oldest American. *Geological Society of America Abstracts with Programs* 24:A26.

Madole, Richard F. 1986. Lake Devlin and Pinedale glacial history, Front Range, Colorado. *Quaternary Research* 25:43–54.

———. 1991. Colorado piedmont section. In *Quaternary Nonglacial Geology: Conterminous U.S.*, ed. Roger B. Morrison, 456–462. Boulder, Colo.: Geological Society of America, Centennial Volume K-2.

———. 1995. Spatial and temporal patterns of late Quaternary eolian deposition, eastern Colorado, U.S.A. *Quaternary Science Reviews* 14:155–177.

Malde, Harold E. 1960. Geological age of the Claypool site, northeastern Colorado. *American Antiquity* 26:236–243.

———. 1984. Geology of the Frazier site, Kersey, Colorado. In *Paleoindian Sites of the Colorado Piedmont*, ed. Adrienne B. Anderson, 13–16. Boulder, Colo.: American Quaternary Association Field Trip Guidebook.

Mallouf, Robert J. 1994. Horace Rivers: A Plainview campsite in the northeastern Texas Panhandle. 52nd Plains Anthropological Conference Abstracts, 74.

Mandel, Rolfe D. 1992. Soils and Holocene landscape evolution in central and southwestern Kansas: Implications for archaeological research. In *Soils in Archaeology: Landscape Evolution and Human Occupation*, ed. Vance T. Holliday, 41–100. Washington, D.C.: Smithsonian Institution Press.

———. 1994a. Geoarchaeology of the Horace Rivers site, northeastern Texas Panhandle. 52nd Plains Anthropological Conference Abstracts, 74.

———. 1994b. *Holocene Landscape Evolution in the Pawnee River Valley, Southwestern Kansas.* Lawrence: Kansas Geological Survey Bulletin 236.

———. 1995. Geomorphic controls of the Archaic record in the Central Plains of the United States. In *Archaeological Geology of the Archaic Period in North America*, ed. E. Arthur Bettis III, 37–66. Boulder, Colo.: Geological Society of America Special Paper 297.

Martin, Charles W. 1993. Radiocarbon ages on late Pleistocene loess stratigraphy of Nebraska and Kansas, Central Great Plains, U.S.A. *Quaternary Science Reviews* 12:179–188.

Martin, Charles W., and William C. Johnson. 1995. Variation in radiocarbon ages of soil organic matter fractions from late Quaternary buried soils. *Quaternary Research* 43:232–237.

Matthews, John A. 1980. Some problems and implications of 14C dates from a podzol buried beneath an end moraine at Haugabreen, southern Norway. *Geografiska Annaler* 62A:185–208.

———. 1985. Radiocarbon dating of surface and buried soils: Principles, problems and prospects. In *Geomorphology and Soils*, ed. K. S. Richards, R. R. Arnett, and S. Ellis, 269–288. London: Allen and Unwin.

May, David W. 1989. Holocene alluvial fills in the South Loup Valley, Nebraska. *Quaternary Research* 31:117–120.

May, David W., James B. Swinehart, David Loope, and Vernon Souders. 1995. Late Quaternary fluvial and eolian sediments: Loup River basin and the Nebraska Sand Hills. Lincoln: University of Nebraska–Lincoln, Conservation and Survey Division Guidebook 10.

Meade, Grayson E., Glen L. Evans, and John P. Brand. 1974. *Mesozoic and Cenozoic Geology of the Southern Llano Estacado.* Lubbock, Tex.: Lubbock Geological Society Guidebook.

Meltzer, David J. 1983. The antiquity of man and the development of American archaeology. *Advances in Archaeological Method and Theory* 6:1–51.

———. 1986. The Clovis Paleoindian occupation of Texas: Results of the Texas fluted point survey. *Bulletin of the Texas Archeological Society* 57:27–68.

———. 1988. Late Pleistocene human adaptations in eastern North America. *Journal of World Prehistory* 2:1–52.

———. 1991. Altithermal archaeology and paleoecology at Mustang Springs, on the Southern High Plains of Texas. *American Antiquity* 56:236–267.

———. 1993. Is there a Clovis adaptation? In *From Kostenki to Clovis: Upper Paleolithic–Paleo-Indian Adaptations,* ed. Olga Soffer and N. D. Praslov, 293–310. New York: Plenum Press.

Meltzer, David J., and Michael R. Bever. 1995. Clovis Paleoindians of Texas: An update on the Texas Clovis fluted point survey. *Bulletin of the Texas Archeological Society* 66:47–81.

Meltzer, David J., and Michael B. Collins. 1987. Prehistoric water wells on the Southern High Plains: Clues to altithermal climate. *Journal of Field Archaeology* 14:9–27.

Meltzer, David J., and Bruce D. Smith. 1986. Paleo-Indian and early Archaic subsistence strategies in eastern North America. In *Foraging, Collecting and Harvesting: Archaic Period Subsistence and Settlement in the Eastern Woodlands,* ed. Sarah W. Neusius, 1–30. Carbondale: Southern Illinois University, Center for Archaeological Investigations.

Myers, Thomas P. 1987. Preliminary study of the distribution of fluted points in Nebraska. *Current Research in the Pleistocene* 4:67–68.

———. 1995. Paleoindian occupation of the eastern Sand Hills. *Plains Anthropologist* 40:61–68.

Neck, Raymond W. 1987. Changing Holocene snail faunas and environments along the eastern Caprock escarpment of Texas. *Quaternary Research* 27:312–322.

———. 1995. Molluscan remains. In *Stratigraphy and Paleoenvironments of Late Quaternary Valley Fills on the Southern High Plains,* by Vance T. Holliday, 59–67. Boulder, Colo.: Geological Society of America Memoir 186.

Nicholson, John H. 1960. Geology of the Texas Panhandle. In *Aspects of the Geology of Texas: A Symposium,* 51–64. Austin: University of Texas at Austin, Bureau of Economic Geology Publication 6017.

NOAA. 1982. *Climate of Texas.* Asheville, N.C.: National Climatic Data Center, Climatography of the United States 60.

Nordt, Lee C., Thomas W. Boutton, Charles T. Hallmark, and Michael R. Waters. 1994. Late Quaternary vegetation and climate changes in Central Texas based on the isotopic composition of organic carbon. *Quaternary Research* 41: 109–120.

O'Brien, Michael J., and R. E. Warren. 1983. An Archaic projectile point sequence from the southern Prairie Peninsula: The Pigeon Roost Creek site. In *Archaic Hunters and Gatherers in the American Midwest*, ed. James L. Phillips and James A. Brown, 71–98. New York: Academic Press.

Oldfield, Frank. 1975. Pollen-analytical results, part II. In *Late Pleistocene Environments of the Southern High Plains*, ed. Fred Wendorf and James J. Hester, 121–147. Taos, N.Mex.: Publication of the Fort Burgwin Research Center, no. 9.

Oldfield, Frank, and James Schoenwetter. 1964. Late Quaternary Environments of Early Man on the Southern High Plains. *Antiquity* 38:226–229.

———. 1975. Discussion of the pollen-analytical evidence. In *Late Pleistocene Environments of the Southern High Plains*, ed. Fred Wendorf and James J. Hester, 149–177. Taos, N.Mex.: Publication of the Fort Burgwin Research Center, no. 9.

Olson, Edwin A., and W. S. Broecker. 1959. Lamont natural radiocarbon measurements V. *American Journal of Science Radiocarbon Supplement* 1:1–28.

Parker, Wayne. 1983. Preliminary notes on a Clovis point associated with mammoth tusk fragments in Hockley County, Texas. *La Tierra: Journal of the South Texas Archaeological Association* 10:31–35.

Patrick, Ruth. 1938. The occurrence of flints and extinct animals in pluvial deposits near Clovis, New Mexico, part V: Diatom evidence from the mammoth pit. *Proceedings of the Philadelphia Academy of Natural Science* 90:15–24.

Patton, Leroy T. 1923. *The Geology of Potter County, Texas*. University of Texas Bulletin 2330.

Patton, Peter C., and David S. Dibble. 1982. Archeologic and geomorphic evidence for the paleohydrologic record of the Pecos River in west Texas. *American Journal of Science* 282:97–121.

Pearce, William M. 1936. A survey of the sand-hill camp sites of Lamb and Bailey counties. *Bulletin of the Texas Archeological and Paleontological Society* 8: 184–186.

Phelps, Elisa, Joan Few, Betty P. Gatliff, D. Gentry Steele, and Frank A. Weir. 1994. Burial to bronze: Excavation, analysis, and facial reconstruction of a burial from the Wilson-Leonard site, Texas. *Bulletin of the Texas Archeological Society* 62:75–86.

Pierce, Harold G. 1974. The Blanco beds. In *Guidebook to the Mesozoic and Cenozoic Geology of the Southern Llano Estacado*, ed. Grayson E. Meade, Glen L. Evans, and John P. Brand, 9–16. Lubbock, Tex.: Lubbock Geological Society.

———. 1987. The gastropods, with notes on other invertebrates. In *Lubbock*

Lake: Late Quaternary Studies on the Southern High Plains, ed. Eileen Johnson, 41–48. College Station: Texas A&M University Press, College Station.

Polyak, Victor, and Monty Williams. 1986. Gaines County Paleo-Indian projectile point inventory and analysis. *Transactions of the Twenty-first Regional Archeological Symposium for Southeastern New Mexico and Western Texas,* 25–95.

Prewitt, Elton R. 1981. Cultural Chronology in Central Texas. *Bulletin of the Texas Archeological Society* 52:65–89.

―――. 1982. *Archeological Investigations at the Loeve-Fox, Loeve and Tombstone Bluff Sites in the Granger Lake District of Central Texas.* Denton: North Texas State University, Institute for Applied Sciences, Archaeological Investigations at the San Gabriel Reservoir Districts, Central Texas 4.

―――. 1983. From Circleville to Toyah: Comments on Central Texas chronology. *Bulletin of the Texas Archeological Society* 54:201–238.

Price, W. Armstrong. 1944. The Clovis site: Regional physiography and geology. *American Antiquity* 9:401–407.

Pye, K., N. R. Winspear, and L. P. Zhou. 1995. Thermoluminescence ages of loess and associated sediments in central Nebraska, USA. *Palaeogeography, Palaeoclimatology, Palaeoecology* 118:73–87.

Rancier, James, Gary Haynes, and Stanford Dennis. 1982. 1981 Investigations of Lamb Spring. *Southwestern Lore* 48:1–17.

Ray, Cyrus N. 1942. Ancient artifacts and mammoth teeth of the McLean Site. *Bulletin of the Texas Archeological and Paleontological Society* 45:151–190.

Ray, Cyrus N., and Kirk Bryan. 1938. Folsomoid point found in alluvium beside a mammoth's bones. *Science* 88:257–258.

Ray, Louis L. 1942. Symposium on Folsom-Yuma problems. *Science* 95:22–23.

Redder, Albert J. 1985. Horn Shelter no. 2: The south end. *Central Texas Archeologist* 10:37–65.

Redder, Albert J., and John W. Fox. 1988. Excavation and positioning of the Horn shelter's burial and grave goods. *Central Texas Archeologist* 11:1–12.

Reeves, C. C., Jr. 1965. Chronology of west Texas pluvial lake dunes. *Journal of Geology* 73:504–508.

―――. 1966. Pluvial lake basins of west Texas. *Journal of Geology* 74:269–291.

―――. 1972. Tertiary-Quaternary stratigraphy and geomorphology of west Texas and southeastern New Mexico. In *Guidebook for East-Central New Mexico,* ed. Vincent Kelley and Frederick D. Trauger, 108–117. Socorro: New Mexico Geological Society Guidebook 24.

―――. 1973. The full-glacial climate of the Southern High Plains, west Texas. *Journal of Geology* 81:693–704.

―――. 1976. Quaternary stratigraphy and geological history of the Southern High Plains, Texas and New Mexico. In *Quaternary Stratigraphy of North America,* ed. W. C. Mahaney, 213–234. Stroudsburg, Pa.: Dowden, Hutchinson and Ross, Inc.

―――. 1990. A proposed sequential development of lake basins, Southern High

Plains, Texas and New Mexico. In *Geologic Framework and Regional Hydrology: Upper Cenozoic Blackwater Draw and Ogallala Formations, Great Plains*, ed. Thomas C. Gustavson, 209–232. Austin: University of Texas at Austin, Bureau of Economic Geology.

———. 1991. Origin and stratigraphy of alkaline lake basins, Southern High Plains. In *Quaternary Nonglacial Geology: Conterminous U.S.*, ed. Roger B. Morrison, 484–486. Boulder, Colo.: Geological Society of America, Centennial Volume K-2.

Reeves, C. C., Jr., and William T. Parry. 1969. Age and morphology of small lake basins, Southern High Plains, Texas and eastern New Mexico. *Texas Journal of Science* 20:349–354.

Reider, Richard G. 1990. Late Pleistocene and Holocene pedogenic and environmental trends at archaeological sites in plains and mountain areas of Colorado and Wyoming. In *Archaeological Geology of North America*, ed. Norman P. Lasca and Jack Donahue, 335–360. Boulder, Colo.: Geological Society of America, Centennial Special Volume 4.

Renaud, E. B. 1931. *Prehistoric Flaked Points from Colorado and Neighboring Districts*. Denver: Proceedings of the Colorado Museum of Natural History 10, no. 2.

———. 1932. *Yuma and Folsom Artifacts, New Material*. Denver: Proceedings of the Colorado Museum of Natural History 11, no. 2.

Roberts, Frank H. H. 1937. New developments in the problem of the Folsom Complex. *Smithsonian Institution Explorations and Field Work in 1936*, 67–74.

———. 1940. Developments in the Problem of the North American Paleo-Indian. Washington, D.C.: Smithsonian Miscellaneous Collections 100:51–116.

———. 1942. *Archaeological and Geological Investigations in the San Jon District, Eastern New Mexico*. Washington, D.C.: Smithsonian Miscellaneous Collections 103(4).

———. 1943. Edgar Billings Howard. *American Anthropologist* 45:452–454.

———. 1951. Radiocarbon Dates and Early Man. In *Radiocarbon Dating*, by Frederick Johnson, 2–22. Washington, D.C.: Society for American Archaeology Memoir 8.

———. 1953. Earliest men in America. *Journal of World History* (*Cahiers D'Histoire Mondiale*) 1:255–277.

Roper, Donna C. 1991. A comparison of contexts of red ocher use in Paleoindian and Upper Paleolithic sites. *North American Archaeologist* 12:289–301.

Rosholt, John N. 1958. Radioactive disequilibrium studies as an aid in understanding the natural migration of uranium and its decay products. *Second International Conference on Peaceful Uses of Atomic Energy, Proceedings* 2:230–236.

Russell, Richard Joel. 1945. Climates of Texas. *Annals of the Association of American Geographers* 35:37–52.

Saunders, Jeffrey J. 1980. A model for man-mammoth relationships in Late Pleistocene North America. In *The Ice-Free Corridor and Peopling of the New World*, ed.

Nathaniel W. Rutter and Charles E. Schweger, 87–98. Edmonton, Alberta: Canadian Journal of Anthropology 1.

Saunders, Jeffrey J., and Edward B. Daeschler. 1994. Descriptive analyses and taphonomical observations of culturally-modified mammoths excavated at "The Gravel Pit," near Clovis, New Mexico in 1936. *Proceedings of the Academy of Natural Sciences of Philadelphia* 145:1–28.

Saunders, Roger S., and John T. Penman. 1979. Perry Ranch: A Plainview bison kill on the Southern Plains. *Plains Anthropologist* 24:51–65.

Schaffer, James B. 1958. The Alibates flint quarry of Texas. *American Antiquity* 24:189–191.

Scharpenseel, H. W. 1971. Radiocarbon dating of soils. *Soviet Soil Science* 3: 76–83.

———. 1979. Soil fraction dating. *Radiocarbon Dating, Proceedings of the 9th International Radiocarbon Conference,* ed. Rainer Berger and Hans Suess, 277–283. Berkeley: University of California Press.

Schoenwetter, James. 1975. Pollen-analytical results, part I. In *Late Pleistocene Environments of the Southern High Plains,* ed. Fred Wendorf and James J. Hester, 103–120. Taos, N.Mex.: Publication of the Fort Burgwin Research Center, no. 9.

Schultz, C. Bertrand. 1943. Some artifact sites of Early Man in the Great Plains and adjacent areas. *American Antiquity* 8:242–249.

———. 1948. Memorial to Erwin Hinckley Barbour. *Proceedings of the Geological Society of America Annual Report for 1947,* 109–117.

Schultz, C. Bertrand, and W. D. Frankforter. 1948. Preliminary report on the Lime Creek sites: New evidence of Early Man in southwestern Nebraska. *Bulletin of the University of Nebraska State Museum* 3:43–62.

Schultz, C. Bertrand, Gilbert C. Lueninghoener, and W. D. Frankforter. 1948. Preliminary geomorphological studies of the Lime Creek area. *Bulletin of the University of Nebraska State Museum* 3:31–42.

Sellards, E. H. 1916. Human remains and associated fossils from the Pleistocene of Florida. *Florida Geological Survey, 8th Annual Report,* 123–160.

———. 1917. Further notes on human remains from Vero, Florida. *American Anthropologist* 19:239–251.

———. 1938. Artifacts associated with fossil elephant. *Geological Society of America Bulletin* 49:999–1010.

———. 1940. Early Man in America: Index to localities and selected bibliography. *Bulletin of the Geological Society of America* 51:373–431.

———. 1952. *Early Man in America.* Austin: University of Texas Press.

———. 1955a. Fossil bison and associated artifacts from Milnesand, New Mexico. *American Antiquity* 20:336–344.

———. 1955b. Further investigations at the Scharbauer site. In *The Midland Discovery,* by Fred Wendorf, Alex D. Krieger, and Claude C. Albritton, Jr., 126–132. Austin: University of Texas Press.

————. n.d.a. The Milnesand site, New Mexico. Unpublished manuscript on file, Texas Memorial Museum, Austin.

————. n.d.b. The Ted Williamson site. Unpublished manuscript on file, Texas Memorial Museum, Austin.

Sellards, E. H., and Glen L. Evans. 1960. The Paleo-Indian cultural succession in the Central High Plains of Texas and New Mexico. In *Men and Cultures,* ed. Anthony F. C. Wallace, 639–649. Philadelphia: University of Pennsylvania Press.

Sellards, E. H., W. S. Adkins, and F. B. Plummer. 1933. *The Geology of Texas (vol. 1), Stratigraphy.* Austin: University of Texas at Austin Bulletin 3232.

Sellards, E. H., Glen L. Evans, and Grayson E. Meade. 1947. Fossil bison and associated artifacts from Plainview, Texas. *Geological Society of America Bulletin* 58:927–954.

Semken, Holmes A., Jr., and Carl R. Falk. 1987. Late Pleistocene/Holocene mammalian faunas and environmental changes on the Northern Plains of the United States. In *Late Quaternary Mammalian Biogeography and Environments of the Great Plains and Prairies,* ed. Russell W. Graham, Holmes A. Semken, Jr., and Mary Ann Graham, 176–313. Springfield: Illinois State Museum Scientific Papers 22.

Shelley, Phillip H. 1993. A geoarchaeological approach to the analysis of secondary lithic deposits. *Geoarchaeology* 8:59–72.

Singer, Michael J., and Peter Janitzky, eds. 1986. *Field and Laboratory Procedures Used in a Soil Chronosequence Study.* Washington, D.C.: U.S. Geological Survey Bulletin 1648.

Slaughter, Bob H. 1975. Ecological interpretation of the Brown Sand Wedge local fauna. In *Late Pleistocene Environments of the Southern High Plains,* ed. Fred Wendorf and James J. Hester, 179–192. Taos, N.Mex.: Publication of the Fort Burgwin Research Center, no. 9.

Smith, Fred H. 1976. The skeletal remains of the earliest Americans: A survey. *Tennessee Anthropologist* 1:116–147.

Soil Survey Division Staff. 1993. *Soil Survey Manual.* Washington, D.C.: U.S. Department of Agriculture Handbook 18.

Speer, Roberta D. 1978. Fossil bison remains from the Rex Rodgers site. In *Archaeology at MacKenzie Reservoir,* ed. Jack T. Hughes and Patrick S. Willey, 68–106. Austin: Texas Historical Commission, Archeological Survey Report 24.

————. 1986. Archeology of the MacKenzie Reservoir area. In *Geomorphology and Quaternary Stratigraphy of the Rolling Plains, Texas Panhandle,* ed. Thomas C. Gustavson, 79–81. Austin: University of Texas at Austin, Bureau of Economic Geology Guidebook 22.

————. 1990. History of the Plainview site. In *Guidebook to the Quaternary History of the Llano Estacado,* ed. Vance T. Holliday and Eileen Johnson, 79–92. Lubbock: Texas Tech University, Lubbock Lake Landmark Quaternary Research Series 2.

Stafford, Thomas W., Jr. 1981. Alluvial geology and archaeological potential of the Texas Southern High Plains. *American Antiquity* 46:548–565.

Stafford, Thomas W., Jr., A. J. T. Jull, Klaus Brendel, Raymond C. Duhamel, and Douglas Donahue. 1987. Study of bone radiocarbon dating accuracy at the University of Arizona NSF Accelerator Facility for Radioisotope Analysis. *Radiocarbon* 29:24–44.

Stanford, Dennis. 1978. The Jones-Miller site: An example of Hell Gap bison procurement strategy. In *Bison Procurement and Utilization: A Symposium*, ed. Leslie B. Davis and Michael Wilson, 90–97. Lincoln, Nebr.: Plains Anthropologist Memoir 14.

———. 1979. The Selby and Dutton sites: Evidence for a possible Pre-Clovis occupation of the High Plains. In *Pre-Llano Cultures of the Americas: Paradoxes and Possibilities*, ed. Robert L. Humphrey and Dennis Stanford, 101–123. Washington, D.C.: Anthropological Society of Washington.

———. 1983. Pre-Clovis occupation south of the ice sheets. In *Early Man in the New World*, ed. Richard Shutler, Jr., 65–72. Beverly Hills, Calif.: Sage Publications, Inc.

Stanford, Dennis, and John Albanese. 1975. Preliminary results of the Smithsonian Institution excavation at the Claypool site, Washington County, Colorado. *Southwestern Lore* 41:22–28.

Stanford, Dennis, and Frank Broilo. 1981. Frank's Folsom campsite. In *Archaeological Essays in Honor of Mark Wimberly*, ed. Michael Foster, 1–13. *The Artifact* 19.

Stanford, Dennis, C. Vance Haynes, Jr., Jeffrey J. Saunders, George A. Agogino, and Anthony T. Boldurian. 1990. Blackwater Draw Locality 1: History, current research, and interpretations. In *Guidebook to the Quaternary History of the Llano Estacado*, ed. Vance T. Holliday and Eileen Johnson, 105–155. Lubbock: Texas Tech Museum, Lubbock Lake Landmark Quaternary Research Series 2.

Stanford, Dennis, Waldo R. Wedel, and Glenn R. Scott. 1981. Archaeological investigations of the Lamb Spring site. *Southwestern Lore* 47:14–27.

Stephenson, Robert L. 1965. Quaternary human occupation of the Plains. In *The Quaternary of the United States*, ed. H. E. Wright, Jr., and David G. Frey, 685–696. Princeton, N.J.: Princeton University Press.

Stevens, Dominique E. 1973. Blackwater Draw Locality No. 1, 1963–1972, and its relevance to the Firstview Complex. Master's thesis, Eastern New Mexico University, Portales.

Stock, Chester, and Francis D. Bode. 1936. The occurrence of flints and extinct animals in pluvial deposits near Clovis, New Mexico, part III: Geology and vertebrate paleontology of the Quaternary near Clovis, New Mexico. *Proceedings of the Philadelphia Academy of Natural Sciences* 88:219–241.

Stuiver, Minze. 1993. Editorial comment. *Radiocarbon* 35:iii.

Stuiver, Minze, and G. W. Pearson. 1992. Calibration of the radiocarbon time scale, 2500–5000 BC. In *Radiocarbon after Four Decades: An Interdisciplinary Perspective,* ed. R. E. Taylor, A. Long, and R. S. Kra, 19–33. New York: Springer-Verlag.

Suhm, Dee Ann. 1960. The Beidleman Ranch site: An Early Man kill site in Stonewall County, Texas. *Bulletin of the Texas Archeological Society* 31:207–212.

Suhm, Dee Ann, Alex D. Krieger, and Edward B. Jelks. 1954. *An Introductory Handbook of Texas Archeology.* Austin: *Bulletin of the Texas Archeological Society* 25.

Tankersly, Kenneth B., and others. 1995. They have a rock that bleeds: Sunrise red ocher and its early Paleoindian occurrence at the Hell Gap site, Wyoming. *Plains Anthropologist* 40:185–194.

Taylor, R. E. 1987. *Radiocarbon Dating: An Archaeological Perspective.* Orlando, Fla.: Academic Press.

———. 1992. Radiocarbon dating of bone: To collagen and beyond. In *Radiocarbon after Four Decades: An Interdisciplinary Perspective,* ed. R. E. Taylor, A. Long, and R. S. Kra, 375–403. New York: Springer-Verlag.

Thies, R. M., and T. A. Witty, Jr. 1992. The Archaic of the Central Plains. *Revista Arqueología Americana* 5:137–165.

Thomas, George B. 1978. A survey and assessment of the archeological resources of Fort Hood, Texas. *Bulletin of the Texas Archeological Society* 49:195–240.

Thomas, Ronny G. 1972. *Geomorphic Evolution of the Pecos River System.* Waco, Tex.: Baylor Geological Studies Bulletin 22.

Thompson, Jerome L. 1987. Modern, historic, and fossil flora. In *Lubbock Lake: Late Quaternary Studies on the Southern High Plains,* ed. Eileen Johnson, 26–35. College Station: Texas A&M University Press.

Thompson, R. S., C. Whitlock, P. J. Bartlein, S. P. Harrison, and W. G. Spaulding. 1993. Climatic changes in the western United States since 18,000 yr B.P. In *Global Climates since the Last Glacial Maximum,* ed. H. E. Wright, Jr., J. E. Kutzbach, T. Webb III, W. F. Ruddiman, F. A. Street-Perrott, and P. J. Bartlein, 468–513. Minneapolis: University of Minnesota Press.

Thoms, Alston V. 1992. Late Pleistocene and early Holocene regional land-use patterns. A perspective from the preliminary results of archaeological studies at the Richard Beene site, 41BX831, lower Medina River, south Texas. In *Late Cenozoic Alluvial Stratigraphy and Prehistory of the Inner Gulf Coastal Plain, South-Central Texas: Guidebook for the 10th Annual Meeting of the South-Central Friends of the Pleistocene,* ed. Rolfe D. Mandel and S. Christopher Caran. Lubbock: Texas Tech Museum, Lubbock Lake Quaternary Research Center Series 4, draft copy.

———. 1993. Knocking sense from old rocks: Typologies and the narrow perspective of the Angostura point type. *Lithic Technology* 18:16–27.

Thoms, Alston V., and Rolfe D. Mandel. 1992. The Richard Beene site: A deeply stratified Paleoindian to late Prehistoric occupation in South-Central Texas. *Current Research in the Pleistocene* 9:42–44.

Thurmond, J. Peter. 1990. *Late Paleoindian Utilization of the Dempsey Divide on the Southern High Plains.* Lincoln, Nebr.: Plains Anthropologist Memoir 25.

Tiffany, Joseph A. 1993. Introduction. In *Prehistory and Human Ecology of the Western Prairies and Northern Plains,* ed. Joseph A. Tiffany, 1–3. Lincoln, Nebr.: Plains Anthropologist Memoir 27.

Tunnell, Curtis D. 1977. Fluted point production as revealed by lithic specimens from the Adair-Steadman in northwestern Texas. In *Paleoindian Lifeways,* ed. Eileen Johnson, 140–168. Lubbock: *Museum Journal* (West Texas Museum Association) 17.

Turner, Ellen Sue, and Thomas R. Hester. 1993. *A Field Guide to Stone Artifacts of Texas Indians,* 2d ed. Houston: Texas Monthly Fieldguide Series, Gulf Publishing Co.

Turpin, Solveig A., Leland C. Bement, and Herbert H. Eling, Jr. 1992. Big Lake: A playa bison kill site in west Texas. *Current Research in the Pleistocene* 9:45–46.

Walker, Jimmy R. 1978. *Geomorphic Evolution of the Southern High Plains.* Waco, Tex.: Baylor Geological Studies Bulletin 35.

Warnica, James M. 1961. The Elida site: Evidence of a Folsom occupation in Roosevelt County, eastern New Mexico. *Bulletin of the Texas Archeological Society* 30:209–215.

———. 1966. New discoveries at the Clovis site. *American Antiquity* 31:345–357.

Warnica, James M., and Ted Williamson. 1968. The Milnesand site—revisited. *American Antiquity* 33:16–24.

Waters, Michael R. 1992. *Principles of Geoarchaeology: A North American Perspective.* Tucson: University of Arizona Press.

Watt, Frank H. 1978. Radiocarbon chronology of sites in the central Brazos Valley. *Bulletin of the Texas Archeological Society* 49:111–138.

Wayne, William J., et al. 1991. Quaternary geology of the northern Great Plains. In *Quaternary Nonglacial Geology: Conterminous U.S.,* ed. Roger B. Morrison, 441–476. Boulder, Colo.: Geological Society of America, Centennial Volume K-2.

Webb, T., III, P. J. Bartlein, S. P. Harrison, and K. H. Anderson. 1993. Vegetation, lake levels, and climate in eastern North America for the past 18,000 years. In *Global Climates since the Last Glacial Maximum,* ed. H. E. Wright, Jr., J. E. Kutzbach, T. Webb III, W. F. Ruddiman, F. A. Street-Perrott, and P. J. Bartlein, 415–467. Minneapolis: University of Minnesota Press.

Wedel, Waldo R. 1983. The Prehistoric Plains. In *Ancient North Americans,* ed. Jesse D. Jennings, 203–241. San Francisco: W. H. Freeman and Co.

Wendorf, Fred, ed. 1961a. *Paleoecology of the Llano Estacado.* Santa Fe: Museum of New Mexico Press, Publication of the Fort Burgwin Research Center, no. 1.

Wendorf, Fred. 1961b. An interpretation of late Pleistocene environments of the Llano Estacado. In *Paleoecology of the Llano Estacado,* ed. Fred Wendorf, 115–133. Santa Fe: Museum of New Mexico Press, Publication of the Fort Burgwin Research Center, no. 1.

————. 1961c. Invertebrate collections. In *Paleoecology of the Llano Estacado*, ed. Fred Wendorf, 105–114. Santa Fe: Museum of New Mexico Press, Publication of the Fort Burgwin Research Center, no. 1.

————. 1970. The Lubbock Subpluvial. In *Pleistocene and Recent Environments of the Central Great Plains*, ed. Wakefield Dort and J. Knox Jones, 23–36. Lawrence: University of Kansas Press.

————. 1975a. The modern environment. In *Late Pleistocene Environments of the Southern High Plains*, ed. Fred Wendorf and James J. Hester, 1–12. Taos, N.Mex.: Publication of the Fort Burgwin Research Center, no. 9.

————. 1975b. Summary and conclusions. In *Late Pleistocene Environments of the Southern High Plains*, ed. Fred Wendorf and James J. Hester, 257–278. Taos, N.Mex.: Publication of the Fort Burgwin Research Center, no. 9.

Wendorf, Fred, and James J. Hester. 1962. Early Man's utilization of the Great Plains environment. *American Antiquity* 28:159–171.

————, eds. 1975. *Late Pleistocene Environments of the Southern High Plains*. Taos, N.Mex.: Publication of the Fort Burgwin Research Center, no. 9.

Wendorf, Fred, and Alex D. Krieger. 1959. New light on the Midland discovery. *American Antiquity* 25:66–78.

Wendorf, Fred, Alex D. Krieger, Claude C. Albritton, Jr., and T. D. Stewart. 1955. *The Midland Discovery*. Austin: University of Texas Press.

Wheat, Joe Ben. 1967. A Paleo-Indian bison kill. *Scientific American* 216(1):44–52.

————. 1972. *The Olsen-Chubbock Site: A Paleo-Indian Bison Kill*. Washington, D.C.: Society for American Archaeology Memoir 26.

————. 1974. First excavations at the Lubbock Lake site. In *History and Prehistory of the Lubbock Lake Site*, ed. Craig C. Black, 15–42. Lubbock: *Museum Journal* (West Texas Museum Association) 15.

————. 1976. Artifact life histories: Cultural templates, typology, evidence, and inference. In *Primitive Technology and Art*, ed. J. S. Raymond, 7–15. Calgary, Alberta: University of Calgary Archaeological Association.

————. 1979. *The Jurgens Site*. Lincoln, Nebr.: Plains Anthropologist Memoir 15.

Wheeler, Richard P. 1954. Selected projectile point types of the United States. *Bulletin of the Oklahoma Anthropological Society* 2:1–6.

————. 1995. *Archeological Investigations in Three Reservoir Areas in South Dakota and Wyoming, Part 1: Angostura Reservoir*. Lincoln, Nebr.: Reprints in Anthropology 46.

White, Ralph W. 1987. The Muncy site in the Oklahoma Panhandle: Indian cultural evidence over a long time span. *Bulletin of the Oklahoma Anthropological Society* 36:39–103.

Willey, Gordon R. 1966. *An Introduction to American Archaeology, vol. 1: North and Middle America*. Englewood Cliffs, N.J.: Prentice-Hall.

Willey, Patrick S., and Jack T. Hughes. 1978. Archeological methods. In *Archeology at MacKenzie Reservoir*, ed. Jack T. Hughes and Patrick S. Willey, 45–48. Austin: Texas Historical Commission, Archeological Survey Report 24.

Willey, Patrick S., Billy R. Harrison, and Jack T. Hughes. 1978. The Rex Rodgers site. In *Archeology at MacKenzie Reservoir*, ed. Jack T. Hughes and Patrick S. Willey, 51–68. Austin: Texas Historical Commission, Archeological Survey Report 24.

Wilmsen, Edwin N. 1965. An outline of Early Man studies in the United States. *American Antiquity* 31:172–192.

Wilmsen, Edwin N., and Frank H. H. Roberts. 1978. *Lindenmeier, 1934–1974: Concluding Report of Investigations.* Washington, D.C.: Smithsonian Contributions to Anthropology 24.

Winkler, Dale A. 1987. Vertebrate-bearing eolian unit from the Ogallala Group (Miocene) in northwestern Texas. *Geology* 15:705–708.

Winsborough, Barbara M. 1988. Paleoecological analysis of Holocene algal mat diatomites associated with prehistoric wells on the Texas High Plains. *Geological Society of America Abstracts with Programs* 20:132.

———. 1995. Diatoms. In *Stratigraphy and Paleoenvironments of Late Quaternary Valley Fills on the Southern High Plains*, ed. Vance T. Holliday, 67–82. Boulder, Colo.: Geological Society of America Memoir 186.

Wormington, H. M. 1948. *A Proposed Revision of Yuma Point Terminology.* Proceedings of the Colorado Museum of Natural History 18(2).

———. 1957. *Ancient Man in North America*, 4th ed. Denver: Denver Museum of Natural History, Popular Series 4.

———. 1984. The Frazier site, Colorado. In *Paleo-indian Sites of the Colorado Piedmont*, ed. Adrienne B. Anderson, 12–13. Boulder, Colo.: American Quaternary Association Field Trip Guidebook.

Wright, H. E., Jr., J. E. Kutzbach, T. Webb III, W. F. Ruddiman, F. A. Street-Perrott, and P. J. Bartlein, eds. 1993. *Global Climates since the Last Glacial Maximum.* Minneapolis: University of Minnesota Press.

Wyckoff, Don G. 1984. The foragers: Eastern Oklahoma. In *Prehistory of Oklahoma*, ed. Robert E. Bell, 119–160. Orlando, Fla.: Academic Press.

———. 1989. Accelerator dates and chronology at the Packard site, Oklahoma. *Current Research in the Pleistocene* 6:24–26.

———. 1993. Gravel sources of knappable Alibates silicified dolomite. *Geoarchaeology* 8:35–58.

Wyckoff, Don G., and Lyonel Taylor. 1971. The Pumpkin Creek site: An Early Archaic site on the Southern Plains border. *Plains Anthropologist* 16:20–51.

Young, Diane E. 1988. An osteological analysis of the Paleoindian double burial from Horn shelter no. 2. *Central Texas Archeologist* 11:13–115.

Zier, Christian J., Daniel A. Jepson, Michael McFaul, and William Doering. 1993. Archaeology and geomorphology of the Clovis-age Klein site near Kersey, Colorado. *Plains Anthropologist* 38:203–210.

Index